PRAISE FOR

Real Estate Valuation and Strategy

This book provides readers with a great way to understand the real estate appraisal process without getting bogged down in a lot of unnecessary technical details. It might be viewed as a book about appraisal for nonappraisers, although beginning appraisers could also benefit from its practical examples and review of key valuation techniques. It is especially useful for the target audience of financial advisors who want to understand enough about the appraisal process to explain the appraisal report to their clients.

—Dr. Jeffrey D. Fisher, Professor Emeritus, Finance and Real Estate, Indiana University, and Chairman of the Homer Hoyt Institute

This is a must-read book for financial advisors and high-end real estate investors. It is an invaluable reference guide that will become the standard against which all subsequent efforts will be judged.

—Dr. Ko Wang, Clayton Emory Chair, Real Estate and Infrastructure, Johns Hopkins University, and editor, *Journal of Real Estate Research*

John serves as a highly respected advisor, guest speaker, and adjunct faculty member for the finance and real estate programs here at WSU. He is one of the most knowledgeable and insightful people I know in the world of real estate valuation, and his communication style is very well received by students.

—Dr. David A. Whidbee, Omer Carey Chair in Financial Education and Chair of the Department of Finance and Management Science, Washington State University

Real estate is an incredibly complex asset to hold. It is multidisciplinary and this book provides a comprehensive analysis of the things that a family business owner or high net worth investor should know if they are going to invest in real estate. It is a must read for anyone venturing into the wonderful world of real estate.

—Dr. Elaine Worzala, Director, Carter Real Estate Center, College of Charleston

Dr. John Kilpatrick, a nationally known appraiser and economist, has written a text that should be invaluable to high-end investors and their families.

—The Honorable Charles Bernstein, retired Circuit Court judge, Baltimore City

This is an invaluable work on real estate. John brings to the world of real estate investing decades of experience as a practitioner coupled with advanced training at the PhD level. Rarely have I seen theory and practice so seamlessly intertwined in a book that covers a domain of knowledge so comprehensively and expertly. There is advice in these pages for all types of real estate investors: from those buying their first residential property to those considering serious commercial real estate investments.

—Dean Peter Brews, Darla Moore School of Business, University of South Carolina

Dr. John Kilpatrick is the nation's go-to expert on real estate valuation. When a family office is about to acquire or dispose of a high-amenity "trophy" property or a corporate owner seeks to optimize a business-related real estate asset, it's John to whom I always refer them. His *Real Estate Valuation and Strategy* will undoubtedly be the resource they and I will consult as the bible on the topic.

—Marc J. Lane, JD, President, Marc J. Lane Wealth Group

Accessible conversational style + distillation of conventionally received wisdom of valuers + practical street smarts + implications of sophisticated high finance = wisdom beyond value. This book is packed with stories, mini-case studies from the author's wide-ranging advisory practice, and mini-analytics examples. One of real estate's smartest pros—who knows the numbers yet knows that real estate is so, so much more than numbers—provides a gift of inestimable value to neophytes and experts alike: a wide-ranging introduction for the former and thought-provoking insights for the latter.

—Dr. Stephen E. Roulac, CEO, Roulac Global, and Distinguished Visiting Professor of Global Property Strategy, School of Built Environment, University of Ulster, Belfast

REAL ESTATE VALUATION AND STRATEGY

A GUIDE FOR FAMILY OFFICES AND THEIR ADVISORS

JOHN A. KILPATRICK, PHD

McGraw Hill

New York Chicago San Francisco Athens London Madrid
Mexico City Milan New Delhi Singapore Sydney Toronto

1 2 3 4 5 6 7 8 9 LCR 24 23 22 21 20

ISBN: 978-1-260-45904-3
MHID: 1-260-45904-7

e-ISBN: 978-1-260-45905-0
e-MHID: 1-260-45905-5

Library of Congress Cataloging-in-Publication Data

Names: Kilpatrick, John A., 1954– author.
Title: Real estate valuation and strategy : a guide for family offices and their advisors / John Kilpatrick.
Description: New York : McGraw-Hill Education, [2019] | Includes bibliographical references and index.
Identifiers: LCCN 2019027027 (print) | LCCN 2019027028 (ebook) | ISBN 9781260459043 (hardcover) | ISBN 9781260459050 (ebook)
Subjects: LCSH: Real property—Valuation. | Real estate investment.
Classification: LCC HD1387 .K4185 2019 (print) | LCC HD1387 (ebook) | DDC 332.63/24—dc23
LC record available at https://lccn.loc.gov/2019027027
LC ebook record available at https://lccn.loc.gov/2019027028

To my wife, Lynnda, who honestly knows
more about real estate than I do.

Contents

Acknowledgments

THIS BOOK WOULD not have been possible without the constant support and assistance of my wife, Lynnda Kilpatrick, our family, and my teammates at Greenfield Advisors. Much of what is here comes from my various classroom lectures and public appearances, and Lynnda in particular has encouraged me to write down these ideas for years. She's been amazingly patient with the long and involved process of taking my mental meanderings and turning them into something actually readable. I continue to marvel that she puts up with me.

My agent, Tim Brandhorst, at the Law Offices of Marc Lane in Chicago, has encouraged me throughout the process. He took on the thankless role of reading every word of this, chapter by chapter. Even though this is not my first time to the writing rodeo, I've learned much from Tim about how to structure this morass of ideas. Looking back, the first draft of the outline and the early chapters were unreadable, and it was only with Tim's help that this really became something with structure and organization. Of course, without Tim, this book would never have landed on a desk at McGraw-Hill!

Which brings me to my very excellent editor, Noah Schwartzberg. He believed in this book from the onset. His team there—and particularly the folks in production—made this one of the smoothest projects imaginable.

I also want to thank Dena Russell, my proofreader. She came to this late in the game, when we realized we needed another set of eyes, and managed to digest this tome in record time with terrific results.

It would be impossible to list all of my great real estate and finance mentors over the years. Even a short list would be a book in and of itself. However, I would be remiss in not mentioning three groups in particular. First, my colleagues at the Real Estate Counseling Group of America have been a constant sounding board for advanced ideas in valuation theory and practice. I don't always agree with all of them—and they rarely all agree with each other—but the intellectual stimulation from them has been a constant. Second, I want to give a shout-out to the Appraisal Institute, which I've mentioned at some length in the text. Over their 85+-year history, they've morphed from a simple professional association to a very real society of experts on the complex topic of real estate investment. I continue to serve on the review board for their flagship publication, *The Appraisal Journal*, and I'm constantly learning from that process.

Finally, I have to give a shout-out to my alma mater, the Moore School of Business at the University of South Carolina. I thought I was a pretty good finance guy when I showed up at their door to work on a PhD nearly 30 years ago. After all, I'd worked on Wall Street, been CFO of a successful development company, and run my own consulting practice for several years. Little did I know that for the next four years, they would upend everything I thought I knew about how money and the economy actually worked. I've had the very real pleasure of staying in close touch with them, and they've continued to grow and improve as an academic institution over the years. A couple of years ago, they invited me back to deliver the keynote for their graduate hooding process. I got to meet the then-current crop of newly minted advanced graduates. What a terrifically bright group!

This book is about using real estate appraisal tools to find, manage, and optimize the investment process. This is an ever-changing dynamic, with big stakes, complex models, and long time horizons. At the least, the final result should provide healthy diversification and good risk-adjusted returns in the portfolio. But real estate is anything but a "buy and forget" asset. It requires regular monitoring and nurturing, but the rewards make all that worthwhile. Remember, if you sleep indoors tonight, you are a participant in the real estate investment market. Hopefully, I've helped you optimize that participation.

1
The Real Estate Valuation Cycle

Buy Low, Sell High . . . Any Questions?

ANY INVESTMENT, SUCH as a share of publicly traded stock or a bond, entails three phases of ownership. To risk oversimplification, it includes buying or acquiring the investment, enjoying gains, dividends, interest, or some other ownership benefits over time, and then disposing of the investment either through sale, inheritance, maturity (in the case of a bond), or some other normal means. (Admittedly, there are other endgames for stock—to the day he died, my father-in-law, a pilot, had a framed stock certificate for Pan Am Airlines on his office wall.)

An oversimplified real estate ownership cycle would be:

1. Purchase or acquisition (which can also be an inheritance or some other nonpurchase event)
2. Management over time
3. Reversion, which can be a sale, some other disposal, or some change in nature or use

This broad paradigm covers very nearly every type of real estate ownership and provides a useful template for thinking about valuation issues at each point in this cycle. Baked into this is a level of involvement and understanding which is somewhat greater than stock or bond ownership. If I own a share of Ford Motor stock or a Ford corporate bond, I really don't need to know how an F-150 truck is built. But if I own real estate, a basic understanding of real estate marketing, finance, development, and even construction and maintenance would prove helpful, if not vital in many situations.

Professionals in the field have extensive study and experience, and grasp the situation-specific nuances of these topics. Nonetheless, a solid understanding of nomenclature and methods will aid every investor, and every investor's advisors, and help those dependent on real estate to become better participants in this aspect of their portfolios. In a recent meeting with family office managers, I heard the phrase "the fruits of actions can be architected"—meaning, the outcome of a real estate purchase can be designed by a knowledgeable investor. Real estate is fairly unique among asset classes in that the value can be improved or diminished by the actions or inactions of an individual investor. The informed investor has enormous influence on value over time.

In this chapter, I will introduce concepts of the real estate ownership cycle. A beginning reader will be left wanting more—every topic in this chapter begs for a deeper and more thorough discussion, and I will regularly reference subsequent chapters where these topics are explored in more depth. These core concepts are:

- You make money when you buy real estate, not when you sell.
- Use and enjoyment are unique benefits that flow during ownership.
- Real estate enjoys capital gains over time.
- Real estate investments must consider public, private, and economic restrictions.
- The endgame strategy must drive valuation optimization decisions.
- Accounting values differ from economic values.
- Investors must understand "Value to whom? Value of what?"

The rest of this chapter provides a brief overview of each concept, to give you context as we dive deeper in Chapter 2 and beyond.

1. You Make Money When You Buy Real Estate, Not When You Sell

This may be the core thesis of this book. If you buy real estate at the right price, you can weather bad markets, idiosyncratic property problems, and systematic disruptions in the real estate sector. If you overpay for a property, no amount of inflation will ever catch you up to where you should have been.

This leads to an important concept: a property may have a given *market value*, but a very different *investment value*. The investment value, to a particular investor, is defined by the investor's strategic goals. Some disagree with this and suggest that any property purchased at or below its market value is a good deal. For an investor with a specific investment strategy in mind, nothing could be further from the truth.

Take, for instance, purchasing a single family residence for personal occupancy. Strategically, do you plan to simply occupy the house for the rest of your life (use and enjoyment benefits), or are you going to live there a few years and move up or out to another home? The choice may dictate the type of neighborhood (long-range stable or early stage gentrifying), the home size (a smaller home in a neighborhood will sell more readily than a larger one), the amenities (do you anticipate a growing family over the coming years, or are you single?), the home condition (buying a "fixer-upper" may have short-term use and enjoyment limits but will sell better after remodeling), or the home construction quality (we will address "superamenities" in a later chapter on the cost approach).

There was a study a number of years ago of small, family-run groceries in New York City. Some stores were hugely profitable and resold at a significant profit. Other stores, almost identical, were less profitable and rarely sold at all. The researchers found out that the store owners had diametrically opposite investment strategies. In the first case, investors viewed the store as short-term "flips." They looked for rapidly gentrifying neighborhoods, bought troubled stores, kept them open for extended hours, and waited for the resale market to peak. The others were bought by families who viewed the store as a multigenerational "hold and operate" investment. They looked for stores in established neighborhoods, typically operated during the day and early evening, and tended to stock less-profitable, specialty items. The stores—and the families who owned them—aimed to become centers of community life, were more likely to extend credit, and had subjective ownership benefits disconnected from the cash income or income growth.

Hence, the first strategy was to maximize resale value, a function of high and growing cash income but disconnected from any sort of subjective ownership benefits. The second strategy was totally focused on the subjective ownership benefits.

In farming states, many tracts are purchased purely to be rented as farm or grazing lands. The owners will rarely live on the properties. The purchase decisions consider optimizing cash value (usually a function of the land productivity), the proximity to wholesale markets, and the market cycle for the crops themselves. A family farm, on the other hand, may trade off maximizing income for other subjective benefits, such as proximity to amenities.

To further illustrate, consider a typical real estate cycle, starting from the end (some sort of disposition) and working our way back to the beginning.

The Endgame

There are really just two "endgames" for real estate—either you get rid of it or you don't. If you get rid of it (the formal word is *reversion*), you may sell it, give it away, convert it into some other use (and *then* sell it or keep it), subdivide it and sell part, combine it with other property into a portfolio and then sell *that* (or some of it), etc. Reversion covers a whole lot of ground, but for the time being we will focus on two options, sell or keep.

If you plan to eventually sell, you consider potential trade-offs between ultimate reversion value and current income. From a valuation perspective, the two can be viewed as a balancing act, although a dollar of forgone current income is worth less than a dollar of reversion value thanks to the time value of money. For example, Figure 1-1 shows an oversimplified but illustrative cash flow scenario for a real estate investment. Our investment will pay us a small cash return each year, growing significantly each year, and then we plan to sell the investment at the end of the fifth year for $10,000. Our desired investment return is 12%. Under this scenario, the project is worth about $10,600 today (called the *net present value*, or *NPV*). In short, we can invest $10,600, collect these cash flows, pay the debt off, and we will enjoy the required 12% return.

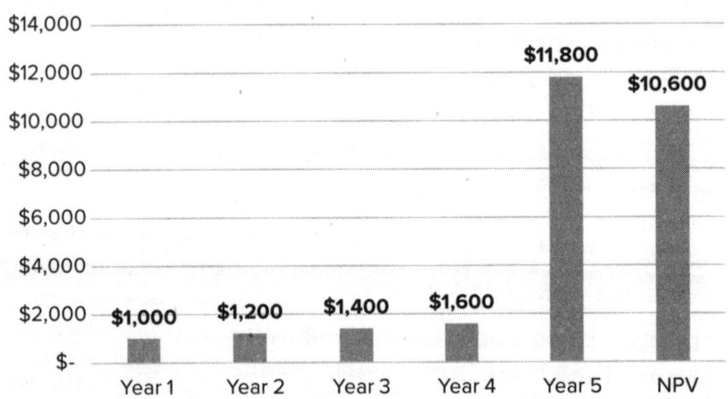

FIGURE 1-1 NPV with 12% Discount Rate

Now, let's say our desired rate of return is a bit higher—14%. This project is no longer worth $10,600, but rather $9,800 (Figure 1-2). This won't work—at that number, we can't make the investment today.

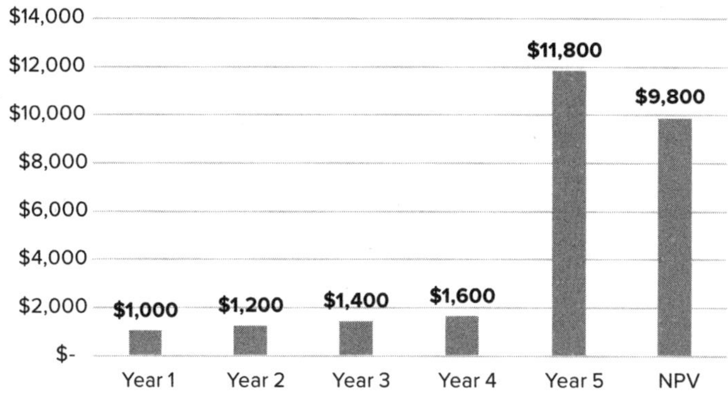

FIGURE 1-2 NPV with 14% Discount Rate

So we go back to the drawing board and redo the project to have greater current income but less reversion value. In practice, there are a number of strategies to make this sort of trade-off, and we will explore a few of those in later chapters. Now, the lower reversion value coupled with the higher current period income brings our project back into sync again (Figure 1-3).

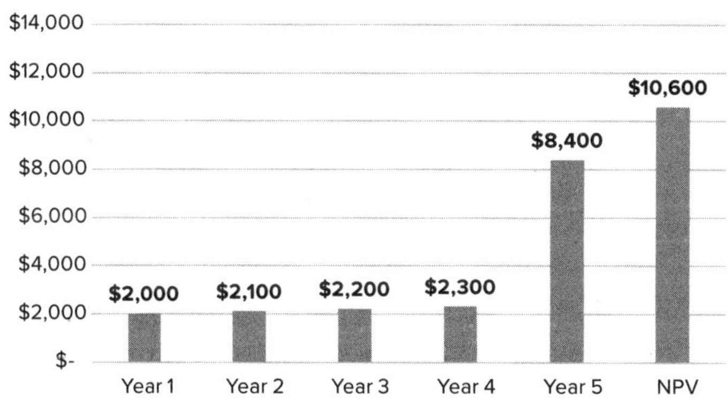

FIGURE 1-3 NPV After Adjusting Cash Flows

This wildly oversimplified example illustrates that we can vary the ingredients and end up in the place we need to be. Not every project will have this level of flexibility, but this also illustrates the valuation scenarios that can be examined before getting into a project and provides the launchpad for a sensitivity analysis on the overall returns.

Considering the endgame will dictate such aspects as ownership structure, degree of leverage, and physical life span of the investment itself. An investment that is planned to be owned for the rest of the investor's life, and then passed on to heirs, will have an ownership structure that facilitates tax-advantaged intergenerational transfers. Or, a real estate investment that is linked to a business investment may be bifurcated from the business itself so that the business can be sold free of the real estate asset, or vice versa.

Disposition Decisions Drive Leverage Decisions

Most real estate is appraised with "market normal" financing. Valuation and pricing assumes that most buyers will enter the market with approximately the same expectations about financing. This is one of the least understood concepts in real estate valuation, even among the most experienced and sophisticated professionals. Let's assume that you want to buy a small income-producing investment property, such as a rental duplex. Most investors in the market will put up 30% to 40% equity and finance the remainder. The market value—and pricing—assumes that. However, you have excellent credit and favorable treatment at the bank, due to your other relationships with that lender, and you can borrow a much higher portion of the purchase price, say 80% or even 100%. When mortgage interest rates are lower than investor equity rates of return (and they certainly are as of this writing), you have a significant advantage over other buyers, and this duplex has an *investment value* for you that is higher than for other buyers in the marketplace. All things being equal, you can outbid other buyers in a hot market.

Of course, debt has to be repaid, and this higher investment value is specific to *you*, not to other buyers to whom you might want to sell this property. If you're thinking about a quick fix-up and flip on this property, you may be better off financing a different way. Let's say you want to buy a distressed investment property and sell it for a gain in a few years. If you pay all cash, then you could be in a position to offer seller financing to a buyer, perhaps at better-than-market rates. Thus, a buyer of *your* property will now enjoy a higher investment value, and may be able to pay *you* more than that buyer might pay some other seller.

Conversely, if you plan to hold the property forever, or build up a portfolio of such properties, then leverage can be a useful tool. Of course, caution is always key—building up a large portfolio of rental properties, each financed with debt, puts you in an awkward position if vacancy rates systematically cycle up in your market. We'll look at cyclical vacancy rates at the end of the chapter.

Physical Life Cycles Must Be Considered in the Context of the Endgame

Your endgame will influence decisions about the physical life cycle of acquired properties and have a very real impact on valuation. Generally, depreciation falls into three categories—physical, functional, and external (sometimes called "economic"). The first category, physical, is just wear and tear on the structure itself. For example, a new building has a new roof. A 20-year-old building may be near needing a roof replacement, which can be an expensive proposition.

The second category—functional—considers the ways a property may be out-of-date. An older high-rise building may have less functional elevators, an out-of-date fire suppression system, or inadequate electrical or heating services. These can be expensive to bring up-to-date.

External obsolescence includes those things beyond the property owner's control. A neighborhood may have been nice many years ago when a property was constructed, but may be run-down and shabby today.

An investor with a "buy and forget" strategy, for a long-term hold, may want to buy brand-new properties with no depreciation. Investors with shorter-term, capital appreciation strategies may think differently. The purchase price of depreciated properties may, at times, be discounted well below the reasonable costs of renovation. There is risk and entrepreneurial effort involved in such strategies, and the valuation equation will need to price those carefully.

There are many other endgame issues that influence the investment decision. The few examples I've presented here only scratch the surface. Later in the book I will present more detailed endgame strategies to maximize capital gains as well as holding benefits and income.

That leads us to a second core concept (or, more accurately, a category of related concepts) I'd like to explore and will discuss further later on in the book.

2. Use and Enjoyment Are Unique Benefits That Flow During Ownership

Certain benefits can be received during the ownership period of real estate. If you buy a share of stock or a bond, you expect capital appreciation over time and in some cases cash income. In the case of real estate there are a variety of potential benefits to the investors. Some are easily valued, such as incomes from rents. Others, such as the subjective benefits from a personal residence or recreational property, may be harder to value. Some property, such as owner-occupied business property, provide current income (or at least implicit income from forgone rental expenses) plus the potential for subjective synergies with the business.

Examples of use benefits include, but are certainly not limited to, the following.

Personal Residence

The use and enjoyment includes the occupancy benefit. This is often mistakenly quantified by only measuring the forgone rent. In fact, studies find benefits accruing to owner-occupant homeowners are significantly higher than forgone rents, and the quantitative measures of these benefits vary widely. The most common variation is by residential value. Upscale residences, not surprisingly, have use and enjoyment benefits far in excess of the rental values.

Raw Land

Many investors find carefully chosen raw land as a beneficial place to store wealth. Land, when properly valued and managed, tends to appreciate over time. The use and enjoyment benefit over time may simply be that appreciation. Investors may also get significant subjective benefits from the land investments, and can even receive tax credits as discussed in a later chapter. Land can also be rented for farmland, hunting land, or recreational space. While annual agricultural rental rates are fairly low, the current income coupled with capital gains over time makes this an attractive investment for some.

Development Project

This can be a residential subdivision development, commercial building development, or a variety of real estate projects. The development project should be approached like any other business enterprise, with start-up costs, minimal cash flows in early periods, then significant cash flows in later periods. Investors with a higher tolerance for risk may enjoy higher returns.

Seasoned Income-Producing Property

This is a common scenario for most investors. Typically such investments carry lower risk but commensurately lower levels of income (Figure 1-4). Such income is often uncorrelated with other income investments, such as bonds, and often exceeds bond income even on a risk-adjusted basis.

Business-Related Property

As noted above, the forgone rents alone explain the benefit of owning the real estate for an investor's business. Business tenants usually find that rents increase over time—landlords enjoy built-in escalation clauses in the leases.

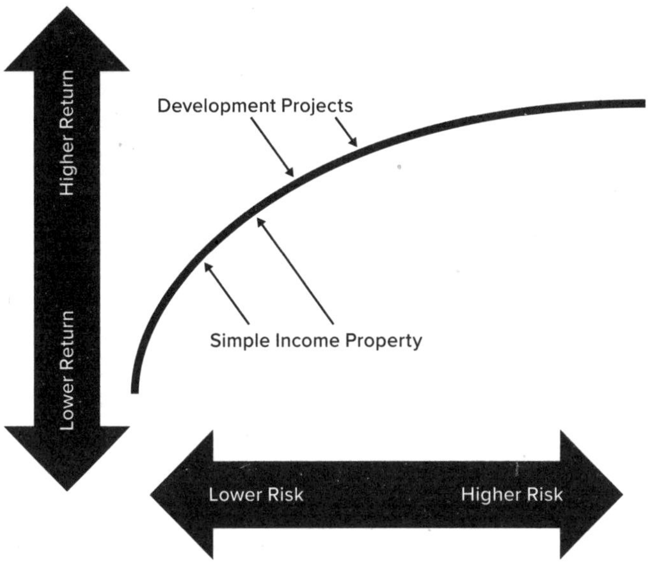

FIGURE 1-4 Relationship Between Risk and Return

Well-chosen and well-maintained commercial property often increases in value over time, so the landlord is enjoying both income and capital gains increases over the lease life. Conversely, the business owner who also owns the real estate moves these benefits back into his or her own pocket. As an added benefit, business owners who also own the real estate may tailor the property more closely to the specific business needs and enjoy other synergies over time. Finally, the business owner can bifurcate the ownership and pay him- or herself rents. There are significant tax and estate planning advantages to such arrangements.

3. Real Estate Enjoys Capital Gains over Time

Investors have flexibility *in some situations* for fine-tuning the benefits between current cash and long-term capital gains. When choices are available, this is often a function of tax implications, although some investments, such as development projects, may have different return structures for capital gains versus current income. For a given project, the capital gains portion may have a higher overall rate of return than the current income, often designed to induce the investor to leave the cash in the project, providing developmental liquidity for a longer period of time.

Capital gains may arise from:

1. Entrepreneurial effort expended by the developers.
2. Simple appreciation over time affected by normal real estate cycles. (At the end of this chapter, I will discuss specific market cycles and how they differ from an individual property cycle.)
3. Short-term market cycles, buying on the upswing.
4. Property improvement over time, such as a tired building in a great location renovated to enjoy higher rents.
5. Tactically structuring higher rents with long-term tenants in "out" years with low early-period rents and escalation clauses, giving the investor a built-in capital gain over a predictable period.

While real estate prices generally trend upward over time, these trends are rarely continuous. Prices for most properties, and in most markets, tend to cycle around those trends during the intermediate term (Figure 1-5). There is some predictability to these cycles, and while investors are encouraged not to try to "catch a falling knife," the savvy investor can spot market cycles and take advantage of those for short- and intermediate-term capital gains.

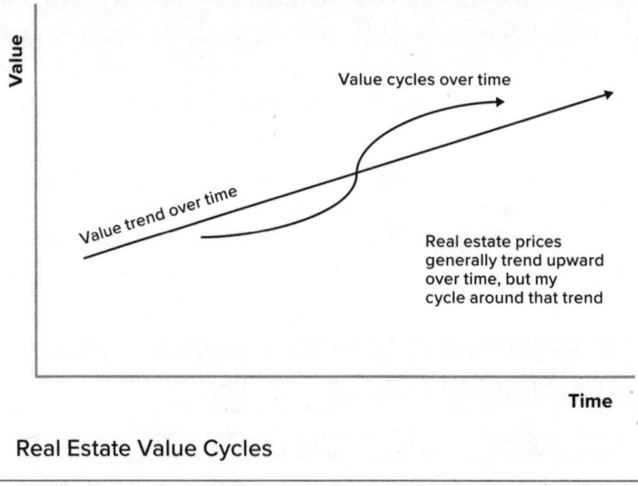

FIGURE 1-5 Real Estate Value Cycles

Real estate cycles are usually driven by rents and occupancy. Savvy investors will seek properties at the cycle trough with leases soon expiring. Those properties will rent-up with increasing escalations in the intermediate term, and result in higher values at the cycle peak. On the other end of the investment spectrum, some not-so-savvy property owners will chase occupancy by offering long-term, fixed-rate leases at the real estate cycle bottom to lock in tenants. Those landlords will watch other properties increase in value as the market exits the cycle, while their property will stagnate in value, burdened by below-market lease rates.

Buy Low and Sell High—or Never Sell at All

Monitoring local market cycles can be extraordinarily profitable in the long run, but requires a certain staying power—the winner's curse, as it is known in economic circles. Fine-tuning the timing of up and down cycles can be risky. If the cycle is real and can be monitored with some degree of confidence, then buying on the down side of the cycle and holding or even selling on the up side is a proven strategy. Of course, playing that strategy requires the investor to keep a lot of dry powder.

I knew a very successful home developer in a medium-sized market who was in it for the long haul. He recognized that there was a tremendous amount of money to be made in up markets, and money could easily be lost in down markets. When he sensed a down market, he simply quit building entirely and went fishing for a year or two. It was a strategy that made him quite wealthy over time.

All sorts of properties may be substantially improved over time, and in fact monitoring and taking advantage of local market cycles can give investors not only buying opportunities but rehab and remodeling opportunities, as well.

Commercial Properties Are Categorized by Quality and Location

Commercial property is often categorized as "A," "B," and "C" grade, depending on the quality of the property, amenities, and resulting levels of rents. A central business district office tower, with high levels of security, architectural stylings, excellent views, and top grade amenities may be an "A" building locally and command top rents. A similar building, but without quite the same level of amenities and located in a suburban office park, may be a "B" building and may command somewhat lesser rents. Finally, "C" buildings are usually in third-tier locations, have few if any amenities, and may be near the end of their physical and functional lives. Naturally, this categorization may be different from one market to another. A suburban office building in Seattle, D.C., San Francisco, or Los Angeles may be significantly better than the nicest office tower in the downtown of a smaller city.

Additionally, location is an important valuation concept for investors. A Class "C" building in a Class "A" location is a much better investment than a Class "A" building in a Class "C" location. In the former scenario, the investor has the opportunity to rehab or remodel up the valuation curve. Perhaps the building can never become a Class "A" building, but secondary and tertiary tenants may look for less desirable space close to their Class "A" customers. A great example of this is in the suburbs of Redmond, Washington. Many secondary tenants need space near Microsoft and are willing to pay a premium over what the office building might bring if located in a less desirable place. In the down portion of real estate cycles, these "C" buildings in "A" locations are often the first hit, as "C" tenants find that they can move up to "B" buildings at the same or even lower prices. Savvy investors use those opportunities to acquire "C" buildings and bring them up to "B" status in preparation for the next up cycle. Of course, the converse is true—investors are well advised to recognize that cycles cycle—a Class "B" building that is not maintained well can become a "C" building during the next down cycle. Investors are constantly monitoring the investments with an eye to portfolio positioning, tax implications, and new investments.

Investment decisions are driven by rents and occupancy cycles, but are aimed at capital appreciation and income. These factors require constant monitoring and management, and can be architected through careful planning and understanding of the valuation metrics.

And that brings us to another major concept we will cover in greater detail in later chapters, but would like to explore now.

4. Real Estate Investments Must Consider Public, Private, and Economic Restrictions

Real estate valuation is subject to a myriad of restrictions, some jurisdictional, some by mutual assent, and some by force of economic realities. In a later chapter, we will discuss the concept of "highest and best use" (HBU) and how it applies to a given property. For the present, it is sufficient to understand the first step in an HBU analysis is determining legally permissible uses for the property by analyzing the public, private, and economic restrictions.

Real Estate Is Subject to Public Restrictions

The most common public limitation is zoning. Most jurisdictions provide for use restrictions or allowances for particular areas to ensure commonality of use. A small neighborhood of single family residences would be negatively impacted if a waste dump was suddenly located nearby. Similarly, industrial properties may be faced with unexpected liabilities if single family residences were built on the same street. These zoning restrictions provide commonality of use and help reduce economic depreciation, a topic that will be explored more fully later.

A second common restriction is the institution of building codes. Most jurisdictions have adopted a common building code with local adaptations. Structures built in Florida have restrictions based on the hurricane season. Those same structures built in the Pacific Northwest will have earthquake restrictions. Otherwise, the building codes throughout the United States are fairly similar, detailed, and specific to particular property uses.

Many jurisdictions will place size limits on development, over and above zoning ordinances. For commercial properties, these are usually limitations on what is called a floor area ratio (FAR), the ratio of the building size to lot size, along with height restrictions.

Public restrictions often consider services, ingress/egress, and parking. These limitations can be complex, and for a commercial building will almost certainly require a certified land planner, an architect, and some negotiations with the municipal authorities.

Even building a house will require navigating local restrictions. In addition to zoning, common restrictions include density, height, and maximum number of bedrooms or bathrooms. Communities govern housing development to make sure crucial public services (schools, transportation, sewer and water, storm water drainage, etc.) are adequately provided. Density restrictions may limit development to a certain number of units per acre, which will dictate whether single family detached houses (lower density) or apartments or condos (higher density) will be allowed.

Many communities will have environmental restrictions to protect wetlands, natural areas, habitats, waterways, and even tree canopies. Key West, Florida, will only allow tree removal upon payment of a fee and planting replacement trees on either private or public spaces. In areas of significant natural habitat, no-growth protection zones, wetlands buffers, and view easements may exist. Many areas, particularly on the West Coast, are subject to extensive and complex growth management ordinances.

Real Estate Uses May Also Be Subject to Private Restrictions

Private restrictions typically include:

- Easements
- Use restrictions (typically through covenants)
- Lease restrictions (typically contractual)
- Encroachments

The most common restriction is an easement, which places specific restrictions on a defined portion of a property. The most common is granted to a utility, such as an easement for overhead or buried power or telecommunications lines. The property owner is restricted from constructing anything that interferes with the utility's right to access and maintain its power lines. Similarly, underground easements may be acquired for these same purposes, plus water, sewer, natural gas, or storm water drainage purposes. In some places, underground easements are acquired for more exotic uses, such as mining or transportation tunnels. Both the easement holder and the surface holder have specific rights and restrictions as specified in the easement and local ordinance or common law.

Many properties come with use restrictions outlined by covenants attached to the deed, although some such restrictions may be a matter of public or even private record separate from the deed itself. Buyers and users of real estate are cautioned to make close examination of public records for private restrictions. Such restrictions may be similar to easements, but will usually restrict or give rights to the entire property. A shopping center was anchored by a grocery store, and this anchoring was an important component to the shopping center value. Across the road was a vacant tract of land suitable for another similar shopping center or a stand-alone grocery. The shopping center owner purchased the land and then resold it to a new buyer with a covenant that the land could never be used for a grocery.

Real estate investment can be exceptionally profitable, and adaptive reuse of real estate, either through development, rehabilitation, or conversion to another use, can be a significant way to enjoy tax-advantaged gains during the holding period. Property valuation either at the acquisition stage or during the ownership phase should take into account optimum strategies for adaptive uses. Public and private restrictions can change over time. Public authorities can impose new zoning or building requirements. While most new public restrictions include "grandfathering" of prior uses, such is not always guaranteed and may be highly restrictive. Private restrictions, such as easements imposed via eminent domain, can occur without significant warning and can have very real impacts on the property itself and the property uses.

And that leads us to the next important set of concepts—all that happens at the property life cycle end.

5. Reversion—the Endgame Strategy Must Drive Decisions

The term *reversion* is a catchall for the various valuation scenarios at the end of a property's life cycle. From an investor's perspective, reversion may take on many different forms:

- Continued ownership as part of an estate
- Sale to another investor or investors
- As a stand-alone investment
- As part of a portfolio
- As part of a business transaction
- Part sold and part retained (physical subdivision)
- Part sold and part retained (legal subdivision)
- A combination of physical and legal subdivisions (such as a syndication)
- Conversion to another use (which restarts the property cycle clock)
- Substantial rehabilitation or remodeling (which restarts the property cycle clock)
- Complete demolition to a raw land state (which restarts the property cycle clock)

Plans may change, and a property purchased with the intent to retain may end up being sold, and vice versa. Nonetheless, every property, to be properly and accurately valued, needs to have some anticipated endgame.

Continued Ownership as Part of an Estate

This is one of the most common estate tools for wealthy families. Real estate is a place to store wealth. It has counterinflationary value trends and generally emerges from down cycles intact, if wisely acquired and properly managed. Indeed, residential market value appraisal techniques assume a residence will be owned in perpetuity. For commercial properties, the net operating income is capitalized with a perpetuity metric, not unlike the valuation of preferred stock. Details and examples of such valuation appear in a subsequent chapter.

Sale to Another Investor

If the property is planned to be owned for a short or intermediate term, then the proper valuation techniques include some sort of discounted cash flow, with an estimate of the reversion cash flows (the net cash from the sale or conversion). Even in situations with a high degree of confidence, the estimate and timing of reversion cash flows may be a moving target. Constant monitoring and management of the endgame cash flows is needed to optimize the investment strategy.

Part Sold and Part Retained (a Physical Subdivision)

A common physical subdivision is a shopping mall or shopping center, in which the primary investor retains certain common areas, parking, "outparcels," and the smaller units, while selling the anchor tenant units to those retailers. The larger retailers control their spaces and guarantees of unfettered parking, while the primary investor retains the rights to the somewhat more lucrative smaller units, all the while benefiting from the halo effect of the permanent anchor. Not all shopping centers are organized this way, but this scenario is increasingly common.

Part Sold and Part Retained (a Legal Subdivision)

Primary investors may sell tenant-in-common shares to smaller investors, or may sell rights, such as shared parking rights. A city built a parking garage and sold a guarantee of a certain number of parking spaces to a major downtown office tenant to encourage job creation. Indeed, parking rights are often bought and sold. Another common legal subdivision is air rights. The Trump organization purchased the air rights above Tiffany's to construct Trump Tower in Manhattan. Valuation of such rights can be problematic, as comparable (or "comp" in the appraisal vernacular) transactions are rare, and the cost/benefit estimates can be huge. In this example, the Trump Tower simply could not have been built without those air rights. What was the value of those air rights to Tiffany's? To the Trump organization? Those two numbers may have been very different.

Conversion or Substantial Rehabilitation

Various endgame uses of real estate are not mutually exclusive. In the 1920s, John and Mabel Ringling built a wonderful trophy residence in Sarasota, Florida, called Ca' d'Zan. After their death, the residence, gallery, and grounds were left to the State of Florida. The property fell into massive disrepair, as can be seen in the 1998 movie *Great Expectations*, largely filmed in the house. After that movie, funds were raised to rehabilitate the property and convert it into a museum and public art gallery.[1]

Many properties, particularly high-end commercial properties, will undergo substantial conversion and rehabilitation as part of the ownership cycle. First-class hotels and resorts are constantly being renovated, with portions frequently converted to other uses.

Complete Demolition

Valuation optimization may mean conversion back to raw land. A property may be best used to provide open space, view space, parking, or permanent easement dedication. In a famous project a few years ago, the Hearst family dedicated many thousands of acres of the Ranch at San Simeon, including miles of Pacific coastline, as permanent open space. They enjoyed significant tax credits as a result. Indeed, there are open space and preservation tax credits available in many circumstances.

6. Accounting Values Differ from Economic Values

Up to this point, I've used the term *value* with only a few qualifiers. We have noted that there is a difference between market value and investment value, and later in the text I will expand on that more fully. For now, I'd like you to understand the difference between value from an economic perspective and value from an accounting point of view.

Accounting is largely *historic* cost oriented, with depreciation calculated by formula rather than by economic realities. Land cannot be depreciated, but buildings can be written off over a specified period of time (usually less than their actual economic life). Certain other improvements to real estate, such as fixtures, may also be depreciated by other formulas. Only under certain circumstances are these depreciation calculations tied to economic realities. Land is assumed to be valued in perpetuity at its historical acquisition cost.

Conversely, economic value is *prospective* and is focused on cash flows. Land and improvements are rarely bifurcated for valuation, and then only if there is some economic reason. Depreciation is tied to economic realities, and is divided between curable and incurable components. Curable components may be repaired or renovated to generate higher returns.

Over time, there may be a very real disagreement between book value and actual value of real estate owned. See Figure 1-6 as an example.

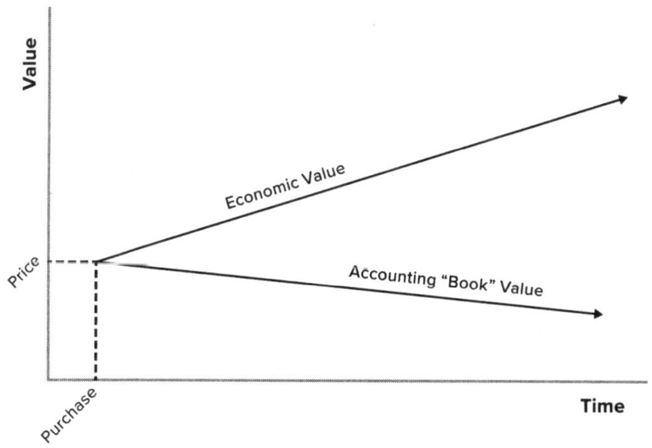

FIGURE 1-6 Economic Value Versus Book Value

The historic book value may be a useful metric for tax purposes, some estate decisions, or even monitoring the remaining property economic. On the other hand, the touchstone for investment management is market value. This is what the investor wants to maximize, or at least optimize, for real estate to be a storer of value, a diversifying portfolio hedge, and a profitable investment.

7. Investors Must Understand "Value to Whom? Value of What?"

The next important concept discussed at length in later chapters has to do with two important questions that need to be answered in estimating the property's value: who is the likely property buyer, and what is actually being bought and sold?

Consider the Ringlings' trophy home in Sarasota—56 rooms, thousands of square feet, an expansive waterfront with a dock for the Ringlings' yacht, a world-class gallery for their art collection, and storage buildings for circus memorabilia. Passing without heirs, they left this to the State of Florida. It begs the question, though, who would buy this? Thus, from a valuation perspective, who would have been "the market" had the property been appraised?

Any investment real estate decision has to take into account the prospective market, even if the asset is assumed to be held in perpetuity. A problem arises when investors fall in love with a property that no one else particularly likes. The biggest house in the neighborhood, unique properties, and properties with very specific uses cause valuation problems. Conversely, I recently examined a very desirable family estate located in a wealthy suburb of New York City. This particular township considered a 5-acre lot as a building site, and taxed it at a significant rate. The estate sat on 25 acres, and so the township, for tax purposes, considered that the family had one residence (on 5 acres) and four other building lots. Their tax bill was enormous. The family protested, saying that they would never subdivide or sell the properties, but their appeal fell on deaf ears. Fortunately, we were able to suggest a solution—an open space easement that gifted away the development rights in perpetuity.

> At every real estate cycle phase, the notion of the market and the property being owned, managed, and sold must be taken into account. The values depend on clearly defining the property and the property rights, and the market in which that property may be bought, leased, managed, redeveloped, and/or sold.

8. Summary—Key Points

Any individual property investment, or portfolio of properties, has a property-specific life cycle. The property is bought, it is owned and managed, and it has some anticipated endgame. These factors should and must be considered at the onset, but will inevitably change over time. The valuation metrics must take into account the anticipation at the onset, the changing dynamics over time, and the impact on value of those changing dynamics.

Property ownership should take into account the public and private restrictions. Buying a property, and optimizing its use and disposal, will happen within the context of those restrictions. Restrictions, public and private, are also dynamic. Property management may necessitate relationship management with outside forces imposing such restrictions.

Finally, the endgame for a given property can be a myriad of options, the most obvious being a "buy and hold" strategy in perpetuity. Real estate requires constant management and attention, and the physical deterioration aspect of real estate negates a pure "buy and hold" strategy in most cases. Multiple options can be considered, and various strategies are not mutually exclusive over the asset's life.

9. A Final Note—Real Estate Market Cycles

A given market goes through cycles, consisting of four phases: expansion, hypersupply, recession, and recovery.

Expansion. Rents rise rapidly, stimulating new construction. It takes a while for construction to catch up, so there is high rent growth with declining vacancy rates.

Hypersupply. New construction catches up with demand. Rents continue to grow, but at declining rates. Developers see the market becoming saturated and pull back on new projects. Vacancy rates slowly rise.

During expansion and hypersupply periods, new construction is financially feasible on a cost versus rent basis.

Recession. New construction has surpassed demand, and vacancy rates rise above levels where new construction is feasible. Rents fall. There is no new construction.

Recovery. Natural growth in the market begins to absorb excess supply. Rents start to grow again, although at rates below inflation. New construction is still not feasible until occupancy surpasses long-term averages. At that point, the recovery turns into an expansion phase and the cycle continues again.

We define a market geographically, such as by the metropolitan market area, or by property type, such as hotel, industrial, or retail. Within the property types, we can also look at subtypes, such as suburban offices, full-service hotels versus limited-service hotels, and neighborhood shopping centers versus shopping malls.

This sort of information informs the investment decision. Naturally, it is not the only or even the primary decision tool for a savvy investor. The underlying concept, that a local market and a type of property in a local market can be tracked using vacancy rates, rents, and supply/demand metrics, is an important tool for acquisition strategies and property management and disposal decisions.[2]

2
A Simple Real Estate Investment Example

Real estate cannot be lost or stolen, nor can it be carried away. Purchased with common sense, paid for in full, and managed with reasonable care, it is about the safest investment in the world.

—Franklin D. Roosevelt

IN CHAPTER 1, I explored the life cycle of real estate to demonstrate that an investor should measure and influence value at each stage. To illustrate this, I will walk through a typical office building development project. *While this example is based on several actual case studies, its purpose is to focus on key elements in the value metrics. In practice, this case study would deserve a book all to itself.*

The property in this example was previously a low-end, fully depreciated, one-story retail store on a fairly large lot. The store fronted a busy street, and the neighborhood was rapidly redeveloping. The principal economic driver was a dot-com business relocating to a several-city-block complex of new buildings being constructed nearby. To accommodate the growth and redevelopment, the city opted to widen the busy street from four lanes to six and would need to "take" the property under eminent domain. A portion of the property would be used for the road widening, and then the remainder would be sold at market value in an auction. After extensive negotiations, the prior owner was compensated by the city. The remainder would be sold off in public auction after the road construction.

The city was interested in job-creating, higher-density development for the neighborhood. To foster this, the remaining lot and the sites nearby were rezoned for commercial high-rise development. This suggested a number of options, including:

- A mixed-use building, with retail on the ground floor and several stories of office space above
- A multistory retail, such as an interior-facing mall
- A pure office building, with no retail on the ground floor

Before even considering the site value, we have to consider which use would be optimal. Naturally, the optimal use would drive the price a buyer would bid at the auction.

1. Optimizing the Use

I previously talked about public and private restrictions on land use. Here, the key element is zoning—use restrictions, height restrictions, floor area ratio restrictions, and parking requirements.

The lot in question is 20,000 square feet, or about a half-acre. The city has zoned the area with a height restriction of 120 feet, which suggests about 10 stories. The same zoning ordinance requires a floor area ratio for commercial development of no more than 5 times the land area, suggesting a maximum development of 100,000 square feet above ground. Underground parking is not included in the floor area requirement, but the depth of a parking garage (and so, the number of spaces) is severely limited by the soil's quality and engineering issues. Figure 2-1 shows a very rough schematic of the tower and the underground parking structure.

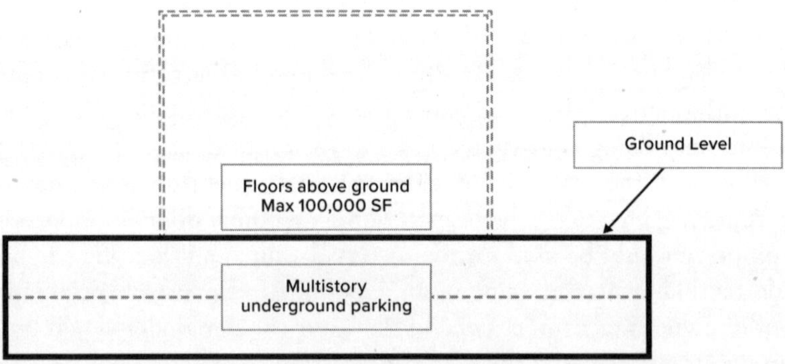

FIGURE 2-1 Simple Schematic of a Multistory Building with Parking

The city encourages subterranean parking. The entire lot can be excavated for a 20,000-square-foot (nominal) parking garage footprint. Each parking space will require about 400 square feet, including driveways, ramps, and such. We consult with an engineer who has worked in this area regularly, and he tells you that the underground area is problematic. We could go down two stories for parking, but no more. Thus, we can excavate the lot and build 40,000 square feet of underground parking, or about 100 spaces. The city requires one parking space for every 1,000 square feet of office space, so this will just barely work.

If we put in a mixed-use property, with retail on the ground floor, the parking requirements change. We'll now have nine stories of office, requiring 90 parking spaces, but the city has different requirements for retail—one space for every 500 square feet. Thus, the ground floor retail by itself will require 20 spaces. The subterranean garage will only accommodate 100 spaces, so to put in ground-floor retail, we'll have to give up not one but two floors of office.

> Just taking a peek forward, the office space you lose will be the tenth floor. Higher-level offices typically rent for more than lower levels, thanks to the view and the ambiance. Hence, we're losing the best floor of office rents to pick up one floor of retail.

2. Valuation at Acquisition

From a purely rent perspective, the ground floor retail will gross $50 per square foot, or $500,000 per year. The office space will gross $20 per square foot for lower floors, $30 for middle floors, and $40 for upper floors. Ground-floor office space would rent for $15 per square foot.

Table 2-1 (see next page) provides a synopsis of rental alternatives.

From a purely gross rent perspective, a 10-story office building provides a better gross income and estimated net operating income than a 9-story office/retail building. However, a 9-story building will cost less to build than a 10-story building. Assuming the cost of construction is linear (which is rarely true!) a 9-story building will cost 10% less than a 10-story building. Thus, under this oversimplified scenario, a 1.6% decrease in rents is coupled with a 10% reduction in construction costs, and hence an increase in overall value.

TABLE 2-1 Rough Rental Estimates

	Office	Office + Retail
Retail (@ $50/SF/year)		$500,000
Floor 1 ($15/SF/year)	$150,000	
Floors 2 & 3 (@ $20/SF/year)	400,000	400,000
Floors 4–8 (@ $30/SF/year)	1,500,000	1,500,000
Floor 9 (@ $40/SF/year)	400,000	400,000
Floor 10 (@ $40/SF/year)	400,000	
Parking (100 spaces @ $200/month)	240,000	240,000
Annual Gross Rent	3,090,000	3,040,000
Vacancy and Collection (5%)	(154,500)	(152,000)
Expense Ratio (35%)	(1,081,500)	(1,064,000)
Estimated Net Operating Income	$1,854,000	$1,824,000
Difference Between the Two	1.6%	

In real life, a more detailed pro forma is developed to examine the costs and benefits of various scenarios. In all likelihood there are numerous bidders for this property, particularly in a "hot" market, and all of them are looking at approximately the same data. It is likely that the various bids will all come in close to one another.

It is important to understand that these rents assume *stabilization* and *seasoning*. These are two related but different topics, and are heard repeatedly when developing and selling income-producing real estate. Stabilization is the period necessary to rent the property at a desired threshold of occupancy. This varies from property type to property type, and often the permanent financing is contingent on achieving stabilized occupancy and rent goals. The developer will aggressively try to prelease a building and move tenants in as soon as practicable, even if this requires concessions. Seasoning refers to a period of time after stabilization when tenants pay rents in a timely fashion, the "bugs" are all worked out, and the developer demonstrates that the property is performing as predicted. Many funds that buy income-producing assets want a period of seasoning before closing the deal.

Now we think we know the optimal mix—a nine-story office building with retail on the ground floor and eight stories of Class B office space. We have yet to consider what the land is worth—how much we will bid at auction. There are two useful methods, one very reliable but fraught with data problems, and the other more complex but potentially more useful in the absence of good data.

The first is a simple sales comparison. We are buying 20,000 square feet of dirt zoned for a 10-story commercial tower in a rapidly growing part of town. If similar sites have been sold recently, this will give us a good idea of what other investors think this site might be worth. Finding truly comparable land sales can be a challenge. As noted, this is a rapidly changing neighborhood, with new city-provided infrastructure. A land sale a year ago might not tell us much about the value of land today. Also, developers will pay top dollar to aggregate a developable site. For example, imagine that a city block in this neighborhood has six parcels. You want to develop the entire block, and you own five of those six parcels. You will pay a king's ransoms to get the last parcel, and in practice that last parcel may sell for five or six times as much as was paid for the first parcel on the block.

Most investors will begin with a *land extraction*. Land extraction assumes that we can bifurcate the entire project value between the building value and the land value. Buried in both values is a factor for *entrepreneurial profit* as well as holding costs during the land development and rent-up period. Hence, estimating the land value will also require estimating those two factors as well. Admittedly, at this point we are dealing with very rough estimates. In a rapidly changing land market, this may be the only way to determine the land value in this project.

Let's start with a project value as a whole. In Table 2-1, I showed that the net operating income for the project, at stabilized and seasoned occupancy, would be about $1,824,000. I glossed over that number, but now it may be wise to explore just what it means. First, I estimate the gross rents. Those rents assume the building is optimally occupied. Full occupancy rarely happens, however, and when it does, it may be a signal that rents are too low! Thus, we deduct a factor for vacancy and collection issues. This factor is usually locally determined, but as a general rule of thumb, in healthy markets, this will be about 5% to 10% of gross rents.

> Technically, Table 2-1 leaves out a step. Gross rents minus vacancy and collection losses equals *effective rents*. In practice, this is an important step, because management fees and some other expenses may be tied to this.

I then deducted expenses. In valuation, unlike accounting, I am only interested in actual, anticipated cash expenses *with one exception*. I also deduct an estimate of future repair costs, called the *reserves for replacement.* These reserves include, but are not limited to, any major repair to the structure that is the landlord's responsibility. For an office building, this will usually include any repairs to the mechanicals (heating and air, hot water, ventilation), the structure itself, and particularly the roof, which will generally need to be replaced on a fairly well-defined schedule. Stand-alone, single-tenant buildings such as warehouses, big-box retails, and stand-alone office buildings are usually rented on a "net" basis. The landlord provides the structure, and the tenant is responsible for all expenses including such reserves for replacement. Often, there is some negotiation, and any major structural replacement, major mechanical replacement, or roof replacement may be left to the landlord on a case-by-case basis.

Long-term office rents usually have a provision for *tenant improvements* (e.g., paint, carpet, wall coverings, even new kitchens and specialty or custom hardware) that are specific to the tenant spaces themselves. At the lease inception or renewal, these are usually negotiated on a tenant-by-tenant basis. Tenant improvements can be quite costly—for a long-term lease with a great tenant, it is not uncommon for a landlord to spend a year's gross rent on tenant space improvements.

Accounting for tenant improvements is tricky. Generally accepted accounting principles require that tenant improvements be capitalized and amortized over the life of the lease. From a valuation perspective, prospective tenant improvements can be treated as reductions in gross rents (thus prospectively amortizing anticipated tenant improvement costs) or expensed. For purposes of this exercise, I will assume tenant improvement costs and leasing fees are already accounted for in the gross rent structure.

Now, going back to the expense ratio—an actual valuation will be much more exacting about the expenses, breaking each one down into constituent components and estimating future expenses for each category based on market comparisons and best estimates from the developer. For an existing building, actual historical expenses will be compared to market norms. Common categories of expenses include, but are not limited to:

- Management fees
- Utilities
- Day-to-day maintenance
- Custodial and engineering services
- Property taxes
- Insurance
- Security services
- Reserves for replacement

Two important things are *not* on the list—debt service and income taxes. Valuation is agnostic to the specific debt service or investor/owner tax situation. In the non-real-estate world, the analogy is EBITDA, or earnings before interest, taxes, depreciation, and amortization. The analogy in securitized real estate is FFO, or funds from operations.

High-rise office buildings and many multitenant retail establishments are rented on a *gross rent* basis (as assumed in this example). The landlord pays essentially all expenses and simply charges the tenant a single monthly fee. In a *net rent* situation, the tenant pays for all expenses and a significantly lower monthly rent. There are, of course, various middle-ground scenarios. In a long-term lease, the landlord may include a rent escalation clause (either a fixed annual increase or an increase tied to the inflation rate) and may also include an *expense stop*. This means that the landlord will pay all expenses up to a fixed level (either a dollar level, a dollar level with an inflation factor, or a percentage of the gross rent), and the tenant may be responsible for expenses beyond that limit. Expense stops were very popular a few decades ago when inflation rates were higher for expenses than for rents. Now, these are not as common.

Developers and landlords have some control over these expenses. One large office real estate fund found that they could use artificial intelligence to proactively predict utility, engineering, and maintenance issues. They were able to reduce their expense ratio by 3%. While this does not sound like much, this particular fund has over $1 billion in annual rents. A 3% reduction in expenses adds up!

We are left with NOI, or *net operating income*. This assumes stabilization and seasoning. A more detailed analysis would develop a more detailed set of cash flows, both in and out, on a monthly or annual basis through the life of the acquisition, development, and eventual sale, after seasoning. Cash flows during the development and rent-up period would be discounted at a higher rate to reflect inherent riskiness (development, financial, and marketing risk to name a few). Entrepreneurial profits would be earned at the permitting, development, rent-up, and project sale phases. For purposes of this simple illustrative example, however, we will take a few shortcuts. As will be seen in later chapters, these shortcuts actually get us pretty close to the same answer that the more detailed analyses would find.

I assumed a bit earlier that the cost of building the 9-story retail/office building would be about 10% less than the cost of the 10-story building. You might argue—with some merit—that we're not building a 9-story building, but rather an 11-story one with two floors underground, and indeed you would be correct. Those two underground floors replace a foundation that would otherwise have to be built! This isn't to say that underground parking isn't expensive, but it is a very good use of space and concrete, assuming the engineering plays out.

In Table 2-2, I return to the comparative income analyses and *capitalize* the income at the prevailing rate. Capitalization of income assumes income perpetuity at either a constant or predictably increasing (or decreasing) level. The simple formula for capitalization is:

$$Value = \frac{CF_1}{r} \quad \text{EQUATION 2-1}$$

Where CF is the annualized cash flow expected in period 1 (here, the stabilized NOI) and r is the capitalization, or cap rate. Cap rates are linked to the collective rate-of-return expectations of investors in the market. As such, cap rates are usually determined from market transactions—the ratios of NOI to purchase prices of comparable transactions. In a perfect world, Equation 2-2 would also tell us:

$$r = \frac{CF_1}{Price} \quad \text{EQUATION 2-2}$$

Of course, the world is rarely perfect. Comp data can be hard to gather, market conditions can change rapidly, and there can be significant variation among transactions due to hidden conditions. The analyst can also proactively estimate r with what is known as a mortgage-equity analysis. While valuation is agnostic to any particular investor's financing situation (which is why NOI is a before-tax and before-interest estimate), cap rates implicitly recognize market normal requirements for financing and expectations of typical market participants. Hence, as shown in Equation 2-3, r can be estimated as the weighted average of the cost of debt and the expected return to equity investors, weighted by the market normal loan-to-value ratios:

$$r = (LTV)(mortage\ constant) + (1 - LTV)(r_e) \quad \text{EQUATION 2-3}$$

In Equation 2-3, the LTV is the market normal *loan to value ratio*, a fraction between 0 and 1. The market normal LTV on a typical residence is 80%. On most commercial property, somewhere between 50% and 60% is typical. The mortgage constant is the annual (or monthly × 12) factor necessary to fully amortize a commercial mortgage at prevailing rates and terms. The factor r_e refers to the expected rate of return for the equity investors, sometimes referred to as the *equity dividend rate*.

This assumes that the cap rate captures how investors expect the cash flows to increase over time. Finance students may remember the Gordon's Growth Model, which accommodates changing cash flows, as long as the rate-of-change is constant. Equation 2-4 is handy under those situations:

$$\text{Value} = \frac{CF_1}{(d-g)} \qquad \textbf{EQUATION 2-4}$$

where CF is the expected year 1 NOI, d is the discount rate, and g is the growth rate. If we let $r = d - g$, then we see that it looks like Equation 2-1. In other words, the cap rate is now equal to $d - g$.

"Price" and "value" can be substituted for one another here, although that's not always true! In this case, though, we assume we have found that investors in the current market expect a 10% rate of return and the NOI and property values are expected to grow at 3% per year. Thus, the implied cap rate is 7%. 3% per year, constantly and in perpetuity. The implied cap rate is 7%, as shown in Equation 2-5:

$$r = \frac{\$1\ m}{\$10\ m} - 3\% = 10\% - 3\% = 7\% \qquad \textbf{EQUATION 2-5}$$

Returning to the NOI estimates, and capitalizing by 7%, I calculate values as shown in Table 2-2:

TABLE 2-2 Capitalized Income

	Office	Office + Retail
Estimated Net Operating Income	1,854,000	1,824,000
Capitalization Rate	7.00%	7.00%
Indicated Value (rounded)	$26,486,000	$26,057,000

The pure office scenario has a slightly higher value and would be worth more if already built. The office development, however, would cost more to build. We estimated that the difference would be about 10%. At this juncture, we consult with architects, engineers, and land planners, who typically keep up with local construction costs. Cost markets can change rapidly, and so the net value to the developer is actually higher with the office/retail scenario, as shown in Table 2-3.

TABLE 2-3 Land Value Calculations

	Office	Office + Retail
Estimated Net Operating Income	1,854,000	1,824,000
Capitalization Rate	7.00%	7.00%
Indicated Value (rounded)	26,486,000	26,057,000
Estimated Construction Costs	(24,000,000)	(22,000,000)
Land Value	$2,486,000	$4,057,000

The land has a higher contributory value in the second scenario (office + retail) than in the first. This is not unusual, and it is one reason why this sort of mixed-use development is common when it is possible. The bottom line, of course, is *not* the bid price on the land. The estimated construction costs, in a perfect world, take into account the entrepreneurial profits and holding costs associated with the construction project itself. (I assume here that the construction costs have a 15% annual entrepreneurial profit built in and a factor for holding costs such as interest expenses. I will address this in more detail in a later section.)

The land value estimate does not take into account profits and holding costs associated with the land itself. For purposes of this example, I assume the developer wants to earn 15% annually on this project, and the holding costs are 10% annually (until the entire project reaches stabilization). I further assume this takes about two years. With that in mind, I examine a proposed purchase price for the land, as shown in Table 2-4.

TABLE 2-4 Determining the Price for the Land

	Office + Retail
Estimated Net Operating Income	1,824,000
Capitalization Rate	7.00%
Indicated Value (rounded)	26,057,000
Estimated Construction Cost	(22,000,000)
Land Value	4,057,000
Entrepreneurial Profit (15%/yr)	(876,312)
Holding Costs (10%/yr)	(584,208)
Indicated Purchase Price (rounded)	$2,596,000

The actual "bid" price for the land is slightly under $2.6 million, even though the contributory value at stabilized occupancy is over $4 million. The difference includes the holding costs while the project is not earning income ($584,208) and the profit expected by an entrepreneur for taking on the risk of development ($876,312).

3. Returns and Valuation During the Holding Period

I am purposely skipping an important valuation component—the development itself. Development projects require significant oversight, management, and value engineering. Usually, on a project this size, an architect and an engineering team will provide continuous oversight from project inception to completion and "punch out." The developer, owner, and/or investor (who may all be the same person!) will be in regular contact. In the military, they say no battle plan survives first contact with the enemy, and likewise no development plan survives intact from inception to conclusion.

To be useful, the development oversight process would fill a book all on its own. However, a brief outline provides a good on-ramp into the holding period analysis. The development began with an idea of what could be built on the site. In real estate, it is said that there are sites looking for uses or uses looking for sites. I've glossed over this decision process, but the development of real estate is frequently a bit of both. Most developers have a degree of specialization—apartments, office, industrial, to name a few—and are constantly looking for sites to ply their trade. Conversely, some sites, such as in this case, cry out for developers to look at them as a result of the city's investment. Given the zoning requirements, the developers who were looking at this site were all probably in the office or mixed-use business, and all knew more or less what a 9- or 10-story building would cost to build. They have the contacts, the team of professionals, the financing, and the contractors all ready to move when and if one of them was able to buy the site at auction.

Since this is most likely a well-honed team who have probably worked together before, the actual development process requires little in the way of new invention. The cost numbers are fairly well known to this group, and they would have been conducting preliminary permitting investigations in parallel with the financial analysis in the preceding section.

> Early in my career, I had the opportunity to work with a developer who specialized in low-rise (three-story) suburban office buildings near tertiary cities. He owned the marketing, design, development, financing, and even the construction companies. He worked off the same set of plans and specifications throughout the United States, with only slight modifications as needed for terrain differences, and typically built 5 or 10 buildings adjacent to one another in a large suburban office park. Many modern developers are like this, and view construction more or less as an assembly-line process.

Shortly after the land purchase (which is often *optioned* or joint-ventured with the seller rather than purchased outright), the permitting process begins in earnest. As soon as the developer sees that the permitting process will be successful, a timetable is developed, final plans and specifications are drawn up, and construction bids are let. Successful construction bidders (a general contractor and major subcontractors) finalize timetables. Specialty products, such as steel and glass, are ordered. In parallel, construction financing is finalized.

> Construction and permanent financing typically go hand in hand. Many lenders and financial sources only want one piece of the financing rather than the whole bundle. This reflects on different risk/reward needs by different financing sources.

At some point, the building will be "nearly" finished and ready for occupancy. Typically, "finished" means a shell with supporting walls in place. With a new building, preleasing allows the tenant improvements to be constructed along with the building shell, saving everyone time and money. These improvements will be capitalized and amortized over the life of the tenancy, which will be different from the depreciation period for the rest of the building.

After building completion, there are usually small issues on a "punch out" list. This is the list of items that do not conform to the contract specifications, even though the project or building is substantially complete. These items may or may not be completed before occupancy. Often, these will include minor repairs to finishes, cleanup, and any outstanding installations remaining. In some cases, the punch list will also include final additions to cope with new last-minute details.

The city requires parking, but it is silent as to how this gets allocated. Office tenants will expect us to rent "availability" (but not necessarily a specific space) at market normal rates, which for this example are estimated at $200 per month per space. Requirements for the retail tenants vary from market to market. Generally—but not always—the allocation of parking space to a specific retail tenant will carry with it higher rents. Most parking garages like this will have key entry for the tenants and credit card entry (and exit) for visitors, who pay by the hour.

In a hot market, landlords can be a bit choosy about tenants, but in a soft market, landlords may have not have this luxury. In the previous chapter, I discussed local market cycles. In a perfect world, we would want to have our new office building ready for rent near the top of an up cycle. However, it is rarely a perfect world, and catching a falling knife can be dangerous. Basic leases are 5 to 10 years or more. Longer leases are usually rewarded with greater discretion in tenant improvements. Landlords also want tenants with good credit and "staying power"—replacing a tenant, or suffering with a tenant who fails to pay rent—can be costly and troublesome. We may want a mix of tenants so that systematic economic cycles do not cause widespread problems among a project's tenants. Imagine the problems in the suburbs of Redmond, Washington, and Palo Alto, California, during the dot-com bust!

As for the "light" retail clients, they usually focus on serving the shopping needs of building tenants and tenants of neighboring buildings. Common light retail in Class A and B office space includes restaurants, barbers, convenience stores, newsstands, and coffee shops. Usually, these are not "destination" retail, in that these shops do not expect customers to drive in from a distance and park to shop there. Rather, these shops and stores rely on walk-in trade from the tenants of nearby buildings.

Modern "new urbanist" thinking intersperses office and retail with high-rise apartments and condominiums. The ground-level retail in these high-rise buildings will need to service a broader variety of customers, and may include some types of retail normally thought to be "destination" stores, such as large groceries, banks, medical offices, and even schools.

Once the building is finished and stabilized occupancy is achieved (estimated at 95% or so), we have two choices: hold the building in our investment portfolio or sell the building to another investor after seasoning. Both have merits, but common practice is to separate the "development" from the "investment-ownership." These two sit at very different places on the risk/reward curve (see Figure 2-2), and pure cash-flow investors

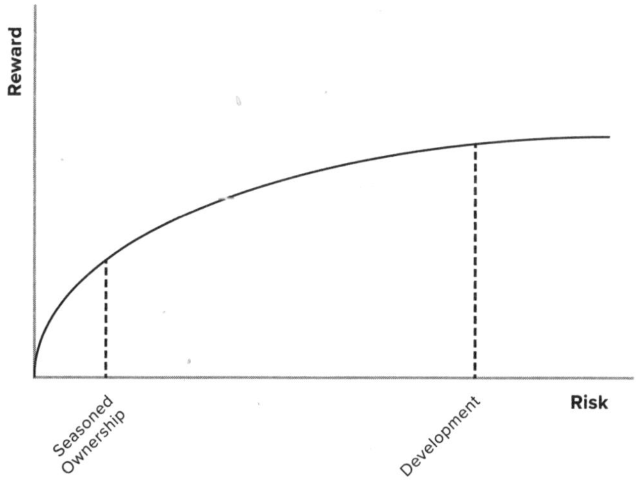

FIGURE 2-2 Risk and Reward, Seasoned Ownership Versus Development

typically prefer lower risk with stable, predictable rewards. Developers, on the other hand, are willing to assume risk for the higher entrepreneurial profits, acknowledging that the development (and risk management) process requires significantly more day-to-day input.

Risk versus reward deserves some explanation. The exact shape of this curve is constantly changing. At any given point in time, the relationship between the two points may be greater or less than shown. The general truism holds, though, that higher rewards usually require assuming higher degrees of risk. Perhaps even more important, there is a limit to the degree of reward associated with ever-increasing assumptions of risk. This second truism is important whether the investor is looking at real estate, stocks and bonds, or just hiding money in a mattress. There are certain risks associated with any investment or use of funds. Real estate provides a number of solutions to this problem that can fit into nearly any diversified portfolio.

During the seasoning process, the developer will ready the building for sale to a prospective long-term investor. The two key elements any investor will examine are net operating income (sustainable, long-term, forward-looking) and capitalization rate. Going back to the earlier equations, investors will negotiate based on a number of metrics, but ultimately the value will be very close to NOI divided by market-normal cap rate.

So, how does the developer optimize these two metrics? Taking the latter one first, developers (and investors) tend to be price *takers* with respect to cap rates. In other words, they have little control over the cap rate in the market. Market cap rates—the ratio of income to price—are dictated by competing properties in the marketplace. No investor wants to be ahead of that curve, and arbitrage keeps undervalued properties in check.

That leaves optimizing the NOI. At the top line, developers who want to sell a property in the short term have a somewhat different strategy from investors who might want to own the property over the long term. A short-term "flip" would entail maximizing net rents rather quickly. Many tenants would prefer lower rents in the short run with a trade-off of higher rents in later periods. Consider two scenarios, as shown in Table 2-5. In Scenario 1, building rents are maximized today, with escalation clauses at the expected inflation rate (2%) in later years. In Scenario 2, building rents are somewhat lower (10% lower) today, but with a 5% escalation in later years.

The differences in the two scenarios are astonishing and insightful on several levels. First, the "develop and hold" strategy yields a much higher value in year 5, but with a trade-off of a lower value today. This can be problematic if financing is a function of *pro forma* values, but if not this can yield a value enhancing solution. More to the point, direct investors (the potential buyers of this project) are well advised to seek out purchases where

TABLE 2-5 Five-Year Comparative Metrics

	Escalation at Inflation		5% Escalation Clauses	
	Office + Retail Today	**Office + Retail Year 5**	**Office + Retail Today**	**Office + Retail Year 5**
Retail (@ $50/SF/year)	$500,000	$552,040	$450,000	$574,327
Floors 2 & 3 (@ $20/SF/year)	400,000	441,632	360,000	459,461
Floors 4–8 (@ $30/SF/year)	1,500,000	1,656,121	1,350,000	1,722,980
Floor 9 (@ $40/SF/year)	400,000	441,632	360,000	459,461
Floor 10 (@ $40/SF/year)				
Parking (100 spaces @ $200/month)	240,000	240,000	240,000	240,000
Annual Gross Rent	3,040,000	3,331,426	2,760,000	3,456,230
Vacancy and Collection (5%)	(152,000)	(166,571)	(138,000)	(172,811)
Expense Ratio (35%)	(1,064,000)	(1,165,999)	(966,000)	(1,209,680)
Estimated Net Operating Income	1,824,000	1,998,856	1,656,000	2,073,738
Cap Rate	7.00%	7.00%	7.00%	7.00%
Indicated Value	26,057,000	28,555,000	23,657,000	29,625,000
Present Value		$20,359,000		$21,122,000

there is significant upside potential in the rent, particularly when a property can be upgraded with a small investment on the front end. In this case, the second scenario has a present value (discounted at 7%) which is $773,000 higher than the first scenario, or about 3.75%. Thus, if this was an "older" building with deferred maintenance and corresponding lower rents, the buyer/investor could purchase, put in $773,000 of improvements, raise rents 5% per year, and be as well off as with the new building with initially higher rents.

Other scenarios to maximize net operating income all focus on the expense column.

Minimize Vacancy and Collection Losses

This isn't as simple as it sounds. Academic studies suggest that there is a profit-maximizing level of vacancy. At 100% occupancy (0% vacancy), the landlord is probably charging lower-than-market rents. Most investment scenarios consider something between 5% and 10% to be optimal and likely.

Management Costs

Self-management or owning a captive management firm may provide some benefits. In most major cities there is an active commercial rental brokerage community who expect to be paid commissions when they bring in a tenant. A landlord certainly has the privilege of relying on a captive management and marketing team, but at the cost of alienating the local brokerage community.

Property Taxes

For a commercial property, this can be one of the biggest expense line items. The tax appeal industry is thriving by representing major property owners, particularly large trusts or retail chains, in their property tax management issues. Few areas in the expense ratio can have such dramatic and direct impact on the bottom line and hence on the valuation.

Insurance

Insurance management is a constant struggle, particularly downtown core and "trophy" properties that may be targets of litigation or vandalism. Buildings with modern construction or located in suburban areas may enjoy lower rates. Policy specifics vary from state to state, and as either a developer or investor you will want to have your insurance broker involved at the earliest possible time.

Utilities

Modern commercial buildings are designed to comply with energy requirements, and many tenants look for buildings with LEED or Energy Star certifications. Since energy costs may vary significantly, and may increase faster than rents, a proactive stance on energy and other utility costs, including water recycling, is part of value engineering at the design phase. An investor in an older building will be well advised to consider improvements that can be made to retrofit such energy saving components.

4. Maximizing Returns at Reversion

Optimizing the "current rent versus future rent" mix has impact during the holding period and during the lead up to sale or reversion. Other tips for improving the returns at sale include, but certainly are not limited to the following.

Catch Up on Property Maintenance

Even short periods for seasoning can entail some maintenance and short-term depreciation issues. Key issues include the mechanicals (boilers and other HVAC, elevators, garage facilities), Americans with Disabilities Act compliance, roof structures and drainage, and simple cosmetic issues such as landscaping and signage. Buyers will often discount more than the repair costs due to the hassle associated with these issues.

Conduct an Environmental Audit

Buyers will nearly always order an environmental "Level 1" audit (more formally known as a Phase 1 environmental assessment), and if it is even vaguely suspected that the property has environmental issues, then a Level 2 will be required. What are these? A Level 1 is basically a public records search to see if there is any likelihood of environmental contamination, and a Level 2 actually pokes holes in the ground. If a Level 2 finds anything, then a Level 3 begins the remediation process.

> The ISO 14000 Standard outlines the requirements for such an audit. Real estate investors are encouraged to have at least a cursory familiarity with such standards.

Understand Investor Motivations

Developers and investors often speak two different languages, and exist on two different points on the risk/reward spectrum. Investors typically want predictable, inflation-hedged cash flows with the security of capital preservation. Risk needs to be removed, to the extent possible, and indeed this is the purpose of stabilization and seasoning. On the other hand, developers tend to be more risk-takers, and anticipate higher levels of returns.

5. Summary and Key Points

The purpose of this chapter was to introduce real estate investors to issues confronting project development. These issues, and the techniques for analyzing and confronting them, are common to most real estate development projects, from the smallest (building a single house) to the largest (a whole planned community). We have purposely examined how the developer and the investor/owner sit at different places on the risk/reward curve. The issues in this chapter are important for these market participants—even the simplest pure investment will have redevelopment issues sometime in the property life span.

With that in mind, you should have five key takeaways at this point:

Real estate values are largely baked in at the acquisition stage. The key element here was finding the right price for the land acquisition. If we make a mistake and overpay, the project may not bail us out. If we make a mistake and underpay, the land will go to someone else. Most bids for this property will probably come in very close to one another.

The best property use is highly influenced by local legal constraints and market conditions. Developers and investors have to work within the constraints of zoning, engineering, and construction requirements. In a later chapter, I will explore the concept of *highest and best use* in detail. For now it is sufficient to understand that value maximization takes place within the set of constraints. Successful investors understand how to maximize value within those boundaries.

Building the biggest building isn't necessarily the value-maximizing choice. We could have built a 10-story office building, but opted instead for a 9-story mixed-use building. Consider a typical residential neighborhood—the most valuable house in the neighborhood may not be the biggest one. The "Mona Lisa" is a small painting, but it is one of the most valuable—if not *the* most valuable—at the Louvre.

Charging max rents may not be the value-maximizing solution. Developers and investors need to consider the entire property and lease life cycle. Rents in future years may be more valuable than rents today.

Controlling expenses is a key element. NOI is a function of net rents and total expenses. To the extent those expenses can be controlled, the cash flows directly to the bottom line and is multiplied by the cap rate into value.

6. A Final Note—Leverage or Not?

One great advantage of real estate is the ability to *leverage*—to borrow significant sums toward development or acquisition. Indeed, since returns from real estate (on a percentage basis) generally exceed the cost of debt (again, on a percentage basis), the concept of leverage makes a lot of sense. Plus, debt expenses (interest and other costs associated with the debt) are tax deductible, so the after-tax cost of debt is actually:

$$R_{at} = R_{bt}(1-t)$$ EQUATION 2-6

Where R_{at} is the after tax cost of debt, R_{bt} is the before-tax (the actual, nominal interest rate on the loan), and t is the borrower's marginal tax rate. Even tax-hedged entities such as REITs and limited partnerships benefit due to the tax shelter flow-through.

If this is the case, then why isn't every real estate investment leveraged to the maximum loan-to-value ratio allowed by the lenders? The answer, simply put, is *risk*. Long-term investors tend to be risk averse, looking for simple, steady flows of cash. To the extent leverage assists in meeting internal return targets, leverage is useful. Otherwise, though, leverage increases the riskiness of an otherwise low-risk investment.

Take a look at Figures 2-3 and 2-4 (see next page). In Figure 2-3, increases in rent impact the bottom line (before tax cash flow, which is NOI *minus* debt service) only after the cost of debt is satisfied. The lender has first claims to the profits, and has a preemptory claim if the cash flows are not sufficient.

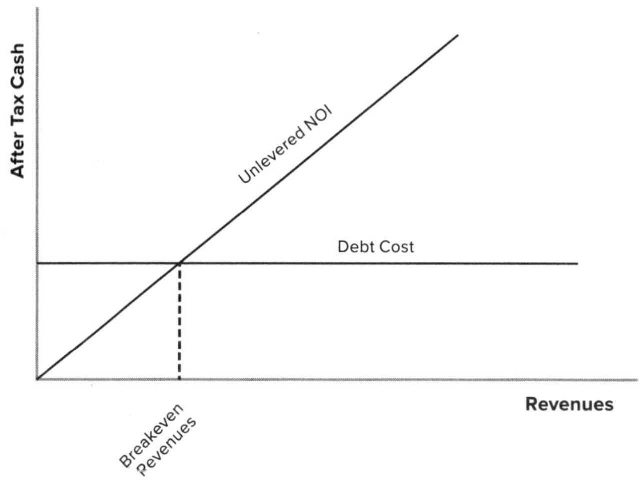

FIGURE 2-3 Breakeven Revenue with Debt

As shown in Figure 2-4, leverage has a significant impact on return on investment (ROI). The slope changes dramatically, all things being equal, and above the leverage advantage point, levered ROI is much higher than unlevered. Of course, the risk is that below the breakeven point, levered ROI can be costly.

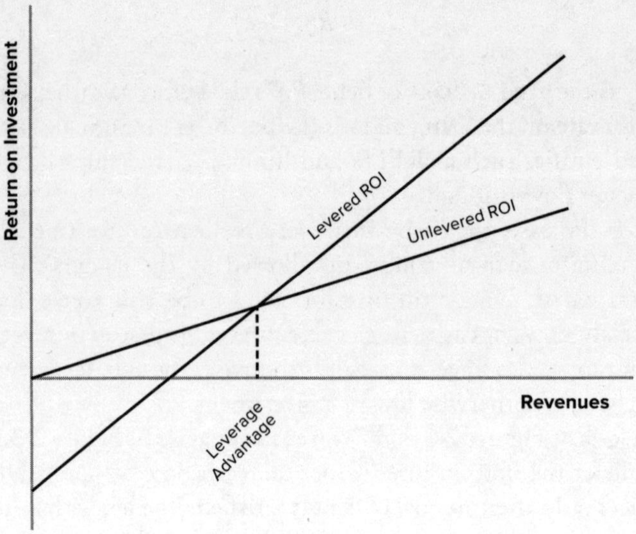

FIGURE 2-4 Levered Versus Unlevered ROI

Calculating the exact leverage points requires a sensitivity analysis, well beyond the scope of this simple exercise. Later in the text we will examine such sensitivities in a more detailed discussion of leverage.

3

Reflecting on Why We Buy Real Estate

> Buying real estate is not only the best way, the quickest way, the safest way, but the only way to become wealthy.
>
> —Marshall Field

IN CHAPTER 2, I examined a real estate development deal from the perspective of the developer (higher risk, higher rewards) but also with an eye to the requirements of the long-term investor (lower risk, stable long-term rewards). Both perspectives consider real estate as a return-generating investment.

There are many reasons to invest in real estate. The *market value* is the same whether you buy it for income or buy it for personal satisfaction. Personal perspectives, specific investment needs, and portfolio strategies will certainly affect the *investment value* of real estate. Careful consideration of value metrics allows the investor to maximize the market value *and* the investment value.

I knew an investor who enjoyed a particular coastal city. He was extraordinarily wealthy and could buy whatever house he wanted in this particular town. He was also gregarious and enjoyed the company of others. In the words of Rhett Butler, "I prefer to stay in a well-managed hotel." So, the investor bought one of the nicer hotels in this town and dumped a good bit of money into it. He stayed in the penthouse suite, which was outfitted to his liking, whenever he was in town. He stayed there until the end of his days, enjoying the coastal sunrises every morning. The investment turned out to be quite good, and the hotel was eventually sold by his estate for top dollar. The market value during his lifetime was of little importance to him. That said, he was indeed able to have it both ways—a great market value investment and a great personal investment value.

The rest of this chapter describes other non-return-generating reasons why we buy real estate and the implications for valuation.

1. Personal Real Estate

In the simplest of terms, personal real estate consists of personal residences, vacation property, and recreational holdings. For most Americans, the personal residence is the only property they own. For more upscale investors, the personal holdings can be complex and intertwined.

The choice of an upscale personal residence has a lot to do with lifestyle, well beyond the scope of simple valuation metrics. Even geographic differences count—try comparing a large luxury residence in a rural area (think the Ewing mansion in "Dallas") with a similarly sized luxury residence on the shores of Lake Washington outside Seattle. The choice of a family residence—and we are really talking about estates here—also carries issues of intergenerational stability. While purchase or construction decisions should be made in a value-optimizing fashion, the successful family typically has little or no interest in the eventual resale value. If indeed the residence is to be sold, this is a matter for subsequent generations.

The decisions about location, size, features, and amenities have more to do with the family structure. Is it a large family or a small one? Does the family entertain large groups at the home? Conversely, is the family home just a place for the family's senior members to live and entertain small groups of friends and family?

Some decisions with value implications will include:

- Location (part of the country—often a family cultural decision)
- Life span and lifestyle of the principal residents (Will there be a need for live-in staff?)
- Proximity to amenities (Is the family lifestyle more outgoing or introverted?)
- Proximity to transportation (Will the family travel regularly?)
- Proximity to business interests (Are family members still active?)

I once counseled a retired, childless couple who entertained very little and enjoyed a bit of a hermit lifestyle. They built an architecturally wonderful home on an island quite some distance from transportation. It was accessible, but only via a convoluted route. Shortly after retiring, the husband, a retired multinational company CEO, agreed to consult to some businesses in his industry. The consulting fees were secondary to remaining active and respected in an industry where he'd spent his career. While much if not most of his consulting could be done online and by phone, he regularly needed to travel to meet with colleagues. Just getting to a major airport required a one-hour drive, a half-hour flight via a small commuter plane (only in good weather, by the way), and then another half-hour drive to the major airport. The couple really loved their home, the view, and the ambiance, but his postretirement lifestyle hardly fit with their location decision.

Location

Historically, the part of the country or part of the world for the family residence had an important legacy component. Families who lived in the Northeast had probably lived in the Northeast for many generations. Post–World War II, and particularly the twenty-first century, put pause to many such legacy decisions. The newly wealthy families consider "home" to be far removed from where their ancestors lived. Indeed, home base may be a function of where they made their money—Wall Street or Silicon Valley, for example.

Life Span of the Principals

Everyone wants a long life span. The point is, will the principal family members live in this residence for the rest of their lives? Will the family home pass on to the next generation? Will the principal family members require live-in staff in later years (e.g., nursing assistance)?

Proximity to Amenities

Amenities could include the environmental ambiance of an island home but could also include proximity to the arts, culture, and performance venues, implying an urban location. As the principals get older, they may value proximity to healthcare. If the principals are still active in business, proximity to an airport may be critical, which is also important for those who value recreational travel. For some, seeing the mountains every day is critically important, but for others a view of the sea is a must-have. Notably, proximity to amenities carries with it a high value component, and it may be critical if the long-range plan is to sell the residence.

> One client built an extraordinarily expensive home in a fairly remote area, far away from amenities, business assets, and even transportation. He eventually needed to put a value on the home. As it turned out, the original construction costs far exceeded the value. He had simply built too much home in too little location.

Proximity to Transportation

Bill and Melinda Gates built their home on the banks of Lake Washington, and of course have a private jet (actually, more than one) at Boeing Field in downtown Seattle. The driving time between Gates's house and his jet can be a couple of hours in bad Seattle rush-hour traffic. (Whoever thought up the term "rush hour"?) Gates's time is extraordinarily valuable, but regulations (remember those from Chapter 1?) prevented him from building a helicopter landing pad on his property. The solution was a custom-built floating helicopter pad. It can taxi up to his dock, pick him up, motor out into the lake, and dispatch a helicopter with Gates and whatever entourage he requires. His travel time from his back door to the airport is suddenly reduced to 10 minutes or so. By the way, based on an 8-hour day, 5 days a week, and 10% ROI, if you're worth $50 billion, more or less, an hour is worth about a quarter million dollars. Yes, proximity to transportation is a pretty valuable thing.

For the average John and Jane Millionaire, proximity to transportation is critical to business, to family interests, and to recreation. A remote primary residence, with a near-hermit existence, may sound attractive to some, but as a practical matter, it begins to pale.

Proximity to Business Interests

The very concept of retirement is an oxymoron among the new moneyed set. As of this writing, Tom Johnston, the 71-year-old Doobie Brothers lead singer, is talking about going back in the studio to cut a new album. Warren Buffett is 89 as of this writing. Tony Bennett is still crooning at 93. Dr. Ruth Westheimer, at 91, has embarked on a new lecture series. More to the point, when Dwight Eisenhower was sworn in as the thirty-fourth president, he was 62 and considered elderly. Fast-forward to the present, and the forty-fifth president was 70 when he was elected. His opponent was 69, and no one thought a thing about it. The simple fact is, older people are active well into an age where prior generations would have been in an "old folks home."[1] With that, the primary residence for the principals in a family may need to be proximate to business interests. The length of an active, productive life span is far different from what it was a generation ago, and the likelihood is this trend will continue. As such, Granddad and Grandma may want to be proximate to the business or other interests core to the family wealth.

Indeed, many "business interests" morph into personal interests. Bill and Melinda Gates, in their sixties, now find fulfillment through their personal foundation. It is no accident that their foundation headquarters is located a scant 20 miles from Microsoft's headquarters, and the Gates home is halfway between the two.

Richard Florida, the great urban economist, notes that creative people live where they want to live, and business interests have to chase them. It comes as no surprise that there is a Pacific Northwest culture, a Silicon Valley culture, and so forth. People who make their fortunes in a particular part of the world are drawn to live there. Since wealth breeds wealth, these very wealthy enclaves tend to be places where the newly wealthy families have put down roots.

In short, there are a myriad of considerations for acquiring the principal family residence. These considerations are multiplied for families with multiple residences—vacation homes, recreational property, and extended estates. How will these be managed? A large estate requires full-time management. Second homes and beyond will require ongoing services, even if just for seasonal maintenance and security issues. Haphazard residential acquisition and management can become a deadweight cost on the family portfolio.

> One family office manager, who advised four families each with about $500 million in total assets, estimated that each family had about a quarter of their wealth in real estate, on average. He confided that he had little understanding or interest in advising on real estate, and the four families were basically "on their own" with respect to these holdings. This was an astonishing admission, as he simply failed to recognize how badly acquired and badly managed real estate could quickly dissipate a family fortune. Conversely, well-acquired and well-managed family estates can be an asset and an excellent storer of value.

2. Intergenerational Issues

> It is estimated that wealthy families will transfer $19 trillion in assets to the next generation in the next three decades. To put that in perspective, the US gross domestic product (GDP) in 2017 was also $19 trillion.[2]

This leads into consideration of multiple generations of a family and their attitude toward the family real estate holdings. The preceding section focused entirely on the family personal assets, such as a family home and recreational properties. Multi- and intergenerational issues encompass the whole range of real estate that a family may acquire and manage.

Much is written about intergenerational transfers, which have tax and legal implications. These implications vary by state, and recent attention to inheritance taxes and other estate issues suggests that these implications will vary from time to time into the future. Intergenerational real estate transfers cannot be separated from other intergenerational transfers, including business assets, investments, art, and anything storing wealth. Families with tax implications consider these issues well in advance of probate and make ownership decisions accordingly.

This text is more focused on valuation issues, with an emphasis on acquisition and management, rather than disposition issues. All too often, though, families only consider the intergenerational issues in the context of disposal—either probate or transfers in anticipation of probate. Recent practical research into the subject suggests ownership issues have other implications for family cohesiveness, wealth maximization, and even family reputation.

One study noted that, "Gifts of real estate . . . may represent far more than just a monetary value. They symbolize family history and reflect processes of intergenerational reproduction as tangible family property is passed on.[3] Intergenerational considerations in real estate ownership have often been blamed for increased concentration of wealth, but research does not support this. Another study compared intergenerational links in the United States, where wealth tends to be relatively concentrated, and Sweden, where less concentration occurs. Researchers found that society and families consider intergenerational links to provide important subjective values to the family."[4] Surprisingly, even though there is a great deal of anecdotal information and public debate about wealth concentration and intergenerational wealth transfer issues, there is an actual dearth of true data and academic studies on the issue.[5]

On the other hand, significant evidence shows that poor planning and preparation is the greatest threat to successful intergenerational wealth transfer and maintenance. There is recent increasing emphasis on the nature of the successful family—the "ties that bind"—and issues of family unity and harmony. Proactive families consider their assets in the context of identifying family values, developing a family mission statement for their wealth and assets, aligning estate plans with this family mission statement, identifying needs and roles of individual family members, developing qualifications and performance standards for asset management, and preparing family members to fill various roles:[6]

Identifying Family Values

This transcends every aspect of family wealth holdings, particularly real estate holdings. Choices made say something about the family, its priorities, and its vision of itself. One large, wealthy family I met with endows an annual family vacation so that every family member from all corners of the globe can come together at least once a year to renew family ties. For families like this, the personal real estate holdings have a lot to do with facilitating this extended family community. Similarly, business holdings, such as the Walmart stores owned by Walton family members, provide a common bond—the source of personal and family wealth—that ties family members together and provides a common external face for everyone named Walton. The nature, type, and manner of making real estate investments speaks volumes about a family, its priorities, and its values.

Developing a Family Mission Statement

Positive decisions are not enabled by accident. From Chapter 1, these things can and have to be architected. Part of that architecture, perhaps the beginning step, is a written family mission statement. Top-down missives rarely work. As much as families may outwardly venerate the words of Grandma or Granddad, the family mission statement needs to be something with broad family concurrence and internal discipline. Family members need to buy into this statement and continuously return to it as a touchstone for investment decisions.

Identifying the Needs and Roles of Family Members

Not all family members are created equal. Many family members can take on leadership and management roles within the family real estate investments, while others may have lesser roles or may even find themselves supported by the family, making little or no obvious contribution at all. While the notion of "from each according to his abilities, to each according to his needs" did not work at Jamestown, it works quite well if there is broad concurrence and a positive internal dynamic in a family. Many folks named Ford have held leadership roles at Ford Motors, but many more have not. The Kennedy Family Trust, dating back to 1927, is estimated to have over $1 billion invested, much in real estate. While Kennedy family members provide strategic oversight to the trust, day-to-day management is left up to professionals. Notably, the nature and mission statement of the trust has evolved significantly since the days when Joseph Kennedy ran it personally.

Developing Performance Standards for Asset Management

As with the Kennedys, professional managers or advisors are a must, but family oversight is a key element. Part of the family mission statement will include the expectations of those real estate managers and advisors, and will outline the manner in which managers and advisors are selected and oversight provided.

Preparing Family Members for the Roles They Will Fill

Eventually, the torch will be passed from one generation to another. Having a well-organized real estate management system in place provides the training ground for future generations to understand how the family assets were accumulated, nurtured, and preserved. Haphazard organization and management of key family assets leads to dissipation and eventual loss of family wealth.

Family real estate holdings say a lot about who the family members are and where they come from. The aforementioned Hearst Ranch continues to be a touchstone for that family, dating back over 150 years. Many great families are associated with family compounds that provide a home base for multiple generations. Family trophy property, whether it is the family residence, a second residence, a trophy recreational property, or a pure trophy investment, can make a statement about the family for many generations.

With that in mind, family acquisition of top-tier investment-grade personal real estate will continue to be mindful of the rules of acquisition—valuation at purchase with an eye to long-term management and maintenance costs, plus an eye to long-term value. Implicit in this, of course, are the subjective values. These include, but are certainly not limited to, the intergenerational relationships, the family's public image, and the collectibility of the real estate itself.

3. Homeownership, Second Homes, and Such

In a prior section, I discussed some of the selection criteria for a family home. Now, I want to dive deeper into the complexities of estate ownership, second home or vacation property ownership, and recreational property ownership, always from the perspective of valuation.

Homes are a bit like children, in that having two is probably three times as complicated as having one. If the math does not make sense, think about the issue of residence management. Even a small home requires constant attention. What happens when a pipe bursts? When the electricity goes out and the alarm system needs to be reset? Who mows the lawn, or oversees the person who mows the lawn? Keeping track of two sets of emergency contacts (plumbers, electricians, heating and air, septic tank service, lawn care) can be a full-time job! Of course, many multi-home owners opt for a property or estate manager, but finding a good one can be a complex task. At the upper end of the spectrum, full-time personal assistants may be needed to keep up with the chores of household management and moving family members—and their belongings, pets, and detritus of life—back and forth from one house to another.

A simple solution is a condominium or co-op apartment. If the main—or even secondary—home is in Manhattan, this will be a likely solution. In many cities, there are services to keep the apartment clean, ready it for the principals when they arrive, and stock the refrigerator and pantry. Of course, there are trade-offs with apartments or condos. First, upscale units do not exist in every market, and indeed some states do not have enabling legislation for co-ops. Finally, there are lifestyle choices. Many people simply do not want to be in such close proximity to their neighbors, even in a vacation or second home. This means that owners who opt for detached properties will also opt for the maintenance and management headaches associated with multiple property ownership.

These choices have valuation implications. Well-managed properties retain and improve their value relative to poorly managed and maintained ones. Thus, the true cost of maintenance and management must be offset against the maintenance of property values over time.

The management complexity increases with different types of personal real estate. Owning two nearly identical homes in the North and South, a common practice for "snowbirds," will entail some complexity, even though management issues with both houses are similar. Heat and air need to be managed with the season and serviced regularly, light bulbs changed, new batteries put in smoke detectors, security systems tested, and so forth. Now, imagine that we add a third house to the mix—one that fronts on the ski slope in Whistler. Insurance, taxes, even security become complex issues. Some wealthy families acquire complex properties specifically for the uniqueness. At one time, the largest number of "mainland" property owners on Kauai, the westernmost of the Hawaiian Islands, came from only one US county. The remoteness, the beauty, and the peace and quiet of Kauai attracted a tsunami of mainlanders, who adopted the island as their own.

In large part, second home ownership follows a fairly conservative pattern. According to one recent study, the top five cities in the world for wealthy families to own second homes are:

- London
- New York

- Los Angeles
- Monaco
- Miami[7]

Within the United States, the pattern is more diffused. The Census Bureau asks how many homes are owned for seasonal, recreational, or occasional (SRO) use. Nationwide, the 2010 census counted 132 million housing units, of which 4.6 million, or 3.5%, were self-reported for SRO use. This was up by about a million homes from the 2000 census. The largest percentage goes to Maine, with 16.4% of dwellings reported for SRO use, followed closely by Vermont and New Hampshire. Florida has the largest number (657,000) but only the eighth highest percentage of SRO homes (7.3%).

There is little data on where these homeowners come from, but it is clear that they are looking for seasonally interesting climates. From a value management perspective, these extreme climates have interesting problems. Maine, Vermont, and New Hampshire are all known for intriguing winters, and one can surmise that these SRO homes are probably located near winter recreation. Conversely, those 657,000 homes in Florida are all in the path of large circular storms that occasion the Southeast in the summer.

> By the way, according to a recent study by Zillow, the community with the largest percentage of SRO homes is Ocean City, New Jersey, where 31.6% of homes, or 50,490 dwellings, are SRO.

The concept of second or vacation property implies a home, or at least something that resembles a home. Many second, third, and subsequent SRO properties are less "home" and more "camp." The idea of a lake or mountain cabin has long been a favorite of families of all stripes. Many families own properties that can be enjoyed recreationally but only in a "camping" or "day-trip" sense. This will be explored more fully in the next section, but any recreational properties have management and valuation implications.

All this leads to some consideration of property disposal, either sale, conversion to some other family use, or probate. Many valuable and unique properties contribute value to an estate through gifts or bequeath to charitable organizations, reducing the tax bill on the estate and at the same time garnering positive public relations for the family name. In a previous example, the Ringling Estate in Sarasota, Florida, was gifted to the state. While it took many years for this to come to fruition, the estate now anchors a regionally important arts and performance venue, forever memorializing the Ringling name.

In a perfect world, the vacation or second home will continue in a family estate with a trust established to maintain it in perpetuity for the family to enjoy. This implies that the SRO property was acquired with an eye to family enjoyment, and that a large number of family members will want to continue to enjoy it. In the previously mentioned slope-side home in Whistler, British Columbia, it is assumed that children and grandchildren will all enjoy skiing. Many Florida homes will be enjoyed for vacations for generations to come. However, the world is far from perfect, and often the second and SRO homes will be sold and the clock started over with another generation.

Before I conclude this section, I want to stress two points. Throughout this text, little emphasis is placed on sales of properties other than those developed purposefully for sale. I have a bias in favor of accumulating and holding properties with a family mission theme. Sales of properties carry significant deadweight costs to the sellers, often as much as 10% of the sales price, including commissions, excise taxes, and fees. This does not even consider the income taxes associated with sales, which can be substantial, even with long-term capital gains treatment. Conversely, in probate, real estate may have favorable valuation treatment. Properties owned for many years or generations may be passed at a very low value compared to the cash sale price. Clearly, from a wealth accumulation perspective, the family is benefited if properties can be accumulated and not dissipated.

Second, as of this writing, there have been recent and significant changes to the federal tax laws that may have implications for local burdens in some states as well. We know that the long-term impact of tax law changes are usually not felt for many years. Investors and families are well advised to consult with proper counselors on these issues before acquiring or disposing of any real estate, and particularly family vacation or SRO properties.

4. The Care and Feeding of Trophy Property

In a pair of articles in the *Appraisal Journal* in 2002 and 2003,[8] the famed real estate economist Bill Mundy set down a set of criteria for determining, evaluating, and valuing *trophy* real estate. In short, Mundy observed that within any category of real estate, the top 2½%, from a value perspective, fell in the trophy category.

The Mundy criteria recognize that a property can have trophy, or "collectible" characteristics regardless of property type. This flies against common wisdom, which would typically consider a trophy or collectible property to be something like a famous mansion, pristine forest land, or seashore holdings. However, under the Mundy criteria, properties like Rockefeller Center in New York; the famed Boeing Plant[9] in Everett, Washington; the Sears Tower in Chicago; or the U.S. Steel building in Pittsburgh might all have collectible qualities.

For appraisers, the normal criteria hardly apply. Much like trophy artwork, the ownership transcends the economics of the property itself. Economic benefits derive from the resale values, although in practice these properties are collected without an eye to resale.

Valuation methodology is fairly standard, but the data used has to accommodate the far-flung market for trophy property. As a simple example, consider the nicest house in any town compared to the average house in that same town. The market for that average house may be very localized to people who want to live in that school district or near work or near other amenities. Comps used to value the average house would probably come from the same neighborhood. Conversely, the top home in the city would draw its market at least from throughout the region, if not beyond.

Applying the top 2½% rule takes into account the concept of the market. Consider "hot" cities in the world, such as London, New York, and Paris, or even secondary "hot" cities such as Seattle, Charleston, and Miami. These are destinations for buyers that Richard Florida labels the *creative class*. A significant number of Miami homes, and particularly in Miami Beach, have *trophy* characteristics. Ironically, in these tony destination cities, valuation becomes simpler—the local market has a plethora of trophy homes sold on a regular basis. Valuing a historic mansion in Savannah, Georgia, is somewhat easier than valuing a historic mansion in Seattle, Washington.

More typically, the concept of trophy property refers to collectible real estate. This includes very high amenity forest lands, ranch lands, and properties with historic or architecturally valuable features. Owning these includes not only the qualitative benefits of art collection but frequently other economic benefits and burdens. A historic home in Savannah, Georgia, may be listed on the National Trust, but the owners are expected to maintain the home and its facade in original condition. Finding materials and craftspeople can be a burden, and historic materials and styles may not provide modern comforts, such as insulated windows. Tax benefits are frequently available, but these may not fully offset the functional disutility.

Some very ordinary property may become "trophy" very suddenly. The rancher who found the "dinosaur named Sue" on his property, the most intact T. rex skeleton, triggered a real-life Jurassic Park saga, discussed later in this text. The property continued to be valuable as a trophy site, not only from the halo effect of Sue's discovery but also from the demand by the world's top paleontologists to find out what else might be there.[10]

On the other hand, the Farnsworth House in Plano, Illinois, was designed to be a trophy property from inception. Built for Dr. Edith Farnsworth in the late 1940s by acclaimed Belgian architect Ludwig Mies van der Rohe, the squabble between designer and owner reached such a pitch that van der Rohe declared the house to be the last (of three) he would ever build in the United States. Of course, his declaration simply drove up the value of Dr. Farnsworth's trophy investment. Eventually, the home was acquired by a British trophy property collector, Baron Peter Palumbo, and was auctioned in 2003 for $7.1 million to an anonymous bidder who donated the property to the National Trust for Historic Preservation.[11]

Trophy property value may be influenced by the owner's actions—"architected," so to speak. The Hearst family donated the famed Castle at San Simeon to the State of California in 1957, but retained ownership of the 83,000-acre ranch, which includes over two miles of pristine Pacific coastline. In 2005, the family appraised the development value and donated those rights to a permanent preservation trust. The family enjoyed a substantial tax benefit while at the same time preserving a land-trust legacy going back to Senator George Hearst's 1865 land grant purchase.[12]

Much like art, well-curated real estate holds its value very well. It provides significant subjective benefits and can provide economic benefits as well. Like any art piece, there are maintenance and management costs for trophy real estate. Nonetheless, there seems to be no shortage of trophy property buyers, and the market remains strong. Like any investment, purchase decisions are key. The long-term property value trend needs to be carefully considered at the onset of the acquisition.

5. Hybrid Trophy-Recreational Property

Can Ted Turner really ride his horse from Canada to Mexico without leaving his own property? Somewhere in between personal recreational property and trophy property lies a set of recreational properties filling both bills. In the western United States, trophy ranches have become popular, and they combine a storer of value with a high-amenity recreational site.

I recently consulted on a trophy island owned by a private equity investor. The island itself was several thousand miles from his home base, but it was situated in the middle of some of the best trophy (there's that word again!) sport fishing in the world. Rather than simply buying a marina slip to store his 125-foot custom-built fishing boat, he bought an entire island and had it outfitted with private generators, a private water and sewer system, and a world-class freshwater dock for his boat.

Trophy recreational property meets the same definition as any other trophy real estate—it is in the top tier of properties in that category. The valuation challenge is recognizing that the market for such property is worldwide. An island in the Caribbean, or a ranch on a mountaintop in Wyoming, or a horse ranch in Santa Fe will all find a global market, will all provide top-tier recreational value, and will all, if purchased correctly and with an eye to value, provide an excellent storer of value.

The history of Kuleanas is unique to Hawai'I, and the reader might think that this history has little impact on real estate valuation anywhere else on the globe. Nothing could be further from the truth, and the story of Kuleanas has implications for every single family that owns personal real estate.

First, it is important to understand some history of the westernmost of these United States. My apologies to my friends in that great state[13]—a thorough history is exciting and well beyond the scope of this book. Dialing back to the 1830s, Hawai'I was a kingdom, ruled by Kamehameha III. Governance was though a network of local Chiefs. Responsibility for nurturing the land was considered to be the responsibility of the King or the Chiefs. This responsibility did not necessarily carry with it the concept of ownership as we might think of it today. Indeed, the concept of land ownership was foreign to the Hawaiians, since nature could not be owned.

Sadly, though, the concept of ownership was not foreign to foreigners, and the King could see the handwriting, so to speak, on the palace wall. The Constitution of 1840 assured that the lands belonged to the people, to be managed by the King on their behalf. The goal of the King and the Chiefs was to assure that the Hawaiian natives had continued tenure in their lands. In 1848, the King proposed the Great Mahale, which provided actual ownership—called a Kuleana—to each Hawaiian for the lands they currently occupied. The law required that the Hawaiians register their claims within two years, and most failed to do so. In 1850, while the King was away, the legislature passed the Alien Land Ownership Act, providing that non-Hawaiians could own lands. Today, only about 4% of Hawaii is actually owned by native Hawaiians.

The broader lesson learned from the Kuleana experience is how the value of land, land ownership, and land tenure can vary between families and cultures. In most places, there is a fairly predictable relationship between rent and value for most homes—it is called the *gross rent multiplier*, and I will discuss it further in a later chapter. For now, though, it is sufficient to recognize that for most homes in a given market, this ratio is going to be fairly constant, and the gross rent multiplier is fairly constant across most markets in the United States.[14] At the upper end of the scale—remember trophy properties?—this relationship breaks down. Exceptionally valuable homes and other trophy properties tend to rent for far less than would be suggested by the underlying property value. The concept of ownership, and the fact of owning something that has intrinsic value beyond simple utility, has value unto itself. Indeed, the difference in what an upscale home actually rents for versus what would be suggested by local gross rent multipliers is a measure of trophy markup.

6. It's Four O'Clock Somewhere[15]

With apologies to Alan Jackson and Jimmy Buffett, vast swaths of American real estate are devoted to recreation. In 1982, the US government set up an inspection point in Florida City, Florida, a choke point for all traffic headed to the Keys. The government of Monroe County declared their independence—creating the Conch Republic—in no small part because the beer trucks could not get through. The coastline of Florida is replete with upscale recreational properties, with something to fit nearly every price point. Similar recreational enclaves exist across the Gulf Coast all the way to Mexico.

Recreational real estate prices and values are highly sensitive to economic shifts. Florida was one of the states worst hit by the real estate meltdown that started in 2007, although many upscale properties fared quite well. Deep sea fishing, recreational boating, and similar water-based recreation is popular today, but those industries are constantly looking to the future, with all that demographic shifts might entail. Sustaining real estate in the Gulf is the burgeoning retirement age bracket. Even this has undergone a significant shift in the past generation. The famed Del Webb communities were hugely successful catering to the Greatest Generation with moderately upscale retirement homes in communities dedicated to their desired lifestyles. In the 1990s, when 50,000 Beatles fans in the United States started turning 65 every day, the Del Webb community recognized that the same retirement lifestyle would not satisfy the baby boom generation. The shift in retirement lifestyle was precipitous and dramatic.

The same is true of basically any recreation-based lifestyle real estate, which tends to dominate the second home and retirement home market. Ski-related real estate has prospered in recent years, while hunting and fishing seem to have waned a bit. Not many years ago, there was a brief flirtation with university-based recreational homes, second homes, and even retirement homes. This fad seems to have passed by the wayside.

The lesson learned here, from a value perspective, is to look at long-term trends with a critical eye. Families and investors who look to real estate as a storer of value may be perplexed a dozen years from now when they discover that the "hot" recreational market of a past generation draws little interest in the next one. One fix for this is to only invest in real estate from a multigenerational perspective. What does the family—over several generations—enjoy doing? Where are markets with long-term values? These are keys to acquiring personal real estate, and for that matter all property investments, with an eye to the future and to sustained value.

7. Summary and Key Points

The focus of this chapter was on personal real estate—the family residence, vacation or recreational property, collectible or trophy property, and other properties that fall outside investment or business categories. Often, even in the most successful and well-advised families, these properties are the worst bought, the worst managed, and the worst sold. Decisions are frequently made for purely subjective and discretionary reasons. Even when the long-term family estate has been inherited, the family can make significant decisions to optimize value and tax implications of ownership and intergenerational passage.

This has also been the least quantitative chapter in this book, and that was on purpose. Value-optimizing decisions about personal real estate are often made very subjectively. Guiding those value-optimizing decisions requires not a small amount of understanding of those subjective processes. Nonetheless, even in that subjective world, the *goals* are quite objective.

8. A Final Note—Yachts, Airplanes, and the Care and Feeding of Toys

I recently went to a charity fund-raiser at a friend's warehouse. He rents and maintains a very large warehouse simply to curate his collection of toys—motorcycles, cars, pinball machines, and the like. He uses the warehouse for fund-raising parties, or simply parties, or I guess to pour a beer and imagine he's Jay Leno. This wasn't my first toy-warehouse party. Another collector I met specializes his curation on muscle cars from the 1960s. I lost count, but he appears to have about 40. Just to round things out, his warehouse also has a killer bar, a small but extremely functional kitchen, and two extremely nice pool tables. Another collector has nothing but pinball machines. He is apparently one of the nation's premier collectors, and yes, he has a very nice bar in his pinball warehouse.

This chapter has been about curated real estate, but often wealthy investors use—indeed need—real estate to curate other things in their lives. The east side of Boeing Field in downtown Seattle is often referred to as "Billionaires Row," and from the runway side of these hangars, they are often architectural masterpieces. (One is purposely designed and painted to resemble a Costco store. Guess who owns it?) Business jets are an important business tool, and a necessary way to get around the country and schedule the myriad of meetings that fill a CEO's calendar. Which of course explains why the late Paul Allen (co-founder of Microsoft) hangered 31 planes, mostly from World War II, including a Hawker Hurricane, several Messerschmitts and Focke-Wulfs, and a Mitsubishi A6M Zero.

Finally, there was a point in time when a wealthy individual *might* own a yacht. Today, it's "yachts," plural. All of these—and yes, many are business assets—require care and feeding. From a real estate perspective, the curation of these assets is not an inexpensive proposition. At a minimum, even the smallest boat big enough to be called a yacht will require a dock, and increasingly these are owned rather than rented or leased. In many cities, there is real estate development (often in condominium form) that includes moorage coupled with a building providing lodging and office space for the full-time captains.

In short, the "toy" collection has expensive real estate implications. As of this writing, even a small hangar at a third-tier airport will cost several hundred thousand dollars and will be built on leased land. A jet-capable hangar at a towered airport (the preference for all-weather operations) will be several million. Condominiumized dock space is frequently $15,000 per foot or more, and for bigger yachts, the prices increase exponentially. The location of the yacht or airplane or toy collection is a lifestyle function—an investor in Miami will not be in the market for a yacht slip in Los Angeles unless he or she owns two yachts. (As many do!) These real estate investments have value implications, and amazingly enough, many of these decisions are made without the same consideration normally given to a seven-figure real estate investment.

4
Valuing the Personal Residence

Price is what you pay. Value is what you get.

—Warren Buffett

WHETHER THE PERSONAL residence is a midmarket home or an upscale mansion, certain truisms should be understood by buyers and their advisors. First, every dwelling acquisition, even if it is for a short term, should be made with an eye to long-term value maximization. Buyers should take into account trends in the market (the overall housing market and the local or regional one); the relative utility of the dwelling versus the proportion of the purchase price buried in the land; and the fact that not all "fix-up" costs are created equal.

Any given purchase price can be allocated between the land value and the improvements value, just as shown in the office building development example in Chapter 2. For most residences in America, land value will fall somewhere between 20% and 40% of the total price. At the lower end of the spectrum, there is the real danger that the house is overbuilding the neighborhood. At the upper end, the land should really contribute something important to the value, such as world-class views (waterfront, mountaintop, etc.). Above 40%, and there is a likelihood that the dwelling is significantly depreciated. Of course, depreciated dwellings can be excellent investments if purchased wisely with an eye to curing the depreciation. As noted below, not all depreciation can be cured.

Following are the most important principles in buying and valuing the personal residence.

1. Buying the Best Deal in the Neighborhood

This is the simplest lesson in this book. Quite a few years ago, I was CFO of a homebuilding and development company. We were fairly well vertically integrated for the time. We bought land, developed that land into finished lots, built the houses, and sold them through our captive brokerage firm. Our "sweet spot" was buying distressed subdivisions—ones where some other builder/developer got in over his or her head or got overextended. We did phenomenally well turning those situations around.

Eventually, we ran out of distressed subdivisions to sustain our business, so we had to rely more heavily on our development arm. We decided to systematize what we did and brought in several consultants to advise on marketing strategy. One charged us a shockingly large amount of money to give us the information in the next two paragraphs. If you have read this far in the book, then this information is yours for whatever price the publisher has charged you.

As a real estate developer, there is a profit-maximizing selling price for homes. As it turns out, that price is not at the market top, but at the 90% point in the market (Figure 4-1). This balances the price against selling time, marketing costs, and carrying costs. The most expensive house in the market will rarely sell quickly, at least in a market at equilibrium. The costs associated with selling will offset any marginal additional profit for a developer (assuming both the 100% house and the 90% house are built to sell with approximately the same percentage net profit on sales). For a developer/builder, the task is to itemize all homes in the broad market

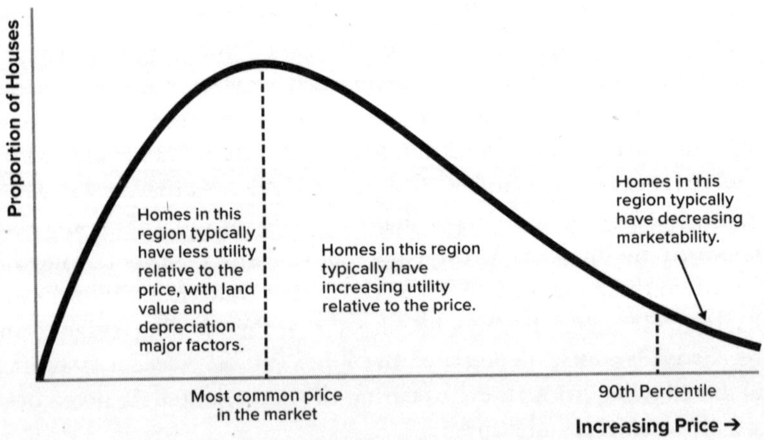

FIGURE 4-1 Distribution of House Prices in a Given Market

that compete with this one. This is typically done by examining competing neighborhoods and tabulating all sales for the past year in those competing neighborhoods or among houses that would be likely to compete with the homes being built by this builder/developer. Naturally, 90% is an approximate range, but the successful builder/developer will aim for that range.

From a buyer's perspective, the goal is to find the house in the market that will hold its value, appreciate at or above the market trend, and be easy to sell if and when that eventuality happens. The 90% rule generally takes this into account. This overcomes several other issues:

- The smallest or least expensive house in the neighborhood probably has issues. Either this small or less expensive house has disutility issues or the price is disproportionally representative of land rather than usable home space.
- The largest house in the neighborhood will compete with houses in the next nicest neighborhood. In short, do you want to buy the biggest house in this neighborhood or the midsized house in the nicer neighborhood? Usually, that decision ends up being adverse to the biggest house.
- In between the middle (the most common prices in the market) and the ninetieth percentile, homes are generally increasing in utility (relative to price) and marketability, but at an ever-decreasing rate. Empirically, this trade-off is usually optimized somewhere around that ninetieth percentile mark.

Naturally, these are generalities. In specific cases, there can be good reasons to own one of the smallest or least expensive homes in the competing market, or conversely to own the biggest or most expensive. However, as a general rule of thumb, the ninetieth percentile is somewhere near the optimizing point for homes in a given market.

At the market bottom, the diminished utility/price trade-off is often a function of excessive depreciation. Recall the three categories of depreciation:

- Physical
- Functional
- Economic

The first category has old homes with substantial repair problems. Often, these repair problems are incurable, such as sagging beams and joists, settling foundations, or other problems that would be economically impractical to cure. Some of these problems are curable, such as a fully depreciated roof, the need for yard work or other "curb appeal" issues, or other simple cosmetic problems. The Ringling Mansion at Sarasota, Ca' d'Zan, is an example of a structurally sound home that fell into massive disrepair. The cost of repairing Ca' d'Zan was economically difficult to justify, but the restored mansion is now the centerpiece of a culturally important regional arts center. In short, careful shoppers may find orphan properties in the low end that can be brought up to the upper end through judicious addressing of curable physical depreciation. (Beware: the "house flipping" television shows have made this task look much easier than it really is.)

Functional disutility includes attributes of design and construction that are often much more difficult to cure. Older dwellings (1970s or earlier) may have asbestos or lead-based paint. Homes built before the middle of the 1900s may have dangerous knob-and-tube wiring, or may have fuse or breaker boxes insufficient to meet modern appliance needs. Older dwellings will often have inadequate insulation or weatherproofing. Homes from the 1800s may not have adequate ingress or parking for automobiles, or the accommodation of automobiles may diminish the historic or architectural quality. Indeed, maintenance of a historic or architecturally preserved residence entails significant costs.[1] Curing functional depreciation can be expensive, but it can prove very profitable if amortized over a long holding period.

External disutility (sometimes called external obsolescence or economic depreciation) comes from issues outside the direct control of the property owner. A common example is an obnoxious nearby property use, such as environmental contamination or a down-zoned use (i.e., building an industrial building in what used to be a residential neighborhood). An increasingly common inconsistent land use is an airport. While few new airports are being constructed today, the rapid increase in air travel worldwide, and particularly in the United States, increases the likelihood of annoyance from airplane traffic. A property owner who finds that his or her home is diminished in value from a neighbor's land use may pursue legal claims for the stigma loss, may petition for a reduction in property taxes, or may find ways to mitigate the stigma.[2]

While external disutility may impact all homes in a given neighborhood, it will not impact the homes in the competing market. A dwelling at the ninetieth percentile of the entire city probably competes with homes throughout the city and perhaps throughout the region. Top-of-the-market homes in a stigmatized neighborhood will decline in value after announcement or revelation of a negative externality compared to competing homes in other neighborhoods. Homes at the market's lower end typically do not compete with homes further away. These homes often already suffer from physical or functional disutility, and potential buyers or tenants are frequently locationally restricted (work, transportation, amenities, etc.). Thus, while a stigmatizing event will systematically impact home values in a neighborhood, upscale homes may be impacted to a greater extent.

> Price and value can become disconnected in a rapidly changing market. We know from the recession-related real estate meltdown that began in 2007 that home prices in "hot" markets become irrationally high relative to their long-term intrinsic values. The same disconnect happens when sudden negative things hit value. Many homeowners cannot afford to sell because they owe more than the diminished value of their properties. Some buyers wistfully ignore the issues. In general, it takes a period of time for prices to stagnate down to the new equilibrium levels. Thus, after a negative event in a neighborhood or a market, some buyers may be lulled into submission by prices that stay healthy, even in the face of reduced sales volumes, greater marketing times, or buyer reluctance. These "soon after the event" buyers end up paying too much and watching their investments winnow away.

So, the best deal in the market is probably near the market top, somewhere around the ninetieth percentile, but probably not above that mark. Homes at lower prices with easily curable physical depreciation may be "deals," but buyers need to beware of homes with functional or economic disutility, or physical disutility that cannot be easily cured.

2. Maintaining Value

Why do some homes seem to hold their values while others do not? Clearly, there are decisions made at the purchase that can influence long-term value. But some homes just seem to be maintained better than others. There are five key elements homeowners frequently overlook that have significant and sometimes permanent impact on value. These elements are:

- The roof
- The heating and air system
- The appliances
- The floors
- The curb appeal

Each of these should be considered at the purchase, particularly the long-term cost associated with each element. At the lower end of the economic spectrum, homeowners experience sudden costs that they cannot afford. A leaky or damaged roof can be a costly surprise for anyone. Selling a house with a damaged roof will engender a discount far beyond the actual cost of repairing the roof. The likely buyer will want a discount for the roof cost, the hassle of having to handle repairs, and the risk associated with the fact that there may be other issues (latent defects) that were caused by or associated with the roof damage.

This book is aimed at the upscale real estate investor and the advisors who help that investor maintain and manage assets. The quality of these conditions will be taken into account at the time of acquisition. A roof that is 18 years into a 20-year life span should be factored into the purchase price. While upscale investors are generally more likely to be able to handle "surprise" expenses such as roof failures, this book is also about very long-term, intergenerational investments. A family that wants to buy the family estate and hold it through multiple generations will need to establish a management plan to address these issues in future years.

> For the upscale homeowner, day-to-day management will often be invested in a professional estate manager or management firm. The owner will need to know what these key elements are to be conversant with the estate manager.

The Roof

Average roofs for average houses have expected life spans of 20 years. When replaced, there will typically be some underlying decking damage (rot, old age). Upscale homes usually have roofing materials with longer lives. These may include, but are certainly not limited to, cedar shakes, faux shakes (made from metal, ceramics, or even concrete), tiles, metal, or other complex materials. Even upscale fiberglass "architectural shingles" are expected to last longer than 20 years. Underlying decking for expensive homes may be something more expensive than plywood or composite board. It is not unusual for an upscale home to have an expected roof life of 50 years.

Regular inspections are a must. In high-wind or storm areas, these inspections may be annually required by insurers. Insurers in high-wind areas may require an invasive roof inspection on older homes to determine if the roof is properly connected to the structure by acceptable hurricane strapping.

If this cannot be performed, the wind insurance policy may be more expensive. Regular maintenance may also include cleaning, and replacing certain components that have worn out at unexpected intervals. The downside to roof failure can be significant. Even without a significant storm event, a failing roof can leak, and frequently these leaks are isolated to the attic, thus going without detection until other obvious or even latent problems arise.

Heating and Air Conditioning System

A functioning air conditioning system is literally a life-or-death issue in many regions. A functioning heating system is generally required for a certificate of occupancy in most parts of the United States.

Of course, an upscale residence will require a system beyond the minimums required for legal compliance and simple creature comfort. An upscale residence may frequently be used for entertaining. An adequate system for daily household needs may prove wholly inadequate for an afternoon party with 100 guests. System adequacy will be a mandatory inspection before purchase.

Regular inspections and filter cleanings are a must—typically every six months. In most locales, there are service providers that schedule such inspections. This needs to be included in the maintenance plan and budget. Heating and air systems have an expected life span—a major overhaul every five years is not unusual.

> One upscale client found an artesian well on his property with a constant water temperature about 50 degrees Fahrenheit. He used this to power a heat pump dedicated to his wine cellar. It was a very, very nice wine cellar.

Appliances

Upscale homes come with upscale appliances. An upscale kitchen remodel can easily cost six figures. Upscale appliance maintenance carries upscale price tags. The repair bill on a top-of-the-line multidrawer dishwasher will significantly exceed the replacement cost of a low-end dishwasher. The same is true for top-of-the-line refrigerators, trash compactors, cooktops, wine storage, ovens, and so on. For the upscale residence, it is not uncommon to have a separate catering kitchen. At acquisition, an inventory should be made of built-in kitchen appliances with ages and current maintenance status. Replacements should be planned and budgeted accordingly.

Floors

This is one of the most overlooked (pun intended) areas. Most upscale homes will have some type of hard flooring (tile, granite, hardwood) that is usually thought to be permanent. However, even hardwood will warp and have to be replaced if there is significant water intrusion.

Underlying the flooring material there is usually some sort of base material, such as plywood or planked hardwood. In most upscale dwellings, this is built on a floor joist system (unless the ground floor is on a slab of some kind), and the floor joist system may serve as the ceiling system for whatever is below (another floor, a basement, or a crawl space). Even minor events, such as small earth tremors or other geological events, natural settling, water intrusion, or improper utility installation can undermine the floor system integrity. Regular inspections are needed, and particularly at the first sign of damage, such as warping or cracking of the surface layer.

> One very upscale residence we recently consulted on—a vacation home—had a foyer floor designed by an artist with a backlit inlay resembling a stylized map of the nearby coastline. The floor itself was a valuable objet d'art, but subject to the potential wear and tear of a recreational home foyer. Regular maintenance was necessary to preserve the value of this entranceway.

Curb Appeal

It should go without saying that an upscale residence is measured by its curb appeal, but a surprising number of residences in this category ignore this fundamental issue. Sometimes there is a legitimate reason—such as owners who value their privacy live at the end of a long driveway and couldn't care less what the curb end of that driveway looks like. Unfortunately, the neighbors and potential buyers think differently. Upscale neighborhoods often have provisions in the covenants and regulations for maintenance of outwardly visible portions of the property. Again, budgeting for regular maintenance and management is a must, and failure to do so can prove expensive. Restoring the outward view of an upscale residence can be a significant undertaking.

> Many Gulf Coast cities were targeted by volunteers with chain saws right after recent hurricanes. Unfortunately, these folks knew little about the trees they were trimming, and they frequently did more damage than

good. An upscale yard should have a qualified arborist on retainer with regular tree inspections. Really good, expensive foliage requires years of expert maintenance and management, and it is not a job for amateurs.

Everything Else

There are a countless number of other things that need to be maintained in the upscale residence. Nowadays, these include the security system, cameras, sound system, Wi-Fi system, and entertainment system. Many services integrate all these, and more, into one computer-controlled system. These systems require regular updating to keep up with current standards. A security system that was considered state-of-the-art 10 years ago is now nearly out-of-date.

In the 1999 remake of *The Thomas Crown Affair*, burglars are astonished that billionaire Crown has a 10-digit pin code for his home burglar alarm. Today, Crown's system would be hopelessly out-of-date.

3. Leverage?

Most upscale residences are purchased for cash, or nearly so. The tax code, and particularly the 2017 updates, severely limits the benefit for upscale buyers to leverage personal residences. There are often good reasons to leverage a home purchase, such as the usefulness of low-cost money when the investor has high-return opportunities elsewhere. While the mortgage on an upscale residence will look very traditional, the lending decision is more often made on the borrower's creditworthiness or preexisting relationships. Most banks do not want to foreclose on a multimillion-dollar estate.

Is leverage a good idea? When money can be borrowed at 3% or 4% long term and the investor has double-digit investment opportunities, this would seem to be a no-brainer. However, is it really? This sort of money arbitrage ignores some very fundamental differences that exist at different places on the risk-reward curve.

For one, investments turn sour. A fundamental tenant of portfolio theory is that most investments in the portfolio will work out just fine, but occasionally one will go belly-up. We are willing to take risks that way with our investments to enjoy the benefits of the successful ones.[3] Putting the family residence in the portfolio mix may be quite a different story. Implicitly, by using the house as collateral for capital to invest in other, riskier projects, I am cross-collateralizing the risky investment with the most risk-averse thing I own. If I have other sources of funds or income to cover the mortgage costs, then the risk is somewhat ameliorated, but more risk-averse investors build a solid wall around certain investments, the family home being one of them, in such a way that they can never be touched.

Second, the news day hardly ends without the head of a wealthy family or major business being killed in a plane crash, or in a car crash, or by a sudden heart attack on the golf course. It may seem trite, but mortgages on the principal family residence should be offset with dedicated insurance policies.

Finally, many (if not most) upscale families need to have a line of credit, and may want to be able to buy very large things that require a banking relationship. It's nice to be able to buy that beach house for cash, but one may need to float a short-term loan from the friendly banker until some bonds mature. Even the friendliest of bankers know that the loan on the personal residence will be paid off, in full, before the loan on the new airplane or yacht is paid. Thus, the banker is a lot friendlier about maintaining an open line of credit for the upscale borrower if the banker knows the line of credit will be "first in line" to get paid off.

4. Valuing the Residence Before You Buy

The core of the valuation process is gathering and analyzing a series of comps that bracket the subject property in terms of size, amenities, and anticipated value. If the subject is a five-bedroom, five-bath, 5,000-square-foot home anticipated to be worth $1 million or so, then I would gather several (at least three, preferably six or more) sales of nearby homes within about 10% or 15% of the square footage, with four to six bedrooms, four to six baths, and selling for plus or minus 10% to 15% of the anticipated price. I would make heuristically determined albeit informed analyses to estimate the difference in contributory value between four baths and five, or between five and six, and adjust the comp prices to an "indicated value." Adjustments are also made for any special financing, for the time difference between the original sale and the effective appraisal date, and any other conditions that affect value.

> Tobler's First Law of Geography—Everything is related to everything else, but near things are more related than distant things.

My completed appraisal report will include sketches of the floor plan, photos of the property and the comps used, and maps to indicate the location of the subject property relative to the comps. These addenda help the reader understand the data used and the processes followed.

Finally, I reconcile my findings. The indicated values of the adjusted comps are compared to one another, and the most weight is usually given to the one qualitatively and quantitatively most like the subject. I will usually give weight to physical proximity and to the recency of the comp sale.

Comparing the appraisal cost to the home's purchase price is a fairly inexpensive tool to aid in formulating an offer price on a home or evaluating an asking price. An appraisal may be necessary for property tax appeals and will almost certainly be necessary for estate management purposes.

5. Tax Appeals

There are 3,141 counties in the United States, and each one of them has some form of tax assessor.[4] Assessors produce estimates of value on which property tax assessments are based. In some jurisdictions, there are assessment ratios. Owner-occupied residences may be assessed at a smaller fraction of market value than non-owner-occupied residences. Local taxing authorities (counties, cities, school districts, other districts) then determine a tax rate, called a "millage," that is multiplied against the assessed value to produce a property tax amount for each property in the jurisdiction. Yet another local authority, typically a county treasurer, will send out and collect tax bills.

From our perspective, the entry point is the tax assessor's value estimate. Most assessors determine this with some type of mass appraisal model. These models can be called "CAMA" models ("computer assisted mass appraisal"), "AVMs" ("automated valuation models") or some variant of these. These are statistical models that use a large number of comps, combined with periodic inspections and updates from building permits and other public records, to develop individual estimates of value for each home in the jurisdiction. Most states have very specific requirements about these values. Many states require periodic testing of the mass appraisal values against local sales to determine a measure of accuracy.

In most jurisdictions, there is a process for appealing property tax assessments (and hence the tax). These are not insignificant amounts of money, particularly for upscale homes that are not primary residences. In states with no income tax and notably high-valued homes (Washington and

Florida, for example), the property tax burden can be substantial, and thus appeals are common. Property owners can certainly represent themselves in the process, but there are specialized advisors, often attorneys or real estate consultants, who have expertise in this arena. They will usually represent a property owner for a contingency fee, usually a portion of the reduction in the tax levy. An appraisal is usually required, but appraisers are prohibited by appraisal standards[5] from representing clients for a contingency fee.[6]

The specific appeal process varies from jurisdiction to jurisdiction, but in essence relies on an appraisal based on recent comps in the marketplace. Critiquing the assessor's methodology and findings is generally not a winning strategy. The appellant must show that the actual transactional data in the marketplace does not support the assessor's findings. During periods of rapidly falling prices, or in neighborhoods that are suddenly impacted by negative external obsolescence, such as ubiquitous contamination or stigma, or for an individual property that is suddenly damaged or stigmatized in some fashion, the effort may prove very worthwhile.

6. Insurance Appraisals

Loss or damage due to an insured incident may require an appraisal. Insurance companies have been the subject of significant litigation in recent years due to their preference to rely on the opinions of insurance adjusters rather than an appraisal. The adjuster will assess the cost to cure the problem but may not take into account the actual property value loss. Careful review of the insurance policy may reveal that the latter should be the basis for the insurance claim rather than the former.

One key issue is the difference between *repair* and *replacement*. Replacement cost can be impacted by the degree of estimated depreciation prior to the damage. Assume that a covered event damaged the roof to the extent that the roof required complete replacement. Was the roof brand-new prior to the event, or was it near the end of its economic life?

In parts of the country subject to hurricanes and tropical storms, the homeowner's policy may have a "named storm exclusion." It is popularly thought that flood insurance satisfies the gap left by this named storm exclusion, but there may also be a wind exclusion in the homeowner's policy. In that case, a separate wind policy may be needed. Assume that the named storm in question caused water damage inside the house. Did the water enter the house from below (a flood) or from above (a damaged roof due to the wind)? The answer to this question is of no small importance in determining exactly who pays the claim. Also, does the homeowner's policy exclude specific high-valued property, such as artwork, valuable furniture, or jewelry?

Insurance companies may invoke an "adjustment" immediately after a loss. If the homeowner prefers an appraisal to a simple adjustment, then the courts have held that the demand must be made in a timely fashion, although courts have not specified exactly what "timely" means. However, in one frequently cited case, a demand 72 days later was ruled to not be timely.[7]

While appraisers are obligated to be unbiased, insurance companies typically draw from a regular pool with whom they have prior experience. Given that, many homeowners and their attorneys hire more independent appraisers for this task.

Three topics will be of particular interest to the homeowner, the appraiser, and the homeowner's attorney:

- Replacement cost
- Depreciated replacement cost
- Insurable replacement cost

These may be *very* different numbers. The replacement cost is simple enough—it is the cost of rebuilding the structure with something that provides the same or better utility. *Replacement* is not the same as *replication*. Replicating a 50-year-old house may be difficult, given the changes in building materials and construction methods, and may be in violation of building codes. By the way, many insurance policies separately quote a line item for building codes—this is coverage to bring the residence "up to code" if the damage is such that the local building officials require such be done. In short, a replacement for 50-year-old, a 5,000-square-foot, five-bedroom, five-bath house may look like the old house, but it may be a very different house indeed. Who wants 50-year-old plumbing, heating, air conditioning, wiring, and insulation?

Depreciated replacement cost can be a real problem for older dwellings or structures with significant functional or preloss physical depreciation. Finally, insurable replacement cost may leave a substantial gap in the ability to restore the home. Upscale investors and their attorneys will need to carefully consider the nuances of property insurance policies. No one wants to plan for an insurance loss. A careful review of policies with a competent legal advisor is probably a handy, periodic process, much like reviewing any other estate plan facet.

7. Valuation When You Sell

In a perfect world, investors accumulate real estate over time and pass it on to successive generations. However, this is a luxury, even for the wealthiest families, and properties are occasionally sold for a variety of reasons. Determining the optimum sales price is simple for typical homes and properties—a broker's price opinion is often sufficient. This book is not about typical homes, but about upscale residences, trophy properties, and investment-grade collectible real estate. Determining an optimal selling price can be much more difficult.

First, what is the competitive market for this home or estate? True trophy property will be sold to a global market and may compete with properties that are fundamentally very different. A buyer seeking a waterfront mansion may find quite different opportunities on an island in the Caribbean, on the Pacific Coast near San Francisco, or in the Hamptons. A buyer seeking a collectible "trophy" property may buy an island, a pristine forest, a stretch of desert, or a mountaintop.

Second, what are the sale goals? Normally, profit maximization is the key, but are there other considerations at play? If the personal residence has historic or architectural amenities, are these to be preserved in some fashion? Are there specific restrictions on the use? Many trophy properties are sold with a remainder interest held by the seller or subject to a previously granted conservation or preservation easement. Is this a non-arm's-length[8] sale simply to transfer ownership among family members or acquaintances? Is the sale to a trust, a charity, or some other charitable beneficiary? These questions affect sales prices in complex ways.

Finally, who will intermediate this sale? For 99% of sales, "a broker" is the straightforward answer, but how will you vet the broker? The complexity (and resulting commission) for the sale of a fairly standard $250,000 home is quite different from the complexity—yes, and resulting commission—on a $10 million estate. The latter will undoubtedly require a detailed marketing plan. The seller—and the seller's advisors—will probably solicit presentations from several competing brokers. Many wealthy sellers opt to hire a real estate consultant for the simple expedient of handling this vetting and making a recommendation.

8. Inheritance Valuation

The valuation in probate will almost certainly require an appraisal. The rules of probate, such as effective dates and such, are matters for competent probate attorneys. There are several key valuation elements that should be considered.

Was the property solely or jointly owned? If jointly, was it a joint tenancy with rights of survivorship (which simplifies matters) or some sort of family trust? Is the entire interest being sold, or a part interest?

Is the property subject to any leases, contracts of sale, or pending options? Most appraisals assume a fee simple interest (the most complete bundle of rights). If a property or a portion (say, hunting or farming rights) is subject to a long-term, below-market lease, then there are interesting legal and valuation issues at play.

Was the property subject to complex financing arrangements? If the property is owned outright, or had a market normal mortgage, this is irrelevant. Trophy property, upscale estates, and other complex properties often have financing issues that transcend the normal appraisal experience. Was the property pledged or in some other way liened for business financing? Was the property comingled with other properties in a financing arrangement? Was a portion of the property pledged as an asset? A forest, purchased as a personal land holding by the decedent, may have the timber pledged for financing but not the land.

Is the real estate subject to any other claims? The probate laws vary from state to state, and the appraisal experts assisting the estate attorneys will need to ask the right questions and provide the right feedback. Florida provides that a primary residence passes from the decedent to either the spouse *or minor children* free of any unperfected liens. Other states may not be so generous, and this is an important consideration for wealthy families when structuring ownership.

Are all real estate holdings in the United States? There are complex estate law issues regarding holdings abroad, implying complex valuation issues. As a simple example, would a personal real estate holding in Canada be valued subject to US appraisal standards or Canadian? These are decisions that may need to be made by the estate attorneys.

Undervaluation of estate properties is a temptation, and one that is being aggressively pursued on many fronts. The IRS does not separately break out reports on estate investigations, but as a comparative example, in the past few years the British government has initiated over 10,000 investigations into undervalued estate properties. Large estates are naturally targets for investigation, and careful valuations are critical components to a clean, simple probate process.

9. Summary and Key Points

Valuation of the personal residence includes careful estimation of the purchase value, continued maintenance and management with an eye to value optimization, and valuation at the sale or inheritance of the property. Danger zones include overbuying in a market (buying the biggest or most expensive property is always going to engender resale marketing issues), buying a heavily depreciated property (not just physical but functional and external factors), properties with unique or hard-to-market features, and properties with complex ownership structures.

Owners will need appraisals on occasion, for purchase or sale decisions, for insurance or tax issues, and to settle estates. Most appraisers, and most brokers for that matter, are unskilled at dealing with the complexity of upscale or trophy real estate. This is an area where specialized consultants can intermediate these issues and usually end up saving money, time, and effort.

10. A Final Note—the Family Trust

A successful investor we knew owned a *lot* of commercial real estate, and had purchased every piece of it in his own name, personally. No LLCs, LPs, Incs, Ltds, and particularly no trusts. He started planning his affairs, and it took a battery of lawyers about 10 years (I'm not making this up) to sort things out and get his estate ready.

Structuring the ownership of real estate is a significant decision, which should be reached with consultation from legal, tax, and other experts, and is generally beyond the scope of this book. We will touch on these issues from time to time, if only to remind the reader to get good counsel.

Even the best structured family investment portfolio often fails to properly structure the personal residence and other "family" holdings. Implicit is our bias toward accumulating and holding real estate as an intergenerational asset. Many families, even wealthy, sophisticated families, fail to consider *family trusts* in their estate plans. A family trust is a legal entity created to hold ownership of real property, in this case the personal family holdings. The purpose is to make these assets easier to pass on to subsequent generations. Generally, during the lifetime of the original trustees, the trust can be revoked. The specifics of a particular trust, and the needs of a particular family, are matters to discuss with your advisors.

Advisors often fail to consider the upkeep and maintenance of the family real estate. The trust should include provisions for management of these assets, ensuring that the family holdings provide the desired utility to subsequent generations without burdening them with the expenses. This maintains value across generations. Often, heirs have dissimilar abilities to support the family homestead. Some descendants may be perfectly able to pony up their share of the utility bill or the cost of a new roof, while others cannot. The stresses on subsequent generations cannot be understated, and may result in the sale of the property, counter to the wishes of Mom and Dad, simply to pay the bills.

Finally, many family trusts set up boards of family members to manage the property. This can be good and bad. Obviously, family members should have some say-so in the strategic oversight of properties owned, but the talents and abilities of subsequent generations to manage complex properties should, and indeed must be taken into account.

5
Valuing Rental Property

Landlords grow rich in their sleep.

—**John Stuart Mill**

THE MARKET FOR small rental property, such as houses and duplexes, is huge and growing. Several real estate investment trusts (REITs) are in a buying mode, particularly in fast-growing Sunbelt cities where there is a steady demand for workforce housing. Even in so-called affordable markets, the cost of construction and other constraints is putting the "starter" home out of reach of a new family. Investors with long-term appreciation goals and less emphasis on immediate income find rental housing to be a great addition to the portfolio.

In any city, rental houses are going to be at or near the bottom of the single family housing market. Usually "starter home" neighborhoods and older neighborhoods are dotted with rental houses. Notably, there has also been a fascination among investors recently with mobile home parks. This is a very distinct market segment and has operational characteristics outside the scope of this book.

For families with significant cash investable assets who look for direct property ownership, rental houses can be a significant addition to the portfolio. Current income may not compare well to other investments, but the proper way to view these is as an annuity. In the previous chapter, we discussed pairing a family residence trust with an income stream designed to fund the maintenance and management of that family residence. A properly constructed portfolio potentially provides such an income stream, is tax advantaged, and has certain advantages in probate (or preprobate, in a trust).

Senator Mitt Romney famously bought several rental houses in Houston a few years ago , with the profits accruing to his sons. His total original investment of about $300,000 is a tiny fraction of his estimated quarter-billion-dollar net worth. His original deal was a "rent to own" investment that turned out quite differently during the mortgage meltdown. The "rent to own" portion died, as the market values fell below the outstanding loans. The rental viability remained intact, however, and reportedly the Romney family still owns the properties and continues to collect rents. The investment continues to be a family object lesson.

1. When, What, Where, and Why to Buy

Let's take the last question first. Buying a portfolio of rental houses can be viewed as a long-term, tax-advantaged annuity. Values and rents should increase over time.[1] In America today, and particularly in choice markets, there is a steady growth in households but home ownership at the entry level has become problematic. Many newly formed households rent apartments, but if and as those households grow and mature, particularly the ones that have children, apartment living begins to cramp.

Fixer-uppers are a part of the investment equation. This book is aimed principally at the upscale investor for whom fixing a broken toilet is simply not part of the equation. This investor will almost certainly have a contract with a property manager who doubles as a real estate broker. The property manager will generally have a suite of contractors who specialize in this sort of work, and who are able to deliver repairs at an affordable price. They are typically familiar with the level of work quality and materials needed to satisfy this market tranche. Fixer-uppers usually come at a substantial discount off of "as if new" market value. There is no universal rule of thumb, but as an example, a rental house that would sell for $200,000 if in completely "move-in" condition but requires $20,000 in repairs (10%) might sell in the range of $160,000. In this offhand example, the discount is actually greater than the expected out-of-pocket expenses. Demand and supply will dictate this level of discount, but some discount should be expected in every situation. A portion of the discount, of course, is dictated by the lost rent during the period of repairs.

There is also a social good here. There continues to be a shortage of workforce housing. Institutional investors with a focus on housing are generally more interested in apartments, leaving a gap in the market between apartments and houses with yards.

REITs and private equity funds are focused on growing, secondary Sunbelt cities like Phoenix/Scottsdale, Austin, Houston, and Orlando. Many of these cities suffered significantly during the recession as a result of overbuilding (thus providing "deals" for savvy buyers) and infrastructure constraints limiting starter homes. As such, these institutional analysts view these markets as long-term recession proof.

That leaves many secondary and tertiary cities with little interest from institutional investors. These cities often have slower-growing house prices but are faced with the same cost structure as faster-growing cities. For that reason, home ownership and new construction is solidly constrained in these tertiary markets. Savvy investors look for markets where the ratio of rents to replacement cost makes new rental property construction financially inefficient. The secret in such markets is to buy solidly built existing properties in stable blue-collar neighborhoods. Often, these houses will require substantial renovation, and this is not a place to cut corners. Rental houses will generally suffer more wear and tear than owner-occupied homes. Thus, look for older brick or "real wood" sided homes (as opposed to vinyl or composite siding) with minimal but real wood cabinets and other built-ins, ceramic bathroom fixtures, and hardwood flooring. *Until the mid-1980s, these were minimal standards expected for FHA-insured homes.*

Investors will probably want to concentrate on one city at first, and perhaps even one part of one city. Engage a good local property manager because the city will probably *not* be where you own a principal residence. (Although there may be tax advantages to "inspect" investments in a city you regularly visit for pleasure or for family vacations.) Concentrating in one city provides a critical mass of business with a property manager and contractors who help repair and maintain the houses. Owning 10 houses in one neighborhood is preferable to owning one each in 10 different towns. At some point, though, diversification may be recommended. Systematic issues that hit a particular town can be diversified across multiple geographies. As a general rule, diversification probably should not be undertaken until some sort of critical mass of homes are owned in one market. What is a critical mass? That can be situationally dependent, but we have observed nice portfolios of 10 or 12 houses in midsized (half million population) American cities. At $200,000 each, that is an aggregate investment of $2 million, which gets the attention of property managers anywhere.

As with any investment, the buyer will analyze net operating income versus sales price. There is a little confusion as to where these investments lie on the risk-reward curve. In the short term, the risk can be substantial, because rental houses have significant income variance over a short-term horizon. Taking a much longer view, the risk tends to ameliorate, and the risk-adjusted returns in the long run can be quite handsome. Further, these investments are rarely correlated with securities, and so provide significant diversification benefits.

Later in the chapter, we will discuss financing risk. Many investors prefer to be cash-only with their rental property investments. Arguably, the after-tax cost of money can be pretty low. However, the fixed costs of financing these properties can make short-term returns and financing risks look unattractive. In the end, the decision to finance or not finance may be investor-specific.

Typically, buyers find three kinds of buying opportunities:

- ***"Tenant ready" homes,*** often brand new, built as either starter homes or built specifically for the rental market.
- ***"Fixer-uppers,"*** which can be foreclosed homes, bank repositions, or rental properties being sold by other investors or estates.
- ***Distressed sellers,*** who may be in arrears on their mortgages but want to stay in the homes. These can often be bought as rent-to-own situations, although the history is not very good for distressed buyers actually salvaging their situations.

Tenant-ready homes are often built specifically for the rental market, but are indistinguishable from homes aimed at the owner-occupied market. Optimally, these homes should be ruggedly constructed, recognizing that the rental market homes will not get the same level of care as owner-occupied ones.

Most rental property investments will be fixer-uppers. Sources include regular real estate sales and listings, foreclosure auctions, private sales from bank real estate owned (REO) portfolios, and sales from other investors who can no longer keep up with the property. This latter category bears further discussion. Many investors try to self-manage property and become active landlords, fixing broken toilets and remodeling houses in between tenants. For them, rental property is more a business than an investment. Property management becomes a full-time job, or at least a profitable hobby income. They eventually reach a point (or their heirs reach a point) where property management is no longer in the cards. These properties get sold when the landlord has given up (or died) and the properties in question are in a state of disrepair (hence, the "give up" part).

Overworked owner-managers or the heirs of owner-managers are just one category of distressed seller. Technically, a bank REO or a foreclosure sale is generated as a result of distress. Shrewd investors will try to bypass this route, and even bypass normal real estate listings, seeking out property owners in arrears or ready to sell at a discount. There are some large national companies that target certain markets looking for these sellers. How many readers have seen small signs in some parts of town advertising, "We buy ugly houses?"[2] This sort of mass marketing is emblematic of the value attached to buying and fixing up distressed property. At the other end of the spectrum, many investors research county records for homeowners in distress. In many jurisdictions, banks must file preforeclosure paperwork providing notice to other creditors. This book is not aimed at investors involved at such a granular level. A hungry real estate agent could be directed to do this search for an investor with cash at hand, and the payoff can be substantial. The investor picks up property at a discount, and the in-arrears homeowner gets a lifeline to avoid the cost of foreclosure.

In many markets, there are well-advertised teams of real estate agents who specialize in distressed, foreclosed, REO, and auction properties. They monitor the markets, have contact with specialists who help ascertain optimum prices, and may even be able to provide estimates of rehab costs and connections with niche-focused repair contractors. These folks can be extraordinarily valuable resources for the first-time investor as well as the seasoned pro. If you want to dive into this market, you are well advised to make contact with these folks early. The good ones know that their stock-in-trade is educating investors.

The "when" is complicated since there are long-term trends at work in the market, shorter-term cycles, and of course investor-specific timing concerns. Carefully chosen investments can be made at any time. Clearly, investments immediately prior to the 2007 bubble-burst were ill-timed from a capital gains perspective, but investors with staying power found that rents actually ran up in many markets after the crash as a result of the displacement of many former homeowners. Of course, many tertiary markets, where bargains can always be had, felt less of the bubble and so less of the crash.

By the way, most jurisdictions recognize a joint tenancy that avoids probate. Some states, such as Arizona, provide a "transfer upon death" deed avoiding probate without any joint ownership problems. Real estate may facilitate estate tax opportunities, particularly when the ownership interest is less than 50% and the estate can take advantage of minority interest and marketability discounts. Details are investor-specific and should be planned well in advance with competent estate planning counsel.

2. Geography—the Rent/Cost Relationship

As mentioned, many private equity firms and REITs are focused on Sunbelt, secondary cities. These REITs need cash flow *and* year-over-year net value increases. The hot markets in the Sunbelt (pun intended) are expected to deliver gains well into the future.

This leads to two important investor-specific questions: First, are you looking for rents, capital gains, or both? Second, is your time frame current or more permanent?

The accumulation of a healthy property portfolio should be at the core of every family's estate. Many investors, particularly those in the real estate business or who joint venture with others or other families, will have shorter-term horizons for investment performance. For these investors, following the crowd and looking at secondary Sunbelt cities may be the best idea.

For investors building a rental house portfolio, and for whom wealth preservation is primary, future income is secondary, and current income is even further down the list, following the crowd may be a mistake. I discussed tertiary cities, but without good definition. Miami is clearly one of the world's premier cities and would be categorized as a primary city. Indeed, in the Southeast there are probably only two major, primary cities: Miami and Atlanta (although there is a strong argument for New Orleans and Charlotte to be on this list). But returning to Florida, Orlando would certainly be a secondary city, as would Tampa and perhaps Jacksonville when viewed from a worldwide perspective. Then we get into the tertiary cities, which arguably would include Gainesville and Tallahassee.

Tertiary cities have interesting economies and valuation metrics. First, many are fairly small. Gainesville is the county seat with just over a quarter million people. Tallahassee, the state capital, has a slightly larger metro area at 380,000. Both cities have major universities (Florida State and U. Florida). Both have economies that are on a solid, if boring footing. Neither has the skyrocketing growth of Seattle or Austin, but both are fairly recession resistant.[3]

There is a boring but strong, stable rental house market in both cities. The university halls need to be swept, the fast-food joints staffed, and someone needs to do whatever gets done in the state capital. This implies a large cadre of rental property occupants with slow-growing incomes. The prices of rental properties in comparatively boring cities can be fairly low relative to the rents. Further, the cost of new construction in Gainesville is not much less than it is in Miami. Hence, owning a rental house in Gainesville means that you will have little in the way of competitive supply, a solid and slow-growing demand, and less chance of systematic economic problems.

America is dotted with cities like this. Here are some key elements:

- State capital
- University location
- Very solid local employment base
- Large demand for blue-collar workers
- High cost of new construction relative to local incomes and to the purchase cost of homes
- Availability of solidly built homes at a discount from replacement cost
- Stable neighborhoods

There are risk markers that should send up red flags for any investor. Neighborhoods in negative transition, with significant and increasing vacancy, or neighborhoods that evidence something other than stable households would be problematic. Of course, the investor will want to pay close attention to crime rates and local employment trends. A city dependent on one industry, particularly if that industry is on a shaky foundation, could be a concern. That said, an investor recently shared with me that he invested heavily in a "one industry" city, but at the bottom of the rental market. When the major employer relocated to Mexico, his investments continued to pay off, since the bottom of the market still had tenants.

Despite great returns, solid but boring markets generally do not attract REITs and private equity firms, and so investors in these markets will face less competitive demand for properties. Notably, the same lack of competition limits investment resale potential. Experience dictates that portfolios may need to be sold piecemeal and over time to achieve maximum returns.

3. The Gross Rent Multiplier

In short, the gross rent multiplier, or GRM, is a quick, shorthand way to compare differently priced properties. I touched base on this metric in a prior chapter. The GRM is the ratio of the purchase price to the gross rent (either monthly or annually).

Properties with a lower GRM will have more rent "bang" for the buck, while the higher-GRM properties may suggest that expected capital gains are the predominant reason for buying. As a caution, the lowest GRM in the market probably tells you something negative about the property. Why would the seller knowingly leave money on the table? All things being equivalent, lower GRMs are preferred to higher ones, but the details deserve close inspection. It may be that the low GRM turns into a high one after considering remodeling or fix-up costs.

4. Net Operating Income for Rental Properties

Once a property is being considered for investment, a thorough and complete net operating income (NOI) analysis is required. I will walk through an example, showing the calculations typically made in evaluating a rental property (Table 5-1), and then explain how and why these calculations (and NOI) will be useful for you to understand.

TABLE 5-1 Illustrative NOI Calculations

	Monthly	Annual
Gross Rent	1,500.00	18,000.00
Vacancy & Collection Losses	–240.00	–2,880.00
Effective Rent	1,260.00	15,120.00
Operating Expenses:		
Management Fees (4%)	–50.40	–604.80
Brokerage Commissions	–31.25	–375.00
Reserves for Replacement	–166.67	–2,000.00
Property Taxes	–166.67	–2,000.00
Insurance	–83.33	–1,000.00
Utilities	–16.67	–200.00
Total Expenses	–514.98	–6,179.80
Net Operating Income	745.02	8,940.20

Gross rent exists only in a perfect world—where every property rents for actual fair market rent, the property is fully occupied, and the tenant pays on time, in full, every month. Gross rent is simply the starting point for the analysis, nothing more. In this example, we use a hypothetical monthly rent, and then simply multiply by 12 to get an annual figure. Most other calculations begin with the annual number and work backward to the monthly.

V&C is shorthand for "vacancy and collection costs." This combines forgone rent when a property is vacant, plus the collection costs associated with late rents, evictions, etc. For rental houses, 15% is not uncommon and 20% is not abnormal. There are ways to "tweak" this with security deposits and first/last month's rent in advance, but the simple fact is that rental houses have surprisingly short tenure, even with one-year leases. Our example assumes a vacancy of one month per year, and loss of one month's rent for collections, thus totally about 16%.

In many markets, landlords can rent via local housing authorities, Section 8 vouchers, or other public programs that ameliorate some of this collection risk. However these are not universally available options.

Effective gross rent (EGR), sometimes called "net rent," is the difference between gross rent and V&C losses. It is important because management fees are usually calculated as a percentage of EGR. This provides the manager with some incentive to keep V&C low. Managers work on a negotiated fee, which commonly includes a fee for management and a fee for finding tenants. In this example, we have broken out the two separately and assume the payment of one rental commission of 25% of a month's rent each year.

Below the line, we see a series of actual out-of-pocket expenses. Noncash expenses are not included (such as depreciation). Property taxes are included, but income taxes and debt service are not. Reserves for replacement, in this example, are based on experience with these kinds of properties and assume basic cleanup and fix-up after each tenant plus the replacement of at least one major appliance or system every year. Note the line item for utilities. When a tenant moves out, the owner will probably need to pay a month's utilities during the cleanup/refit period.

Those are the inputs. What does the NOI help you *do*?

In the end, the NOI is analogous to funds from operations in a securitized model, or earnings before interest, taxes, depreciation, and amortization (EBITDA). If you're going to finance, the ratio of NOI to debt service is called the debt service coverage ratio (DSCR). When financing income-producing property, this is of vital importance to lenders, and it should be of vital importance to borrowers as well. Generally, lenders look for a DSCR in the range of 1.35 or higher if they are going to rely on the collateral (the house itself) as the primary basis for the loan. With lower ratios, the bank will place more emphasis on the borrower's personal credit. Many banks have DSCR thresholds below which they simply cannot consider this as a loan secured by real estate. Of course, borrowers with deep pockets, balances on deposit with the lender, or negotiable securities managed by the lender (say, in its trust department) and longstanding relationships with their banker will be able to avoid this complexity.

Further, NOI minus the debt service gives us before tax cash flow (BTCF). This is *not* taxable income on the property because it does not include depreciation. Further, NOI includes a provision for reserves that may not be the same as actual expenditures for repairs anticipated by those reserves. If you annually reserve $1,000 for repairs, but your repair bill this year was actually only $500, the IRS may disallow the unspent portion of the reserves for cash-basis taxpayers. Conversely, the IRS *will* allow deductions for depreciation. Finally, the IRS considers losses to be deductible against other income only under certain circumstances. Again, your tax advisor can fill you in on the details.

Finally, NOI is the numerator in an important valuation equation:

$$Value = \frac{Net\ Operating\ Income}{Capitalization\ Rate}$$ **EQUATION 5-1**

The value of a perpetuity (such as a share of preferred stock or, in this case, an income-producing property) is emulated by the ratio of the NOI to a capitalization rate. Technically, net present value analysis (which we will touch on later in the book) is preferred when cash flows are changing at an irregular rate. As we will show in the next section, this cap rate analysis does a pretty good job of zeroing in on the market value of real estate, even if results of future years are unknown.

5. The Capitalization or "Cap" Rate

The cap rate is simply the denominator in a fraction (see Equation 5-1). Assume we found an absolutely perfect comparable rental property, and we knew its annual net operating income and either its value or recent sale price.[4] Let's rearrange Equation 5-1 as follows:

$$Capitalization\ Rate = \frac{Net\ Operating\ Income}{Value\ or\ Price}$$ **EQUATION 5-2**

See? The cap rate is just the ratio of NOI to the sale price. Now, to revisit middle school math, since NOI is typically lower than the sales price, cap rate is a fraction, usually expressed as a decimal, somewhere between 0 and 1. Since decimals can be easily converted to percentages, real estate agents and appraisers like to express cap rates as percentages.

If I could find several perfect (or nearly perfect) comparables, and knew exactly what their NOIs and sales prices were, and was assured that the sales prices were all at arm's-length market value, then perhaps I could use Equation 5-2 and some weighted averages to estimate the cap rate for our property. Indeed, that's what appraisers try to do, and what banks expect us to do.

Another common method is the "mortgage-equity analysis," sometimes referred to as the "band of investments" method. It takes a weighted average of the payment rate on a typical mortgage in the market and the equity dividend rate (EDR, which is the rate of return) expected by investors. The weighting is the market-typical loan to value ratio. In effect, it emulates the computation of weighted average cost of capital (WACC) for financial firms. The equation is a bit more complicated than we have seen up until now, so we will start with the equation itself and then dive into the parts.

$$Capitalization\ Rate = (LTV)(Loan\ Constant) + (1 - LTV)(EDR)$$

EQUATION 5-3

The end product is the cap rate, the simple weighted sum of the expectation of investors plus the expectation of mortgage lenders. In Equation 5-4, I put some actual numbers to this to illustrate.

$$Capitalization\ Rate = (0.75)(.0948952) + (0.25)(0.12) = 0.1012\ or\ 10.12\%$$

EQUATION 5-4

The factor for mortgage payment is the most complicated part of this method. It assumes an interest rate and a given number of payments. This formulation assumes a fully amortizing loan. Many commercial loans have a payment based on full amortization (say, 15 years) but a balloon in a shorter period (say, 5 years). Equation 5-4 assumes a 15-year fully amortizing loan at 5% annual interest. Since payments are usually computed on a monthly basis, but cap rates assume annual, the common method is to compute the monthly payment rate and multiply by 12.[5]

This assumes a 75% loan-to-value ratio. The equity investor is putting up 25% of the cost, and technically has a 25% claim to the residual income. This is flawed on a number of levels. The equity investor owns a residual claim to all income above debt service. If things work out as planned, and if indeed the DSCR is substantially above 100%, then the equity investor owns much more than 25% of the cash flows. However, the equity investor stands behind the lender in priority, and will not be paid unless and until the lender is paid. Of course, the equity dividend rate (EDR) is a somewhat higher percentage than the loan rate, because equity investors recognize they are standing last on the list for residual claims.

Solving for the EDR is the hard part. Some sources suggest an empirical approach, which requires estimating NOI and sales prices of competing properties, estimating their debt service, and backing into realized EDR. There are numerous fallacies with this. First, estimating the NOI for competing properties can be troublesome. Small errors in this estimate can lead to significant errors in the estimate of EDR.

More to the point, empirical estimates of EDR are subject to the market whims. In good years, NOI is high and the empirical estimate of EDR is high. In bad years, the converse is true. Indeed, if the market is suffering a systematic slump, EDR calculated this way can be negative! This leads to the second major problem with empirical estimates of EDR—these estimates have nothing to do with the long-range expectations of market participants. Instead, they are snapshots of points in time.

I prefer two alternative methods and recommend them to you. First, a survey of local investors, real estate brokers, appraisers, or other knowledgeable parties can yield a treasure trove of information. Second, there are several services that conduct nationwide surveys of investors and other knowledgeable parties to elicit exactly this sort of information. PricewaterhouseCoopers (PwC), for example, publishes a quarterly real estate market digest that is a must-read for active real estate investors. They track not only nationwide investment metrics but also produce periodic in-depth studies of property types (e.g., office market, regional malls, housing, etc.).

6. Capitalized Net Income

The natural extension of the previous two sections is the capitalization of NOI to arrive at a value.[6] The end result of this exercise is important. This is one of the best metrics for determining the optimum offering price. During a due-diligence period, NOI will need to be reevaluated based on the prior owner's actual experience versus your anticipated experience.

Differences in NOI and perceived cap rate (influenced by your own EDR versus the seller's) can be substantial. The seller may be an "owner-landlord" who manages the property. On the books, the seller has no management fees, and repair costs ignore "sweat equity." These are not realistic selling points, since a typical investor would pay those fees. In short, the seller is enjoying both a real estate income and a business income acting as a manager and a repair contractor. It is always essential to make these calculations using your own assumptions and not rely on another party's computations or claims.

Taking the NOI determined in Table 5-1 and the cap rate determined in Equation 5-4, we can estimate value as shown in Equation 5-5:

$$Value = \frac{\$8{,}940.20}{0.1012} = \$88{,}367 \qquad \text{EQUATION 5-5}$$

In the next section, we will examine the sales comparison approach for estimating value as a way of triangulating in on the actual purchase price.

7. Sales Comparisons

The key here is to use comps that are actually competing rental properties. Owner-occupied properties will have been purchased with a very different mindset.

Key metrics for rental properties are location of the property, number of bedrooms, number of baths, square footage of living area, and parking. There are some amenities that are important for owner-occupants that do not have the same weight for rental properties. These include the size of the yard beyond some minimal size, yard fencing, and the difference in value between a carport and a garage. Studies indicate proximity to mass transit is very important to rental property value. Renters are marginally more likely to have school-aged children, so the quality of the school district is important. Built-in appliances are important, since renters generally have few if any appliances. Note whether comps include refrigerators, washers, dryers, and other stand-alone appliances.

Rental properties nearly always rent on a bedroom/bathroom basis. Three-bedroom, two-bath units in the neighborhood will generally rent for about the same, all things being equal. The core of the sales comparison approach is to find comps based on those metrics.

Problems in the sales comparison approach include trying to find comps for unique properties. Large rental houses (more than four bedrooms, more than three baths) or properties in unique parts of town, where there are few comparable rentals, can be difficult. Neighborhood is very important—prospective tenants tend to have very narrow locational windows, and access to transportation can be critical.

This may not have been clear in the preceding chapter, but there is a subtle difference between *quantitative* adjustments and *qualitative* adjustments. The former include such factors as square footage, number of baths, and lot size. These can be easily quantified. The adjustment amount may not be linear, but it can certainly be quantified. On the other hand, location, quality of construction, and property condition are more qualitative. The typical solution is to rank-order comps and see how the subject property fits within the mix. Adjustments for qualitative variables can be highly subjective.

In the end, we are left with several comps with adjusted indications of value. If the comps were good, then the various indicated values should coalesce around a central point, the indicated value. In a market where good comps are rare and adjustments are difficult to determine, the adjusted values may be all over the map. The valuation exercise now depends on determining which comps are most like the subject property being valued.

8. Cost Analyses

The cost approach is usually considered the least useful, but it may indicate a "not to exceed" value for new homes. The underlying theory is that an investor would not pay more for a property than he or she could pay for another property that would provide the same utility. Hence, if the cost of constructing a property (say, the reproduction cost) is higher than the cost to buy the property, this tells us something very important about the investment value.

Insurance companies will often require that the basis for the landlord's loss policy be the reproduction cost of the dwelling. Many landlords, particularly those who are cherry-picking in tertiary markets, are shell-shocked at the estimate of reproduction cost versus purchase price of an existing dwelling. Coupled with this, we have seen many nice blue-collar neighborhoods with vacant lots. The lots are often for sale at fire-sale prices (pun intended). These are usually homes that have burned down without fire insurance, and the local economy simply does not support building a new house on the vacant lot.

This is a real balancing act. If you plan to buy workforce housing in this market for a long-term investment, then the disparity between construction costs and purchase price works in your favor. Over time, the lack of competitive supply will enhance the value of your holdings, and rents should move up over time, further enhancing value.

9. Summary—Key Points

Rental properties can be good investments if approached in the right manner and with an attitude toward long-term holdings and long-term appreciation. The institutional money is currently chasing properties in hot secondary markets in the Sunbelt, but there are deals to be had in the tertiary cities, particularly those with stable local economies.

Appraising rental real estate is different from valuing owner-occupied houses. More emphasis is paid to the income analyses (gross rent multiplier and net income capitalization). The sales comparison approach and the cost approach are less informative, due to the problem of finding truly comparable rental properties and due to the price/cost disparity in many markets.

Costs can be optimized by focusing on building a portfolio. Short-term goals are problematic in this space, but long term, this investment strategy can fit in a variety of portfolios.

10. A Final Note—Building a Tax-Advantaged Portfolio at Any Point in Life

When is the best time to start investing? Tomorrow morning.

Seriously, though, there is an underlying assumption in books like this that investors are fairly early in their lives relative to retirement and "estate planning" issues. Indeed, a driving force behind this book was our study of young investors who are "suddenly" rich and do not have long-term, trustworthy relationships with good advisors.[7] Unfortunately, many begin building their portfolios later in life and are dismayed at the poor returns expected from public securities, bonds, annuities, and the like.

Rental houses, with a long-term (10+ year) horizon, provide a useful and potentially profitable alternative that can build wealth and postretirement income. The tone of this chapter has been aimed at the investor who turns all of the management over to a professional property consultant, although many investors with ample spare time find that the business of managing a real estate portfolio can be a very profitable side venture.

There is a secondary benefit to personal, direct management of the portfolio. Tax law (and again, this is *not* to be construed as authoritative tax advice) gives preference to active real estate managers as opposed to passive ones in the ability to write off losses against other income. An investor with time on his or her hands, and some free cash to invest in a portfolio of rental houses will want to have this conversation with his or her tax advisors and attorneys.

6
Approaches to Value

Buy on the fringe and wait. Buy land near a growing city.
Buy real estate when other people want to sell. Hold what you buy!

—John Jacob Astor

In previous chapters, we have touched on valuation methods including income analyses, sales comparisons, and cost approaches to determine value. It may be handy at this juncture to summarize these methods.

I cannot stress too greatly that this book is *about* real estate valuation, but not written with the anticipation that the reader wants to become a real estate appraiser. However, investors in real estate will regularly be faced with the need to read, review, and understand appraisal documents. This book explores the nuances of valuation from the perspective of that investor, and this chapter explores the even more specific nuances of the appraisal process and appraisal report, again from the perspective of that investor.

Previous chapters illustrated appraisal methods that may be used by appraisers for analyses and conclusions for single residences or small residential properties. In practice, the appraisal results for larger commercial investments and large, complex residential estates—the sort the reader of this book will usually see—will be reported in a narrative, written appraisal report. Often these appraisal reports are highly stylized, aiming at readers who are more intimately familiar with organization of the documents. Investors often throw up their hands at these appraisal reports since, from an investor's perspective, they are so difficult to penetrate.

Consider the stylized format of a financial prospectus. The appraisal is, unfortunately, just as mind-numbingly stylized, with too much verbiage, intentional complexity, and inconsistent narrative.

Since no two narrative appraisal reports are alike, attempting to present a "typical," understandable template would be futile. Rather, this chapter will point to some key elements that the reader might want to look for or have highlighted in the document. By the chapter's end you should have a basic understanding of some key elements underscoring nearly every narrative appraisal report, such that you can more knowledgably communicate with the appraiser.

1. The Principle of Substitution

All investments are intermediated in some fashion, and more inefficient investments require greater intermediation. If I want to buy a share of publicly traded stock, then the price—and the market value—is published continuously on a myriad of websites, and then daily summarized in various periodicals. The underlying, intrinsic value of stock may be different from the current transaction price, but if an equilibrium of buyers and sellers coalesce around that current transaction price, that is the best estimate of market value.

The internet has led to substantial disintermediation of many complex investments. Searching for an investment previously required a broker's assistance, with access to private information. Today, the broker serves a process function rather than a search function. Appraisers continue to provide a regulatory-required function in mortgage lending, and frequently a consulting role in addition to the simple act of determining value.

Real estate is a complex investment. Since each individual parcel has a unique value, dictated in no small part by its locational monopoly, then determining the value requires some analysis. Appraisers are guided in large part by applying the *principle of substitution*, which holds that a buyer will pay no more for a property than it would cost to obtain an equally desirable property. This principle holds for all types of real estate. An investor will pay no more for an income-producing property than for a property with an equivalent return.

Given the principle of substitution, the *sales comparison approach* looks for recent sales of equally desirable properties and, through a marginal-contribution adjustment process, focuses in on the price that would be paid for the subject property. *Cost approach* analyses examine the dollar outlay to buy a tract of land and construct a building of equal utility. Finally, *income analyses* are essentially based on the required rate of return and find the price that would be paid for a given income stream in the context of that ROI.

There are a lot of caveats baked into this principle, and they are important to the concept of valuing any type of property. First, what is meant by *value*? We have already pointed out that there is a stark difference between market value and investment value. There are a lot of other kinds of value bouncing around in the marketplace, some of which define a price that may be higher than market (such as investment value) and some of which may be lower than market (liquidation or foreclosure value).

Even the phrase *market value* itself may have slightly different meanings, depending on the context. Tax assessors are usually required to make a determination of *fair market value* as the basis for property taxes, and this definition may vary from state to state. The IRS proffers a definition of value for appraisals in conjunction with federal tax matters:

> Fair market value (FMV) is the price that property would sell for on the open market. It is the price that would be agreed on between a willing buyer and a willing seller, with neither being required to act, and both having reasonable knowledge of the relevant facts.[1]

In the accounting world, there is a similar definition of what accountants call *fair value*:

> The price that would be received to sell an asset or paid to transfer a liability in an orderly transaction between market participants at the measurement date.[2]

Most commonly, though, in the transactional real estate space, the term *market value* is applied as defined under the Financial Institutions Reform Recovery and Enforcement Act of 1989 (FIRREA).[3] An exposition of FIRREA is beyond the scope here, but FIRREA's definition of *market value* provides guidance across a broad spectrum of transactions:

> Market value means the most probable price which a property should bring in a competitive and open market under all conditions requisite to a fair sale, the buyer and seller each

acting prudently and knowledgeably, and assuming the price is not affected by undue stimulus. Implicit in this definition is the consummation of a sale as of a specified date and the passing of title from seller to buyer under conditions whereby:

(1) Buyer and seller are typically motivated;
(2) Both parties are well informed or well advised, and acting in what they consider their own best interests;
(3) A reasonable time is allowed for exposure in the open market;
(4) Payment is made in terms of cash in US dollars or in terms of financial arrangements comparable thereto; and
(5) The price represents the normal consideration for the property sold unaffected by special or creative financing or sales concessions granted by anyone associated with the sale.[4]

Whew. That's a mouthful. Nonetheless, this definition is so important, and baked into the operational processes of real estate transactions, that it is helpful to take it apart piece by piece.

Most Probable Price

For liquid, publicly traded securities, the "most probable price" is known with a very high degree of accuracy. Either specialists (NYSE) or market makers (NASDAQ) maintain a bid/ask spread throughout the trading day, and even after hours for most securities. For thinly traded or illiquid securities, a bid or ask price is subject to some negotiation. Mortgage loan underwriters are, of course, reluctant to loan money if the value is subject to market whims. Appraisers provide a professional opinion of value based on a heuristic evaluation model, as discussed previously. This is a Bayesian statistic, arrived at with prior knowledge of the market at hand.[5] With the advent of widely available transaction data and cheap computer power, we are seeing the popularization of automated valuation models (AVMs), particularly for simple residential valuation. Mortgage underwriters are increasingly relying on AVMs to produce appraisal reviews and even primary valuations for down-market properties where the cost of a full appraisal is disproportionate to the other transaction costs.

It is that *most probable* price that is sought by the appraiser, not the highest price or the quickest sale price.[6] There is some contradiction in this, because market value assumes that the property is being operated (or at least can be operated) at its highest and best use. Hence, if the property is currently a house, but the highest and best use is a gas station, then the most probable price is the one which would be paid by a buyer who intends to tear down the house and build a gas station. That said, though, the interaction of the market assumes that buyers have alternatives, and at equilibrium the most probable price is not the theoretically highest one potentially achievable.

"A competitive and open market." This is a very important phrase. The competitive and open market differentiates public "market value" sales from private or limited transactions that may result in a price that is not "market."

"Buyer and seller each acting prudently and knowledgeably." Many transactions occur with one or more parties not knowing, understanding, fully appreciating, or acting on information, particularly adverse information. A buyer purchasing a home directly across the street from a waste dump yet paying the same price as would be paid for houses not located across from a dump would probably not be acting "prudently" or perhaps even "knowledgeably." Shortly after Hurricane Katrina, many speculators bought up houses in and around New Orleans at above-market prices, thinking that the shortage of houses would drive up the market. In fact, just the opposite happened, since the loss of supportive economic infrastructure (schools, fire and police protection, utilities) caused demand for these houses to disappear. These buyers were acting without knowledge of the way the market would work, and yet the transaction prices, at least in the short run, would indicate something completely different.

"Each acting in what they consider to be their own best interests." In other words, an arms-length transaction.

"Reasonable time is allowed for exposure." Sales of distressed properties are marked by the lack of exposure time.[7] While we are on the subject, the term *exposure_time* is backward looking. It assumes that the property has been *exposed* on the market prior to the transaction consummation.

"Unaffected by special or creative financing." In short, the transaction represents a true, arm's-length sale with nothing sweetening the pot!

Many investors, brokers, and advisors do not pay enough attention to this definition. It is critically important for a reason that may not be totally obvious. The definition of market value establishes the necessary and sufficient conditions for inclusion of comps into the valuation equation. Assume that we are interested in market value, but all of the comps are distress sales (sold quickly without proper exposure time). The prices of the comps would not reflect the true market value.

We also look at the type of ownership, which also dictates the data gathered for the appraisal. If I am attempting to value a fractional ownership (say, a tenancy in common), then I might examine recent sales of other tenancies in common. The type of ownership may dictate the methodologies I use. Fractional ownership valuation may require the application of marketability or lack-of-control discounts. The purpose of the appraisal may dictate that a certain type of ownership is valued, even if that is not currently the way the property is owned. An eminent domain "taking" may require the valuation of the property as if the "fee simple interest" is owned (see below) even though the owner only has a "leased fee" interest (again, see the following).

Fee Simple Interest

The most complete form of ownership available in the United States is *fee simple interest.* Similar ownership forms exist in most other Western countries. Fee simple implies that the owner has three basic rights:

- The right of possession,
- The right of quiet enjoyment, and
- The right of transfer.

These three rights are limited by four public obligations:

- Eminent domain
- Escheat
- Taxation
- Police power

The last of these four encompasses a host of public limitations, which may include, but are certainly not limited to, property taxation, zoning, and the rights of public officials to enter the property for lawful public purposes. Of course, property ownership may also be restricted by private agreement, such as neighborhood covenants, easements, and leaseholds.

Leasehold and Leased Fee

Tenancy may be on a month-to-month basis, may be by encroachment or adverse possession, or may be by easement (either allowed or prescriptive, and either appurtenant or "in gross"). The most common tenancies are created by a written lease. The rights transferred to the tenant are called *leasehold rights*, and the rights reserved by the landlord are called *leased fee rights*. In a normal situation, the landlord rents the property for a periodic payment that is equal to normal market rents. The landlord also retains all the remainder rights (the reversion of property possession when the lease ends). Thus, the leased fee value is the sum of the present value of the lease payments plus the present value of that reversion value. These two sum up to the fee simple value if the rents are at "market." Usually the leasehold has no intrinsic value in and of itself. The tenant pays market rent and receives the use of the property.

If the periodic lease payment is different from market normal, then the leasehold may have a positive value or even a negative value. The leased fee may have a value that is different from the market value of the fee simple interest. Got it? Perhaps an example will make it a bit clearer.

> Many years ago, there was a retailer called Woolworth's. Its managers realized that their business model was simply not sustainable, and so embarked on a carefully planned shutdown of their retailing business. Over the years, Woolworth's had leased some prime properties for very long terms (50 years, in some situations) at surprisingly low rental rates. Landlords were happy to rent to Woolworth's at such low rates because it was a highly creditworthy tenant and served as an anchor tenant for other retail properties nearby (usually owned by the same landlord). During the shutdown, Woolworth's management realized they had something very valuable—those long-term, below-market leases constituted a *leasehold value* that could be translated into something else. Woolworth's ended up subleasing many of those properties and making more money as a landlord (albeit for a short interim period) than it was making as a retailer!

Easements

These are long-term rights of possession, which may be personal (easements appurtenant) or may run with the land (easements in gross). The easement may be temporary, with a lease payment, or permanent. Normally, for an easement to be legitimate, there is some compensation to the property owner (the "servient estate") when the easement is first created. Subsequent buyers with a long-term or permanent easement will simply accept the property subject to existing easements. The easement may significantly affect the servient estate value, if the easement is unusual (e.g., high tension power lines in the backyard). Utility easements, such as cable television, may be put in place, and part of the compensation is providing neighborhood television services. Long-haul transmission corridors, such as fiber optic cables, pipelines, and such, will usually pay a fee to cross the servient estate. Easements may be acquired by negotiation, by eminent domain, or by prescription. If you sell some of your property but the portion sold is "landlocked," then the buyer has a prescriptive right to an easement across your property to access the nearest road. Such easements should usually be part of the negotiation process in the sale. Significant lawsuits arise when subsequent buyers of the servient estate fail to honor the landlocked property's easement.

Reversion Rights

The landlord has a reversion right after a lease is concluded. This can take on some very interesting scenarios. About 2,200 miles of railroads in America are abandoned each year, and the railroad right-of-way converted to some other use under federal "railbanking" laws. In many situations, the original right-of-way only encompassed use of the easement for rail transportation purposes. Congress enacted legislation in the 1980s to "railbank" these properties in case of future need, with a temporary use as hiking or biking trails. The original easements provided that the land would revert to the adjacent fee simple property owners once rail use was abandoned. These "takings" claims are very common today, often involving quite valuable parcels, and are adjudicated in the Federal Court of Claims.[8]

Another common reversion occurs when a person has a legal life estate. In the United States, this most commonly occurs when an older family member transfers fee simple ownership to a trust but retains occupancy rights, either for the remainder of the grantor's life or until some subsequent event occurs. There are frequent grants of use of property for a specific purpose or to a specific user, with the covenant that possession reverts back to the grantor if that specific use or user is no longer valid. Finally, there can be reversions to a third party.

> There is presently a fascinating court case pending in the United Kingdom over the inheritance of an earldom. One party (the earl) gains possession of the castle until he dies, and then possession of the castle reverts via a nobility formula to another party, who may or may not be the normal heir! The 8th Earl Fortescue, for example, only has three daughters, so the manor house may pass to a male cousin. There are actually several cases pending in the United Kingdom under similar situations.

All of this governs and controls the type of data gathered for the valuation process, and the analytical methods used to evaluate that data. The leasehold estate valuation normally requires valuation data from other leasehold estates. Since positive leasehold estates are fairly rare, other data can be used but must be evaluated to extract the necessary information. In even the simplest situation, an office building, apartment, or raw land valuation should be performed with information from similar properties. Apartment rent, which directly drives net income and hence value, may vary widely by the building's location or age. The remainder of this chapter will examine some more common valuation tools and techniques in light of valuations of more complex properties.

2. Sales Comparison Models

Sales comparison models are nearly ubiquitous in real estate for evaluating nearly every type of property. The preceding section examined the necessary conditions for choosing and accepting comparable transactions that can be used to value a subject in any situation. This section will examine the sales comparison model in more detail.

Sales comparison models are not unique to real estate valuation. These models are commonly used for valuations of thinly traded or illiquid assets for which there are no commonly quoted markets. Art, other collectibles, businesses, machinery, airplanes, and automobiles are all valued with some type of sales comparison model. In real estate, we examine comps that are located nearby, have sold recently under similar transactional circumstances, and are physically or economically similar to the subject.

Assume that we want to value a very simple office building, such as the one presented in Chapter 2: a Class B office/retail high-rise in a high-growth corridor. Let's take a quick look at the salient facts of that office building, as shown in Table 6-1 (see next page).

Rents, vacancy, and expenses are not included in these salient facts. The implicit assumption is that the property competes with other Class B office/retail high-rises in this same neighborhood. Comparable properties should rent for about the same, and so a prudent investor would pay no more for this property than he or she could pay to acquire a comparable property of the same size and utility.

Next, note the salient characteristics themselves and the order in which they are considered. What seem to be subjective factors, such as market conditions, are actually dealt with early in the analysis. The transaction

TABLE 6-1 Characteristics of the Investment

Date	1-Jun-19
Rights transacted	Fee simple
Financing	Market normal
Location	New high-growth area
Square Footage	
Ground Floor Retail	10,000
Low-Floor Office	20,000
Mid-Floor Office	50,000
High-Floor Office	10,000
Garage Parking Spaces	200
Lot Size	20,000
Property Age	2 years
Structure Quality	Class B
Structure Condition	Excellent

date informs us about the market conditions adjustments that may need to be made to comps. *Market conditions* are the pricing trend over time. Assume I am appraising a building as of June 1, 2019. I find a perfectly identical comparable that sold in an arm's-length, market value transaction six months ago for $30 million. The market for properties like this, in this neighborhood, has been moving steadily up by about 5% per year. Thus, the indicated value of the comparable as of our effective date (June 1) is as shown in Equation 6-1:

$$Value = \$30mm\left(1+\frac{.05}{2}\right) = \$30.75mm \qquad \text{EQUATION 6-1}$$

The market conditions adjustment would be $750,000. In upward-trending markets, market conditions adjustments are generally positive because comps sold before the subject property. There are situations when market conditions adjustments can be negative, but these are fairly rare.

The next item is *rights transacted*. The most common rights are fee simple, and this guides us to finding comps that were sold with comparable bundles of rights. What about a transaction in which a security—say, a real estate investment trust—is buying several buildings at the same time? Are the same rights being transacted? This may require some closer inspection, and may even require some adjustment from the comp purchase price to find the net asset value.

Financing may be market normal or may be something special. Oddly enough, all cash transactions are generally assumed to be market normal since the purchase price was not influenced by the offer of special financing. Assume that in this market, financing is a loan to value (LTV) of 60% at 5% interest, fully amortized, for 15 years. The seller of our comparable six months ago was very anxious to sell, and for a variety of reasons wanted to maximize the price but was unconcerned with the immediacy of cash. The seller offered to finance the building at 100% LTV, 4% interest, fully amortized for 20 years. The buyer is positively influenced to buy this building, but what is the difference? Table 6-2 examines the present value of the difference in the two cash flows, again assuming a $30 million purchase price:

TABLE 6-2 The Value of Special Financing

	Market Normal	Special Financing
Cash Down Payment	12,000,000.00	0
Annual Payments	1,734,161.18	2,207,452.51
PV of Payments @ 5%	18,000,000.00	27,509,737.50
Total Present Value	30,000,000.00	27,509,737.50
Difference	2,490,262.50	
Equivalent Value	***$32,490,262.50***	

So, market normal financing is indifferent to a cash purchase of $30 million. However, below-market, favorable financing results in a favorable cash outflow, from a present value perspective, of nearly $2.5 million. Hence, the buyer would be indifferent between a cash transaction of $30 million, a transaction financed at market normal rates of $30 million, or a transaction with favorable financing at $32.5 million. Of course, this scenario assumes the favorable financing is assumable and has no call provisions or other unusual caveats. In practice, these sorts of situations typically arise from related party transactions or transactions with other unusual considerations.

Next is the location. This can potentially be the most important component of value for any type of property, particularly income-producing ones. There are some general guidelines for commercial location, such as central business district (CBD) or suburban. Even within a CBD, there will be choice locations. An office building catering to physicians and other medical practitioners may benefit from being near a hospital, although some types of practitioners, such as dentists, pediatricians, or chiropractors, may want to be near upscale neighborhoods, and particularly neighborhoods with young families and children. Indeed, since medical offices have specific structural requirements and often unique parking requirements, the medical office is now a separate type of office for valuation.

Class A offices will typically be on major streets in the CBD, while Class B offices will be nearby, often on secondary streets. Selection of comps really demands careful examination of the location, the amenities provided (such as ingress/egress, topography, access, views, economic trends, etc.). Making adjustments for location can be problematic, but is often necessary due to lack of actual comps in similar locations.

Quantifying qualitative factors can be challenging. One way is to find comps that bracket the subject with respect to the qualitative condition being examined. In Table 6-3, we examine five different office buildings that vary according to the neighborhood in question. None of the comps are identical to the subject, and none are even identical to each other. I reduce them to a common denominator (in this case, price per square foot) and rank order them. The answer to the problem emerges from the data itself.

TABLE 6-3 Location Adjustments

Property	Location	Size (SF)	Price	Price/SF	Adjustment
123 Elm	Downtown CBD	250,000	100,000,000	400	19.40%
Grosvenor Square	Waterfront	125,000	43,750,000	350	4.48%
The Times Building	Same as subject	130,000	43,550,000	335	0.00%
5th at Blanchard	Downtown Side Street	90,000	27,000,000	300	–10.45%
Bank of Southpark Bldg	South side of town	140,000	40,600,000	290	–13.43%

In practice, I may want more data than this. But as you can see, the value differences based on neighborhood or market are a function of the difference in the price per square foot (all things being equal) for each comparable in a different location compared to the one in the same location as our subject. There are times when there are no sales in the subject neighborhood. In that case, it is not uncommon to make a judgment call—to find neighborhoods that bracket the subject from a qualitative perspective, then arbitrarily put the subject in the middle of that array of comps.

We've dealt with these transactional adjustments first. This is not by accident, but rather this follows a time-honored ordering of adjustments taught in the appraisal process. The transactional matters such as market conditions are dealt with first, and the subject's physical properties are dealt with at the end. This truism holds with all kinds of real estate properties being valued via a sales comparison model.

In a perfect world, we can find comps that exactly match the subject, or at least have very similar physical characteristics, but this is rare. In practice, I need to estimate the adjustments based on matched pairs of comps or based on the rents charged for the space in question. Our subject property has 10,000 SF of ground-level retail. Imagine that instead, we cannot find an identical building, but only buildings that have offices from ground level up. We can compare the total rents for our subject to the total rents for comparable properties and make adjustments accordingly. Table 6-4 (see next page) offers one example of how to accomplish this, although there are many alternatives structures to this solution.

In this analysis, the rents and the square footage result in adjustments. Age is adjusted based on a 40-year estimated economic life of the structure. Rents are adjusted based on an anticipated 5% rate of return. Obviously, there are various ways to make these adjustments—trend lines or regressions across a large number of comps or some sort of matched-pairs analysis may be preferred. Attempting to value a large, complex property with only two comps is foolhardy, but the example is illustrative of the analysis undertaken in the real world. Extend this analysis out to 10 or 12 comps, and this would look like something we would find in a real appraisal report.

To summarize, the sales comparison approach gathers recent sales of comps, examines each for its degree of similarity or dissimilarity, and makes quantitative adjustments accordingly based on the marginal value of each component. If the comparable is slightly larger than the subject, we need to calculate the marginal value of the additional square footage and make an adjustment accordingly. The adjustments are always made in the direction of the subject, so if the comparable is slightly larger, we would expect to make a small *negative* adjustment to the comp's recent sales price. Sometimes these marginal component values cannot be estimated with reasonable precision. In those cases, it may be helpful to use some form of qualitative analysis, such as rank ordering the various comps relative to the component in question to see if there is a measurable trend in value, and then seeing how the subject falls in that rank ordering.

The sales comparison approach is most commonly associated with the valuation of residences, but it is key in the valuation of raw land and is also very useful in valuing income-producing commercial properties.

3. Income Capitalization—Simple Models

I have already discussed income capitalization and gross rent multipliers. The most common method we have not discussed yet is the discounted cash

TABLE 6-4 Adjustments Based on total Rents

	Notes	Subject	Comparable #1		Comparable #2	
		Characteristics	Characteristics	Adjustments	Characteristics	Adjustments
Sales Price	1		$32,490,000		$43,750,000	
Date		1-Jun-19	30-Mar-19	270,750.00	1-Dec-18	1,093,750.00
Rights Transacted		Fee simple	Fee simple		Fee simple	
Financing	2	Market normal	Favorable	(2,500,000.00)	Market normal	
Location	3	New high-grow area	5th/Blanchard	3,395,205.00	Waterfront	(1,960,000.00)
Square Footage						
Ground Floor Retail		10,000				
Low-Floor Office		20,000				
Mid-Floor Office		50,000				
High-Floor Office		10,000				
Total Square Footage		90,000	90,000		125,000	(12,250,000.00)
Blended Rent per SF	4	31.11	29.00	2,204,678.57	30.00	1,562,500.00
Garage Parking Spaces		200	200		150	
Annual Price per Space		2,400				2,400,000.00
Lot Size		20,000	Similar		Similar	
Property Age		2 years	Similar		4 years	2,187,500.00
Structure Quality		Class B	Similar		Class B	
Structure Condition		Excellent	Average	1,624,500.00	Excellent	
Adjusted Selling Price				$37,485,133.57		$36,783,750.00
Notes:	1	5% annual trend				
	2	See Table 6-2				
	3	See Table 6-3				
	4	Difference percentage times comp selling price				

flow analysis. This is extraordinarily powerful and indeed commonly used when periodic cash flows will vary, or when different discount rates need to be applied to different cash flow segments.

Cap rates and discount rates look a lot alike, and they will usually be very close to one another, but they are fundamentally different numbers. The cap rate is the ratio of a single year's NOI to the value or selling price. A discount rate is a weighted average cost of capital—notwithstanding the fact that the mortgage equity analysis in a previous chapter emulated the WACC calculation. Cap rates are more commonly used in real estate analysis, while discount rates will be more commonly used in financial analysis.

In Table 6-5, I examine an investment in an office building that is currently vacant but will have a rent-up period of one year and will be sold after two years of seasoning. The buyer plans to acquire at a 6.5% cap rate to value after the two-year seasoning. Our investment discount rate is 11% until rent-up and then 9% during the two-year seasoning period. For purposes of simplification, rents and NOI are assumed to occur at the end of each year, although in reality these cash flows will occur continuously.

TABLE 6-5 Present Value Accounting for Rent-Up Period

	Year 1	Year 2	Year 3
NOI	912,000	1,860,480	1,897,690
Sale Proceeds			31,628,160
Sum of Cash Flows	912,000	1,860,480	33,525,850
Discount Factor	0.900900901	0.841679993	0.77218348
Present Value	821,622	1,565,929	24,422,743
Sum of the PVs	$26,810,293		

More to the point, though, there are some important guidelines to follow when approaching value from an income analysis perspective. Indeed, these pointers are useful using any valuation approach.

Cap rates are only applicable to stabilized, long-term net operating income. Never include sporadic, one-time, or temporary income or expenses. If faced with a situation of sporadic or one-time income or expenses, use a discount rate.

Be careful to only use income and expenses germane to the property itself. Property valuation generally does not include interest income, such as interest on operating accounts, investment management fees, and fees pertinent to the fund or the trust that owns various properties.

Capitalized income is very sensitive to changes in NOI. At a 10% cap rate, a $100,000 change in NOI results in a $240,000 impact on value. In our 90,000-square-foot building example, this would come from a $1 per square foot per year error in rent estimates.

Property history is extremely valuable. If you are buying an office building with promises of $30 per-square-foot rent, but you find that not a single office has ever been leased for over $28, this is an important piece of information. Take insurance and tax estimates with a huge grain of salt, and actually investigate these expenses—and future trends—yourself.

Get to know the tenants. If this is an office property, find out what they do for a living, their position in their markets, and their financial health. Examine how current and historic rents compare to the market as a whole.

Paid market data sources can be extraordinarily valuable. Many national firms will produce a very detailed local market analysis for a very small fee.

Examine every income and expense item. Compare those items to other properties in the market. What are the chances these items will continue at current or forecasted rates? What's missing?

Where did you get your cap rate or discount rate? Small changes in cap rates can have huge impacts on value. Table 6-6 takes some data from Table 6-5 and shows what happens if the investor decides to pay a cap rate of 7% rather than 6.5%.

Wow—a 0.5% change in the cap rate three years hence has a $2 million value impact today.

Cap and discount rates can be supported by comparables. There are important services that provide surveys of cap and discount rates, and the mortgage equity analysis always allows for a built-up formulation. Empirical, local evidence is probably the most valuable when it is available and of good quality.

TABLE 6-6 Value Assuming Different Reversion Cap Rates

	Year 1	Year 2	Year 3
NOI	912,000	1,860,480	1,897,690
Sale Proceeds—6.5 Cap			31,628,160
Sum of Cash Flows	912,000	1,860,480	33,525,850
Discount Factor	0.900900901	0.841679993	0.77218348
Present Value	821,622	1,565,929	24,422,743
Sum of the PVs	26,810,293		
Sale Proceeds—7.0 Cap			27,109,851
Sum of Cash Flows	912,000	1,860,480	29,007,541
Discount Factor	0.900900901	0.841679993	0.77218348
Present Value	821,622	1,565,929	22,399,144
Sum of the PVs	24,786,694		
Value Difference	2,023,599		

4. The Systematic Market Analysis

Up to this point, this chapter has focused almost entirely on the operations of the valuation analyses. An appraisal *report*—whether it is a simple form for a residence or a complex narrative report for a large commercial property—will spend considerably more time on the market analysis than on the valuation itself. A thorough primer on conducting a market analysis is well beyond the scope of this book, and indeed more than a few good books have been written on the subject.[9]

Real estate analysts recognize that there are two different approaches to this process—a use looking for a site, or a site looking for a use. The tools and techniques are similar, but the focus is very different. The site in search of a use typically starts with a site productivity analysis—physical, legal, and locational attributes. Next, I analyze the competitive supply and demand for properties of this type and the interaction of supply and demand, as measured by *capture rates* and *absorption rates*. All of this can lead to a site valuation at its most profitable use.

A use in search of a site begins with the supply/demand analysis. Following that, we examine the locational, physical, and legal attributes necessary to support the use for which we are seeking a site.

Both processes will inevitably lead to identifying and analyzing at least a few other sales of similar properties that have sold in the competing marketplace. These may or may not end up being comparables in your valuation, but they will give you a good starting point to understand the transactional market and the supply/demand forces at work that will affect the subject valuation. In this process, also identify current and recent listings, options, and contracts. If listings have failed or expired, what happened? This information can be difficult to acquire, but it can yield important investment insights into the competitive market.

Finally, the readers of this book may be more interested in a use or a site as a pure investment opportunity, and thus agnostic to the specifics of either. A systematic market analysis is crucial to that as well but begins with setting certain personal investment parameters. These parameters naturally include return objectives (and preferences for measuring returns) and risk tolerances. Risk/reward objectives for real estate should be compared with risk/reward objectives in other portfolio components. This naturally leads to an analysis of the supply/demand factors, but more with an eye to opportunities that may arise.

5. Holding Period and Reversionary Cap Rates

This section may seem woefully technical, but there is some insight into cap rates and how cap rates are developed and considered by investors that should be discussed, at least briefly. Many investments, such as development deals and turnarounds, are made with the expectation of a finite holding period. The valuation metrics, such as the discount rate, may change dramatically during this holding period. Further, the expected cap rate at the time of eventual resale (the "reversionary cap rate") may be very different from the discount rates applicable during various holding period phases. As such, modest changes in these rates and holding period expectations may have dramatic impacts on the investment's present value.

The cap rate formula is fairly simple, and is repeated here for illustration:

$$r = \frac{NOI}{Price}$$

EQUATION 6-2

This seems to be a fairly normative explanation of how to arrive at the cap rate, with little room for subjective considerations. Recognize that NOI is an estimate and may be the result of a sensitivity analysis. What if the price paid turns out to be speculatively based on a given estimate of NOI, but the actual NOI turns out to be something different? We can sometimes refer to these speculative cap rates as "going in cap rates" and the actual cap rate achieved the "stabilized cap rate." This is particularly true with newly developed properties, but it can also be the case with existing properties when the management and ownership are changing hands. Since r is a constant in these analyses—buyers aim for a given cap rate—then a lower NOI leads to a lower price to achieve a constant cap rate. Conversely, for a given promise of NOI, the cap rate may be increased to incorporate the riskiness, then leading to a lower price (see Equation 6-3):

$$Price = \frac{NOI}{r} \quad \text{EQUATION 6-3}$$

The current NOI (during the building's operation) may be known, and capitalized at a somewhat lower rate. At reversion, the potential buyer may be risk averse at the speculative NOI promises being made. Even if the promise is that the historic NOI will remain constant, risk-averse buyers may look with a jaundiced eye. Thus, the going-out (reversionary) cap rate may be higher than the operating cap rate, and all of this will get discounted via a net present value analysis as shown in the prior section.

Finally, NOI may be predicted to change over time. If the change is forecasted to be constant, then the cap rate may accommodate that via the Gordon's Growth Model:

$$Price\ (or\ value) = \frac{NOI}{r-g} \quad \text{EQUATION 6-4}$$

In this situation, g is the forecasted growth rate over time. If NOI is expected to decline annually, then the denominator would be $r + g$.

6. Discounted Cash Flows and Net Present Values

Calculating net present value, or NPV for short, is a staple of Finance 101. No student should leave a business school without a thorough understanding of how this works. Many if not most commercial development and investment projects will be analyzed with a discounted cash flow methodology. NPV is the core mathematical tool used to discount future cash flows back to the present to estimate value. For that reason, it may be handy to review some basics, just so everyone is on the same page.

Net present value is the sum of the present values of present and future cash flows. Assume you want to buy a tract of land that will cost \$1 million today, and you plan to sell it in two years for \$1.5 million. Your required rate of return, which we will use as a discount rate, is 15%. The formula for the NPV calculation is:

$$\left(PVf_{0.15,\ 2\,yrs} \times \$1.5mm\right) - \$1\ mm = \$134{,}215 \qquad \text{EQUATION 6-5}$$

The secret to this equation is determining the present value factor, or *PVf.* This factor is unique to the discount rate and the time period involved.

Present value factor conceptually derives from the time value of money theory. If this was an advanced text on financial economics, I would spend a few chapters exploring how and why human beings have a preference for current consumption, yet still seem to be willing to save for the future. To induce us to save, there has to be a benefit to it. Hence, a dollar today is worth more than a dollar tomorrow. The quick-and-dirty formula for calculating the present value factor is:

$$PVf = \left(\frac{1}{1+i}\right)^n \qquad \text{EQUATION 6-6}$$

where i is the periodic discount rate (in this case, the required rate of return) and n is the number of periods. If the discount rate is annual, and number of periods is number of years, then all is right with the world. If there is a difference in the units (annual discount rate but n measured in months), some adjustments are in order. Indeed, this can be the most common problem, when there is some fractional number of months to be considered. To alleviate that, there is a simple adjustment, as shown in Equation 6-7.

$$PVf = \left(\frac{1}{1+{}^{i}\!/_{12}}\right)^n \qquad \text{EQUATION 6-7}$$

As long as n is expressed in months, this works just fine. If n is measured in quarters, divide by 4.

Is the Net Present Value the Same as Market Value?

You should recognize that the net present value is related to the investment's present worth. If the required rate of return (i in the *PVf* equation) reflects common market expectations, then yes, the net present value is an approximation of market value. The required rate of return could be investor specific, rather than market driven, in which case the net present value is an approximation of *investment value.* This investment value can be lower or higher than market value, depending on the specific investor's preferences. Take the case of property that supports a very profitable business venture. The return expectations on the property itself may be very low because the owner's principle focus is on the business. Mathematically, the low required rate of return drives up the present value factor, and in turn drives up the net present value. Thus, the investment value may be much higher than the market value.

Why might you be interested in some value other than market? There are a lot of reasons, not the least of which might be knowing what our contributory value is for a business-supportive real estate. Another might be estate settlement. Consider an estate owning one business and two parcels of real estate. One parcel of real estate is "attached" to the business, and one is not. Dividing up the estate implies a unique nonmarket value that may be assigned to the property that supports the business, and thus may be coveted by the heir who acquires that business.

Also, we have situations in which the required rate of return is very high, such as in situations of distressed or environmentally damaged real estate. The higher required return implies a lower price tag that might be paid in a distress sale.

The internal rate of return (*IRR*) is the complement of net present value. In the NPV calculation, we knew the cash flow and the required rate of return, and wanted to solve for the present value. The IRR assumes we know the various cash flows and the present value, and want to solve for *i*. Readers may reflect back on our discussions of cap rates, in which we had a very simple equation (see Equation 6-3) that could be inverted to solve for any one of three factors. If we knew the cap rate, we could solve for value, and if we knew value (or purchase price), we could solve for the cap rate.

With discount rates and complex, changing cash flows, the solution for IRR is much more difficult. Note the NPV determined in Table 6-5. The discount rate was given—11% in year 1, and 9% for years 2 and 3. Based on that and the cash flows we were given, we found that the NPV was $26,810,293. Now, imagine that you have the opportunity to buy this investment for $25 million. What is the *actual* rate of return we will enjoy? That is the IRR, and it is difficult and time consuming to compute by hand. Fortunately, there are common routines in financial calculators and spreadsheets that will do the heavy lifting for us. In this case, the IRR is 13.78%.

IRR can be a vital calculation when offered the choice of two different projects with significantly different costs and cash flows but similar risk profiles. Usually, the decision rule among investments is to choose the one with the highest NPV, assuming the discount rates all incorporate risk profiles. There are often competing investments—a 10-story office building for $25 million versus a 20-story office building for $60 million—that have similar risk profiles and cannot both be bought at the same time. The decision rule then is to pick the one with the highest IRR.

TABLE 6-7 NPV with Varying Cash in/out Flows

	Year 1	Year 2	Year 3	Year 4	Year 5
Cash in/out	1,500,000	1,500,000	–10,000,000	2,000,000	5,000,000
Purchase and Sale	–25,000,000	0	0	0	50,000,000
Sum of Cash Flows	–23,500,000	1,500,000	–10,000,000	2,000,000	55,000,000
Discount Factor	0.900900901	0.811622433	0.731191381	0.658730974	0.593451328
Present Value	–21,171,171	1,217,434	–7,311,914	1,317,462	32,639,823
Net Present Value	$6,691,634				

Often, the cash flows turn from positive to negative and back to positive during the investment's life. Imagine a situation where we are going to buy an old apartment building for $25 million and rent it for two years with an NOI of $1.5 million per year while slowly moving the tenants out. We then shut it down, remodel it in year 3 at a cost of $10 million, rent it with an NOI of $2 million in year 4, and $5 million in year 5, and then sell it as a seasoned investment at the end of year 5 for $50 million. If our required rate of return is 11%, the NPV is calculated as shown in Table 6-7.

The net present value here is something like $6.7 million, which tells us that if our required rate of return is 11%, then this is a good investment and we should go for it. But, what is the IRR? This might be handy to know if we have several different projects competing for our attention at the same time. The textbook definition of IRR is the discount rate, which causes the net present value to be zero. As it happens, the true IRR of this problem is actually higher than 11%, and in fact is 14.41% in this example.

Mathematically, there is a glitch in many spreadsheet and calculator algorithms that solve for IRR. When the sign on the annual cash flows changes from year to year (as it does from year 2 to 3, and again from year 3 to 4), the math of IRR may give you two different solutions. It is best to solve this problem a couple of different ways to make sure the number you are getting is the right one.

7. Cost Approaches to Value

This book generally has a US/Canadian focus, although most tools and techniques are useful worldwide. It is interesting that the *cost approach* is favored in many parts of the world where markets are less efficient, and real estate appraisal is viewed as an engineering task rather than a financial one. In the United States and Canada, the various methods that are lumped into the cost approaches are considered supportive of the principle value determination, but rarely are cost analyses the main focus.

Like any generalization, there are exceptions to this rule. One is the valuation of special purpose buildings, such as theaters, churches, airports, and stadiums. As of this writing, the Seattle Mariners—a beloved and successful local baseball franchise—are in negotiations with the local government over a subsidy for their stadium. The simple fact is, sports stadiums are rarely profitable, even in a sports-centric town like Seattle, thus negating the income analyses. Of course, there are hardly any comparable stadiums, so valuation has to depend on the cost analysis.

Another exception to the rule is when developing a building or some sort of subdivision (either residential or even industrial). The principal analysis for financing is the sales comparison, and the principal analysis for investment is an income analysis. However, buried somewhere is a detailed analysis of costs over time to ensure that the estimates of value make sense.

Whether I am valuing a simple single family house or a baseball stadium, the general paradigm for the cost approach remains the same, as shown in Table 6-8.

TABLE 6-8 General Model for the Cost Approach

Land Cost		$xxx,xxx
plus Improvement Costs		xxx,xxx
minus Depreciation		
Physical	x,xxx	
Functional	x,xxx	
External	x,xxx	–xx,xxx
Indicated Value		$xxx,xxx

I visited this model back in Chapter 2, when I was examining the office development project and wanted some insight into the land value. If I begin with the land value, then I can add to it the improvement's cost and the resultant sum is the value *as if new* and without consideration of depreciation. There are generally two different methods for determining the improvement's cost. For simple projects, such as houses and small, standardized commercial buildings, there are per-square-foot cost estimates provided by services on a localized basis. Thus, if we want to know the current estimates for building a 10,000-square-foot warehouse in Orlando, Florida, we can get a pretty good estimate of that on a per-square-foot basis from one of the cost services. For larger, more unique, or more complex projects, a segregated cost method is preferred, and there are specialists who provide cost estimates based on blueprints, specifications, and localized information.

For properties that are not new, or have some functional or external (economic) disutility, the depreciation will have to be calculated. Physical depreciation is the wear and tear on the building (but not the land) caused by age or by stress or damage to the physical members. The estimate of physical depreciation may be the result of age-life analysis (more or less the same as accounting depreciation) or by a more detailed analysis of components that are ripe for repair or replacement. Functional depreciation is an operative part of the building that would normally be expected but is missing, and the depreciation is typically some function of the cost to restore that operative part. Common functional items include a lack of sufficient elevators, insufficient fire and safety equipment, inadequate parking, or inadequate electric, HVAC, or plumbing services. These may or may not be curable, depending on the specifics. Finally, external obsolescence stems from a changing neighborhood or a negative externality being located nearby.

Buried in the land value and the improvements cost is some measure of entrepreneurial profit. While Table 6-8 does not break that out separately, it may be appropriate to analyze that as its own line item or line items. If the development will require some significant time from land acquisition to profitability, the land cost may need to include some return during the holding period. The contractor will probably want some overhead and profit, and the developer, if separate from the investor, may also want to be paid.

From an investor's perspective, these cost approach tools are rife with information. For one, this is where we identify depreciation and other disutilities that may be cured. An older building may lack modern amenities, but similar older buildings in the same market have been rehabilitated and modernized for significant profit. This is the opportunity to identify those areas where modernization may be profitable—or not! This is also the opportunity to examine the relationship between improvements and land values. Is the site under- or overdeveloped? Is there excess or surplus land? Does this have implications for improving the value? The cost analysis provides that opportunity.

> Even professional appraisers often fail to understand the difference between "excess" and "surplus" land. Imagine a 15,000-square-foot building on a 10,000-square-foot site. The local floor area ratio requirements are 2 to 1, so only 7,500 square feet of land was needed to legally support the building. The additional land—2,500 square feet—is excess. This excess land could possibly allow the owner to add 5,000 square feet to the building, which may be a profitable opportunity. The minimum square footage for a building in this example is 2,500 square feet. Assuming all other zoning restrictions are met, this excess land could be sold off as a new building site. This is the definition of surplus land—a parcel that is not needed to support the existing property but can be separately sold off.

8. Triangulating on the Truth

Appraisers call it "reconciling." There are several methods to examine the value of a real estate investment, such as income capitalization, sales comparable analysis, and cost analysis. While these approaches to value can each stand alone, they are intertwined in many ways. The income analysis depends in no small part on gathering recent sales and/or rent comparables so as to examine how the market is behaving. The sales comparison approach requires examining the cost of various components that may be different from our subject property. A proper cost analysis will examine the pricing of comparable land, comparable construction costs, and the functional utility of comparable properties, among other things.

So how do I reconcile differences in findings among the various approaches? A simple averaging may seem tempting, but that is rarely a proper solution. One approach may be preferred to other approaches. For example:

- Approaches and methodologies may vary in the quality of data input.
- Among comparables uses, one may be a "dead ringer" for the subject property.
- Different methods and approaches may require varying degrees and qualities of assumptions.
- Some analytical processes may be better grounded than others.
- The overall statistical quality and reliability of one methodology may be superior to the others.

There is a certain degree of judgment and experience required, but the reconciliation must be grounded in a solid and carefully explained process. The final result will be a quantitative finding; it may be a point estimate, a range of values, a value with a confidence interval, or even something else. The process for arriving at this quantitative solution must itself be well thought out and quantitatively explained.

9. Summary—Key Points

The principal purpose in this chapter was to synopsize methodologies that had been touched on in prior chapters—the underlying principles behind valuation, the various approaches to value, and the reconciliation of those approaches. Subsequent chapters will address each of these topics in more detail. Three key points should be takeaways from this chapter.

There are many different meanings to the word *value.* A value conclusion can represent market value, liquidation value, investment value, or many others we did not enumerate here. Determining which value we are interested in is a critical decision right up front because it drives the data gathered in the appraisal process. For example, if we end up finding investment value when what we really wanted was market value, the entire process was a wasted effort.

Ownership—and valuation—of property must take into account a host of public and private restrictions. The utility of a property, and hence its value, may be limited in a myriad of ways. From an investment perspective, a savvy investor may be able to manage those limitations, or even get them amended or changed so as to improve the property's value. The good asset manager will keep a wary eye toward new restrictions that may negatively impact value.

Finally, there are a many ways to value a property, and the valuation process should use several and reconcile those based on the data quality, the reasonableness of the underlying assumptions, and the rigor of the analytical processes.

10. A Final Note—the World Trade Center Paradox

You are probably all too familiar with the 9/11 attacks on the World Trade Center. Unless you were personally involved, you may have forgotten news in the aftermath about insurance settlements. The insurance litigation dragged on for years, involving the developer and nine insurance companies. Even the decision to employ real estate appraisers was litigated, with the court finally deciding that appraisals were necessary and important to the settlement process.

There are some excellent writings on terrorism insurance and appraisal in an insurance setting both in the scholarly and the popular literature. I do not want to reexamine the 9/11 attacks and the World Trade Center itself. There are, though, a few features of this settlement that stand out and have implication for real estate investors.

For some background, everyone attached to the insurance settlement process hired an appraiser, and those appraisers approached this problem in various ways. They may all have arrived at the same answer, but sorting through those various approaches and reconciliations would have been a massive undertaking. Eventually, everyone agreed to pick one appraiser and run with it. As it happened, the appraiser in question realized that the cost approach would be very illustrative for finding an appropriate solution.

Figuring out the replacement cost and accumulated depreciation of this "wonder of the world" complex was in and of itself a monumental task. Myriad features of the WTC simply fell outside of the norm. When the WTC was first built and leased up, there were several investment firm tenants who, at the time, raised significant amounts of money for movie deals. In the 1970s and early 1980s, financing movies was a great tax write-off. The 1986 Tax Act killed a lot of those projects, and so many of those deals went away. However, that wasn't the case when the buildings were built, and to accommodate the investment-firm tenants, there was a fully functioning movie theater in the basement of the WTC. By the time 9/11 came, the theater was nearly vacant, and only used about four times per year.

So, how did he appraise this theater? Was it a valuable asset? (Remember—we're talking about a multimillion-dollar theater.) Was it physically depreciated? Were there any comparable theaters located in large office complexes restricted to showing movies to investors? Was there any additional income paid to the landlords as a result of the use of the theaters?

In the end, the appraiser computed the construction value of the theater (a cost approach methodology) and then wrote off all of it as an example of functional disutility. We normally think of functional disutility as something missing—such as an old office building without an elevator or without an adequate fire sprinkler systems. Functional disutility can also come from the addition of something that costs money to reproduce but is no longer used. Imagine appraising an old farmhouse with a stable. The stable might be attractive, but might add nothing to the value of the residence. Indeed, the need to maintain the stable may actually have a negative impact on value.

So, functional disutility is an often overlooked facet of real estate. It can consist of missing features but also features that are a waste of space or a waste of reproduction cost.

7
The Paradox of Highest and Best Use

Ninety percent of all millionaires become so through owning real estate.

—Andrew Carnegie

HOW CAN WE find undervalued properties? How can we identify properties that, with sufficient time and resources, can be nurtured toward a higher value? In this chapter I will discuss a useful tool for these activities.

When you buy stock or bonds, you have a general idea of what the company does. There is an implicit assumption, baked into the stock's market price, that the management is putting the company's resources to work in the best way possible. To use a somewhat antiquated example, if the company manufactures stuff, then we assume it manufacture things that can be sold to maximize the company's profit. If the company is not operating at its maximally productive capacity, then it may be ripe for a takeover and the stock might be bought at a significant discount.

But discount to what? We already know that in highly liquid markets, the market price is an approximation for the intrinsic market value. So, if the stock is selling at a low price due to poor management or improper allocation of resources, is this still an approximation of market value, or is it an approximation of something else?

In real estate, the appraisal is usually to find that intrinsic market value, and one tenet of market value is that the property is being used at its highest and best use or at least that highest and best use is known or determinable.

Hence, the most probable price (the price to be offered by the most probable buyer, and likely to be accepted by the seller) assumes that highest and best use. Comparables used in the valuation process are drawn from properties that are being used at that highest and best use.

A downtown vacant site could potentially be used to build an office building, an apartment building, or a hotel. With some investigation, we determine that the office building will give us the highest value for the site, so we appraise it accordingly. Of course, and as we've already discussed at length, real estate is a complex asset with significant market inefficiencies. It comes as no surprise that determining the highest and best use has some complexities.

We have developed a handy paradigm for determining the highest and best use (HBU) of real estate. The remainder of this chapter will present and discuss that paradigm. *This is more than just a handy valuation tool. Understanding the nuances of HBU determination can aid an investor in finding undervalued properties, or properties that can be nurtured to a higher value with some investment of time and resources.*

1. The HBU Paradigm

- What property uses are *legally permissible*?
- Which legally permissible uses are *physically possible*?
- Which ones of those are *financially feasible*?
- Finally, which one—and only one—provides the *maximum return*?

For a given parcel, this analysis should be performed twice: once *as is* and once *as if vacant*. This dual analysis takes into account the cost to demolish and remove whatever improvements are there. Imagine a house that is nearly fully depreciated but still livable. The lot, and several adjacent lots, are in the crosshairs of development to aggregate the land for a shopping center. Which is the best property use—which use obtains the highest value? Should I appraise the property as if it will continue to be used as a dwelling, or as if it would be purchased, demolished, and aggregated into a larger tract to accommodate a retail center?

The actual *ex post* outcome is irrelevant. This is entirely an *ex ante*, prospective analysis. Let's say the house—as a residence—was worth $100,000 but the land as a potential retail site would be worth $115,000 (accounting for demolition and rezoning costs). The property's market value is $115,000, *even if the property owner continues to live there.* The market value is a determination of the most probable price that would be paid in a competitive equilibrium. If buyers know that the site's best use is for shopping center development, then they will "bid up" the price accordingly. Of course, the seller, if well informed and acting prudently, will accept no bids lower than $115,000. Hence, the highest and best use dictates the most probable price.

This raises two questions with very practical implications. First, if the value "as if vacant" is higher than the value "as is," then the value must take into account the cost of demolishing the existing improvements and carting them off. In the aforementioned example, we have buried the fact that there is a very real cost associated with demolishing and rezoning. Let's say that the shopping center development would actually pay $120,000 for this site, but the estimated conversion costs are $5,000. The value is the difference, or $115,000.

The second question is a bit more theoretical, although it has some practical implications. The HBU estimates the highest value, or the highest price that could be obtained. Market value is interested in the *most probable price* that would emerge from a competitive market. Up to this point in the book, we have basically ignored the fact that real estate exists in a bid-ask spread world just like other assets. In short, the "ask" price for real estate might be the highest price determined by the HBU, but the most probable price in a competitive market might be something a bit shy of that.

One recent study finds the longer a property stays on the market, the higher the price obtained. There is a cost associated with longer marketing times, namely the holding costs of hanging on to the property. Sellers may be willing to forgo maximizing the price to minimize the holding costs. For that reason, HBU value is not necessarily market value, but likely something slightly higher.[1]

2. Legal Permissibility

In the last chapter, we discussed the various restrictions on real estate ownership, which included public and private restrictions. We have also discussed in prior chapters how such issues as zoning, building codes, floor area ratios (FARs), height restrictions, parking requirements, private agreements, easements, and a myriad of other issues may affect what can be developed in a particular place or how an already developed property may be used. The good news is that there are generally land use experts, architects, and even engineers available to assist in making these determinations.

An exhaustive list of considerations would be impossible—so much of this is locally determined and situationally specific. In complex markets, the legal permissibility issues facing a commercial development may be radically different from the ones facing a proposed development right across the street. There are some common considerations facing any legal permissibility examination that provide food for thought on other issues.

Grandfathering

Many properties have historic and continuous uses that are in violation of recently enacted zoning ordinances. Local laws and regulations vary. One danger is that any significant remodeling, reconstruction, or modification may require conformity to the new ordinances. The specifics are locally determined—what can be done in two cities may be very different. There are instances when a grandfathering is permitted only to the owner at the time of the zoning change. A sale or other ownership change may trigger a loss of the use permit. The most common such nonconforming uses are commercial establishments (restaurants, grocery stores, gas stations) in neighborhoods that are now zoned residential.

Density Requirements

For residential subdivisions, land is usually permittable at a certain number of units per acre. Single family detached developments may be in the range of four units per acre to eight units per acre, but in some areas, two acres or even five acres per site may be required. For condominiums and apartments, we will usually see something like 20 to 30 permittable units per acre, or even greater in urban high-rise areas. This is extraordinarily important for determining value, but also a two-edged sword. Higher residential densities mean more houses per acre, but those houses are usually lower priced than houses in lower density neighborhoods. A developer aiming closer to the market top may actually *underbuild* the zoning requirements to achieve higher prices on the finished lots and houses.

Easements and Encroachments

Let's say you own a one-acre vacant parcel and your neighbor wishes to acquire a one-tenth-acre slice along one side to use as a driveway. The entire acre is worth $100,000, so a price of $10,000 may seem reasonable, right? Well, that may be the case if the easement has no impact on the subsequent property developability. If local ordinances require one acre for a building site *net of easements*, then you're left with an unbuildable parcel. If this sounds far-fetched, the 1992 US Supreme Court decision in the *Lucas* case hinged on similar issues.[2] Lucas purchased waterfront lots planning to build residences. Shortly thereafter, the state enacted building setbacks to protect the coastal dunes—a public preservation easement. This inverse condemnation left Lucas unable to build or use his property in any legal fashion other than perhaps picnicking or camping.[3] Public easements, such as wetlands or sensitive areas ordinances, historic district preservation ordinances, and easements for highways and alleys can impact a property's utility.

Height Restrictions

This mainly impacts high-rise buildings but can even impact residences in restricted neighborhoods. One not-so-obvious corollary is the minimum height above a flood plain datum. In flood zones, coastal areas, and some other floodway areas, there may be minimum requirements set either by local ordinance or by insurance requirements.

Open Space and Air Restrictions

Trump Tower, on 5th Avenue in Manhattan, was designed by Der Scutt of the architectural firm of Swanke, Hayden, and Connell. The only way they could build such a big building on this site in 1983 was buying the air rights (the vertical development rights) above the adjacent Tiffany's. A few years later, Donald Trump named his daughter Tiffany, perhaps in honor of that purchase.

Prospect of a Zoning Change

There is money to be made if I can buy property subject to less profitable zoning and then rezone to something more profitable. There is a good bit of risk to that sort of business move, but savvy real estate investors do it all the time. When can an appraiser consider the prospect of a zoning change to be reasonable? Do I consider only the currently effective zoning, or can the property be valued based on some likely zoning change? This is situationally and locationally dependent. This question will arise in eminent domain matters, when the value of a property being "taken" by local authorities is actually much higher than implied by the current use or the current zoning. Typically, appraisers will rely on the new zoning if there is a reasonable chance the rezone will occur. But, what is a reasonable chance?

Appraisers consider zoning trends and the local history of rezoning requests. Other considerations include the local comprehensive or master plan. The most problematic rezones are from residential to commercial, but even these may be reasonable if other nearby properties have received a similar rezone recently or if the comprehensive/master plan calls for a change. Other evidence includes competing rezone applications, transcripts from zoning hearings, and interviews with local officials.

Legal permissibility is important for valuation and investment decision making. If I am handed an appraisal, particularly for a property with development or redevelopment potential, my very first question is, "What can we legally do with this?" The answer to that question may very well be the most important component to the decision.

3. Physically Adaptability

An acre is 43,560 square feet. Now imagine that you are offered a one-acre residential lot in a neighborhood with one-acre legal minimums. A nice square site, or nearly so, may be the optimum—a little over 200 feet by 200 feet. Now instead you find out that the lot is 22 feet wide by 2,000 feet long. This is physically unadaptable for building anything. Indeed, this links back to the *Lucas* decision.

Often, the size will tie back into the legal permissibility determination. Parcel shape may also impact whether something can be built there at all. Note that shape is three-dimensional; a one-acre on flat terrain is very different from a one-acre on the side of a steep slope!

Key issues in physical adaptability also include:

- ***Geology.*** Is the soil sufficiently compactible to support a foundation?
- ***Ingress/egress.*** Will users be able to conveniently enter and exit?
- ***Air and subsurface rights.*** These do not just include legal examples (e.g., Trump Tower) but also the ability to have views, subterranean parking, or foundation supports not disturbed by either overhead or subterranean issues, such as a tunnel or an overhead avigation easement.[4]
- ***Accessibility.*** In addition to ingress/egress, will the property have desirable visibility or, conversely, privacy?
- ***Availability of services.*** These include utilities and linkages to other necessary or complementary uses. For residences they may include access to schools, shopping, and transit.
- ***Natural disasters.*** Is the property in a flood zone, a hurricane or tornado alley, or near an active or potential volcano?

> The active volcanos on the big island of Hawai'I have been in the news lately. Proximity to these volcanos impacts the physical adaptability of land on the island. Monroe County, Florida, consists mainly of the Florida Keys. The property values there seem not to suffer as a result of occasional hurricanes.

One big contribution the appraiser makes at this juncture is to analyze and opine about nonobvious physical limitations. These may be a function of local knowledge and experience, and may also be informed by other experts (engineers, land planners) with whom the appraiser is familiar.

4. Financial Feasibility

Legal permissibility and physical adaptability may indicate "go" or "no-go" decisions, or perhaps some problems that may require more time on the drawing board. Financial feasibility brings in more nuanced asset and investment management issues.

Finding the best or highest value may require valuing several different scenarios. Of the various uses that are legally permissible and physically possible, which are also financially feasible? Which have positive net operating incomes and allow for amortization of the capital needed to build the project? If the site is legally adaptable for residential development, can homes be profitably built?

Rarely do we need more than a few alternatives, and generally this examination does not require a full-blown financial analysis of those alternatives. Appraisers are interested in a variety of potential uses to determine the best one, but most investors are interested in a narrow array of uses. An experienced apartment developer, looking at a site, is generally only interested in the feasibility of an apartment development. There may be little interest in the feasibility of an office project.

Conversely, if I am agnostic to the final use but only interested in optimizing my return on a risk-adjusted basis, I may consider the feasibility of a variety of potential uses. An investor who has come into possession of property that is suboptimally used, such as a hotel with high vacancy rates or a shopping center losing top-tier tenants, may want to know the feasibility of a number of different alternatives. *This also drives the asking price if I am going to sell the property.*

I am interested in the financial feasibility of whatever I intend to add to the existing site, but not the site cost itself. Let's say I find that a vacant site can be used for building an office. I examine the potential office NOI *plus* the cost of amortizing the capital needed to construct the office (either the payment on a hypothetical bank loan or a return of principle and ROI to a cash investor). If this analysis gives me a positive net return, then it becomes the basis for the raw land value. If I want to buy or convert an existing property to another use, then I need to include the cost of demolishing or converting whatever is currently there.

What if the current use, continued as is, is one of the potentially legal and adaptable uses? Then I am only interested in whether or not the current use has a positive NOI. At this juncture I am not comparing uses to one another or rank ordering them. I will do that in the final stage of the analysis.

Probably the most common error in feasibility analyses is what I call *financial myopia.* In short, investors fall in love with internal analyses and fail to take into account the competitive market forces.

Anyone who has read a lengthy appraisal report will have noticed that an inordinate amount of ink is devoted to local market information. The appraisal presents local employment trends, local personal income, the availability of public transportation, school quality, and even prevailing wind directions.[5] This market data is supposed to support a comprehensive market analysis, which in turn is supposed to feed the feasibility study. In reality, the data is often quite good but the analysis and linkage may be lacking.

Appraisers follow a six-step process for market analysis:

Define the property, including physical, legal, regulatory, and locational attributes. Locational attributes should include linkages to nearby properties and changes in land uses over time.

Delineate the market and competitive area, including transportation distances for shopping or employment and the area encompassing competing or substitute properties. Techniques include gravity models[6] and simple customer spotting.

Analyze demand. The most probable customers should be identified ("segmented demand"). Behavioral, motivational, and psychological factors come into play. Use historical growth and absorption to infer demand changes over time. This leads to a demand forecast based on major demand drivers, including population (households), income (retail buying power), and employment (office/industrial users).

Analyze competing supply. Delineate the existing stock of competing properties. Add competing properties under construction, taking into account potential, proposed, and probable additional construction. Consider the attributes and characteristics of competing properties.

How do supply and demand interact? This defines the environment in which this subject property will compete.

Forecast market penetration. How much market will we capture?[7]

Timing is of the utmost importance in any of this. I am trying to value property today, but these alternative uses may have very different timing issues. Some uses may be put in place immediately (current zoning, immediate demand) while other uses may have to be delayed into the foreseeable future. This gives rise to two important feasibility analysis components:

Net present value. Covered in the prior chapter, but worth repeating here. NPV allows me to convert future cash flows or future values to a present value. When faced with a situation of disparate uses with different time frames, the NPV allows me to compare apples to apples.

Interim uses. So I've decided to build an apartment building on this lot that currently has a house, but I can't break ground for two years. What do I do with the house in the interim? Typically, I will want to rent the house for a limited period, building a "drop dead" date into the lease. This has income and expense implications, and the NOI from this interim use, *even if negative*, must be built into the feasibility study.

What if feasible rent is more than market rent? For an investor, this basically means the project is worthless. In short, the project cannot be rented for a price that will make it financially feasible. Many investors "inherit" a money-losing property and naturally order an appraisal as a starting point for figuring out how to either dump the beast or turn it around. The capitalized difference between feasible rent and market rent should equal the total depreciation on the property as revealed in the cost approach analysis. This is a pretty powerful tool for turning this property around. Remember that total depreciation is made up of physical, functional, and external attributes. Parsing this difference among those subcomponents is the starting point to determine if there are reasonably efficient "fixes" for this rent disparity.

I should now be left with an array of potential uses that are legally permissible, physically possible, and financially feasible. Some uses may require creative changes to render them financially feasible. A particular use may be feasible but only if I can get a zoning variance. Another use may be feasible but only if I can rid myself of a troublesome easement or handle a complex ingress/egress problem.

My client owned a wonderfully located 10-acre site—at the intersection of a major arterial and an interstate loop in a high-growth sector of the metro area (Figure 7-1). The other three corners of this intersection had been developed as profitable suburban office parks by a REIT that also wanted to purchase this site.

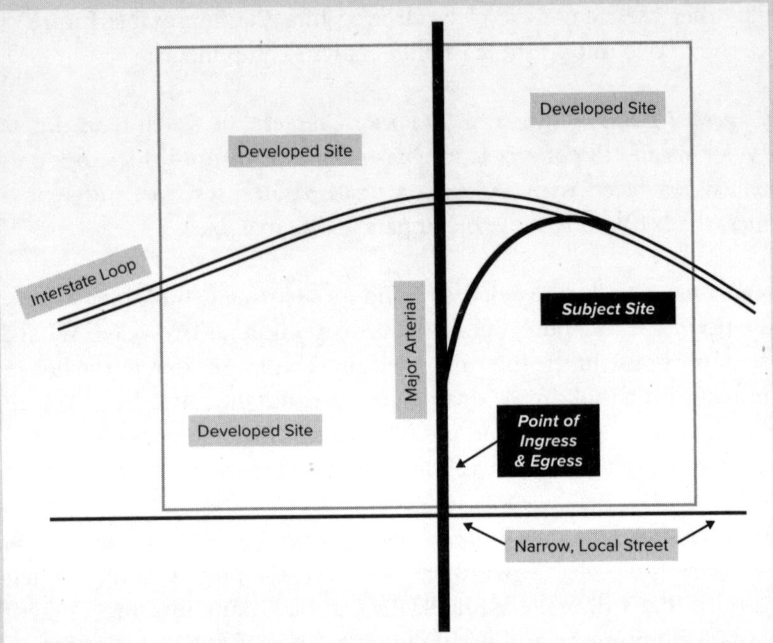

FIGURE 7-1 Ten-Acre Development Site

Unfortunately my client's site only had one physically possible point of ingress/egress *on the major arterial* due to an interstate on-ramp. There was a very narrow secondary road bordering the site to the south that could potentially offer ingress/egress, but this was much less desirable. Unfortunately, the site's southwest corner—right where the ingress/egress was located—had been leased to a gas station with leaky underground storage tanks. The state prohibited the construction of permanent pavement over this contamination plume until remediation was complete. This remediation had been ongoing for 10 years with no completion in sight. The eventual solution was to reevaluate the parcel—nine acres without the polluted corner and with ingress/egress on the narrow street—and negotiate a settlement with the responsible gas station party.

In the end, the financial feasibility analysis is really the core of the HBU determination. This is where various alternative uses can be evaluated.

More important, this is where uses can be carefully analyzed for important nuances that may improve value or even turn negative values into positive.

5. Maximally Productive Use

Of the financially feasible uses, which one and only one will provide the maximum value? The decision rule here is financial—which one provides the maximum dollar value. However, real estate is owned for a lot of reasons, some of which are not financial. Indeed, as I've discussed, there are a myriad of reasons for owning real estate, some of which are not necessarily net present value decisions. For example:

- Does this property investment support other business assets?
- Does this property support subjective family goals?
- Does this property complement existing ownerships?
- Does the property in question make a statement about the family?

Any of these may be qualitative reasons to prefer a particular use or a particular property over other uses or potential investments. Nonetheless, appraisals will be bound by a strict profitability metric and will examine the financially feasible alternatives in that fashion. The investor will read that for what it is worth and make decisions accordingly.

6. Summary and Key Points

The highest and best use analysis, fed by a well-developed market study, is replete with information to aid the decision maker. All too often, readers of appraisal reports focus on the bottom line and ignore the contributing data. Appraisers themselves are often at fault by not stressing the appraisal report as a dynamic decision tool rather than simply a report of a point estimate of value.

The market data in an appraisal report is only worthwhile if it leads to a well-developed supply/demand analysis. Markets are dynamic, and the proposed use of this property will interact with other properties and other proposed properties in the competing market. The demand side is constantly changing with changes in the number of households. The value is a function the market's size and geographic scope. I noted that retail market areas can be measured by a gravity model. From how far away does a shopping center draw customers? Other property uses, such as office and industrial, also draw demand from a geographically dispersed area. Consider a dental office. From how far away do people drive to a dentist? How many people—and particularly, how many families—will live in that gravity area?

A supply dynamic affects property. How many competing properties are there, how many are being developed, and how many are being proposed? Earlier I discussed the dynamics of market cycles, and how robust markets lead to new development, driving up vacancy and driving down rents. Where are we relative to competing supply and the normal and expected market cycle?

All of that leads to the most desirable property use, or given a set of alternatives, the most desirable investment choice. Noting that families often make decisions based on factors other than maximizing net present value, the best investment use may or may not be the one that is at the top of the financial ladder. Real estate should always be thought of as preserving wealth, not dissipating it. The HBU analysis may not point to the property to be acquired, but it certainly will point to properties to be avoided.

7. A Final Note—Marketing Time Versus Exposure Time

This is really linked to prior topics, but it is often discussed in the HBU context. Market value assumes a market normal exposure time *prior* to the effective date of market value. This can prove to be one of the least understood topics in the determination of market value. The exposure time is retrospective, not prospective. Marketing time generally refers to a prospective period *after* the date in question. The difference may seem pedantic, but has some real-world implications.

Consider the difference between a *foreclosure sale* and a *market value*. In the former, the property has been sold in a hurry to turn the property into cash as quickly as possible. Now think about gathering comps to value a subject property. Were these comps—all of which are actual sales—exposed in the market for an adequate period of time to achieve market value, or were they sold quickly to get cash in a distress sale? Thus, the determination of whether a comparable was a market value sale is at least in part determined by the *retrospective* time period for which the property was exposed on the market.

Of course, there is a paradox here. We are valuing something that is not yet sold, and may not be sold. Thus, we are making an assumption about exposure time in the market prior to our effective date of value, even though the subject property itself might never have been exposed in the market. This mental meandering misses the point. The question is about the retrospective exposure time for the comparables that are used to value the subject, not about the subject itself.

If this topic seems unimportant, there is some good news. Most often, indeed nearly all of the time, appraisers get it right. The problem, of course, is in rapidly changing markets or markets that are replete with distressed properties and distressed sales. In those situations, care must be taken in the examination of data used in the valuation process.

This chapter was largely about market research and HBU analysis. Market research also feeds the comparable selection process. Hence, the examination of competing properties, and the recent sales of competing properties, must take into account the nature of the equilibrium in which those properties were sold.

> We recently consulted with an investor regarding a medium-sized business, heavily in real estate, that needed to be sold. The complexities of "exposing" this to the market were numerous. Then, in the middle of the process, the investor made a huge mistake—he died! Since this asset was the bulk of his estate, his family was anxious to liquidate it in a hurry. Fortunately, the property had already been "exposed" prior to his demise, and potential buyers already identified. Had the family been in the unfortunate position of selling in distress, the ultimate price would probably have been much lower. This example, while a bit strained, illustrates the significant difference that a reasonable and proper exposure time has on the ultimate selling price.

8
Various Other Tools and Techniques

> Every person who invests in well-selected real estate in a growing section of a prosperous community adopts the surest and safest method of becoming independent, for real estate is the basis of wealth.
>
> —Theodore Roosevelt

UP TO THIS point, I have focused on fairly common investments, such as residences and income-producing office buildings. Successful investors may have a variety of property types in their portfolio. Common income-producing properties are all fairly straightforward to value, such as:

- Offices
- Apartments
- Retail (either stand-alone or some type of shopping center, including restaurants)
- Rental houses
- Industrial, including mini-warehouses
- Medical specialty properties (such as nursing homes and assisted living)
- Hotels

Such properties are bought and sold regularly. Valuation—finding good comparable data—is routine, and finding an appraiser with skills in these areas is a simple task.

I have seen other acquisitions by wealthy, successful investors that are significantly more complex. These include, but are certainly not limited to:

- Trophy real estate
- Brownfield redevelopment projects
- Marinas, golf courses, and other recreational sites
- Transportation or utility infrastructure
- Mining and mining operations
- Manufacturing
- Open space (either agricultural, forest, or preservation property)

Finding an experienced and talented appraiser with expertise in these tasks can be challenging. In the last category, there are plenty of experienced agricultural land appraisers, but very few have expertise if the property is going to be preserved or dedicated. Since agricultural land value is a function of its productivity for either grazing or growing crops, the notion of returning the land to a fallow state, either for preservation or recreation, flies in the face of the normal valuation tools and techniques used. In addition, forest land valuation usually requires two appraisals—one for the land and one "timber cruise," as it is called, to value the standing timber. Rarely is the same professional experienced in both assignments.

In this chapter, I will explore some questions that arise in valuing complex real estate. If you do not anticipate investing in complex properties, you may be tempted to skip this. However, much of what I cover here is applicable to the valuation of more straightforward properties. This chapter should be considered an extension of the previous two chapters, building directly on the ideas outlined there. I would add that revaluation on a periodic basis is a must. Normal economic metrics rarely apply to these complex properties, and monitoring values is a critical component of portfolio management.

1. Valuing Raw Land

Of the unique challenges, perhaps the most common one for wealthy investors will be the valuation of open space, or raw land. Typical situations include the following:

- Agricultural land, either for crops or grazing, as a pure investment vehicle
- Forest land, either as an investment, for recreation, or for preservation/conservation
- Raw land for eventual development

Up to this point, the most common unit of comparison has been square footage. In the office building example, I made adjustments based on the number of rentable square feet of space. The same was true in our discussion of buying residences. Agricultural land is often valued differently. Assume I have the choice of buying one of two different grazing fields for a herd of cattle. One field can sustain 100 cattle grazing year-round, while the other can only sustain 50 cows. In this admittedly oversimplified example, which field would be more valuable, irrespective of size?

Fields that are used for growing crops (other than grass for grazing) vary significantly in value on a per-acre basis, depending on the crops that can be suitably grown on the land. Since different crops grow in different parts of the United States, it comes as no surprise that crop land values vary widely from state to state. At the end of 2015 (the latest year for which nationwide data is available), the Agriculture Department (USDA) found that the nation's least valuable farmland was in Arizona, at about $510 per acre. The most valuable was in Rhode Island, at $13,800 per acre. In the traditional agricultural midlands of America, Iowa came in at the top at $8,000 per acre.[1]

Anyone familiar with Iowa and Arizona will immediately recognize that the principal difference is the availability of water. Iowa borders major rivers, while Arizona is largely parched. The IRS recommends several bases for selection of comps to value farmland, including:

- Similarity of soil (a soil survey and soil productivity index)
- Whether the crops grown would deplete the soil similarly
- The types of soil conservation techniques that have been practiced
- Whether the properties are subject to flooding
- The slope
- The livestock carrying capacity
- If any timber is comparable
- Whether the property is unified or segmented, and if segmented, the access among the different segments
- The number, types, and conditions of buildings and fixed improvements
- Availability of transportation facilities (cost and proximity)[2]

These points can be extremely exacting and require locally specialized knowledge. Purdue University agronomists measure different soil conditions throughout Indiana. Their productivity index varies from 0.5 to 1.28. Not surprisingly, farms with a productivity index at the higher end of this range are more valuable than farms at the lower end.

When valuing using income capitalization, again the IRS provides substantial guidance. Recall from Chapter 5 that the income capitalization methodology tells us:

$$Value = \frac{Net\ Operating\ Income}{Capitalization\ Rate}$$

EQUATION 8-1

NOI is tough to measure in an agricultural context. Thus, capitalization rates can be difficult to derive. The IRS provides a formula that is more commonly used:

$$Value\ per\ Acre = \frac{Comparable\ Rental\ Rates\ per\ Acre}{Average\ Annual\ Interest\ Rate\ on\ Federal\ Land\ Bank\ Loans}$$

EQUATION 8-2

Both factors—comparable rental rates and the average interest rate—are based on the year-end averages for five years. The choice of comps has to be defended in the context of the IRS regulations.

> Farmland does not sell often, and much agricultural land in America has been aggregated by a few large holdings. Modern methods such as computer-assisted mass appraisal (CAMA), geographic information systems (GIS), and automated valuation models (AVM) can take into account the myriad of complex adjustments and develop accurate values, even when those values vary within a single tract.

By the way, as of this writing, a surprisingly large swath of middle America is owned by the top 25 landowners in the country:

- Flitner Family, Wyoming based, owning 300,000 acres
- Nunley Family, Texas and New Mexico, 301,500 acres
- Pat Broe, New Mexico, 310,000 acres
- Collins Family, 312,188 acres of timber from Pennsylvania to Oregon
- Hughes Family, Texas, 325,000 acres
- Malone Mitchell, Texas, 350,000 acres
- Robert Earl Holding, many states including Wyoming and Montana, 400,000 acres
- J. R. Simplot Heirs, Idaho, 408,663 acres
- Drummond Family, Oklahoma, 440,076 acres
- Philip Anschutz, Kansas, Wyoming, and Colorado, 434,493 acres

- D. M. O'Connor, Texas, 500,000 acres
- W. T. Waggoner Estate, Texas, 535,000 acres
- Briscoe Family, Texas, 560,000 acres
- Lykes Brothers Heirs, Texas and Florida, 615,000 acres
- The Ford Family, Oregon and California, 625,000 acres
- Stan Kroenke, Montana and Wyoming, 740,000 acres
- Reed Family, California, Oregon, and Washington, 770,000 acres
- Pingree Heirs, Maine, 830,000 acres
- King Ranch, Texas and Florida, 911,215 acres
- Singleton Family, California and New Mexico, 1.11 million acres
- Irving Family, Maine, 1.2 million acres
- Brad Kelley, Texas, New Mexico, and Florida, 1.5 million acres
- "Red" Emmerson, California and Washington, 1.84 million acres
- Ted Turner, 12 states plus Argentina, 2+ million acres
- John Malone, Maine, New Hampshire, and New Mexico, 2.2 million acres[3]

To put this in perspective, Delaware and Rhode Island *combined* have a total land area of 1.9 million acres. Clearly, wealthy families have found that raw land is a handy place to store wealth. For many families, the land was accumulated over a long period of time and was itself the source of wealth (ranching, oil and gas exploration, timber). For other families, the land has proven to be an important place to simply store money. For some investors, land holdings continue as ranches or farms, while others let the land sit fallow, let it be used for recreation, or turn it into timberland.

This leads to the special case of valuing timberland. When a buyer invests in simple farmland, the crops are generally annual events, and so do not attach to the land. The contract to buy farmland will typically address the proceeds from the current cash crop. Timber takes a long time to grow and has a long-term value attached to the land. Further, the value of a freshly planted timber stand today is different from what it will be at maturity.

Tax laws are complex on this subject, recognizing three reasons for owning timberland:

- Personal use (personal enjoyment) in which there is no particular anticipation of profitable timber sales
- Investment use, in which the property is managed for eventual profit from the timber, but this is not a principal source of income for the investor
- Business use, in which growing and harvesting timber is a primary line of business

Most investors will fall into the first two categories. However, the third category deserves a bit of expansion. Like any real estate holding, the timber business can be either *active* or *passive*. The rules for an active business interest are set forth by the IRS and are similar to those for active real estate investments. Further, the IRS has specific rules regarding the *profit motive* on timber businesses, and for that matter on any farm. If a timber business fails to meet certain specific criteria, then it can be declared a *hobby*. Further, a timber farm is not treated like a regular farm for tax purposes. Of course, the 2017 tax law changes made all of this even more complicated.

Timberland is often valued with a variant of net present value called *land expectation value* (LEV). The assumption is that the bare land will be put in perpetual timber production. Of course, if the bare land already has a stand of trees growing on it, the timber *as it exists today* will need to be valued. The act of valuing the timber itself, separate from the land, is called a *timber cruise*. It is usually done by a professional forester with experience in local timber valuation.

The formula typically used in the LEV calculation is as shown in Equation 8-3:

$$Value = \frac{Expected\ Cash\ Flow\ Every\ t\ Years}{(1 + cap\ rate)^{t} - 1} \qquad \text{EQUATION 8-3}$$

This looks a lot like the perpetual capitalization formula, except it accounts for the payment received every *t* years. Let's put some numbers on that to see how it works. I'll assume a particular stand of timber will throw off \$400,000 every 40 years, measured in today's dollars. The current rate of return, *i*, expected by investors is 5%.

$$Value = \frac{\$400,000}{(1 + 05)^{40} - 1} = \$66,225 \qquad \text{EQUATION 8-4}$$

That answer may seem odd at first—the property value is less than the periodic timber revenue. But, remember that the first installment of timber revenue won't be received until 40 years from now, and otherwise we simply have a vacant tract of land suitable for planting baby trees.

Second, I do not consider the tract size. The periodic timber revenue implicitly includes the total acreage and the productivity per acre of timber. A 200-acre tract that is very productive and a 400-acre tract that is only half as productive have the same value when measured in this fashion. Also, revenue is net of all expenses or interim incomes. If a site is completely bare, there are costs of site preparation and tree planting. Tree farms are periodically thinned, and there are income flows attached to those thinning opportunities. Table 8-1 shows how the future value is actually computed in practice.

TABLE 8-1 Net Future Value Example

	Year	Amount	FV formula	Future Value
Site Prep	0	(3,000)	(1.05)^40	(21,120)
Planting	0	(3,000)	(1.05)^40	(21,120)
Thinning	20	30,000	(1.05)^20	79,599
Thinning	30	45,000	(1.05)^10	73,300
Annual Property Tax		(500)	[(1.05)^40–1]/.05	(60,400)
Final Harvest	40	350,000		350,000
Net Future Value				400,259

Finally, this land valuation assumes that the tract is bare. The timber cruise will determine the value of timber actually on the site at present, and the two will be added together for a total investment value. As an example, assume that the site was planted 35 years ago and is now 5 years from harvesting. The site prep, planting, and two thinnings have already been accomplished. The only things left now are five years of property taxes and the sale at harvest. Table 8-2 shows the current "timber in place" value:

TABLE 8-2 Timber Value Example

	Year	Amount	FV formula	FV/PV
Annual Property Tax		(500)	[(1.05)^5–1]/.05	(2,763)
Final Harvest	5	350,000		350,000
Net Future Value				347,237
Present Value	5	347,237	(1/1.05)^5	272,069

So, the timber in place is worth $272,000 and the land itself is worth $60,000. Hence, the value is the sum, or about $332,000. Without belaboring the point, these values are highly dependent on the market expectation of return. Currently, agricultural and timber resources are highly in demand in the United States, and cap rates have been reported as low as 4% or even 3% in some cases. Our example assumed a 5% rate of return. What happens if we change that to 3%? The value goes from $332,000 to over $485,000, an increase of 46% in value. Most of that comes from the increase in the land value. The net future value is slightly higher but is discounted at a much lower rate.

Many large forest landholdings, particularly in South America, have been acquired as a result of *carbon tax credits*. Following the Kyoto Protocols

(1992), some investors acquired large timber to develop and trade tax sequestration credits. The United States is not a party to Kyoto, and so these have no monetary value in this country. However, there are active markets in carbon trading, particularly in London, and many holdings have been purchased with this in mind. This market has yet to coalesce, and there is little agreement at this juncture on exactly how to value the carbon units, or for that matter the exact definition of what a carbon unit really is.

Timber investing has become extraordinarily popular, not only as a direct investment but also through public and private REITs and private equity funds. The valuation can be a real head-scratcher, and hopefully I have illuminated a bit. More important, I am trying to illustrate the complexity of valuing compound assets, where the real estate is simply a conduit for buying other assets. Consider a hotel, including land (often a net ground lease, with leasehold and leased fee implications), the building, personal property (furniture and fixtures), franchise value or goodwill, and a business enterprise value. When purchasing or investing in a hotel or any compound business asset, the determination of purchase price and the allocation of that purchase price among the various components may be completely separate decisions. This section demonstrated one method for determining the value—or purchase price—for a timber investment. However, the allocation of that price between land, timber, and even business enterprise may be a unique decision between the investor and his or her tax advisor.

We recently consulted on a business acquisition where the price was a function of the real estate and the business enterprise value. Unfortunately, the seller and buyer disagreed on exactly what the allocation was between those two components, and exactly what business assets and goodwill were being sold. This lack of understanding of the components, right up front, led to expensive and lengthy litigation.

2. Valuing Trophy Property

This section may be a bit redundant—raw land and timber land are often purchased as trophy holdings. Much, if not most of Ted Turner's 2+ million acres were evidently purchased as trophy holdings, without particular regard to ranching or timber profits. Indeed, Turner's largest acquisition was the 580,000-acre Vemejo Park Ranch in New Mexico. He removed hundreds of miles of fencing and replaced profitable cattle herds with environmentally friendly buffalo.

In any given category of real estate—homes, office buildings, hotels, timberland—a trophy property holding is usually regarded as one in the top 2½% of such properties.[4] The phrase "trophy property" gets bantered around by advertising copywriters without regard to what actually is or is not a trophy holding and how it should be valued or priced.

The Rockefeller Center in midtown Manhattan or the Embarcadero Center in San Francisco are clearly trophy holdings. Sales of these properties over the past few decades reveal prices that are completely detached from the intrinsic economic value of the buildings themselves. Indeed, recent anecdotal reports from real estate appraisers indicate that homes at the "top of the market" are often priced far different from what the cost approach would suggest for the replacement value. As of this writing, the Penthouse at the Ritz Carleton in New York is available for $95 million. At 5,087 square feet, that works out to $18,675 per square foot. In comparison, the Bill and Melinda Gates mansion on the shores of Lake Washington, near Seattle, is currently valued by the county tax assessor at $127 million. At 48,160 square feet, it is a more reasonable $2,637 per square foot—almost a shack by comparison.[5]

The key selling points for "regular" real estate may not apply to trophy properties. Consider again the Gates mansion. While it has a waterfront location—usually a plus—the quality of its waterfront is not particularly noteworthy. Access is difficult, with a steep slope rendering the 5+ acre site nearly unusable. The 2,000-acre Errol Flynn ranch on the island of Jamaica, valued at about $50 million nearly two decades ago, enjoyed 2½ miles of pristine waterfront. Otherwise it is nearly inaccessible. Trophy ranches in Montana and Wyoming advertise "remoteness" and "inaccessibility" as selling points.

It is important to differentiate between "investment grade" and "trophy." The former is a common term used by institutional investors to categorize top-grade properties worthy of inclusion in a portfolio. However, the category "investment grade" has proven rather inclusionary of late, and by some metrics, up to 50% of commercial properties fall into this category. Plus, with respect to residences, "investment grade" refers to the top tier of rental homes, far removed from what anyone would consider a trophy residence.

Trophy properties are often denoted by unique characteristics, such as unique views (waterfront, mountaintop), unique amenities (fishing, hunting, wildlife), open space worthy of preservation, or even historic, archaeological, or paleontological assets. One example would be the famed

Cook Ranch in Wyoming is unique in its size (117,000 acres) and its variety of natural characteristics, including biodiversity, geomorphology, 17 miles of river frontage with world-class native fish populations, and significant history as a cattle ranch. Other characteristics include privacy, exclusivity, high-quality improvements (the top tier of construction quality, materials, and methods), and in some cases proximity to top-tier urban services.

Trophy properties complete in a worldwide market. There are some notable exceptions, but when Errol Flynn was shopping for a ranch in Jamaica, he may very well have also been looking at Bali and the Maldives. Ted Turner's landholdings not only appear to span the western United States, but are also in Argentina. At one time, it was reported, perhaps with a bit of hyperbole, that the largest nongovernment landowner in New Zealand was a woman from Switzerland.[6]

Thus, gathering comparable transactions can be a worldwide venture. Making adjustments in a sales comparison grid can be wildly problematic. Table 8-3 features 11 of the most valuable single family residences on the market in the United States as of this writing:

TABLE 8-3 Examples of Trophy Homes

Property	Recent Price	Size	Notes
Sagg Pond Estate, Sagaponack, NY	$65 million	11,700 SF	33 acres, 8 bedrooms, 9 baths, 6 fireplaces
Rancho Dos Pueblos, Santa Barbara, CA	$79 million	2,500 SF	2,175 acres, 5 bedrooms, 14 guest houses and barns, private beach, lagoon
Fleur de Lys Mansion, Los Angeles	$125 million	35,000 SF	12 bedrooms, 15 baths, ballroom seating for 200, 50-seat theater
Casa Casuarina, Miami	$125 million	23,400 SF	10 bedrooms, 11 baths, previously owned by Gianni Versace
1220 South Ocean Blvd, Palm Beach	$74 million	20,129 SF	9 bedrooms, 17 baths, oceanfront, dock and pool
Irvine Cove Estate, Laguna Beach, CA	$65 million	18,000 SF	Wine cellar and tasting room, overlooks Pacific
The Beverly House, Beverly Hills	$95 million	50,000 SF	Formerly owned by William Randolph Hearst
The Woolworth Mansion, New York	$90 million	20,000 SF	Dining for 50, designed by C.P.H. Gilbert
Tranquility Estate, Zephyr Cove, NV	$75 million	38,000 SF	210 acres, 16-car garage, 3,200 bottle cellar
The Flood Estate, Woodside, CA	$85 million	9,000 SF	92 acres, designed by Thomas Church
The Bradbury Estate, Bradbury, CA	$79 million	47,182 SF	3D home theater, stocked trout pond

The market for these is nationwide. An investor seriously considering any of these would potentially be in the market for any of the others, or perhaps an estate outside the United States. Also, these are asking prices, and those fluctuate regularly. There is an additional listing for the Rancho Dos Pueblos that removes most of the acreage, leaving only 210 acres and an undisclosed number of barns and guest homes. That listing is for only $48 million. By extension, we can recognize that the final sales of these properties may be many years in the future, and may be at prices far different from these asking prices and with undisclosed terms and conditions.

So valuing these properties via a normal sales comparison is problematic in the extreme. The income approach is not useful—while some are currently rented either by the room or as a whole, the capitalized NOI would be nearly impossible to determine with any accuracy, and probably meaningless. Of course, I've already noted that a cost-based analysis is worthless because very high-end properties usually sell at a significant premium over and above the replacement cost.

I would recommend two methods. First, survey research has proven highly effective. An appraiser who specializes in this type of property will survey top real estate brokers nationwide who sell properties like these. The survey structure is more complicated than it sounds, because to get valuable insight, it is important not to "lead" the brokers into some sort of predetermined price. There are some clever survey research techniques and statistical methods to narrow in on a valid pricing model.

Second, longitudinal models have proven useful if the subject property—or a nearly identical property—has sold in recent years. We then construct a time-series index of competitive properties. Assume I'm appraising a trophy property that sold for $10 million exactly two years ago. I find that prices on competing properties have increased 20%. I can infer that the subject property is probably worth about $12 million. To be valid, I need more data than this, but hopefully you get the point.

I have used residences as an example, but these issues and techniques pertain to all manner of trophy properties. Survey techniques and time-series models can prove useful for valuing a host of other property types when traditional methodologies fail.

3. Valuing Brownfields

At the other end of the spectrum, properties that have been affected by environmental damage are generally referred to as *brownfields*. Books have been written on the subject of understanding, remediating, and valuing brownfields.[7] Many investors find brownfield remediation socially beneficial and financially worthwhile. Also, many successful investors find themselves stuck with a brownfield from time to time. Proper due diligence failed on a commercial purchase, or a tenant contaminated a property, or a third party (external obsolescence) damaged an otherwise clean property. Any such situation will lead to a brownfield issue.

> Brownfields come in all shapes and sizes. A contractor moved the basement fuel oil tank in a home in the Hamptons (yes, in the Hamptons) but failed to move the intake pipe. The delivery truck came for its regular October top-off and pumped directly into the basement. The basement had a sand drain pit, so all the fuel oil flowed under the house. Remediation was time consuming and expensive. What is worse, this not-inexpensive house was now stigmatized, and the spill event would have to be forever disclosed to potential buyers.
>
> One interesting brownfield I examined was a former liquor warehouse. Broken bottles and spillage over the years saturated the surrounding soil with booze. Authorities considered the property to be contaminated.

A contaminated property will go through three phases, with value losses measured differently in each phase:

Contaminated. Loss in value (relative to its value as if uncontaminated) would be a function of expected remediation costs plus the stigma associated with a property such as this.

Remediation underway. The fully contaminated loss in value is ameliorated somewhat, as there is a better idea of total remediation costs, and there is some reduction in additional stigma loss.

Fully remediated. There are no further expectations of remediation, although there are situations when contamination may evidence again in the future, requiring additional remediation. These risks, and any market reaction to a "previously contaminated, but now remediated" property is captured in the post-remediation stigma loss.

The concept of remediation costs is easy enough to understand—the direct out-of-pocket costs associated with removing, capping, or in some way dealing with the contamination. In a simple world, these costs would be known with some certainty and would be directly deducted from the as-if-uncontaminated value. However, these costs are rarely fully understood, even when remediation is underway. There are situations where the remediation costs are greater than the unimpaired property value. Yes, such property is essentially worthless. In those situations, regulatory efforts or litigation may be required to force the responsible party to remediate the site. Further, "responsible party" has its own meaning under various laws and regulations. A party who had nothing to do with the contamination, such as a landlord or a subsequent buyer who did not conduct proper due diligence, may be deemed a "responsible party."

Stigma itself is harder to understand. Measuring stigma often requires survey research to find out just how much pushback the property will receive from potential buyers or other property owners. Court cases, case studies published in the literature, and even academic studies have proven useful in making these determinations. For an income-producing property, understanding the impact of stigma can be very straightforward, although measuring it can still be a problem. As an example, Table 8-4 offers a simple model to help understand how stigma arises.

TABLE 8-4 Simple Example of a Brownfield Value

	As-If Clean		After Remediation	
Gross Rent		$100,000		$100,000
Vacancy & Collection	10%	(10,000)	20%	(20,000)
Effective Rent		90,000		80,000
Precontamination Expenses	30%	(27,000)	27%	(21,600)
Postcontamination Expenses		0	10%	(8,000)
Net Operating Income		63,000		50,400
Cap Rate		7%		12%
Value Indication		900,000		420,000

The gross rent is the same in both scenarios—"as-if never contaminated" and "after remediation." Vacancy and collection problems increase, often doubling, after a property is contaminated. During the "as-is contaminated" and "remediation" times, the vacancy can increase or even go to 100%, depending on the problem's nature and severity. Some expenses may actually decrease in absolute terms and as a percentage. Since vacancy increases, the normal leasing and management costs decrease. Also, these properties are ripe for property tax reductions. However, additional costs come to bear, including monitoring, legal, engineering, and other consulting fees. Additional insurance may now be required for the physical structure and third-party liabilities. Insurance may not even be obtainable under some circumstances.

The big "hit" comes from the increase in "cap" or discount rates. I have used a simplified cap rate analysis, but since cash flows will change over time and discount rates may change as well, a more complex net present value analysis may be required. The increase in the cap rate is substantial. Most investors and even some lenders will shy away from these properties, and so the required rates of return are high. If the investor with "risky" money is willing to take a chance on such properties, there may be a measurable and significant increase in potential returns.

Two other points need to be made. First, the highest and best use of these properties may change dramatically. A vacant tract suitable for residential development before discovering the contamination may now only be suitable for some lower-end industrial properties. The highest and best use (HBU) may change several times during from before the discovery of contamination, to the discovery phase, the remediation phase, and the post-remediation phase.

Second, I've discussed due diligence, but without much elaboration. Every nonresidential property should have what is often called an "Environmental Level I Site Assessment" (sometimes called a Phase I) before acquisition. This is a simplified examination of public records and the property history, conducted by an environmental professional (usually an engineer). The guidance for conducting this is provided by the American Society for Testing and Materials (ASTM). These usually take several weeks and typically cost a few thousand dollars.

If anything is detected, then this moves to a much more expensive "Level II." Sampling is performed, usually with invasive tools (drills) or heavy equipment. Samples are examined in the lab. Even with extensive testing, there is no guarantee. Sometimes a plume of underground contamination can be missed or can be ephemeral.[8] A Level III (or "Phase III") will actually include a remediation plan and feasibility study. Needless to say, this gets expensive fairly quickly.

Arguably, there is no such due diligence expectation for buying a residence, and buyers should beware. If there is any indication that a home might have been in the path of contamination in the past, or may be near a source of contamination now, then further investigation is warranted.

Chapter 18 explores brownfield valuation in more detail.

4. Staying Ahead of the Creative Class

The creative class was the brainchild in 2002 of University of Toronto economist Richard Florida.[9] In the ensuing two decades, it has entered the urban planning lexicon and become shorthand for massive changes in our real estate landscape.

In the old days (before, say, World War II), people were born, lived, worked, and died in nearly the same place. They might have moved away temporarily for military service or such, but generally returned to their roots. Extended family was a must. Their career options were generally limited to the jobs available in their hometowns. In the 1920s and 1930s, about one out of four American workers earned their living on a family farm.

It is generally—although mistakenly—thought that World War II changed all of that. The percentage of farm families in the workforce declined during and after WWII, but at about the same trend that had been evident since the republic's founding. One important thing happened during and after WW-II—*nonfarm* families moved at an accelerated pace to chase jobs. The great mines and factories of the central United States, the coastal shipyards, Seattle's airplane factories, and textile mills throughout the South became destinations for mobile Americans. The key element, and it bears repeating, was that people chased jobs. A business could locate wherever it wanted to—with an eye to minimizing transportation, land, and energy costs—and workers would flood the gates.

Somewhere along the line, workers at the top of the food chain—the group that Florida labeled the "creative class"—began realizing that the opportunities abounded everywhere. If that's the case, they thought, why chase a job? Why not find the best places to live, the places with great amenities, and then figure out what to do when we get there? As such, creative types, numbering in the millions, flocked to great high-amenity places near the best universities, arts and sciences, fun places to live, and each other. That created a challenge for companies that depended on those creative workers. Suddenly, companies needed to chase creative workers.

It comes as no surprise that a critical mass of the most inventive companies in America now exist in a handful of places, like Silicon Valley, Seattle, Portland, Austin, and Charleston. The implications for real estate investors trying to stay ahead of this curve are very real. In a world where Google's, Netflix's, and Microsoft's products are mostly delivered via fiber optic cable, where Amazon's distribution network is wherever FedEx, UPS, and DHL can land a plane, and where even Apple generates billions in revenue from web- and app-based services, old-fashioned concepts like minimizing transportation costs or maximizing customer contact are relegated to textbook dustbins.

When was the last time a reader of this book actually sat down in a bank branch or an investment firm office? Locating investment grade real estate is now heavily dependent on the whims of the creative class. A suburban office park in a hot city, like Seattle, will enjoy much higher rents and long-term prospects than a Class A building in the center of a tired city.

5. The Impact of Transportation Corridors

Transportation access—a good thing or a bad thing? Is transportation *proximity* a good thing or a bad thing? Even in a world where the creative class sell their wares on the internet and locational proximity has less meaning, there is still a need to transport stuff. Tractor-trailer trucking companies are constantly looking to hire, and 11 million long-haul trucks registered in the United States (a number increasing by about 3% per year) currently log more than 400 billion miles on the nation's highways per year.

If your business deals in goods, you need access to transportation for goods and raw materials coming in and going out. If your business requires the aggregation of people on occasion (even Apple and Google have headquarters buildings!), then those folks need some means of transportation to and from that place of work. Does proximity to a transportation corridor enhance or detract from the parcel value?

A long time ago, real estate appraisers focused on the paradox of shopping center proximity influence on residential property values. It is axiomatic that access to shopping is a positive for residential values. This is a chicken-and-egg problem in that retailers want to locate near high-valued (and hence high-income) homes. Indeed, the gravity models depend primarily on such inputs. Similarly, residential developers and builders want to ensure that there are adequate shopping centers (and schools, and so forth) in the neighborhood. People don't want to travel far for a loaf of bread. So, in terms of shopping center proximity, closer is better, right?

Well, not so far. If a home is 10 miles from a neighborhood shopping center, then fetching that loaf of bread may be a pain in the neck. If it is located one mile away, then access to that bread is not so bad. So, what if the house is located directly across the street? Maybe that is not such a good thing after all. Perhaps the access benefit is offset by the negative externality of shopping center noise, lights, and general lack of residential ambiance.

So, back to the highway example. If the homeowner commutes every day for work by auto or bus, then getting to the highway on-ramp or the bus park-and-ride facility is handy. Of course he or she might not want to live across the street from the park-and-ride, but living a mile away might be good. If homeowners drives, then there is some benefit to easy access to that on-ramp, but few want to live immediately adjacent to an interstate highway, a rail line, an airport, or a ship terminal.

This has implications for residential locational strategy, but is also interesting for commercial locations. Land investors will need to account not only for the normal HBU analyses, but also the negative and positive externalities associated with inconsistent land uses.

6. Class A Buildings in Class C Locations

How does this happen? We have seen this time and time again. Someone comes up with a great idea for a building, and then builds it in the wrong place. To illustrate, we will look at first at a Class A office building, but the same can be said for condominiums, hotels, restaurants, apartments, and even top-grade trophy homes.

We have used the terms Class A, B, and C in this book without rigorously defining them. Indeed, there are a variety of sources of definitions of such buildings, and while there is no single authoritative source, the definitions generally coalesce around the following concepts:

Class A

Highly sought-after space, usually in a central business district. Typically one of the largest buildings in the market and home to premier tenants. Top-tier technology, HVAC systems, elevators, and other infrastructure. Amenities may include abundant art and greenery, water features, concierge services, security, adequate on-site parking (usually with some security of its own), food courts, and the best architectural and design features in the marketplace. Common areas, such as lobbies, have a "wow" factor. Older structures are well-maintained and upgraded to modern standards. Typical tenants may include the top law firms in the market, top-tier accounting and investment firms, main offices of major banks, and other tenants who have regular high-end clients as visitors.

Class B

Older (typically 10 to 20 years of effective age). Spaces have been refit as original tenants have moved out. Technology is good, but not the best. Elevators and HVAC are functional. Finishes are above average, but not the best. Typically located in prime market areas, but perhaps on a side street rather than a main arterial. Lobbies are professional and may be attended but without first-rate security. On-site parking, if available, may not be fully adequate. Typical tenants will include second-tier law firms, non-mainstream accounting firms or smaller investment firms, main offices of government agencies, and regional or local banks. Interestingly enough, some potential tenants who could afford Class A space may opt instead for Class B space as a strategic move to mollify clients. Some clients of top-tier law firms would prefer their fees go into actual legal representation rather than fancy offices.

Class C

Typically at least 20 years old (effective age), with a long history of prior tenants. Out-of-date finishes and services. Usually no lobby attendant, and often no lobby at all. Rents are set for no-frills tenants who desire economy rather than location or amenities. Parking may be limited or nonexistent. Typical tenants include not-for-profit agencies, offices of government agencies that actually meet with the public, and operational offices that require lots of space for workers but little if any client contact. Location is of little consideration and may include industrial areas, poor views, or limited access.

So, why do we occasionally see a Class A building in a Class C location? Reasons may be unique to the building itself and the original developer. In one case in a nearby city, the now-wealthy developer had grown up in a poor part of town and felt that building a first-class office building in his old neighborhood might be a stimulus to the area. There are situations where a business needs to open an owner-occupied, first-class office building adjacent or proximate to co-owned industrial properties. When the original tenants disappear, the building is left to its own devices.

So, as an investor, what is the cautionary tale? These buildings may be offered to investors at what appear to be fire-sale prices. Enormous potential cap rates are quoted, with prices that are significant discounts from replacement costs. These Class A buildings inevitably become Class C properties, with Class C tenants. In some rare occasions, these properties can be benefitted by changing neighborhoods. However, the time and patience needed to effect such changes will rarely be of financial benefit.

7. Class C Buildings in Class A Locations

Now, this gets interesting. How did this happen? First, a building was Class A several decades ago, but allowed to decline in quality. In some cities or locales, the perceived Class A quality measures have changed over time. For many years, Bellevue, Washington, was a sleepy suburban town across the lake from its big brother, Seattle. Then Microsoft opened its campus in Redmond, nearer to Bellevue than to Seattle. Bellevue suddenly found itself the center of the economic universe, and the new home to the lawyers, accountants, and investment houses opened to help Microsoft millionaires manage their hard-earned bucks. Many buildings—retail, office, hotels, even apartments and condominiums—were suddenly old and shabby compared to the new and shiny Class A properties coming on line. One famous such transformation was the Bellevue Square Mall, which had previously been a family-owned, simple community shopping center anchored by a local department store. Today, it is a 1.3-million-square-foot central downtown shopping complex featuring valet parking; 250 top retailers such as Tiffany's, Macy's, and Nordstrom; and over 45 entertainment venues. Interestingly enough, it is still owned by the same family.

Other Class C buildings—which may have been Class A previously—sit with reduced occupancy and/or less-than-feasible gross rents, waiting for redevelopment or demolition. Perhaps the most unfortunate are tired condominiums that were market normal for their day but now compete with upscale condos with top-tier amenities, views, and architectural features. The Class C condos in these situations simply stagnate compared to the rest of the market—prices increase as a result of enhanced locale, but not at the same rate as the more upscale market tranches. Ultimately, the expense of living in this new, enhanced neighborhood tends to drive away potential downscale buyers, yet existing owners in the condominium complex are rarely able to do the "rational expectations" thing, which would be to band together and finance an upgrade of the entire property.

A second cause is simple aging. Buildings that may have been stylish a generation ago are now old and shabby. The market has not changed, but the building has. This may be one of the most complicated problems to fix. Not only is the building aging, but the styles, amenities, and other aspects of functional depreciation have not kept up with the times. Sometimes, such buildings can be "fixed up" to Class B status. More often than not, though, when and as the building has reached the end of its economic life, the land value for redevelopment purposes exceeds the present value of fixing up and continuing to operate the existing building.

A third cause, in this nonexhaustive list of possible reasons, is a zoning change. A modern Class A building is often one of the tallest in the central business district. If a city changes height restrictions, then top-tier tenants will be drawn to the tallest buildings. Shorter buildings, which do not fully utilize what otherwise would be Class A locations, are suddenly disadvantaged. They may not quickly become Class C, but certainly they are on the off-ramp to non–Class A status.

There are opportunities and dangers for investors. Investors may find bargains in Class B or C buildings in otherwise Class A locations. These can often be rented profitably while determining the optimum rebuild or rehab strategy. Indeed, in a market down cycle, if investors have significant confidence that the market will turn around (a true Class A location but with a short-term market cycle) then investment and redevelopment opportunities can be very profitable indeed. Another strategy is a simple "buy and hold." There will be demand for well-managed, well-positioned Class B and C buildings in Class A locations, and often these buildings are on the market because existing landlords simply cannot afford to maintain the structures, even in Class C condition. Estate sales, bankruptcies, and other distressed situations can be ripe with such tired but restorable buildings in great locations.

The obvious trap, of course, is to buy and sit on a declining Class A building. Ownership of Class A properties creates a dynamic relationship with the market. Internal (such as functional and physical disutility) and external forces are at play to damage a building's reputation, ambiance, and top-of-the-market status. Savvy investors are always on top of this, monitoring the competitive market and the impact of that market on the value of their holdings.

The not-so-obvious trap is to fall in love with a building. Consider the investor who falls in love with a property. The periodic revaluations tend to be skewed to the favorable side. Every market event is viewed in the light most favorable to holding on to the building. Slight increases in vacancy, pushback from tenants when rents are increased, and rumors of new competing properties entering the market are ignored. Suddenly, one day, the investor opens the news to read the top-tier anchor tenant announcing a planned move to the bright, shiny new building that is being built across the street. Yes, the building that the city allowed to be 10 stories higher that is going to block our waterfront view. *That* building!

8. Summary—Key Points

I can build a successful family real estate portfolio with simple, boring properties. There is a lot to be said for investing in seasoned Class A buildings in first-tier cities. Pricing these investments is simple, periodic appraisals are run-of-the-mill, and if I want to dispose of them, there is a ready market at top dollar.

While seasoned Class A buildings are a great place to *park* money, they may not be the best place to *make* money. Indeed, there are a lot of specialized, niche investments that are not only very profitable, but in the case of preservation or trophy property, can make an important statement about the family's place in this world. There are a host of interesting and worthwhile specialty investments that I will touch on later, including affordable housing (and the accompanying low income tax credits), historic preservation (again, with tax credits), and infrastructure investments (ranging from marinas to airports to private highways, and everything in between).

Understanding the nuances of pricing and valuing these investments can be extraordinarily important for the forward-thinking investor. Even investments that seem boring, like timberland, require periodic value-optimizing decisions. Understanding some complexities of valuing specialized properties can aid in understanding not-so-complex components on simpler properties. Finally, even simple investments, like Class A apartments and offices, can become complex through age, through external factors, or through simple neglect. Knowing how these things happen and how to recognize inflection points in the property life cycle aids in wealth preservation.

9. A Final Note—Integrating Real Estate Values into Financial Statements

Financial reporting of real estate values used to be simple. Businesses recorded real estate at historic cost minus accumulated depreciation. The most complex decisions were about the differences between depreciation for financial reports and depreciation for tax purposes. There were also some tax recapture issues when the property was sold, but none of this was very exciting or even interesting.

Then two things happened at about the same time a decade or so ago to change this. First, the Financial Accounting Standards Board issued FASB No. 157, titled *Fair Value Measurements*. This was in response to the fact that historic cost and market value could be wildly different. This was true not only for real estate assets but for other holdings as well. In addition, values of real estate on financial reports were often measured as a value in use or a historic construction cost, rather than as a market value at the highest and best use. A company might buy a tract of land to build a warehouse at a cost of $1 million. That becomes the historic cost basis, and depreciation reduces even that over time. Had the property been valued at its HBU when constructed, it may have had a market value of $2 million. Further, after 10 years of constant depreciation, the building might be carried on the company books at $750,000, but might actually be worth $5 million because actual value is disconnected from depreciated book value. Since real estate holdings are not trivial for many companies, this difference can be quite meaningful, and hence the shareholders equity on the balance sheet was effectively meaningless. This was particularly important for real estate–focused entities such as REITs.

Then, the other shoe dropped. Starting in 2007, real estate values turned systematically downward. Residential values, particularly in formerly "hot" states, were the worst affected, but all categories and geographies felt the heat.

The requirements of FASB 157 apply to organizations that comply with Generally Accepted Accounting Principles (GAAP). Private organizations that are not GAAP compliant can make a decision which way to go. Tax reporting is still done on a historic-cost-less-depreciation basis, and it may be simpler for private companies to handle things that way. Certainly the cost of periodic mark-to-market valuations is a consideration. That said, GAAP compliance (and tax compliance) become more complex as the real estate holding becomes more complex. The FASB has issued recent pronouncements on the valuation of leases (financial versus operating) and the determination of exactly what constitutes a purchase price.

In the past few years, REITs and other real estate holdings have exploded in size and complexity. REIT IPOs now include traditional assets (offices, apartments) as well as nontraditional (billboard funds, cell towers, data centers). Further, REIT conversions and spin-outs are increasing rapidly. As of this writing, the IRS has put holders of nontraditional real estate on notice that it is studying the very definition of "real estate."

9
Valuation Quirks and Traps

Don't wait to buy land. Buy land and wait.

—Will Rogers

IN THE LAST chapter, I explored common techniques for valuing unique properties. Now, let's explore techniques applicable across a range of common properties. I will differentiate between excess land and surplus land and show how added value can be discovered—or conversely, value can be dissipated—via these conduits. Excess and surplus land problems are common across a wide array of properties and in all types of locations—but, surprisingly, even professional appraisers often do not understand the difference and cannot advise on the investment implications.

I will also explore certain aspects of the cost analysis. This is frequently the least considered of the various approaches to value, yet may contain terrifically useful investment information. Understanding the various nuances of physical depreciation, how to identify and cure functional depreciation, and how to properly value and account for economic depreciation can make a huge difference in finding hidden value in property, or conversely paying too much.

Finally, I will talk a bit about market equilibrium. Prior to the recent recession, residential real estate was thought to constantly increase in value, and commercial real estate was thought to predictably cycle around upward trends. We now know that disequilibrium situations can occur locally and systemically. These are generally marked by disruptions in the value trends and cycles. Identifying and dealing with these situations can be valuable information for the investor.

1. Excess Land

Appraisers and real estate professionals alike are confused by the concept of excess land, yet it is a common issue confounding valuation.

Take the situation in Figure 9-1. The industrial building has a 5,000-square-foot floor area. Zoning requires industrial buildings to have a maximum floor area ratio of 0.5 to 1. For every square foot of building, there must be 2 square feet of land area. The 5,000-square-foot building needs 10,000 square feet of land.

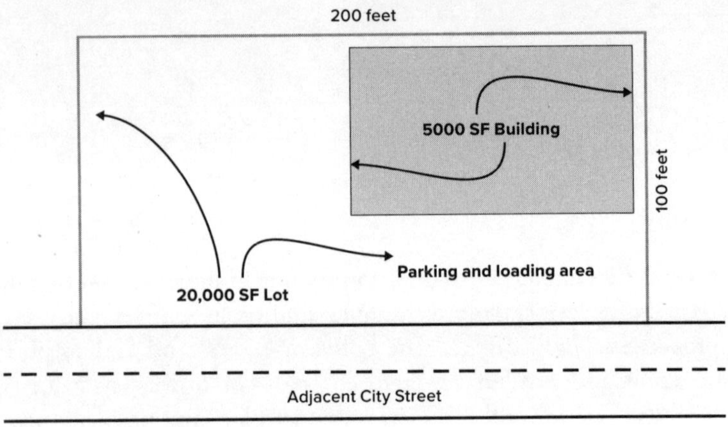

FIGURE 9-1 Typical Industrial Building and Site

The lot area is 20,000 square feet (200 × 100), so the lot would support 10,000 square feet of building. I should appraise this as a 5,000-square-foot industrial building (including the buildable land) plus 10,000 square feet of *excess land*. To put some numbers to this, imagine that industrial buildings of this caliber in this location sell for $50 per square foot and raw land suitable for construction of a new industrial building sells for $10 per square foot. The valuation equation looks like Table 9-1.

TABLE 9-1 Industrial Building Example—Excess Land

	Units	Per Unit	Total
Building	5,000	50	$250,000
Excess Land	10,000	10	100,000
Total Indicated Value			$350,000

I could now leave well enough alone. I have a building with a positive return plus a valuable parcel of excess land. The investor could hold this as a place to store value. The investor could also sell the excess land to another builder-developer who might build an industrial building next door. Assuming selling costs (commissions, fees, and such) are about 8% of the selling price, the investor would net $92,000 on the land sale. The total "worth" from this sale would be the building value ($250,000) plus the $92,000 cleared on the land, or $342,000. The investor has $92,000 to redeploy on something else.

The second alternative might be to double the existing building size. Assuming there were no problems with the existing structure, and the cost of construction for a building of this caliber (adding 5,000 square feet to our existing structure) is $30 per square foot, the new structure would be as shown in Figure 9-2 and the new value as shown in Table 9-2.

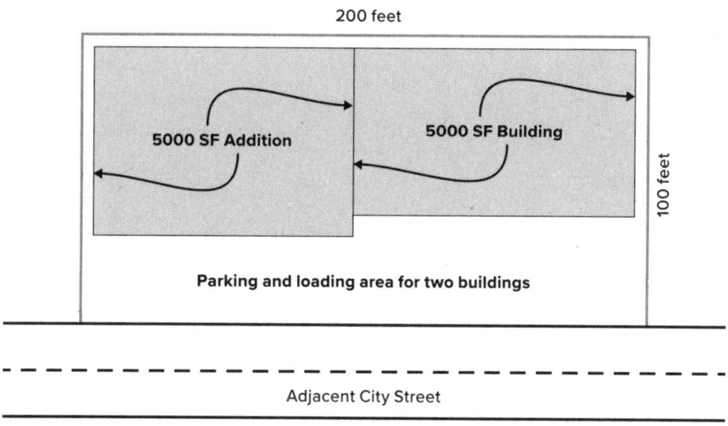

FIGURE 9-2 Industrial Site with Addition

TABLE 9-2 The Value of Using Excess Land

	Units	Per Unit	Total
Building	10,000	50	$500,000
Cost of Construction	5,000	(30)	(150,000)
Total Indicated Value			$350,000

Astonishingly, going to the effort of building a new building, the investor is no better off than before. Rational expectations suggests this makes sense. The entrepreneurial profit associated with the excess land is already captured in the land value. So why build? First, a new building, or an addition to the existing building, turns stored wealth into income. There are a host of reasons why an investor might want to do just that. Second, buildings like this are often owned or developed by merchant builders. A portion of the $30-per-square-foot construction costs flowed to the entrepreneurial developer's bottom line. If we own that merchant builder, then Table 9-2 understates our overall benefit from this transaction. Third, we are putting $150,000 in cash *into* the construction project. If we have excess cash, or lines of credit at favorable terms, this may be an excellent way to take that excess cash and turn it into tax-advantaged income.

Finally—and this is actually the real-life story that stimulated this example—the vacant portion may become an attractive nuisance. This has liability implications for the landowner, and building a new building (or an extension to the old building) in some ways alleviates that attractive nuisance problem.

2. Surplus Land

Let's take that same example I had in Figure 9-1, but instead of 20,000 square feet of land, I have 11,000 square feet (Figure 9-3).

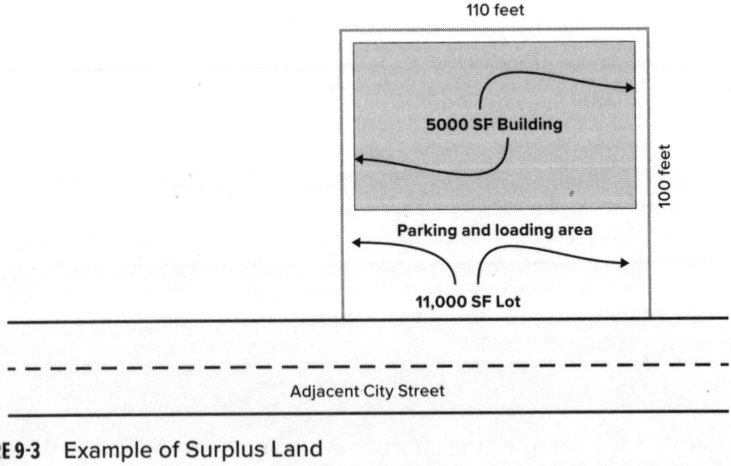

FIGURE 9-3 Example of Surplus Land

This is an example of *surplus land*. The difference between this and *excess land* is often confusing even for professionals. Excess land has a separate highest and best use and may be sold off separately or redeveloped independent of the primary site. On the other hand, surplus land has no separate highest and best use (HBU). In the foregoing example, we redeveloped the excess land as an extension of the existing industrial building. If the HBU of the excess parcel was for development of an office building, there is no reason not to do that. Indeed, the metrics in Tables 9-1 and 9-2 may change dramatically if the excess land was valued at a higher and better use than the existing use for the industrial building.

Surplus land is not needed to support the existing improvements but cannot be separated from the property and developed. Surplus land does not have its own HBU, and it may or may not contribute to value.

In Figure 9-3, the land requirement is 10,000 square feet. Surplus land is 1,000 square feet. We cannot point to a 1,000-square-foot portion and say "Aha! This is the part we don't need!"

In commercial situations, surplus land often gets absorbed into the site's general utility. In Figure 9-3, the surplus land might simply be used for five more parking spaces or landscaping. When valuing any property, with or without surplus land, there is an assumption that the land is adequate to support the improvements. Surplus land does not add to the value—it is simply assumed to be part of the "adequate" land.

Let us go back to Figure 9-3 and reevaluate the property under two scenarios. First, I will value via the cost approach, and recognize that the entire 11,000 square feet of land, if vacant, could be used to build an industrial building with a floor area ratio of 0.5 to 1. Second, I'll value using the sales comparison approach assuming the land is simply adequate, with no excess land that can be separately sold. Table 9-3 compares the two methods.

TABLE 9-3 Valuing Unused Surplus Land

	Cost Approach			Sales Comparison Approach		
	Units	Per Unit	Total	Units	Per Unit	Total
Building	5,000	30	$150,000	5,000	50	$250,000
Land	11,000	10	110,000			0
Total Indicated Value			$260,000			$250,000

What just happened? If I value via two different methods, I get two different answers. How can that be? Well, this is one of those little cracks in the pavement into which coins occasionally fall. The "extra" land is neither surplus nor excess, but something in between. It really cannot be efficiently identified or sold off, and it almost certainly does not have a separable highest and best use. It may be used in this instance to increase the property's value by adding onto the existing building.

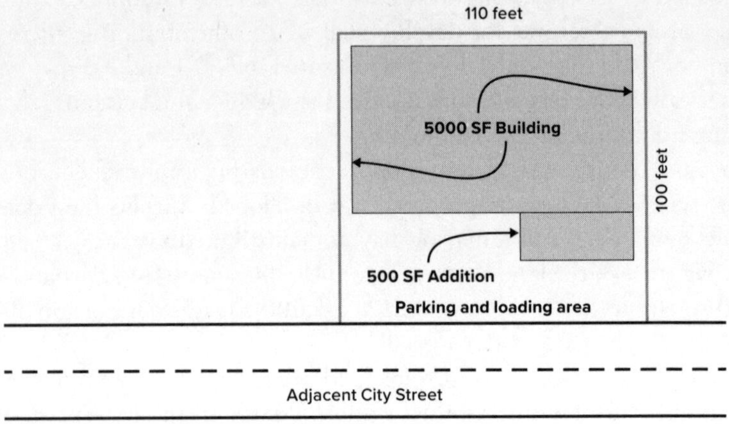

FIGURE 9-4 One Potential Cure for Surplus Land

TABLE 9-4 The Surplus Land Example

	Cost Approach			Sales Comparison Approach		
	Units	Per Unit	Total	Units	Per Unit	Total
Building	5,500	30	$165,000	5,500	50	$275,000
Land	11,000	10	110,000			0
Total Indicated Value			$275,000			$275,000

In Figure 9-4 and Table 9-4, the differential in values is indicating that I can maximize the land's use. Unlike the similar example in the prior section, I cannot capture this land value by selling it off to a separate buyer. However, if I invest in a new addition to the existing building (say, 500 square feet at $30 per square foot) I may increase the overall property value and convert value into income. Arguably, this would be a no-brainer. There are, however, some reasons to leave well enough alone. Often, municipalities are reluctant to permit "site maximizing" buildings and endeavor to force owners to maintain open space. Additional open space, parking, or green space may actually contribute to rents and values. This is a matter for evaluation and consideration.

3. Superamenities

Referred to as the "gold-plated bathroom fixtures" in the vernacular, this problem actually arises in many situations. I showed in Chapter 6 that the movie theater in the World Trade Center was a superamenity and thus constituted functional obsolescence.

On a technical level, a superamenity is anything that costs money to install but does not contribute to value to the extent of the cost. In the prior section, surplus land is an example of a superamenity if we paid for a larger but ultimately not fully usable site. Commonly, superamenities are associated with residences. Any feature or amenity not typical for the market can be a superamenity. Swimming pools in cold climates, an unusually large number of bathrooms compared to the house size, high-end kitchen appliances in a neighborhood where such would be unusual, or a larger-than-normal garage are all common problems.

Beyond the surplus land problem, examples of commercial superamenities are difficult to determine. Some commercial developers will purposely put unusual features in income-producing properties to enhance rents or minimize vacancy. A superamenity may purposely be put in place to satisfy a particularly demanding or desirable tenant. One tenant, a bank, wanted a sky lounge installed in a high floor for bank-sponsored gatherings. To secure a very long-term lease, the landlord installed the pricy sky lounge. *Within a few years, the bank declared bankruptcy and vacated the headquarters building.*

Examples of pricy superamenities include, but are certainly not limited to:

- Excessive parking spaces, particularly for neighborhood retail
- Industrial properties with excess electrical capacity
- Private or executive elevators, particularly in non–Class A buildings
- Private in-room washers and dryers in low-end apartments
- Excessively large or luxurious lobbies in Class B or Class C properties
- Excessive or luxurious office space in industrial buildings

In the residential market, one buyer's superamenity might be another buyer's necessity. In the United States, the market that has become synonymous with superamenities is Miami, although New York City is catching up fast. Intriguingly, the source and nature of potential buyers has come to define whether an amenity actually adds to or detracts from value and salability. Apartments and condos in the super luxury market in Miami have recently featured:

- Private splash pools on each apartment's balcony
- A year-round ice skating rink
- A cigar cellar
- Private recital space
- Auto elevators carrying cars to a private garage adjacent to the condo

While many buyers have been willing to pay for these superamenities, others shy away from the long-term maintenance costs and potential lack of resale value. It is difficult to put a firm value on what may be a "fad" amenity.

Comparable analysis is rarely a good measure of superamenity contributions to value. In other sections, I address survey research and how it is successfully used to value thinly or nontraded properties or aspects of properties. To fully assess the contributions—or lack thereof—of unusual property amenities, a rigorous and thorough survey of market participants may be necessary.

4. Curable and Incurable Physical Obsolescence

Obsolescence falls into three categories—physical, functional, and external (sometimes called economic). I have spent very little time analyzing just how these amounts are determined. These are materially large components of value. For a mature building, perhaps halfway through its economic life, the depreciation can constitute half or more of the building's replacement cost. Understanding this is important for reading and interpreting an appraisal report. Measuring and monitoring depreciation in a real estate portfolio is a critical part of asset management.

Not all depreciation is created equal. Some depreciation may be curable, and there may be value-enhancing opportunities associated with acquiring a mature building. Acquiring and rehabilitating Class C residential units (either houses or apartment buildings) can generate significant tax-hedged cash flow and under some circumstances can shelter other non-realty income. As I discussed previously, taking Class C commercial buildings and turning them into Class B can be an important investment opportunity.

It is helpful to remember: *buildings do not last forever*. Admittedly, there are some stone structures that date back to the dawn of recorded history. However, maintenance and management of those stone monuments is in no way economically feasible. One could nurture virtually any building to have a nearly permanent life. George Washington's home at Mount Vernon was built in an "above average" fashion for its time. The faux stonework on the facade was a decorative device to make the house look more valuable. The 1778 structure was in severe decline a scant 80 years later, when it was saved from ruin by the Mount Vernon Ladies' Association. Similarly, Ringling's famous home, Ca' d'Zan, built near Sarasota in 1926, was near ruin 70 years later when used as the set for the movie *Great Expectations*. Only with great effort and expense were these two historically important and well-built structures saved from natural demolition.

In general, in America, single family homes are built with an expectation of a 50- to 60-year economic life. Upscale homes are built slightly better, but only the very top-tier homes, such as trophy properties, are built with a markedly different set of materials and techniques. So, what does "economic life" really mean? It tells us that with *average* maintenance, a dwelling should be economically viable for 50 to 60 years. Gradually, up to and particularly after that point, the cost of maintenance and repair will generally exceed the economic value. In short, if a home receives *average* maintenance, then it will probably be a candidate for demolition and rebuilding (or at least substantial rehabilitation) in 50 to 60 years. Amazingly, for commercial buildings, the life span is even shorter—sometimes as short as 20 years for retail or high-traffic properties and 40 years for office and industrial properties. Class A office buildings will start to become Class B as they approach that 40-year life span.

This assumes *average* maintenance. What about *above average* maintenance? Well, that may be in the eye of the beholder, with some neighborhood and income considerations. Very nice homes built in very nice, stable neighborhoods will be candidates for above-average maintenance. The general rule of thumb—and this is very general—is that above-average maintenance may extend the economic life of a structure by as much as 100%.

So what constitutes above-average maintenance? Imagine a home built near the end of World War I. A surprisingly large number of very nice homes constructed in America in that era came in two railroad boxcars from Sears Roebuck. The homes had lead pipes, knob-and-tube wiring with 60-amp fuse boxes, single pane windows, no insulation, and lathe-and-plaster walls and ceilings. Heat came from fireplaces or central stoves. Air conditioning was unheard of. The kitchen would feature a woodstove and perhaps an icebox. Most of these would be considered functional obsolescence. However, even if multiple generations of property owners wanted to rough it and maintain the house in original condition, these things would simply wear out over time. At some point, the house would need a physical overhaul, either at one time or piecemeal.

Commercial buildings suffer from much the same set of problems. Roofs need to be replaced periodically. Heating, air, and ventilation systems—indeed, anything mechanical—wears out over time. Structural frames sag, rot, or get infested. Metalwork rusts. Stonework needs to be repaired. Rain, wind, and weather take their toll.

During economic slumps, hotels naturally pull back on maintenance, as do all buildings. During boom times, hotel investors go on buying sprees. One big issue in a hotel is the boiler system. It feeds the kitchen, the laundry, and in some cases even the heating. An out-of-date boiler, with deferred maintenance, can shut a hotel down in an instant, necessitating costly repairs *and* a total loss of revenue for a period, not to mention loss of goodwill with customers. Savvy hotel buyers check the boiler first thing during the due diligence period.

In general, physical deterioration falls into two categories: curable and incurable. There are several defining ways of discerning the difference, but the general rule of thumb is that *incurable* physical deterioration encompasses those items that would not be economically feasible to fix. In a residence, the roof rafters simply do not last forever. Even well-maintained roof systems will sag over time, requiring substantial rebuild. Often, this sort of rebuild is not economically feasible. The contributory value of the rebuild does is not reflected in enhanced or even continued rents.

Replacing a deteriorated piping system or wiring system may also not be economically feasible. On the other hand, replacing a roof (shingles, underlayment, any rotted roof decking), replacing a hot water heater, or replacing the heating and air compressor are expected and may be economically feasible or even necessary. Indeed, even with average maintenance, we expect these items will wear out and be replaced periodically. Thus, *curable* physical deterioration is that which can be fixed or repaired at an economically feasible cost.

Typically, there are three methods for measuring physical depreciation:

- Age-life method
- Market extraction
- Segregated cost, sometimes called the breakdown method

The age-life method is the simplest and resembles what accountants would do in determining cost less depreciation, although appraisers often opt for straight line rather than accelerated depreciation. In the age-life method, the property's reproduction cost, as if new, is parsed between the land cost, which is not subject to depreciation, and the building's reproduction cost. This latter figure should include the builder's overhead and profit, and should be a realistic estimate of how much it would cost to reproduce this property. The appraiser calculates the ratio of the effective age to the total economic life. This ratio, multiplied times the reproduction cost, yields the age-life depreciation estimate. Equations 9-1 and 9-2 illustrate. Assume I have a small office building that would cost $1 million to reproduce today. The building is estimated to have an effective age of 10 years and an expected total economic life of 40 years. We determine the depreciation to be:

$$\$1{,}000{,}000 \times \frac{10 \textit{ years effective age}}{40 \textit{ years expected economic life}} = \$250{,}000$$

EQUATION 9-1

I then determine that the land value is $500,000. The total property value, assuming no other forms of depreciation, is:

$$\$500{,}000 + 1{,}000{,}000 - 250{,}000 = \$1{,}250{,}000$$

EQUATION 9-2

I've used a new term here: *effective age*. A building with average maintenance would become economically infeasible to maintain as it approached the end of its expected economic life. However, above-average maintenance could extend that life and forestall the ravages of time. In short, the *effective age* is a heuristic blend of actual chronological age and a factor for above or below average maintenance. A building with an actual age of 20 years that has recently been substantially remodeled may have an effective age of only 10 years. That same building receiving little or no maintenance and allowed to deteriorate may have an effective age of 25 or 30 years or more.

Age-life is common for average-quality residences. However, it rests on a pile of heuristic assumptions rendering it problematic in complex situations. It assumes straight line depreciation, which is probably not valid, and it depends on rule-of-thumb estimates of effective age. In more complex situations, the market extraction method is preferred. In this method, I find a few highly comparable properties (these may be the most comparable ones used in the sales comparison approach) and then back into the depreciation via the cost approach. Assume that the building across the street is much like ours and recently sold for $5 million. The land under the building would sell for $2 million if the property was vacant, and the reproduction cost, as if new, is $4 million. I can estimate the depreciation amount and percentage via Equations 9-3 and 9-4:

$$\$5{,}000{,}000 - 2{,}000{,}000 - 4{,}000{,}000 = -1{,}000{,}000$$

EQUATION 9-3

Yes, that's a *negative* \$1 million. Remember, depreciation will reduce the value, not increase it! I then compute the percentage depreciation being extracted by the market for a building of this age and caliber:

$$\frac{1{,}000{,}000 \textit{ actual depreciation}}{4{,}000{,}000 \textit{ reproduction cost as if new}} = 25\% \textit{ depreciation}$$

EQUATION 9-4

I do not need to actually compute the expected economic life or effective age of either the comparable or our subject building. The market determines these things for me. The only decision is to find one or more comps of approximately the same age and condition as our property. Market proximity, size, and approximate value would also be good features for finding a market extraction comparable, but they are not necessary if the comps compete for the same buyers.

I can also use a segregated cost method. I break down the building's component into constituent parts, such as those that will need to be replaced soon (short-lived, curable items) and those that will probably not be replaced (long-lived, incurable items). The latter group include structural components. The depreciation for these items will be determined via age-life. For really complex buildings, an architect and/or an engineer is needed. For the short-lived, curable items, I estimate the remaining life of each and the present value of the replacement cost as inputs to the equation.

One confusing issue is the periodic replacement of very short-lived items. Assume a brand-new building with an expected economic life of 40 years. The air conditioning compressor needs to be replaced every 10 years at a cost of \$50,000. In the life of this building, that compressor will be replaced four times at a total cost of \$200,000. However, today it is brand-new, as is every other building component, and so there is no physical depreciation. The periodic replacement is a normal and expected part of the building maintenance. If the building is appraised five years from now, the compressor will have only five years remaining in its economic life. Using the segregated cost method, I determine depreciation of (5/10 × \$50,000 =) \$25,000. At the *next* appraisal, at the 10-year point, how much depreciation is assigned to that compressor? It depends on whether it has just been replaced (in which case, none) or whether it immediately needs to be replaced (in which case, \$50,000). There are more subtleties and complexities to this, to be sure, but hopefully you get the picture.

Measuring depreciation accurately and adequately is an important decision in asset maintenance but also in determining the investment price. Investors will be well-advised to use aspects of all three methods. A property I appraised using either the age-life or market-extraction method may be overvalued if some short-lived components have not been maintained or replaced recently. Conversely, that same building may be undervalued if those components have recently been upgraded or replaced. Recall that air conditioning compressor. At the 10-year point, the segregated cost method would assign it a depreciation of $50,000. However, if an engineer examines it and determines that it still has two years of life left, then the building is undervalued by $10,000 (two years at $5,000 per year).

I once consulted to a church that had a very large, old air conditioning compressor near the end of its life span. The church had recently been remodeled with a new wing constructed blocking the compressor from truck access. The engineers determined that when it came time to be replaced—which would be soon—the only way to remove it and insert a new one would be by helicopter!

5. Functional Obsolescence

I discussed this already, but it deserves a bit more exploration. Functional obsolescence results from a shortcoming in the materials, structure, design, or even building workmanship when compared to other buildings that compete in the same market. A building may have been functionally adequate at the time of construction, but can become unappealing or inadequate as new construction or design standards evolve. The baseline for measurement is the financial feasibility of alternative designs or construction in newer, competing properties.

Imagine a Class A building as it becomes Class B or Class C. Notably, there are several factors that contribute to this evolution, including age (physical obsolescence) or locational factors (external obsolescence). However, as newer Class A buildings come online, with newer design or functional features, the subject property inevitably compares unfavorably to those newer, more modern properties.

The Class A versus Class B or Class C discrimination is not the only pathway. Buildings constructed to be Class B or even Class C in the first place may find themselves competing unfavorably with newer buildings constructed in that same class.

Functional obsolescence includes:

Obsolescence that can be cured with an addition. The building does not have some feature that competing buildings have. The measure is the cost to add this feature. Notably, this is only obsolescence if the market penalizes for not having this feature. An older building may not have a fire suppression system, but do tenants pay less rent than for a comparable building with such a system?

Obsolescence that can be cured with modernization. This results from substandard features. Our building has an elevator, but newer buildings have more modern elevators. The measure is the cost to upgrade or the degree to which rents are diminished as a result of our substandard feature.

Superamenity (or superadequacy). Our building has amenities that exceed market expectations and do not contribute to value, or the cost exceeds the contribution. The superamenity may also have a high ongoing operating cost. The measure is the item's cost or the cost that exceeds the marginal value plus the present value of future carrying costs.

The need to deduct a superamenity as functional obsolescence depends on the methods used to estimate building costs "as if new." The cost approach usually begins with the *reproduction cost*. If that is the case, then the reproduction cost will include an item-by-item reconstruction of the building, including superadequacies. For older or more unique buildings, for which exact reproduction is impossible, a *replacement cost* analysis is used. In this, the costs only include those necessary to deliver a building of equal utility. Since a superamenity is definitionally not needed for equal utility, then the superadequacy will not be included in the first place and will not need to be deducted as functional obsolescence.

Incurable obsolescence. Our building is simply missing a design feature that cannot be cured in a financially feasible manner. Our office building has abnormally low ceilings or inadequate ductwork for the air conditioning system.

An investor may be in a unique position to feasibly cure an otherwise incurable problem. Assume we already own a property with surplus land. The property next door is a small shopping center that cannot expand due to inadequate parking. The shopping center's market value is diminished, but the investor has a unique *investment value* because the already existing surplus land can be used, if combined with the next door neighbor, to cure the parking problem. Suddenly, we find ourselves in the shopping center business!

We've mentioned John Ringling a couple of times in this book. It may seem a bit off the subject, but Ringling learned a lot about railroads by traveling his circus around the country. It thus comes as no surprise that he ended up financing or buying several, including the Oklahoma, New Mexico, and Pacific Railway (nicknamed the Ringling Railroad), which he sold at a handsome profit to the Atchison, Topeka and Santa Fe Railway (AT&SF). He also founded the Ringling and Oil Field Railway Company (which he also sold to AT&SF) and the White Sulphur Springs and Yellowstone Park Railway. Similarly, many real estate investors become experts in the field because of other business interests that steer them in that direction.

6. Economic (or External) Depreciation

External forces can impact value in a number of ways. The existence of those positive amenities is a *sine qua non* of property value. Adequate public utilities, favorable zoning, and access to good transportation are all necessary for a property to have value.

Certain external forces can erupt or systematically grow over time in a way that undermines the relative property value. We stress the word *relative* because the key issue is the value compared to other properties that do not have those negative external forces at work. Except in extreme situations, such as environmental disasters, the property will have some value but will be diminished relative to competing properties that do not have those external forces at work.

Consider a new apartment building located across from an industrial building. The industrial building has always been there, but the developer decides to build the apartment building anyway. Likely tenants are generally going to be less desirous of living in this building than in other nearby apartments. Ignoring whether or not this development is a good idea, or whether it is economically feasible, consider the valuation equation. The market comparable approach would seek out other apartment buildings of similar size, condition, and quality and examine their recent prices. What if those buildings were not located across the street from an industrial building? The value indicated by this approach would clearly be overstated.

Look at it from the income perspective. The starting line is the potential gross rent. Will this new building be able to charge the same rent as competing properties? Perhaps not, lowering the net operating income. Also, prospective investors will be less likely to want this building. Management, marketing, and the general hassle of owning this building will all dissuade potential buyers. The capitalization (or discount) rate will be higher to incorporate the stigma in the marketplace.

The more common situation arises when a noxious or nonconforming use suddenly arises near an existing building. Some sort of environmental issue is the most common—discovering, for example, that a nearby building is leaking contamination in our direction. General neighborhood decline or loss of important neighborhood amenities would also negatively impact value.

Negative externalities can be short-lived or long-lived. Construction of a new building next door can disrupt use and enjoyment of our property for a time, but eventually the problem will be solved. Environmental contamination may ultimately be remediated, although the associated stigma usually lasts beyond the remediation. Loss of an important local service, such as a school closure, may impact values for a long time. Changes in zoning, if adverse to the current use, can have a permanent negative impact.

> Often there is disagreement over what is "permanent" and what is "temporary." The time value of money suggests that a negative impact that lasts several years has nearly as much impact as a permanent one. A dollar, discounted at 10% for 10 years, is only worth about $0.39 today. Thus, a negative externality that renders the subject property unmarketable and unusable for 10 years or more has an impact on value of 60% or more.

In a perfect world, the local neighborhood has other properties similarly affected and recently sold. Those sales, compared to sales in unaffected areas, give some indication of diminution in value. Markets, however, are rarely so robustly full of information, particularly with a new negative externality. Studies have repeatedly shown that prices are "sticky downward"; they do not quickly respond to negative information.

Sometimes, prices actually behave illogically. Immediately after Hurricane Katrina, prices remaining habitable houses in and near New Orleans actually spiked upward—speculators believed the shortage of houses would drive up prices. However, the near total collapse of local public services tanked those prices, and several years passed until those speculators were bailed out of bad decisions.

The impact can be materially large, and this adds to the measurement difficulty. Indirect measurement is usually needed. One common method is survey research.[1] This has been extensively written about in the academic and the practitioner literature and has been shown to be highly accurate in measuring market reactions to negative events and conditions.

Another useful tool is a literature search for scholarly research and case studies. In the former, researchers examine markets at equilibrium for pricing trends. In the latter, practitioners will report recent individual studies and court decisions. These studies can be used in the same manner as comparable data, via a meta-analysis, to determine the locational adjustment warranted in these situations

Investors should be constantly mindful of the market and neighborhood conditions of properties in their portfolios. Sudden impacts, and even the rumor of impending market conditions changes, can require immediate decisions to preserve wealth or maximize advantages.

> After Hurricane Katrina, property prices spiked in nearby Baton Rouge, which was less affected by the storm, as occupancies rose to 100%. Similarly, owners of unaffected properties can benefit by negative externalities impacting competing properties.

By the way, a given externality can sometimes be either positive or negative, depending on its location. The classic example is a neighborhood shopping center. Everyone wants to live *near* one, but no one wants to live *next* to one. Figure 9-5 illustrates the problem.

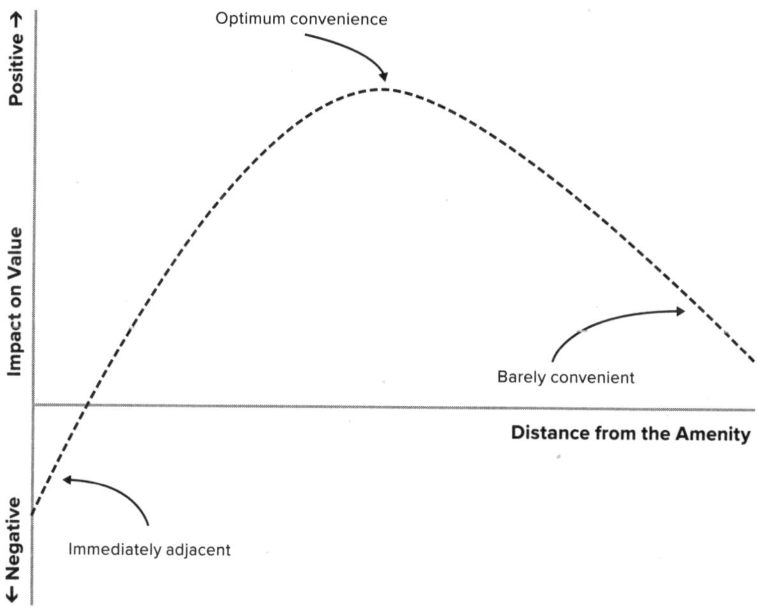

FIGURE 9-5 An External Impact May Be Positive *or* Negative

7. Disequilibrium, or How John Nash Won the Nobel Prize

The movie *A Beautiful Mind* is about the late mathematician John Nash, the 1994 Nobel Laureate in Economics. Nash was interested in something called *game theory*, which helps predict how people and institutions will behave in complex situations. While the focus of Nash's work was trade economics, his theories have been extended to such areas as diplomatic strategy. Of interest here is the implication for real estate market equilibrium.

Nothing puts people to sleep faster than a discourse on market equilibrium, but please bear with me. Nash modeled a market where players know each others' strategies but do not cooperate with one another. There are plenty of "buyers" and plenty of "sellers," and so each is trying to maximize their outcome given a reasonably full knowledge of the playing field. Players may make what appear to be suboptimal choices, given that they know that a bidding war could break out if everyone tried to bid on the same property. Hence, the market reaches an equilibrium with prices that may not, for each individual buyer and seller, be the best price.

This is important for several reasons. Earlier, I noted that market value assumes the *most probable price* even though the highest and best use may look for the maximum. But buyers and sellers competing against one another end up with what are called *pareto-optimal* solutions. Pareto optimality occurs when everyone is "well off" and no move will result in anyone being better off without someone else being worse off. In other words, chasing after the best property in the market may leave me either overpaying or without any property at all.

Another interesting outcome of Nash is that the best property in the market may go without any bidders. No one actually wants to be at the market top because of the 90% rule I mentioned. Hence, the top-tier properties end up being sluggish to sell and selling at larger discounts than the second-tier properties. Go figure.

The implications for wealth optimization are very real. The wealth maximization strategy may *not* be to chase the market top, but instead to look at the tier close to the market top. Some most interesting things will happen there.

A final note on market equilibria. Nash's model predicts that disturbances in the market will not instantly cure. Economics 101 is silent about this, and most basic econ teachers act like it happens immediately. Modern schools of behavioral economics recognize that the marketplace does not act efficiently. When a negative externality emerges, sellers often cannot put their properties on the market at a new, lower price. Instead, they withdraw from the market entirely. Many other sellers fall into the "wishful thinking" zone and hope things will get better. Buyers withdraw from the market, although some speculators do not make rational decisions. Thus, the market size and the scope shrinks, and stagnates over time to a new equilibrium. Figure 9-6 illustrates what typically happens when there is a negative market disturbance, such as emergence of a negative externality.

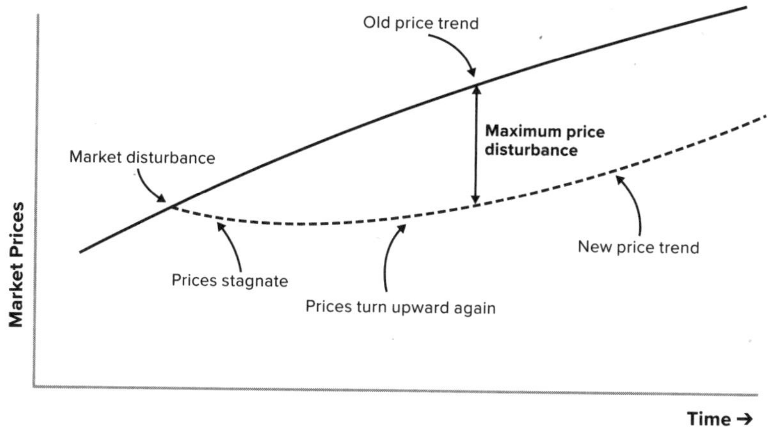

FIGURE 9-6 The Impact of a Negative Event over Time

After some negative disturbance, prices may decline but are more likely to simply stagnate over time. Prices will begin to rise again in the future, and the pricing gap—the maximum loss in value as a percentage of the "normalized" price—may not be evident until after prices have begun to rise again.

Market disequilibrium separates the investors from the speculators. Investors in markets that get hit with such disturbances are advised to pay close attention to market movements. While commercial properties may continue to rent well, values may stagnate or decline (due to lack of buyer interest) and costs will go up (due to increases in management, monitoring, legal, and insurance costs). Investors should seriously consider exit strategies from these situations. Ironically, these markets can provide some investment opportunities, but only very selectively.

8. Summary and Key Points

While these may appear to be advanced topics, these are actual situations that arise regularly in real estate investing. Excess and surplus land, various forms of depreciation, and market disequilibria are all common problems and opportunities facing real estate market participants. Surplus and excess land can be dissipating overhead if not addressed, and yet can be value enhancing if handled properly. Depreciation in all its forms is a market reality, and yet it provides opportunities for investment if properly understood. Of course, marketwide, systemic upsets happen regularly as well and must be monitored and managed aggressively.

9. A Final Note—Conducting a Survey

Survey research is a common tool for complex real estate appraisal. At the most basic form, an appraiser trying to value an office building will survey local brokers for market rents. Conducting a feasibility study for a proposed apartment complex will require surveying market demand and supply. A good bit of what is used for capitalization and discount rates comes from surveys, either conducted locally by an individual appraiser or nationally by one of several data services.

There are two general formats for surveys. First are the direct question-and-answer interviews, often very straightforward and simple. An appraiser wants to know what the current lending rate, loan-to-value requirements, and debt service coverage will be for a 15-year, fixed-rate loan on a small office building. The appraiser phones local banks, and typically gets nearly the same information from each. Another appraiser is interested in the impact of a proposed waste dump on nearby property values. The researcher may call a dozen or so real estate brokers in the market to get a sense of their opinions.

Informal surveys have drawbacks. Respondents may be biased. They certainly do not want to denigrate a neighborhood where their potential clients live! Also, the value impacts of the proposed dump can be complex.

In more complex situations, the researcher follows a formal, prearranged script asking a series of probing questions of market participants. The questions are usually aimed at quantifying the values or the value diminution associated with a particular benefit or detrimental condition. A large number of respondents are surveyed—often in the hundreds. The format follows a very well-developed process, and in the end, the results are tabulated and statistically analyzed.

The most common format is the contingent valuation method (CVM). It was developed to measure the value of nontraded benefits, by estimating the price that respondents would pay (willingness to pay, or WTP) for a particular good. Homebuilders and developers used CVM to measure how much extra homebuyers would pay for new amenities. Once they figure out that buyers would pay more than the amenities cost, the amenities become standard. Developers use CVM to price new homes or even commercial properties in new market niches. Researchers also use CVM to measure the WTP for public goods, such as parks and nature trails.

In market disequilibrium situations, CVM can be valuable to ascertain the reaction of market participants to the negative externality. When prices are stagnated and not telling the full story about eventual market declines, then the WTP to avoid this situation, or conversely the amount needed to induce a buyer to purchase a property in the affected neighborhood, can be invaluable information.

10

A Deep Dive into the Sales Comparison Approach: Residential

The major fortunes made in America
have been made in real estate.

—John D. Rockefeller

INVESTORS WILL ENCOUNTER residential appraisals in a number of situations. An appraisal may be performed on a principal or secondary personal residence, even if those are not financed. If the investor wants to take advantage of the limited deductibility of mortgage interest, then an actual residential appraisal will be required. Appraisals may be useful when purchasing investment properties, and will certainly be necessary for estates and probate work, for property tax appeals, for insurance, and for any litigation, such as eminent domain or inverse condemnations, that may affect the residence.

Residential appraisals depend on a surprisingly large array of heuristic assumptions. Legally, an appraisal is called an "opinion of value." It is the professional opinion of a trained, experienced, and licensed appraiser based on professional judgement. Like any professional opinion—physician, attorney, accountant—the opinion's quality depends on input from the client. If you ask your attorney about a particular contract, the opinion may be affected by information that only you have. The more obvious example is the physician's opinion. If you hide some symptoms, or fail to answer your medical history correctly, the physician's diagnosis—and prognosis—may be materially affected.

You may be more familiar with attorneys and physicians than appraisers. Part of this is a manifestation of pop culture. We grew up watching movies and TV shows about doctors, lawyers, and the police. To the best of my recollection, there have been no TV shows about real estate appraisers. Also, most readers of this text have regular physicals or have interactions with one or more attorneys, either in a business or personal setting.

Understanding how an appraisal comes together, and how assumptions affect the value conclusion, are critically important and have materially large financial impacts. Understanding this process will point to niches and opportunities for the financially savvy investors.

Again, this text is not designed to train real estate appraisers. My goal is to make the real estate owner, when faced with an appraisal, as knowledgeable as a patient going in for a physical or a routine medical procedure.

1. Critical Assumptions and Theoretical Underpinnings

The Holy Grail of appraisal is a model that works all the time with a reasonable degree of accuracy, reliability, and confidence. Mass appraisers, with highly sophisticated automated valuation models, relying on statistical tools, have come very close, using massive reams of data.

The individual dwelling appraisal is less a model and more a valuation paradigm. Proper application of tools and techniques relies heavily on the individual appraiser's experience and expertise. Some facets considered may have applicability in some areas, while those same facets may have no applicability in other markets. A fireplace may be exceptionally valuable in Boston, but not so much in Phoenix. The dwelling's absolute square footage, room count, bedrooms, and bathrooms may be critical issues for "middle market" homes, but will probably have almost no direct bearing on the value of a top-of-the-market trophy property or, ironically, at the bottom.

It is also helpful to understand what an appraisal is and what it <u>is not.</u> For one, appraisers are not generally in the title search business (although many are very familiar with that arena). There is a critical assumption that the property and all comparables have good, marketable titles. Even when liens, encumbrances, and assessments are known, they are disregarded unless this is an issue in the appraisal itself, and the property is assumed to be "free and clear." We also assume that the owners are responsible and the property is competently managed.

Appraisers are usually not trained in the nuances of building inspection. Property examinations are conducted for the purpose of identification and description, and to determine the highest and best use. The appraiser's observations are not a warranty of any property component. Most appraisal reports will include language that the appraiser has assumed the dwelling is structurally sound and all components are in working condition (unless otherwise noted).

If the appraisal report notes any significant adverse conditions, such as unrepaired items, depreciation, hazardous wastes or other toxic substances, the reader should make no assumptions about the completeness or accuracy of those observations. Again, the appraisers are generally not experts in those fields. Of course, appraisers cannot even observe hidden or latent problems.

Much information comes from public information. There is an explicit assumption, usually stated in the report, that these sources are correct. If indeed that assumption is false, then the analysis may fail on that basis.

So, why use an individual appraisal in the first place? There are three principal reasons:

- ***The law often requires it.*** Federally regulated mortgage lending institutions must adhere to appraisal guidance and law set down following the 1980's Savings and Loan crisis. The Financial Institutions Reform, Recovery, and Enforcement Act (FIRREA) of 1991, and enabling regulations, require an appraisal for most mortgages. Often, the prospectuses for mortgage-backed securities specifically cite appraisals as part of loan underwriting and due diligence. The federal government has little incentive to change this, and the appraisal profession has absolutely no interest in seeing this changed. So, there you have that.
- ***Appraisals are efficient.*** For an individual transaction, running an automated valuation model can be expensive and time consuming. Having said that, as of this writing, there are services which are in the process of producing AVM values for a small fee. Some services also produce an accompanying report that outlines the statistical characteristics, market data, and sometimes even the methodology used. None of these services span 100% of the American market, often due to data limitations. Individual appraisals can generally always be used.
- ***Non-mortgage situations*** requiring appraisals include litigation, tax appeals, estates, eminent domain situations, dispute settlements, and investment decisions. The players—attorneys, advisors, CPAs,

courts and judges, local commissions and boards—all understand appraisals and are used to them. Having a local appraiser along for the ride provides a potential expert witness or advisor if and as these situations turn contentious or if further explanation is needed.

Appraisals are vital tools in a variety of situations, and when performed properly, the appraisal report can be valuable in the decision-making process.

2. FNMA/FHLMC Appraisal Forms

This begins a two-chapter arc on the sales comparison approach, often called the market data approach. (This is a misnomer—all of the various methods and approaches use "market data.") In the next chapter, I will explore sales comparison for a simple income property. The format, analyses, and logic for residential versus income properties is somewhat different. For about 95% of residences in America, there are pretty good comps available for the valuation process. For income properties this is not always the case. Income property valuation usually leans more heavily on an income analysis (the "income approach," which I will address later).

Since most residences are fairly homogenous, and since most residential appraisals are performed for mortgage lending, the residential analysis process follows a fairly rigid set of processes promulgated by the Federal National Mortgage Association (FNMA, or Fannie Mae) and the Federal Home Loan Mortgage Corporation (FHLMC, or Freddie Mac). These are two different organizations, but they control the lion's share of the mortgage secondary market in America. Residential mortgage lending is regulated by a complex set of laws stemming from the 1991 Financial Institutions Reform, Recovery, and Enforcement Act (FIRREA) and subsequent promulgations by the Controller of the Currency, the FDIC, and even the National Association of Credit Unions. This regulation is aimed to ensure that every residential appraisal performed in America looks a lot like the others, and that appraisals can be used to support residential mortgage-backed securities (RMBS) issued to provide liquidity for lenders.

FNMA and FHLMC promulgate a rigid set of processes for residential valuation, but also promulgate forms so that the appraisal results can be reported in a systematic and simplified fashion. Residential appraisers are so used to using these forms that they often—indeed, almost always—use these forms to report residential appraisal in nonmortgage situations, such as eminent domain, estate settlement, and tax appeals. The common use of these forms is understandable—the forms are simple and free, appraisers are trained to use them, and most important many of the software packages that appraisers use report the analysis on these forms.

Also, the form reports themselves are not appraisals, they are merely the reporting of an appraisal. Readers may be familiar with Rene Magritte's famous 1920 painting, "La Trahison des images (Ceci n'est pas une pipe)," or "This Is Not a Pipe." It is simply a painting of a pipe. The FNMA/FHLMC form is simply the reporting of an appraisal analysis, not the analysis itself. If this seems trivial, it has an important implication. Often, when filling out any form, we tend to try to fit the data—and the answers—to the form's requirements. But, what if the implications for valuation have nothing to do with any of the questions asked on the form?

3. Key Elements of a Sales Adjustment Grid

Well, first, it would be handy if I defined a "grid." It is simply a stylized spreadsheet, and indeed in commercial valuations, the common spreadsheet is the nearly ubiquitous tool. However, for residential properties, it is common for appraisers to use specialized software packages designed to fill in the blanks of the spreadsheet used on FNMA/FHLMC forms. That spreadsheet is no different from what can be created on any computer screen.

> Old-timers may remember when accountants used huge sheets of line-and-column paper to make financial adjustments and determine end-of-period balance sheets and income statements. For reasons lost in antiquity, these big sheets of paper were usually colored green, with alternating columns and rows shaded different hues of green. The electronic spreadsheet has put all that out of business, along with mechanical calculators.

The first step in any sales adjustment grid is determining what factors contribute to the value of the subject property. Let's take a simple single family residence as an example. Items of interest might include, but certainly would not be limited to, the things arrayed in Table 10-1:

TABLE 10-1 Typical Components of Value for a Residence

	Subject
Special Financing?	No
Date of Sale/Valuation	1/1/2019
Location	Above average
Rights Appraised/Sold	Fee simple
Lot Size (SF)	9,000
View	Backs up to open space
Design Style	2-story, modern, wood
Quality of Construction	Above average
Age	10 years
Condition	Average
Total Rooms Above Grade	10
Bathrooms Above Grade	3.5
Bedrooms Above Grade	5
SF Above Grade	4,800
Basement Finished Rooms	2
Basement Finished SF	400
Basement Unfinished SF	2,000
Functional Utility	Average
Heating/Cooling	Forced air
Garage/Carport	3-car garage
Energy Efficient Items	Modern
Other:	Sports court
	Bonus room
	Sound system
	Security system
	Updated appliances
	200-SF screened porch

This is a fairly limited list. The wall color is not included (except as a particularly horrendous color or paint condition may influence the marketability). The color of the tile or fixtures in the bathrooms, the specific brand of built-in range or dishwasher, or the quality of the carpet are not broken out, but rather lumped into "quality" and "condition" assessments. There are important reasons for this. The goal is to determine features that are valued by the market as a whole. While a particular buyer may value, say, a blue house over a brown house, the market itself may not care.

Some features may be broadly recognized as valuable, but not by an amount greater than a typical rounding error. Built-in microwave ovens are usually considered valuable. However, the actual contributory value of one may only be a couple of hundred dollars. Of course, if every other house in a competing market has a built-in microwave, but this subject property does not, it might affect the appraiser's property quality assessment. Indeed, such a shortcoming may have a material impact on the residence's marketability far beyond the actual cost of the missing appliance itself.

Following the recent residential mortgage meltdown, FNMA and FHLMC, along with their oversight agency, the Federal Housing Finance Authority, significantly increased the guidelines and requirements for appraisals. Starting in 2014, most such appraisals have to use a uniform data set. Before that, determinations of quality and condition were very judgmental. Appraisers in a given market may have a common methodology, passed down from appraisers to their apprentices, but there was little in the way of uniformity across markets. The agencies addressed this with a uniform set of condition ("C" rankings) and quality ("Q" rankings) definitions, as shown in Tables 10-2 and 10-3 (see next pages). Even for properties and situations that do not need to conform to agency requirements, these are handy guidelines for assessing condition and quality.

These definitions are useful even for upscale and trophy properties. The highest quality and condition ratings would probably apply, and would provide guidance for finding comparable "trophy" transactions.

Some entries are duplicative or at least overlapping. We note the square footage (usually called "heated square footage"), but we also count rooms, bedrooms, and bathrooms. Statisticians would have a field day with those notations—clearly larger homes have more rooms, and smaller homes have fewer ones. Also, bedrooms and bathrooms are nearly perfectly colinear. Nonetheless, these facets tell the right story about the quality and value of a dwelling, and have aided appraisers in understanding and communicating the valuation.

4. Finding Comparables—Transactional and Physical Elements

Assume you need to value a painting (for insurance, potential sale, estate settlement, or gifting). The art appraiser will seek out comparable sales of other pieces, looking in the market for such art (collectors, galleries, and curators). Recent sales are preferred, and of course you will want to look at sales by the same artist. If no such sales exist, perhaps you will look at sales from the same art genre and current trends among collectors. You may look at the painting's actual physical attributes—the scale, the intensity, the medium. Some review of critical response to this particular piece or to the artist's work in general will help form a basis for comparison.

TABLE 10-2 FNMA/FHLMC Conditions Definitions

Rating	Description
C1	The improvements have been very recently constructed and have not previously been occupied. The entire structure and all components are new and the dwelling features no physical depreciation. **Note:** *Newly constructed improvements that feature recycled materials and/or components can be considered new dwellings provided that the dwelling is placed on a 100 percent new foundation and the recycled materials and the recycled components have been rehabilitated/remanufactured into like-new condition. Improvements that have not been previously occupied are not considered "new" if they have any significant physical depreciation (that is, newly constructed dwellings that have been vacant for an extended period of time without adequate maintenance or upkeep).*
C2	The improvements feature no deferred maintenance, little or no physical depreciation, and require no repairs. Virtually all building components are new or have been recently repaired, refinished, or rehabilitated. All outdated components and finishes have been updated and/or replaced with components that meet current standards. Dwellings in this category either are almost new or have been recently completely renovated and are similar in condition to new construction. **Note:** *The improvements represent a relatively new property that is well-maintained with no deferred maintenance and little or no physical depreciation, or an older property that has been recently completely renovated.*
C3	The improvements are well-maintained and feature limited physical depreciation due to normal wear and tear. Some components, but not every major building component, may be updated or recently rehabilitated. The structure has been well-maintained. **Note:** *The improvement is in its first cycle of replacing short-lived building components (appliances, floor coverings, HVAC, etc.) and is being well-maintained. Its estimated effective age is less than its actual age. It also may reflect a property in which the majority of short-lived building components have been replaced but not to the level of a complete renovation.*
C4	The improvements feature some minor deferred maintenance and physical deterioration due to normal wear and tear. The dwelling has been adequately maintained and requires only minimal repairs to building components/mechanical systems and cosmetic repairs. All major building components have been adequately maintained and are functionally adequate. **Note:** *The estimated effective age may be close to or equal to its actual age. It reflects a property in which some of the short-lived building components have been replaced, and some short-lived building components are at or near the end of their physical life expectancy; however, they still function adequately. Most minor repairs have been addressed on an ongoing basis resulting in an adequately maintained property.*
C5	The improvements feature obvious deferred maintenance and are in need of some significant repairs. Some building components need repairs, rehabilitation, or updating. The functional utility and overall livability are somewhat diminished due to condition, but the dwelling remains useable and functional as a residence. **Note:** *Some significant repairs are needed to the improvements due to the lack of adequate maintenance. It reflects a property in which many of its short-lived building components are at the end of or have exceeded their physical life expectancy, but remain functional.*
C6	The improvements have substantial damage or deferred maintenance with deficiencies or defects that are severe enough to affect the safety, soundness, or structural integrity of the improvements. The improvements are in need of substantial repairs and rehabilitation, including many or most major components. **Note**: *Substantial repairs are needed to the improvements due to the lack of adequate maintenance or property damage. It reflects a property with conditions severe enough to affect the safety, soundness, or structural integrity of the improvements.*

Source: FNMA Selling Guide, B4-1.3-06: Property Condition and Quality of Construction of the Improvements (April 15, 2014)

TABLE 10-3 FNMA/FHLMC Quality Definitions

Rating	Description
Q1	Dwellings with this quality rating are usually unique structures that are individually designed by an architect for a specified user. Such residences typically are constructed from detailed architectural plans and specifications and feature an exceptionally high level of workmanship and exceptionally high-grade materials throughout the interior and exterior of the structure. The design features exceptionally high-quality exterior refinements and ornamentation, and exceptionally high-quality interior refinements. The workmanship, materials, and finishes throughout the dwelling are of exceptionally high quality.
Q2	Dwellings with this quality rating are often custom designed for construction on an individual property owner's site. However, dwellings in this quality grade are also found in high-quality tract developments featuring residences constructed from individual plans or from highly modified or upgraded plans. The design features detailed, high-quality exterior ornamentation, high-quality interior refinements, and detail. The workmanship, materials, and finishes throughout the dwelling are generally of high or very high quality.
Q3	Dwellings with this quality rating are residences of higher quality built from individual or readily available designer plans in above-standard residential tract developments or on an individual property owner's site. The design includes significant exterior ornamentation and interiors that are well finished. The workmanship exceeds acceptable standards and many materials and finishes throughout the dwelling have been upgraded from "stock" standards.
Q4	Dwellings with this quality rating meet or exceed the requirements of applicable building codes. Standard or modified standard building plans are utilized and the design includes adequate fenestration and some exterior ornamentation and interior refinements. Materials, workmanship, finish, and equipment are of stock or builder grade and may feature some upgrades.
Q5	Dwellings with this quality rating feature economy of construction and basic functionality as main considerations. Such dwellings feature a plain design using readily available or basic floor plans featuring minimal fenestration and basic finishes with minimal exterior ornamentation and limited interior detail. These dwellings meet minimum building codes and are constructed with inexpensive, stock materials with limited refinements and upgrades.
Q6	Dwellings with this quality rating are of basic quality and lower cost; some may not be suitable for year-round occupancy. Such dwellings are often built with simple plans or without plans, often utilizing the lowest-quality building materials. Such dwellings are often built or expanded by persons who are professionally unskilled or possess only minimal construction skills. Electrical, plumbing, and other mechanical systems and equipment may be minimal or nonexistent. Older dwellings may feature one or more substandard or nonconforming additions to the original structure.

Source: FNMA Selling Guide, B4-1.3-06: Property Condition and Quality of Construction of the Improvements (April 15, 2014)

Valuing a house is a lot like that, although regulatory issues impose certain degrees of uniformity and systemization. Gems, businesses, mineral rights, automobiles, yachts, aircraft, and all manner of things people own or collect may be valued by some sort of sales comparison methodology. All of these consider comps and the basis for selecting those comps. This may seem simple and straightforward, and the process is standardized so that any two appraisals may follow the same predictable process.

Somewhat obviously, if my goal is to value a house, then I'll seek recent sales of other houses. At any given point there are a plethora of sales from which to choose, if I broaden my search sufficiently. The process, though, is to *narrow* my search, rather than to broaden it. Of the universe of potential sales I can use, I first examine the nature of the transactions themselves, rather than the physical attributes. I do so in the following order:

Financing Terms

If the task is to determine the subject's market value, I will look for comps with normal market financing. Comps with seller financing, some sort of favorable financing, or situations where normal financing is not available would not be representative of the market. The "comp" buyers may have been paying for certain tax advantages or for a mortgage they otherwise could not obtain.

Motivations, Terms, and Sale Conditions

Were there other forces at play in this transaction? Assume that the house across the street sold last week and is identical in all respects. On the surface, this may be a handy comp. However I find that it was sold by elderly parents to a child. It is likely that the sale price is not indicative of market value. Were the same interests being transacted that are the focus of our appraisal? If I am interested in valuing the fee simple interest in a rental house, but find that the comparable sale is subject to a very long-term, low-rate lease, then the interest sold in that comparable transaction was probably not fee simple.

Recent Sales Are Preferable

There are few hard-and-fast rules, but generally, for residential appraisals, a comparable from the past year is preferred. If my appraisal is to adhere to FNMA/FHLMC standards, then the use of comps over a year old must be explained.

Nearby Sales Are Preferable

A comparable across the street or next door is wonderful, but this rarely happens. In urban areas, comparable transactions should be from within a mile. In suburban areas, three miles should do, and in rural areas, five miles.

I also consider the physical characteristics and approximate range of the value. If the subject is a 4,000-square-foot, two-story, reasonably modern and above average residence, I am implicitly filtering for homes that more or less look like that. After all, casting a wider net would be uselessly time consuming and expensive.

> Since automated valuation models use computer algorithms to supplement appraisal judgment and experience, these AVMs can cast a much wider net, and will filter out the outliers at the analysis stage.

At this juncture, I am left with an array of nearby, recent comps that transacted under similar circumstances and with similar conditions. What if a better comp has a transactional glitch? Assume I am interested in the market value of a fee simple interest, but a comp transacted a leased fee interest. I need to make certain adjustments to the comp sales price accounting for the difference between a leased fee interest and a fee simple interest. What if a comp sold with significant seller financing? Assume the seller agreed to pay 5% of the purchase price toward the buyer's closing costs, which is unusual in this market. I will have to make an adjustment for this nonrealty component in the sale.

The terms "nearby" and "recent" can be troublesome. In a perfect world, all of my comps come from the same neighborhood, or have the same or equal locational features. In practice this assumption is regularly violated. Comparable transaction locations may be superior or inferior to the subject's location. I need to determine the percentage adjustment for the difference in location. Also, if a comp sale occurred several months ago, I will need to determine the pricing trend (often called a *market conditions adjustment*) and adjust the comps accordingly.

For larger, automated models, regressions or statistical trends can help make these determinations, and indeed the location and market conditions adjustments are usually baked into the regression formula. For my simple appraisal, the most common tool is called the *matched pairs analysis*. I find two properties—not necessarily two of the comps—which have recently transacted and have identical characteristics *except for the item in question*. The difference in sales prices should determine the percentage adjustment applicable. I want to find several such pairs, just to make sure. Equation 10-1 demonstrates the method. In this example, Transaction 1 is in the same neighborhood as the subject, while Transaction 2 is in the neighborhood of a comp that may need to be adjusted. Otherwise, the two transactions are of identical homes.

$$Adjustment\ \% = \frac{Trans\ 1 - Trans\ 2}{Trans\ 1} = \frac{\$180{,}000 - \$200{,}000}{\$200{,}000} = -10\%$$

EQUATION 10-1

As you can see, the comp is in a more valuable neighborhood, so I need to adjust comp prices in that neighborhood downward by 10%. I make these adjustments to the comps to find a set of *adjusted prices* that triangulate in on the true value of the subject.

Up to this point, I have discussed using three to six comps. For very simple residences, three may be sufficient, and for more complex properties six or more may be needed to fully ascertain the value implications. In most circumstances, one or two of the comps will be most indicative of the true value, but the other comps are necessary for proper due diligence.

This leads naturally to the concepts of *bracketing* and *qualitative analysis.* There is a fair amount written about these topics, but they are not very well understood, even by appraisers. In Equation 10-1, I was able to very carefully quantify a neighborhood adjustment using nearly identical matched pairs. In practice such matched pairs are hard to find, and comps may come from several different neighborhoods. Trying to set up a matrix of such matched pairs adjustments may confuse the issue more than solve it. A simpler and somewhat more elegant solution reduces houses to some common denominator—say average sales price per square foot—and then rank-orders the various neighborhoods. Our subject neighborhood should be bracketed by the various superior and inferior neighborhoods (Table 10-4). This rank ordering will not be determined by my judgment, but rather endogenously by the data itself.

TABLE 10-4 Bracketing and Qualitative Adjustments

Neighborhood	Avg. $/SF	Adjustment
Comp 1	$250	−12.0%
Comp 2	$235	−6.4%
Comp 3	$225	−2.2%
Subject	$220	
Comp 4	$210	4.8%
Comp 5	$200	10.0%

I end up with a quantitative adjustment, but via a qualitative ranking and bracketing the subject neighborhood.

The average square foot price in the subject neighborhood was $220. One basis for comparison, from Table 10-1, was also square footage. This implies—erroneously—that I will adjust comps by $220 (or something like that) for every square foot difference between the comp and the subject. It's not that easy! The question is the *marginal* value difference, holding everything else equal. Assume two houses, each with an identical complement of bedrooms, bathrooms, fireplaces, garages, and such. One house is 20 square feet larger than the other. That means that the 10-foot-wide utility room in one house is two feet wider in the other. Admittedly, a slightly larger utility room is a nice thing to have, but is it $4,400 nicer for a typical middle-American house? Probably not. In practice, for square footage adjustments, the marginal value will typically be less than half of average value.

5. Longitudinal (Trend) Analyses

Values and prices change over time, requiring a market conditions adjustment. The most common method for determining this is some sort of extrapolation of a trend. In its simplest form, I find two comps (somewhat of a matched pair) that are nearly identical and have sold in the year preceding our date of value. I can then estimate the monthly change in price (as a percentage) and extrapolate accordingly. Table 10-5 and Figure 10-1 illustrate this very straightforward methodology.

TABLE 10-5 Computing Market Conditions Adjustments

	Date of Sale	Price/SF	Adjustment
Subject	1/1/2019		
Comp 1	6/1/2018	$250	
Comp 2	9/1/2018	$255	0.7%

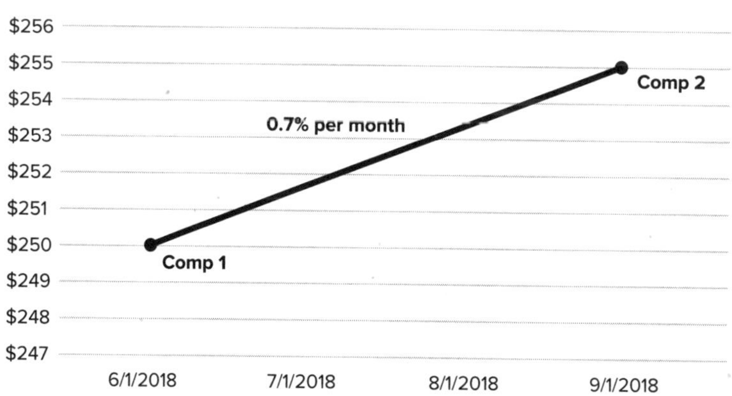

FIGURE 10-1 Market Conditions Adjustment with Two Comps

While two points do mathematically determine a trend line, sometimes real estate data does not conform to the absolutes of math. When I add two more data points—comparables 3 and 4—the 0.7% monthly trend line suddenly does not appear to be correct (Figure 10-2).

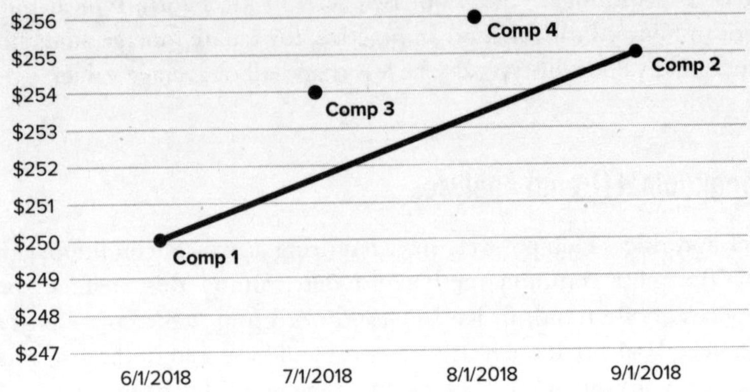

FIGURE 10-2 Market Conditions Adjustment with Additional Comps

The lesson learned here is that the appraiser must often use more than just a single pair of data points to develop these adjustments.

6. Repeat Sales Analysis

This is one of the most powerful tools in the appraiser's arsenal, yet it is often overlooked and misused. Assume that my subject property sold sometime in the recent past, and that there have been no material changes since that sale. (If there have been any changes, I can factor them into my analysis.) I find a few other comps that sold and then resold more recently. I'll reduce these to a price-per-square-foot basis, although in practice it is a bit more complicated. Table 10-6 illustrates this.

I have three comps, each of which sold twice in the past year, and I've averaged the annualized rate of return. This comes to 13.4% annualized. The subject sold for $250 per square foot about 8½ months ago. I adjust the $250 by 13.4% for 8½ months and arrive at $274 per square foot. While this by itself is not an appraisal, it provides an important check for the analysis.

TABLE 10-6 Applications of a Repeat Sales Analysis

	Date of Sale	Price/SF	Annualized	Indicated Value	
Comp 1a	1/1/2018	250			
Comp 1b	2/15/2018	255	16.2%		
Comp 2a	3/15/2018	240			
Comp 3a	3/30/2018	235			
Subject	4/15/2018	250			
Comp 2b	7/1/2018	250	14.1%		
Comp 3b	9/1/2018	245	10.0%		
Today	1/1/2019		13.4%	$274	

There are two very important caveats. First, there is a substantial degree of variation in the annualized returns—from 10% to 16%. However the range of final values is only about 8.5% from low to high.

Second, and this is perhaps most important, during the run-up to the recent mortgage meltdown, rapid-fire sales and resales of residences were often indicative of illegal "flipping." People were buying homes, reselling to colleagues at inflated prices (covered by 100% loan-to-value, frequently fraudulent mortgages), and then walking away with the cash, leaving the investors (the ultimate lenders) holding the bag. An analysis of sales and resales may uncover some very interesting information, particularly if the property's physical condition has changed very little but the prices have skyrocketed outside of the norm.

7. The Sales Adjustment Grid

The actual grid itself is a template for reporting the analysis results. It also makes for a handy illustration and explanation of processes being followed, and a reminder that the transactional issues are dealt with before the physical adjustments are made.

Normally, at least three comps would be used, and the adjustment grid contained on most residential appraisal report forms has space for reporting three comps, plus a continuation sheet for more comps if needed. I will use a simplified illustrative here (see Table 10-7, next page).

Table 10-7 is a continuation of Table 10-1, with space for the first comparable to be analyzed. In practice, an appraiser will probably analyze all of the comps at the same time, since information gleaned from one comparable may influence the analysis of the subsequent ones.

TABLE 10-7 Example of a Sales Adjustment Process

	Comparable 1			
	Subject	**Basis**	**Adjustment**	**Notes**
Price			1,240,000	
Price/SF			238	
Distance from Subject		0.1 mile		
Special Financing?	No	3% seller paid	–37,200	A
Date of Sale/Valuation	1/1/2019	9/30/2018	41,540	B
Location	Above average	Similar		
Rights Appraised/Sold	Fee Simple	Similar		
Lot Size (SF)	9000	9500		C
View	Backs up to open space	Average subdivision view	62,000	D
Design Style	2-story, modern, wood	2.5-story colonial		
Quality of Construction	Above average	similar		
Age	10 years	8 years	–49,600	E
Condition	Average	Above Average	–62,000	F
Total Rooms Above Grade	10	12		
Bathrooms Above Grade	3.5	4	–2,000	G
Bedrooms Above Grade	5	6		
SF Above Grade	4800	5200	–47,692	H
Basement Finished Rooms	2	0		
Basement Finished SF	400	0	23,846	I
Basement Unfinished SF	2000	0	47,692	J
Functional Utility	Average	Average		
Heating/Cooling	Forced air	Similar		
Garage/Carport	3-car garage	4-car garage	–10,000	K
Energy Efficient Items	Modern	Similar		
Other:	Sports court	Swimming pool	–5,000	L
	Bonus room	Bonus room		
	New sound system	Old sound system	1,000	M
	Security system	Similar		
	Updated appliances	Similar		
	200-SF screened porch	None	10,000	N
Net Total Adjustments			–27,414	O
Gross Adjustments %			32%	P
Net Adjustments %			–2%	Q
Adjusted Price			$1,212,825	R

A. The actual price paid for the comp in an arm's-length transaction meeting all of the criteria set forth in the definition of value. For virtually all residential appraisals, the market value of the fee simple interest is the goal. If the occasion calls for some other basis of value, then the comps should conform to that.
B. Comps will precede the subject's date of value, so I will perform a trend analysis to determine the market conditions adjustment. Here I've used data from Table 10-6, adjusted for the three-month difference between the comp sale and the effective date of value. Since the trend line is upward sloping, if all things were equal, the subject is worth a bit more than the comparable.
C. No adjustment was made for the lot size, even though one is somewhat bigger than the other. Recall the discussion about excess and surplus land. In residential subdivisions, it is not uncommon for lots to vary in size. In upscale neighborhoods, the lots may vary widely with negligible impact on value. The exception, of course, is if the lot size difference is so significant that one house enjoys some utility from the larger lot.
D. The subject backs up to open space, which is generally a plus. Even though it was not discussed in the chapter, the appraiser would probably have sought out some matched pairs. Here, I use 5%, measured as a percentage of comp sales price.
E. The comp is slightly newer than the subject. Assuming average maintenance a two-year difference should be equal to about 4% of value. Since the subject is older, the adjustment is negative.
F. Condition and age are tied into one another. The 4% depreciation is based on the fact that the subject is in average condition—it has received average maintenance. The effective comp age is probably much less than eight years due to the above-average condition. While FNMA outlines definitions for categories of condition, it does not specify the actual adjustments to be made. These should be driven by the local market and analyzed by the appraiser on a case-by-case basis. I use a 5% adjustment, which is not unusual.
G. Total rooms and total bedrooms may or may not have an impact on value, depending on the situation. For smaller homes, the difference between three and four bedrooms may be important for marketing purposes, but of course that extra bedroom takes space away from some other rooms in the house. Bathroom count is usually important. I will have measured the differential value between three and a half baths and four full baths. This is actually a bit of a complex measure—the bedroom occupants are enjoying more full

baths, but probably at the expense of a downstairs powder room. If the comp had four and a half baths, the value difference may have been more pronounced.

H. Square footage above grade is often called "heated square footage" or "livable area." Neither term is correct. Total livable area, and total heated area, would include areas in the basement. For purposes of valuation, I break these out into separate categories. Finished basement space is typically worth less than finished space above ground, and unfinished basement space is worth less than that. Here I have estimated the marginal value of a difference in square footage above ground at about half the total price per square foot ($238/2 = $117/SF). Matched pairs analysis is useful here.

I. Determining the marginal value of finished basements can be problematic, even in markets where finished basements are common. Basements are rarely finished to the same quality as the main living areas, and the basement's utility can vary widely ("rec-room" to "utility room" or even "workshop"). In areas where finished basements are uncommon, this may entail simple guesswork and appraiser rules of thumb. In a best-case scenario, I will have some data on local houses with and without basements and can perform a simple analysis (matched pairs, again) to narrow in on the marginal value.

J. Unfinished basements also vary in quality and utility, ranging from unheated but functional utility areas to simple junk storage. The same analyses for finished basements can be used for unfinished.

K. The marginal value of a garage varies across the United States but is almost always a positive contributor to value. Garages may be attached or detached, and they come in various sizes. For upscale homes, larger, attached garages may be a necessity. The garage provides space for certain utility items that would otherwise take up space in the heated area, such as hot water heaters, air handlers for heating/air systems, and storage.

L. So, what is the value difference between a sports court and a swimming pool? In colder climates, the sports court may actually be preferred, because it requires less maintenance and provides a longer period of utility each year. In warmer climates, just the opposite may be true. In recent years, "outdoor living" features have become more and more valuable—outdoor kitchens, covered patios, screened porches, built-in hot tubs, and even more complex outdoor living spaces. Often these spaces are integrated with complex and expensive landscaping. The challenge is to put a contributory value on these features, and to measure the differential contributory value between such features among various different properties.

M. The sound system here is a placeholder for all advanced electronics—simple integrated security and fire detection systems to systems that control the electronic features in a dwelling (including security cameras, sound systems, lighting, heating and cooling, and even opening and closing garage doors via the internet).

N. A screened porch in some markets is a necessity, while in others is a quaint throwback to a bygone era.

O. I now sum the total adjustments—plus and minus. As shown, the net of these adjustments is nearly insignificant and closes to a rounding error.

P. If I take the absolute value of the various adjustments, the sum is quite large. This gross adjustment percentage shows us that, in the aggregate, we have had to make quite a few adjustments—and quite large ones—to reconcile the value of this comparable to the various components of this subject property. Historically, FNMA/FHLMC directed that maximum gross adjustment percentage not exceed 25%, although the agencies recently rescinded that absolute threshold. Above that level, the comparable is perhaps not all that comparable after all.

Q. The net adjustment percentage takes into account the signs of the adjustments (the sum in item O above) and divides by the gross sales price (A above). The FHMA/FHLMC threshold was 15%, before the most recent version of the selling guide.

R. Finally, I have an adjusted value. This, along with other adjusted values from other comps, will be *reconciled* to a final indicated value. Reconciliation is more than just a simple average. Some comps will be better than others, and will be given greater weighting in the final analysis.

8. The Reconciliation

The various comps are *reconciled*. If selected carefully, and the sales adjustment analysis was performed properly and rigorously, the final adjusted values of each of the comps should be very close to one another.

Appraisal standards and methodology are replete with guidance on the reconciliation process. Appraisal standards dictate that the report provide the data used, the methodology followed, and the basis for the conclusions. The reconciliation process needs to be summarized sufficiently that the reader can replicate the work.

Simple averages are generally eschewed. Some sort of weighting is appropriate, since some comps will be more indicative of value than the others. Indeed, for IRS-related appraisals, the comp with the fewest adjustments is generally the one given the most weight.

9. Summary and Key Points

This chapter may seem a bit pedantic—after all, the purpose of this book is not to train real estate appraisers, but rather to help investors and wealthy families understand what an appraisal looks like and how to understand it.

However, the wealthy family is actually likely to run into residential real estate appraisals more frequently than most. Such families are likely to own several properties. While the current US tax laws disfavor loans on personal residences above $1 million, financing up to that level may have a tax advantage. These properties will often be appraised for tax appeals, estate settlements, gifts, and other nonfinancing reasons. It is rare that an upscale residence is "taken" for eminent domain purposes, but these things happen from time to time. Finally, any litigation involving a personal residence will entail some sort of valuation exercise.

More to the point, the sales comparison approach fundamentals set the stage for analysis of investment property. Since a residence is a fairly easy and common example to understand, the tools and techniques can be explored and later applied to all manner of real estate holdings. Single family residences are popular investments themselves, and understanding the valuation nuances is important. Recognize that there was significant room for disagreement, for judgment calls, and for alternative valuation outcomes. Indeed, the comparable featured in Table 10-7 had adjustments totaling 32% of the original purchase price. Within that 32% there are certainly opportunities for alternative determinations and negotiations.

10. A Final Note—Statistical Characteristics

Amazingly enough, there is very little discussion in the literature about the statistical properties of residential appraisals. Since it is a fairly heuristic process, the exercise does not lend itself to the normal statistical outputs one might expect (mean, standard deviation, coefficient of dispersion, etc.). You might consider since an appraisal is supposed to *predict* a sales price, we could conduct a study where a large number of appraisals were compared to the sales prices supposedly predicted to determine the accuracy and reliability of the appraisal exercise.

That has been done, but the answers are somewhat disappointing. An appraisal is supposed to *predict* a sales price, but in most circumstances, the appraiser is aware of the purchase price before beginning the appraisal exercise. Thus, appraisals serve only to *confirm* the preexisting sales price, and the accuracy evaluation falls flat on its face.

Following the recent mortgage meltdown, significant resources were applied to evaluating the due diligence in the mortgage lending process during the housing bubble. The results of this evaluation were disappointing, to say the least. In parallel, the regulatory bodies have instituted new processes to enhance and maintain the integrity of the loan underwriting process. It remains to be seen if these efforts bear fruit.

Two important goals of any statistical evaluation are accuracy and reliability. Reflecting on the exercise in this chapter, the selection and evaluation of comparable 1 appears to result in a fairly accurate determination. The net adjustments are nearly zero (2%), suggesting a level of unbiasedness. This is not to say that higher levels of net adjustments would indicate higher levels of bias, but this at least is a fairly good outcome, albeit one which could be arbitrarily influenced.

The gross adjustments total 32%. This suggests a variation on either side of the mean of 16%. That is not a very good level of deviation and really suggests that the final outcome could have been anywhere in a plus-or-minus 16% range.

Ironically, a high degree of variation is not a bad thing if you are a buyer. This really suggests that there is room for negotiation and room for improvement in the value. In the end, the user is encouraged in the direction of skepticism. How accurate are the results? How much variance is in the final outcome? How much room is there for some change in the results? These are critical questions for any investor to ask in any situation.

11 A Deep Dive into the Sales Comparison Approach: Income Properties

> Real estate is an imperishable asset, ever increasing in value. It is the most solid security that human ingenuity has devised. It is the basis of all security and about the only indestructible security.
>
> —**Russell Sage**

"INCOME PROPERTY" AND "nonresidential property" are often but incorrectly used interchangeably. Not all "nonresidential property" is income producing, and not all "income property" is nonresidential. This begs for a better definition.

Real estate owned for personal purposes—residences, recreational, or even collectible—is not owned for business or investment purposes. Some investment or business property may be owned to support a business, or for long-term capital gains, and thus not held in anticipation of current income. Confounding the problem, as discussed in earlier chapters, residences are popular income-producing investments. With all this confusion, I will use "income" and "residential" as two sides of the valuation coin. *Income properties, for our purposes, are those acquired for business, investment, or other nonpersonal uses.*

This issue may seem trite, but is important for a discussion of sales comparisons and income properties. This approach seeks out recent transactions of comparable property. As noted earlier, the transaction itself must also be comparable. If the transaction (motivations, relationship between or among the parties, financing terms, rights being transferred, market conditions) are materially different, then physical similarities between the subject and comp may be irrelevant. Ironically, though, similarity in the transactional motivation may obviate many physical differences.

Consider two very different office buildings. One is in a less desirable part of town but is bigger and thus produces more income. The smaller one produces less income but is in a more favorable part of the central business district. Both were purchased for investment. The first has a somewhat higher capitalization rate, commensurate with the risk level attached to properties in less desirable locations, while the other has a lower "cap" rate. Through an income analysis, we find that the two properties have nearly identical values. They also have nearly identical transactional features. Are they sufficiently similar to be used as comps for one another, or for a third building being constructed in yet another part of town?

1. Critical Assumptions

The same assumptions that applied to residential property analysis also apply to here, but with one major caveat. Comps used for income property analysis should be *well managed*. This can be a difficult feature to observe or analyze, but it can greatly affect the unadjusted comp price, and hence the indication of value for the subject property.

Recall the important transactional features: motivations, relationship between or among the parties, financing terms, rights being transferred, and market conditions. These are usually assumptions buried in the definition of value. If a residence is not well managed, exactly what does that mean? It may mean the roof has been allowed to fall into disrepair, the yard does not have "curb appeal," the paint is peeling, the window screens are torn, or the hot water heater is overdue for replacement. While in the aggregate, these can have material impact on value, they are easily accounted for under the "conditions" adjustment and generally constitute items of curable, short-lived physical deterioration, the cost of which can be easily obtained.

For an income property, bad management can result in numerous deficiencies not easily valued:

Long-Term Reputational Damage

Consider a badly managed rental building (office, warehouse, apartments, hotel). A Class A or B building becomes B or even C. Recovering the reputational damage can require a massive undertaking, not just curing physical and functional problems but also often a public relations effort. Long-term tenants signed to new leases during the downward slide will be problems until leases renew, and may be reluctant to sign on to higher rents after a physical and reputational rehabilitation. During the remaining lease periods, these tenants will be free riders on the improved building reputation. Some tenants may enjoy a halo effect to their businesses (e.g., lobby restaurants or office tenants who benefit from walk-in trade) without paying the increased rents associated with the cause of the halo.

Domino Effect on the Physical Structure

A badly managed roof leads to leaks, which may lead to structural damage. Failure to adequately inspect systems can result in long-term impacts to the property. Failure to manage ingress and egress to the property, signage, parking, or views may result in encroachment from neighbors that will be difficult to undo. Basement leaks can undermine the physical integrity.

Misstated Expenses

Some mismanagement may include failure to adequately update insurance (leading to irrelevant premiums), failure to manage energy costs, and failure to monitor water usage. A poorly managed building may also have understaffed security and/or parking attendants, or insufficient landscaping. A potential buyer or appraiser cannot trust the expense ledger accuracy.

Transactional Issues

Any appraisal assumes that the comps were transacted in a manner consistent with the value to be determined. If I am trying to determine market value, then the comps should all have transacted in a manner consistent with the definition of market value being used. This usually includes an arm's-length transaction, with no duress, and buyer and seller each acting knowledgeably and prudently. A poorly managed property may not sell that way. Poor management may be indicative of cash flow problems. For example, I recently examined a building that was in very good condition, with good rents and little vacancy. However, the owner was cash-strapped due to problems with other properties and needed to unload this good building in a hurry to solve other cash flow problems. This comp transaction would not at all be evident of market value, since the buyer, having learned the seller's plight, took full advantage of the situation.

In selecting comps, I have to be assured that the comps were well managed and the transaction performed by competent sellers not acting under duress. This can be a time-consuming and expensive bit of due diligence;

in residential valuation, this may not be worth the effort. When appraising income properties, the difference can be substantial and well worth the underlying effort.

> This investigation may lead the investor in a very different direction. An appraisal may reveal other properties on the market that are better deals due to bad management.

The extent to which a comp is badly managed, or managed to less than maximum productivity, will be reflected in the transaction price. In a perfect world, the comp price reflects the market value (if it was well managed) minus the cost to cure the problems resulting from less-than-stellar management, and also minus a deduction for the hassle factor. Actual prices are sometimes a bit higher than this because value-seeking bidders look for these properties, and often compete against one another, in the end actually overpaying for bad properties. Beware of supposed turnaround deals in hot markets with lots of buyers.

2. Quantitative Analysis

Assume I am appraising a 300-acre parcel of agricultural land for an investor who wants long-term income and stable capital growth. The tract is relatively well shaped, with good topography and no intervening problems (such as ditches, cell phone towers, fences, or odd angles) that will inhibit the efficient planting or harvesting of crops. The land fronts on an agricultural farm-to-market road, which also services many nearby farms. There are plenty of farmers in the region who will rent the land on a long-term basis at market rates, and indeed the land is currently rented. I have found four nearby tracts of 250, 500, 1,000, and 500 acres that have sold recently. These sales are considered to be market-value, arm's-length transactions, with no unusual financing, no burdensome leases (all are leased at fair market rents), and no odd transactional problems.

To begin the valuation exercise, I array the subject and the four comps on a table (Table 11-1).

Well, now, that's an interesting situation. The price per acre for these comps ranges from $10,000 to $11,000 per acre, a 10% variance. I know that prices will vary over time, but Comps 1 and 2, which transacted within

TABLE 11-1 Comps for Simple Agricultural Land Example

	Subject	Comp 1	Comp 2	Comp 3	Comp 4
Price		2,500,000	5,500,000	10,800,000	5,200,000
Date of Value	1-Jan-19	1-Oct-18	30-Sep-18	1-Jul-18	31-Mar-18
Proximity to Subject		1.3 miles	1.5 miles	2 miles	1.3 miles
Size (Acres)	300	250	500	1,000	500
Price/Acre		10,000	11,000	10,800	10,400

a day of one another, vary by the widest margin. Noting that Comp 1 is half the size of Comp 2, I might infer a size adjustment is needed, but I do not yet have all the data needed to compute that. Also, I have two comps, Comp 2 and Comp 4, which are the same size but transacted on different dates. Thus, I can easily solve for the time adjustment, assuming that market conditions change over time is linear, as shown in Figure 11-1.

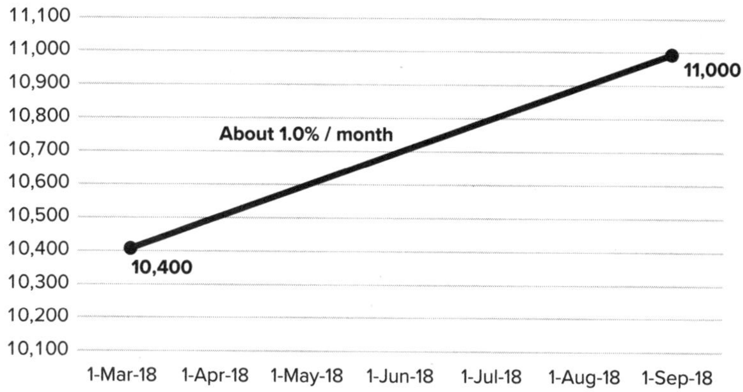

FIGURE 11-1 Market Conditions Adjustment with Two Comps

The market conditions adjustment—the time trend—appears to be about 1% per month. (By the way, this would actually be an abnormally high trend in agricultural land prices, but I use this for illustrative purposes. In practice, an upward trend of just a few percent per year would be exceptionally high.) With this, I can adjust prices to the current market and begin examining the differences in price relative to size. Table 11-2 begins that process.

TABLE 11-2 Time Adjusted Price per Acre

	Subject	Comp 1	Comp 2	Comp 3	Comp 4
Price		2,500,000	5,500,000	10,800,000	5,200,000
Date of Value	1-Jan-19	1-Oct-18	30-Sep-18	1-Jul-18	31-Mar-18
Proximity to Subject		1.3 miles	1.5 miles	2 miles	1.3 miles
Size (Acres)	300	250	500	1,000	500
Value/Acre		10,000	11,000	10,800	10,400
Time Adjusted Price/Acre		10,300	11,330	11,448	11,336

I can rearrange these a bit and examine the trend in prices relative to property size, as shown in Figure 11-2.

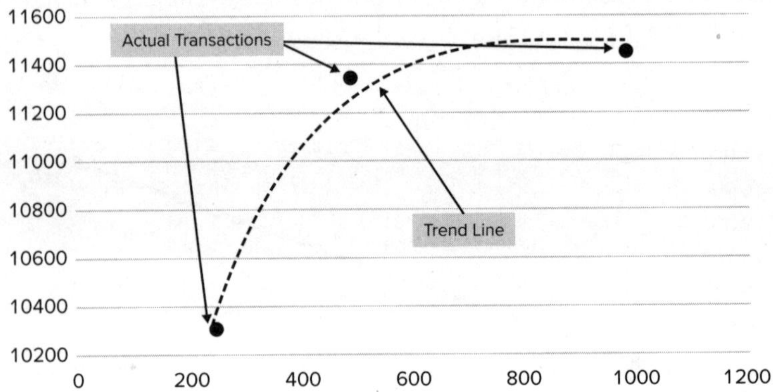

FIGURE 11-2 Price Versus Parcel Size

The size trend is certainly not linear. There appears to be a significant benefit to larger parcels up to about 500 acres, and then a smaller but positive benefit above 500 acres. Why might this be? For farming, in this particular situation, there may be an optimum size for local crops. Below a certain size field, the fixed cost of moving equipment and people may not be worth the effort. It would appear that 500 acres seems to optimize the size constraint, although there is certainly some economy of scale for larger tracts.

Advanced economics classes discuss the notion that economies of scale can actually turn negative—after a point, larger is not better due to management, finance, logistics, and marketing constraints. The same is true for agricultural tracts and is coupled with the issues associated with crop management. There are simply only so many acres a tractor can plow in a day!

My subject is 300 acres, which puts it on a portion of the curve between the 250- and 500-acre comps. The curve is nearly linear at this point, so I can simplify the problem and just extrapolate the per-acre value between these two points. Equation 11-1 shows one way of solving this, although there are other equally good ways to calculate this adjustment:

$$\left(\frac{300-250}{500-250}\right)(11{,}333)+\left(\frac{500-300}{500-250}\right)(10{,}300)=10{,}507 \qquad \textbf{EQUATION 11-1}$$

I use $11,333 as the price point for the 500-acre tracts as the average of the adjusted comp prices. I can add this to the trend line in Figure 11-3 and see that the adjusted price for our subject tract seems to make sense:

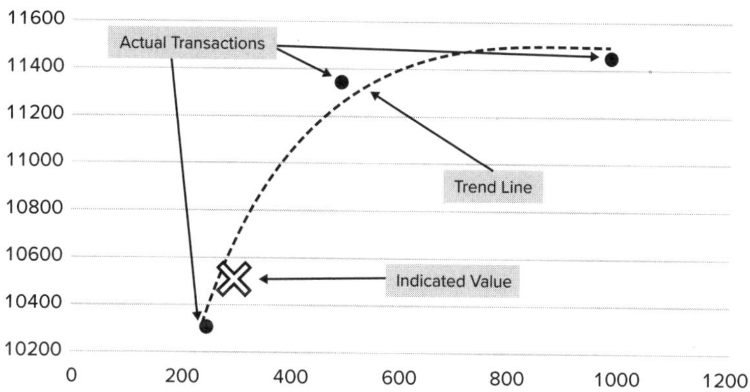

FIGURE 11-3 Indicated Value

A *very* close examination of Figure 11-3 suggest that the linear extrapolation may slightly understate the value, although by less than about 1%. Perhaps $10,600 is closer to the truth. Thus, the value of this proposed acquisition is about 300 × 10,600 = $3,180,000.

This admittedly simplified example is indicative of issues using the sales comparison approach to value income properties. Different types of income properties have different indicia of value. Common traits, beyond the transactional issues, include:

- Location
- Land size (with an eye to excess and surplus land)
- Improvements size (considering various types of improvements)
- Age of improvements
- Parking structures and sizes
- Convenience of ingress and egress
- Topography
- Air and subterranean rights
- Quality of construction
- Condition of improvements
- Functionality
- Nature of existing leases

Apartments may also be compared on the basis of curable physical deterioration (particularly carpets and appliances), on-site or nearby recreation, on-site or in-unit laundry facilities, and the mix of apartment type (bedroom, bathroom, and size count). The nature and existence of security is important—is there some on-site or nearby staff on call and making regular rounds of the facility? Industrial properties vary according to the main floor elevation (are the loading docks at-grade or elevated for ease of truck access?), the roll-up door sizes (at least 16 feet high is usually a standard), the nature and quality of on-site office space, ingress and egress for trucks, and the availability of electric power and other needed utilities.

The search for and analysis of comparables lets the investor see how the subject property fits into the market. Ease and simplicity of adjustments suggests that the investment fits well and will probably be easy to market and eventually resell. Problems with these adjustments suggest that the subject may be unique in some way. This has positive and negative implications, and should be considered in that light. A unique property may meet an unmet demand in the marketplace. Conversely, a unique property may be aimed at a demand that does not exist.

3. Qualitative Adjustments

Going back to my agricultural land example, I ascertained ahead of time that the tract had good topography, with no noteworthy obstructions that would interfere with the ease of cultivation and harvesting. In practice these simplifying assumptions rarely come true. A leisurely drive through the countryside demonstrates that farmland has telephone poles, ditches, interspersed trees or rocks, or irregular shapes. These give farmers problems plowing and planting straight rows, and can materially interfere with harvesting. These problem tracts will be somewhat more difficult to rent, and will probably bring a slightly lower rental rate. Similar barriers to easy rental or use exist for all types of income properties.

But how do I quantify this? If the tract in question already has a good rental history, then this can be compared to other tracts with known rental rates and purchase prices. The capitalized difference in net rents forms the basis of quantitative adjustments. Of course, properties do not always have good, clean rental histories, and cap rates can be tricky to pin down. The subject may have to be rank-ordered among comps to determine just how the subject fits in the scheme of things.

Let's look at another tract of agricultural land, with adjusted comparable prices per acre as shown in Table 11-3.

TABLE 11-3 Size Adjusted Prices of Comparables

	Subject	Comp 1	Comp 2	Comp 3	Comp 4
Price		2,500,000	5,500,000	12,000,000	6,000,000
Date of Value	1-Jan-19	1-Oct-18	30-Sep-18	1-Jul-18	31-Mar-18
Proximity to Subject		1.3 miles	1.5 miles	2 miles	1.3 miles
Size (Acres)	300	250	500	1000	500
Value/Acre		10,000	11,000	12,000	12,000
Time Adjusted Value/Acre	10,600	10,300	11,330	12,720	13,080
Size Adjustment		2.9%	−6.9%	−10.0%	−6.9%
Size Adjusted Value/Acre	10,600	10,600	10,550	11,450	12,175

This completely throws our nice, neat analysis into disarray. The two 500-acre parcels have wildly different prices per acre, and one has a price per acre far above the 1,000-acre parcel. In Table 11-4, I explore these prices a bit further and arrive at some additional facts about the comparables in question. The new observations are all qualitatively measured with reference to the subject property.

TABLE 11-4 Comparables with Qualitative Factors

	Subject	Comp 1	Comp 2	Comp 3	Comp 4
Price		2,500,000	5,500,000	12,000,000	6,000,000
Date of Value	1-Jan-19	1-Oct-18	30-Sep-18	1-Jul-18	31-Mar-18
Proximity to Subject		1.3 miles	1.5 miles	2 miles	1.3 miles
Size (Acres)	300	250	500	1000	500
Value/Acre		10,000	11,000	12,000	12,000
Time Adjusted Price/Acre	10,600	10,300	11,330	12,720	13,080
Size Adjustment		2.9%	–6.9%	–10.0%	–6.9%
Size Adjusted Price/Acre	10,600	10,600	10,550	11,450	12,175
Shape/ Topography		Equal	Equal	Superior	Superior
Location		Superior	Inferior	Superior	Superior
Soil Quality		Inferior	Superior	Equal	Superior
Water Rights		Equal	Equal	Superior	Superior

The first big question arising from these subjective factors concerns the rank ordering. Do all factors have equal weighting, or do some factors have more influence than others? In many situations, weighting will become evident in the analysis. Another important question concerns the span of qualitative factors—did I get everything? Am I missing an important factor? Usually, this is answered by using local or specialized experts to aid in the assessment. If such experts are unavailable, the data may often speak for itself, and a survey of local market participants will prove exceedingly useful. A critical issue—and perhaps investment opportunity—arises when the data does not speak for itself. When there is unmet demand, transactional data may evidence buyers "settling" for second-best choices because first choices simply do not exist. Survey research has proven invaluable for plumbing the depths of local market demand.

In Table 11-5, we begin the process of rank-ordering our subject and the comparables and assigning heuristically weighted adjustment factors.

These adjustments arise from the data in much the same way the solutions to a set of simultaneous equations might be solved. It appears that water rights are somewhat more valuable, but a very superior shape/topography of a property can also be extremely valuable. Individually, the adjustments are not very large, but cumulatively they make a material impact on the price.

TABLE 11-5 Qualitative Adjustments

	Subject	Comp 1	Comp 2	Comp 3	Comp 4
Size Adjusted Price/Acre	10,600	10,600	10,550	11,450	12,175
Shape/Topography		equal	equal	superior	v. sup
Adjustment				*−2%*	*−5%*
Location		superior	inferior	superior	superior
Adjustment		*−2%*	*2%*	*−2%*	*−2%*
Soil quality		inferior	superior	equal	superior
Adjustment		*2%*	*−2%*		*−2%*
Water rights		equal	equal	superior	superior
Adjustment				*−4%*	*−4%*
Adjusted Price/Acre	10,600	10,600	10,550	10,534	10,592.25

The use of agricultural land in these examples has been purely for purposes of simplification. The methodologies are applicable to all types of commercial or income-producing properties. The key lesson from this section is that qualitative factors, which are not easily quantified, can nonetheless have an important impact on the value of investment property. Understanding how these qualitative factors work and interplay can uncover hidden investment opportunities. In the preceding example, superior water rights had a significant impact on value. If such water rights can be negotiated or acquired inexpensively, then property value can materially increase. If an office building has side-street frontage, acquiring a parcel giving the building frontage on a major arterial may be key to changing the building from Class B to Class A. Enhanced landscaping, painting, or decorating may significantly improve the value of a hotel or apartment building. A neighborhood shopping center can be vastly improved by retopping and painting the parking lot, installing new lighting, redemising inadequate spaces, and enhancing signage. These qualitative factors can be identified in the appraisal and can be used to the investor's advantage.

4. What Constitutes a Comparable?

With residential properties, a comp is more or less obvious—another similarly situated residence. Appraisal standards seem to be directed more at residential comparable selection than at nonresidential situations. Even courses taught by authoritative bodies, such as the Appraisal Institute, tend to deal more with *what to do* with the comps than *how to find them*.

The Yellow Book standards, discussed later in the text, actually give some excellent guidance for finding and selecting comps. The Yellow Book is written for appraisals in federal acquisition situations, but it can be informative in a number of situations. One often-overlooked source of a comparable is a prior sale of the subject itself. There are four governing caveats to the use of such a prior sale:

- The sale needs to be relatively recent. Depreciation plus nonlinearity in market conditions trends may make older sales difficult to extrapolate. Notably, *USPAP* actually *requires* an appraisal to report and analyze any prior sale within the past three years. The Yellow Book requires reporting and considering *any* prior sale, regardless of time frame.
- There should be minimal physical changes in the property over time. If economically material physical changes can be priced and modeled, the sale can still be considered.
- Applicable market conditions (price trends) over the ensuing period should be easily modeled.
- The conditions of the prior sale (sale conditions, financing terms, value transacted, legal rights transacted) are all the same as today or are differences known and easily priced.

As for other comps selected, the governing criteria is generally the highest and best use. Even experienced appraisers can get tripped up over this requirement, since the current use of a comparable may not be its highest and best use. This is particularly problematic with marginal properties. Class C offices, apartments, hotels, and other commercial properties may actually have an HBU (highest and best use) as continued use for the economically foreseeable future. Conversely, a nearly identical comp, but located in a superior location, may have an HBU for near-term or immediate teardown or renovation into some other use. The use of this teardown comparable would give a misleading subject value indication.

Comp selection must consider forced sales, distressed sales, litigation or other settlement negotiations, non-arm's-length sales (sales between related parties or entities), and sales involving condemning authorities. Comp selection should also be wary of assemblage sales, where a highly motivated buyer is anxious, usually for financial reasons, to buy a particular parcel. One obvious assemblage situation is the acquisition of the last tract, or last few tracts, to agglomerate a site for subsequent development or redevelopment. Any sale involving next-door or nearby parties may be suspect. Financing terms should also be investigated carefully.

Once these HBU and transactional issues are ascertained, the comparable selection process really falls to three criteria:

- The physical similarity
- The locational similarity
- The recentness of the transaction

For simple properties, such as warehouses, simple apartment buildings or complexes, or Class B or C offices, a direct physical comparison is often adequate. For more complex properties, such as Class A offices, full-service or convention hotels, or high-end luxury apartments, finding adequate comps will be problematic, and the adjustments process will be complex.

Items of comparison will include the size of the site and the improvements and particularly the components, such as parking versus office, retail on the ground floor, and in the case of shopping centers, the mix of tenant pads. Energy certification (LEED, EnergyStar) has become increasingly important. The ability to expand or renovate the property (the current use versus the legally permissible use) may be a factor. Environmental issues and environmental risks are critically important, since nonresidential property owners may, in some circumstances, be liable for past or current actions of third parties.

Easements will also be of interest, and may work in both directions. A comp that is the grantor of an easement to another party will be evaluated for the burdens placed by that easement. Conversely, a comp that depends on an easement for use (common ingress/egress, common parking, common demising walls, etc.) will be evaluated accordingly.

Additional factors in the comparable selection process may include:

- Build-to-suit: the structure was built to the specifications of a particular owner or user
- Deed restrictions
- Deferred maintenance
- Ground lease (both grantor and grantee)
- Historical significance
- Tenant has net versus gross lease
- Options held by tenants or third parties
- Partial interests
- Sale-leaseback considerations
- Shell conditions versus tenant improvements
- Single tenant versus multitenant
- Long-term versus short-term leases

In short, the issues surrounding comparable selection are complex and varied. For simple properties, such as unimproved or agricultural land, simple improved properties, and single use properties, the sales comparison approach is extremely useful, applicable, and straightforward. As properties become more complex, the appraisal will rely more heavily on the income approach and some cost approach tools.

5. Specialized Properties and Topics

> Even though income and cost methods may be preferred for more complex or specialized properties, the sales comparison approach and the sales adjustment grid will almost always be a facet. It is deeply entrenched in appraisal tradition, and indeed would be expected by users even when it contributes little to the final reconciled value conclusion.

Shopping Malls and Other Retail

According to the most recent statistics from the International Council of Shopping Centers (ICSC), there are currently over 115,000 shopping centers in the United States, aggregating over 7.5 billion square feet. The most common categories are shown in Table 11-6.

TABLE 11-6 US Retail

	Number	Average Size (SF)	Segment Share
Superregional Malls	620	1,255,382	10.2%
Regional Malls	600	589,659	4.7%
Community Centers	9,776	197,509	25.4%
Neighborhood Centers	32,588	71,827	30.8%
Strip/Convenience	68,936	13,218	12.0%
Specialty Centers			
Power Center	2,258	438,628	13.0%
Lifestyle Centers	491	335,852	2.2%
Factory Outlet Malls	367	238,060	1.2%
Theme/Festival	159	147,791	0.3%
Limited Purpose			
Airport Retail Centers	62	249,240	0.2%

One challenge valuing a shopping center is disentangling the business value from the real estate value. Smaller centers—such as neighborhood and community shopping centers—tend to be pure real estate investments. Conversely, large superregional malls, with complex leases and large, national anchor tenants, have more complex nonrealty components.

Simple shopping centers can be effectively valued using a few comps, assuming those comps are reasonably similarly situated, draw on similar markets, and are demised in similar fashion. Table 11-7 draws from an actual appraisal of a simple small strip center servicing a neighborhood in a small town. It is a one-story, 7,888-square-foot structure, renovated to like-new condition in 2010, sitting on about a quarter acre of land. It is demised into six units. The basis for comparison is price per square foot, which is normal for small retail, industrial, and office properties. The appraisal's effective date is January 1, 2019.

TABLE 11-7 Simple Retail Example

	Comp 1	Comp 2	Comp 3	Comp 4
Price/SF	247.50	168.75	183.84	171.01
Sale Date	March 2018	Nov 2018	Jan 2017	Sept 2017
Months	10	2	24	16
Time Adjustment/Yr	3%	3%	3%	3%
Time Adjustment/Mo	0.25%	0.25%	0.25%	0.25%
Total Time Adjustment	2.50%	0.50%	6.00%	4.00%
Time Adjusted Price	253.69	169.59	194.87	177.85
Qualitative Adjustments				
Location	5%	5%	0%	5%
Access/Exposure	0%	0%	0%	5%
Parking	–10%	0%	0%	0%
Size	0%	5%	5%	5%
Const Quality	–5%	0%	0%	0%
Age/Condition	0%	0%	–5%	0%
Finish	–5%	0%	0%	0%
Total Adjustments	–15%	10%	0%	15%
Adjusted Price/SF	215.63	186.55	194.87	204.53
Simple Average	200.40			
Units Used	194.87			
Subject Size	7,888			
Indicated Value	1,537,135			
Rounded	1,550,000			

My indicated value is not a simple average of adjusted prices, but relies more heavily on the indication from Comp 3. This comp has the fewest adjustments, although it was the oldest among the four. Other than market conditions (time), all adjustments are determined qualitatively, rather than quantitatively. In practice, for a small non-investment-grade retail property, this is exactly what the sales adjustment grid will look like. For larger, investment-grade properties, more comparables will probably be used, but to basically the same end.

Apartments

According to the most recent statistics, there are about 43 million tenant-occupied dwellings in America, slightly over 31% of the total housing stock. The combination of systemic growth in the population plus the decline in the homeownership rate (from a peak of nearly 69% down to about 63%) means that the demand for apartments has soared recently. After accounting for rental houses, duplexes, triplexes, and fourplexes (all of which are "residential" for valuation purposes), and subtracting mobile homes, this leaves about 21 million apartments, or 17.3% the US housing. According to the National Multifamily Housing Council, citing HUD statistics, there are currently about 684,000 apartment buildings in America. Seven metro areas in America have over one million apartments: New York, Los Angeles, Chicago, Dallas, Houston, Washington, and Miami.

Table 11-8 shows a sample sales adjustment grid, taken from an actual apartment appraisal. The basis of comparison is price per unit, rather than price per square foot, but apartment size is a basis for a qualitative adjustment in the grid. This particular investment has 32 units contained in four two-story buildings situated on 1.25 acres, or a fairly typical 26 units per acre. The buildings were constructed in 1950 but renovated in 1998 and have enjoyed average maintenance. The property is near the middle of its economic life. If the buildings' "bones" are in good shape, then they will probably be renovated regularly and enjoy such tax and financing breaks as may be available from time to time.

Gross living area is 31,680, and net rentable space is 28,800. The difference includes common and access areas, such as stairwells, hallways, and utility spaces. The average apartment is 900 square feet, and has two bedrooms, one bath, central heating and air conditioning, and separate utility metering. Every apartment has off-street, paved, uncovered parking. Everything is considered functionally adequate and comparable to the market. Average rent is $867/month per apartment, and all units are currently occupied. These are all important points of comparison with other comparable apartment transactions. The landlord collects about $12,000 per year in water reimbursements, laundry, and late fees.

I used five comparable apartment transactions, which are summarized in Table 11-8, and the sales adjustment grid in Table 11-9.

TABLE 11-8 Apartment Comps

Comp #	Date of Sale	Sale Price	No. of Units	Price/Unit
1	June 2018	9,500,000	82	115,854
2	Oct 2018	800,000	9	88,889
3	Jan 2018	1,160,000	17	68,235
4	April 2018	855,000	12	71,250
5	Dec 2017	1,681,000	18	93,389

TABLE 11-9 Apartment Sales Adjustment Grid

	Comp 1	Comp 2	Comp 3	Comp 4	Comp 5
Price/Unit	115,854	88,889	68,235	71,250	93,389
Date of Sale	June 2018	Oct 2018	Jan 2018	April 2018	Dec 2017
Months	7	3	12	9	13
Time Adjustment/Yr	6.0%	6.0%	6.0%	6.0%	6.0%
Time Adjustment/ Month	0.5%	0.5%	0.5%	0.5%	0.5%
Total Time Adjustment	3.5%	1.5%	6.0%	4.5%	6.5%
Time Adjusted Price	119,909	90,222	72,329	74,456	99,459
Adjustments					
Location	0%	5%	0%	5%	0%
Size	–10%	10%	5%	10%	5%
Quality	–5%	5%	10%	10%	0%
Age	0%	5%	10%	5%	0%
Unit Size & Mix	–5%	–5%	10%	10%	0%
Condition	0%	–5%	0%	0%	0%
Total Adjustments	–20%	15%	35%	40%	5%
Adjusted Price/ Unit	95,927	103,756	97,644	104,239	104,432
Average Price/ Unit	101,200				
Value Used	104,432				
Total Units	32				
Indicated Value	3,341,832				
Rounded	$3,350,000				

This sales adjustment grid raises several interesting points. I made separate adjustments for size and average unit size/mix. The former deals with the fact that Comp 1 has 82 units. That means there are significant economies of scale, probably reflected in the price. Comps 1 and 2 have a negative adjustment for unit size and mix. This is a combination of the average unit size plus the number of bedrooms and bathrooms. A variation in the offering (number of bedrooms, number of bathrooms) gives a landlord more flexibility.

While Comp 1 might have been sufficiently large to attract the attention of an institutional investor, the others will probably be owned by smaller, locally based landlords. Apartments in tertiary cities can be acquired for fairly small investments and managed effectively and efficiently for a "buy and hold" investor.

Industrial Buildings

Investors purchase these either for long-term income or to facilitate family-owned businesses. Warehouses come in several configurations, although the newer ones, which are most popular with investors, are "tilt-up concrete walls" with high ceilings, raised loading docks, and high loading doors. Key elements of comparison include the percentage and quality of office space, the paved turnaround area for trucks, electrical utilities, clear ceilings, and optimum site use. In any given market, there are optimum sizes, with larger generally being preferred over smaller.

Table 11-10 illustrates a typical sales adjustment grid for an investment-grade warehouse. This 146,342-square-foot (rentable area) steel-frame and steel-clad constructed warehouse has 14,900 square feet (9.9%) of office space. The warehouse site is about 6.7 acres, proximate to major highways near a large metropolitan area. The warehouse has a clear internal ceiling height of 24 feet, and the roof appears to be in good condition. There are 15 large loading docks with truck-height loading bays. The warehouse is 100% wet sprinklered. The site is adequate for 150 auto parking spaces and space for up to 20 trucks to park when not at the loading bays. These are all issues of importance when selecting comps.

I have also computed the gross adjustments, mainly to note that there are relatively few adjustments for Comp 6, which is also the closest in size to the subject. As a result, I weighted this one twice as much as the other five comparable transactions. This has a slight impact on value—about $200,000. Clearly the validity of this shift in value needs to be further analyzed in the income and cost approaches.

TABLE 11-10 Warehouse Sales Adjustment Grid

	Comp 1	Comp 2	Comp 3	Comp 4	Comp 5	Comp 5
Sales Price	7,156,800	6,000,000	5,192,400	8,950,000	6,541,500	13,500,000
Gross Rentable Area	100,000	80,000	74,172	104,000	71,500	175,700
Price/SF	71.57	75.00	70.00	86.06	91.49	76.84
Date of Sale	Aug 2018	March 2018	Aug 2018	Sept 2018	July 2018	Feb 2018
Months	5	10	5	4	6	11
Time Adj/Yr	5.0%	5.0%	5.0%	5.0%	5.0%	5.0%
Time Adj/Month	0.4%	0.4%	0.4%	0.4%	0.4%	0.4%
Total Time Adj	2.1%	4.2%	2.1%	1.7%	2.5%	4.6%
Time Adj Price/Unit	73.06	78.13	71.46	87.49	93.78	80.36
Adjustments						
Location	0%	0%	0%	–15%	–15%	0%
Clear Ceilings	5%	5%	10%	5%	5%	0%
Land/Building Ratio	–10%	0%	5%	0%	0%	5%
Property Size	–5%	–10%	–10%	–5%	–10%	0%
Age/Condition	0%	0%	0%	0%	0%	0%
Net Adjustments	–10%	–5%	5%	–15%	–20%	5%
Gross Adjustments	20%	15%	25%	25%	30%	5%
Adjusted Price/SF	65.75	74.22	75.04	74.37	75.02	84.38
Average Price/Unit	74.80					
Value Used	76.16					
Total Units	146,342					
Indicated Value	11,145,990					
Rounded	11,145,000					

Billboards

Recent IRS decisions have broadened the definition of real estate, particularly for REITs and other tax-advantaged investments. Billboards are an example of a category that may now be called "real estate" even though the asset may be a fixture attached to something that the investor does not own. Continuous increases in automobile traffic and demands for advertising opportunities have increased the demand for billboard space. These assets are regularly bought and sold and have become more and more popular among investors.

Elements of comparison include the placement of the sign unit itself, the road side when viewed from a vehicle (same side or opposite), the distance from traffic when the sign is viewed, the sign angle and the road traffic, whether the sign is viewed by traffic and/or pedestrians, the type of street or roadway, and the sign's physical features (illumination, size, and height above grade). These ratings are outlined by the Traffic Audit Bureau (TAB) for Media Measurement, a trade association of sign companies. TAB also gathers data on cost per thousand impressions, reported by the sign companies. Other key components include annual average daily traffic count (AADT) at a particular location and daily effective circulation (DEC). The former is usually available from state or local authorities. The latter is the number of persons age 18 or older in vehicles passing and potentially exposed to the sign. DEC and TAB ratings are used somewhat interchangeably to measure the quality and comparability of a sign, although in recent years, TAB has come into more favor in the industry.

> Billboards may be owned in fee simple or may be leaseholds. Comparing the value will be difficult and will require a detailed understanding of the underlying leases.

Hotels

According to a 2015 study for the American Hotel and Lodging Association, there are about 54,200 hotels, motels, casino hotels, and other lodging facilities in the United States with a total of 4.6 million rooms. On any given night, 65.5% of those rooms are occupied, generating $245 billion per year in revenues and taxes. From 2005 to 2015, the number of hotels in America grew by 1% per year.

Hotels sell regularly, but are a valuation challenge even for the most experienced in the field. A given hotel appraisal will have several components, including land, improvements, tangible personal property, and intangible business value. This latter component can be further disentangled to include the "flag" value (the franchise), related businesses (convention, conference, bar and restaurant, parking) and third-party leases within the hotel. Hotels are generally divided into vertical categories, such as limited service, extended stay, full-service, and luxury. Even those categories have graduations. Some full-service hotels have valet parking and full-time bell service, while others do not. Increasingly, limited service hotels are offering food and beverages. Lately, some terms such as "select service," "boutique hotels," and "historic inn" have entered the lexicon.

Hotel valuation is usually on a per-room basis within the given category. If I can find several comparable hotels that have sold in comparable markets recently, under comparable terms and conditions, then the price per room *within that category* may give some indication of the subject's value range.

A key element to hotel valuation is market delineation. Markets are ranked and rated by *revenue per available room*, or RevPAR. Thus, a limited service hotel in a high RevPAR market may sell for a higher multiple per room than a full-service or even luxury hotel in a low RevPAR market.

Tables 11-10 and 11-11 illustrate an appraisal of a midsized, full-service hotel under renovation in a major market near a busy airport. When completed, the hotel will have 340 rooms, about 300,000 square feet of usable area, on a 16-acre site, located in a manner complementary to the airport (as an "airport hotel"). The site is adequate for parking and other necessary services (trash collection in the rear, average landscaping, and signage). Renovations were estimated to be about halfway complete. The hotel will be "flagged" with a major, well-known brand. Comps are all currently operating hotels and indicate value at completion and stabilization. As with comparable properties, the hotel will feature a restaurant and bar, conference center and meeting rooms, and an indoor pool and gym. A typical room will have about 420 square feet.

By the way, the term for hotel rooms is "keys." The subject will have 340 keys. While the simple average across the five comps is about $182,000 per key, I place the most emphasis on the value from Comp 3, which has the fewest adjustments. The adjusted prices per key very widely—over 100% from lowest to highest. As such, the income approach (not shown here) will provide the best indication of value.

TABLE 11-11 Hotel Sales Adjustment Grid

	Comp 1	Comp 2	Comp 3	Comp 4	Comp 5
Sales Price (000)	105,000	28,500	25,250	13,350	16,000
No. of Rooms	422	150	160	122	191
Price/Unit	248,815	190,000	157,813	109,426	83,770
Date of Sale	July, 2016	Jan, 2017	July, 2017	May, 2017	Nov, 2017
Months	30	24	18	20	14
Time Adj/Yr	3.0%	3.0%	3.0%	3.0%	3.0%
Time Adj/Month	0.3%	0.3%	0.3%	0.3%	0.3%
Total Time Adj	7.5%	6.0%	4.5%	5.0%	3.5%
Time Adj Price/Unit	267,476	201,400	164,914	114,898	86,702
Sale Adjustments					
Non-Arm's-Length			25%		
Expend After Sale					21,000,000
Adjusted Price/Unit	267,476	201,400	206,143	114,898	196,649
Adjustments					
Location	–15%	–15%	–15%	25%	–15%
No. of Rooms	5%	–5%	–5%	–5%	–5%
Amenities	0%	0%	15%	15%	0%
Adjusted Price/Unit	240,729	161,120	195,835	155,112	157,319
Net Adjustments	–10%	–20%	–5%	35%	–20%
Average Price/Unit	182,023				
Value Used	195,835				
Total Units	340				
Indicated Value	66,584,053				
Rounded	66,585,000				

6. Reconciliation and Summary

In each valuation example, most physical adjustment determinations were made qualitatively, although applied quantitatively. In a perfect world, the appraiser would be able to triangulate in on a central indication of value, but this is rarely the case. This would presume that the appraiser is able to develop a model spanning the materially large components of value, and that each buyer in the market values each of those components in the same way. In larger, more complex models—such as regressions—the law of large numbers ameliorates the idiosyncratic noise in the individual transactions. As such, when dealing with a handful of comparable transactions and attempting to value complex, expensive investments, the appraiser must rely on judgment, experience, and knowledge of specialized transactions.

The comps with the fewest adjustments are usually the most indicative of value or weighted more heavily than the others. Simple comp averages are rarely acceptable. As such, this methodology is replete with assumptions and heuristic adjustments.

So, why do it at all? If other approaches to value are more indicative, then why go through this exercise? The simple fact is that no individual approach is without assumptions and expert judgment. Even if little weight is placed on one approach in the final reconciliation, it still provides support for the other approaches. This "also ran" approach may provide interesting information and potentially useful investment tips and opportunities. The sales comparison approach applies information gleaned from the market analysis, and shows how the subject fits into the competitive landscape. It may also provide information on rents, expenses, and sales prices useful in an income analysis, or provide raw land data necessary for a cost analysis.

Lenders expect to see a sales comparison approach in any appraisal, regardless of how much emphasis is placed on it. Similarly, the sales comparison approach is extremely useful when appealing property taxes, dealing with an eminent domain situation or a zoning ordinance problem, or when plumbing the market depths for a potential property sale. In any situation, though, the sales comparison approach gives a very granular synopsis of the competitive landscape.

7. A Final Note—More on Fee Simple, Leased Fee, and Leasehold Estates

As discussed previously, there are three common bundles of rights transacted in real estate. While there are many other combinations of ownership and occupancy rights, these three are the most common in commercial real estate.

The fee simple estate is the most complete bundle of rights available in America. It does not mean that the property is unencumbered, but only that the property owner is reimbursed at market rates for such an encumbrance. If you own a warehouse, but lease it to a tenant at market rates, then the value of your ownership is the present value of future net rents (net operating income) plus the present value of reversion at lease end. The sum should equal the fee simple value as if unencumbered, even if the discount rates are different. The amount of rent charged for the tenancy should be set in such a way that the values are equalized.

> In the world of rational expectations, a tenant would pay no more for occupancy than they would to acquire ownership, minus the reversion value at lease end. Thus, gross market rents and cost of ownership are related to one another.

What if the tenant has a long-term, below-market lease? Expectations of market rent increases may have been underestimated at the time the lease was signed. Owners of multitenant properties may want to attract anchor tenants who will attract customers to other businesses. The per-square-foot rent for a grocery anchor in a community or neighborhood shopping center is a fraction of what is paid by the smaller tenants. From a tenant's perspective, possession of such a lease carries with it a value, referred to as a *leasehold estate.* The leasehold value is the difference between the net present value of a market lease and the net present value at the actual, existing lease. The landlord has an asset which is worth somewhat less than the fee simple interest. We call that the *leased fee interest.*

Sales comparison examples in this chapter were taken from actual appraisals. Many of those appraisals were for the *leased fee interest* rather than the *fee simple.* The comps used were transactions of occupied properties. The biggest difference would come in the income analysis. The leased fee income analysis would depend on actual contract rents rather than attempting to ascertain market rents.

If the difference between contract rents and market rents is immaterial, then the value implication is immaterial. The report user will be well advised to determine exactly what is being provided. If the appraisal report claims to value a leased fee interest, then the fee simple, unencumbered interest may be higher. This can be valuable information. Conversely, if the appraisal report claims to value a fee simple interest, then the report user will be well advised to ascertain just where the underlying data was gathered.

12
Income Approaches to Value

Look at market fluctuations as your friend rather than your enemy; profit from folly rather than participate in it.

—Warren Buffett

CHAPTER 11 LEFT off noting that the income approach may be more useful for valuing income-producing properties. This not only makes a certain degree of common sense, it also comports to the thinking of typical investors, particularly institutional and professional investors. They are almost always aiming at a particular return level and are less concerned with sales-comparison type factors.

This is not to suggest that thorough inspection and comparison of the investment subject in its competitive market is unnecessary. Far from it—the quality and stability of future returns are in no small part tied to the property's nature and condition within its competitive landscape. Sales comparisons provide a vital tool in that assessment.

For a given category of property, investors will typically aim at a particular return, often measured as its "cap" rate. An institutional apartment investor may seek investments of a particular size (say, greater than 100 units) in a particular location (top-20 markets) with a certain target cap rate. While there will be other due diligence criteria, ascertained with a sales comparison, the income level measured as an ROI or cap rate will be the threshold for consideration of the investment.

The income approach also "makes sense" to analytical types fresh out of MBA school. While competitive market analysis gives some indications about the local investment landscape and the positioning (and therefore quality and stability) of the subject, the various income approach methodologies are consistent with typical financial analysis tools, such as net present value and internal rates of return.

In this chapter, I will take a deeper, more focused dive into some particular nuances of income analyses applied to real estate. I have already used many of these tools in preceding examples, and we will revisit these examples again to show how the two approaches, together, provide a nuanced view of the true value of property under the microscope. As always, the focus of this material is from the perspective of investors—typically a family office or similar fund looking to build, maintain, and manage a diversified portfolio of real estate. To that end, income analysis is key to optimizing values, but with a long-term, asset protection view in mind.

1. A Quick Note on Residential Income Analysis

Income analysis is, quite obviously, geared toward income-producing property. Again, the specific property itself does not need to be income producing. Many nonresidential properties are acquired to supplement another for-profit enterprise, such as a warehouse which will support a related business. Indeed, some warehouses are acquired to curate, maintain, and display a collection, such as comedian Jay Leno's famous garage. However, even Leno's garage can be valued using data from contemporaneous comparable transactions.

But what about residences? In prior chapters, I discussed investments in single family rental properties and noted that duplexes, triplexes, and fourplexes are also appraised using single family techniques. The methodology used for small rental properties relies heavily on determining the following:

Comparable Rental Properties Based on Size, Number of Bedrooms and Bathrooms

In the small-unit rental market, these are the primary determinants of rental rates. The driving force for income comparables would be a set of recent transactions of properties with a similar configuration of rental units. Thus, a duplex with two-bedroom, one-bath, 1,000-square-foot apartments should be valued using other duplexes with similar configuration.

Determining Market Rents

In the small-unit rental business, it is not uncommon for one or even more units to be occupied in a non-arm's-length fashion. Many parents purchase a duplex or a small rental property in a neighborhood adjacent to where a child is attending college. Income maximization is rarely the goal, since success is measured in terms of forgone rents in a dormitory or nearby apartment building. One unit will be occupied by the college student, and in many cases the other units will be occupied by friends or relatives. The investors are perfectly happy to break even and may hang on to the investment after junior graduates or sell it to another set of proud parents. There are many other scenarios, and given that such investments are often held more for capital gains than for income, determining the boundaries of market rents can be problematic.

Determining the Gross Rent Multiplier (GRM)

As discussed back in Chapter 5, the GRM is simply the ratio of sales price to gross rent. In some markets, this is expressed on a monthly basis, and in others an annual basis. The above-referenced duplex may rent for $1,200 per side (a total of $2,400 gross) per month, with separately metered utilities. The landlord is responsible for property taxes, fire insurance, management and collection fees, and normal upkeep. The property sells for $300,000, and the monthly GRM is thus:

$$GRM = \frac{300{,}000}{2{,}400} = 125 \qquad \text{EQUATION 12-1}$$

In most markets, GRMs on small rental properties will range somewhere between 90 and 150. Higher levels of GRM indicate markets with substantial capital gain and rental growth prospects. Lower GRMs are experienced in slow-growth markets.

Examine the GRM Across Several Comparables

Rarely will GRM be perfectly constant, even among highly comparable transactions. In a given market, GRM will vary somewhat according to the same factors noted in the sales comparison approach—location, age, quality, functional utility, condition, parking, and other amenities. A duplex that has recently been renovated—new roof, new windows, and a fresh paint job—may not rent for much more but certainly will sell for more. The goal is to find comparables that bracket the subject and to examine the GRMs that span those comparables to determine the likely GRM range for the subject.

Determine Market Rents for the Subject

The factors that determine market rents may be somewhat different from the factors that determine selling price, but the two are certainly linked to a large extent. The starting point for estimating market rent will be the market rents for nearly identical comps. For unique properties, this will need to be extrapolated or estimated. One- and two-bedroom units are most common, with three bedrooms less so. Four- and five-bedroom rental units (in small multifamily structures) are fairly uncommon. Studio apartments are becoming increasingly common, particularly in urban areas or college towns. One-bath, one-and-a-half-bath, and two-bath configurations are also common. Other factors influencing rents will be the unit size, location (and particularly proximity to mass transit), amenities (central heating and air conditioning), the inclusion of some utilities (Wi-Fi being common in some situations), the inclusion of appliances (stove and refrigerator are normal, with dishwasher, microwave, garbage disposal, and other appliances less common), and even provision of furnishings in some markets.

> Decades ago, the situation of shared bathrooms in what were called "boarding houses" was not uncommon. Today, this is extremely rare but can still be found in some places.

Use GRM and Market Rents to Estimate Value

Once market rents and market GRM are determined, a simple extrapolation will give us an indicated value via the income approach. I'll assume that the 125 GRM holds true, and rental comps tell me that market rents average $2,300 per month. I thus find an indicated value of:

$$Value = 125 \times 2{,}300 = \$287{,}500 \quad \text{EQUATION 12-2}$$

This needs to be substantiated with the sales comparison and cost analyses, but given typical motivations of income property buyers, this is probably the most representative of value.

This GRM can and should be used for any small residential property when the highest and best use (HBU) is for rental income and the local market is replete with rental comps. If I wanted a condo in a building with many condos sold as rental units, then it would be inconsistent to value the condo without consideration of potential rental income.

As other types of properties are condominiumized, the same is true across a variety of property types that might not normally be valued this way. Office condos, parking lot condominiumization, and even condominiumization of marinas give rise to the use of this GRM methodology.

2. Critical Assumptions

The major mortgage market meltdown was a function of many systemic and structural failures. The appraisal profession has spent considerable time and effort since then and continues to improve the standards and quality of appraisals. Users of appraisal reports make assumptions about the underlying research and analytical rigor. Users or investors conducting valuations on their own would be well advised to consider some critical underlying assumptions in an income analysis, including the following.

Properly Defining the Competitive Market

Seemingly obvious, this assumption can be flawed in many ways. Gravity models aid in determining the competitive landscape, particularly for retail. On North Roosevelt Boulevard in Key West, Florida, a city of about 25,000 people, within the span of one mile, there are three major grocery stores. Intriguingly, two are from the same grocery chain. Why? Somewhere along the line, the models showed that this market could sustain three large grocery stores. Because of local land use regulations and opportunities, all three needed to be located close to one another. One chain realized that if they were going to face competition, it might as well be from themselves. They benefit from economies of scale and certain other competitive advantages. If they closed one store, in a flawed attempt to consolidate, then some other chain would invariably open in the market. This gap in the market may not have been obvious before these groceries were opened, but the owners have certainly benefitted from a prescient understanding of the competitive real estate and retail landscape.

Conducting a Thorough Market Analysis

The data used and reported in an income analysis should be thorough, complete, and representative of the competitive market. Boilerplate, out-of-date, or unrepresentative data will be misleading and result in a value that has no credibility or relevance.

Using Relevant Data

Appraisal reports can be filled with excellent market data, but if that data is irrelevant to the investment decision being made, then the data is useless and leads to flawed conclusions. If our investment is an industrial building, then local office rental information may be of only peripheral interest.

Excess and Surplus Land Issues

We discussed this in Chapter 9, and this is an area in which these issues arise. The income analysis—say, an apartment complex—needs to include the income associated with excess or surplus land. If there is land sufficient to be separately rented or sold for other purposes, then this has a very real impact on the income to be derived from the apartments. This could also suggest expansion and has a very real implication for the HBU and future rents. Conversely, if the land supporting the apartments is insufficient to meet the needs of parking, landscaping, signage, or other activities, then rents may not be sustainable.

Continuity in the Analysis

All too many appraisals make leaps in logic—a review of several recent transactions reveals cap rates of 8%, 8.5%, 8.75%, and 9%. The appraiser leaps to a conclusion of an 8% cap rate without any underlying support. Even a simple averaging would require some continuity in the logic.

Understanding the Difference Between Single-Tenant and Multitenant Rents

Big-box retailers, small single-tenant office buildings, stand-alone industrial properties, and nearly everything "built to suit" will have single tenants. These tenants are generally able to negotiate very different rents and lease terms in multitenant scenarios. Using single-tenant rental comparables to value multitenant subject properties, and vice versa, is widely discredited.

Understanding the Implications of Space Demising

Different markets have different demands for space, and these demands may change over time. One investment team, operating in a top-10 market, enjoyed excellent results by seeking out tired community shopping centers in need of an overhaul. Most changes were cosmetic—retopping and painting the parking lot, new signage, and new trim for the storefronts. They also sought out shopping centers where the demising (the unit size) was not meeting the demands of potential tenants. They were able to inexpensively redemise spaces to meet the needs of new renters, get the shopping centers up to full occupancy, and then sell the renovated centers for a handy profit.

By the way, since this sort of "flip" takes a year or more, preferential tax treatment can be a possibility.

Understanding Regional, National, and Even Global Markets

A small neighborhood or community shopping center will look for tenants and customers within a few miles. A major superregional shopping mall will need to understand the national and global implications of multinational retailers and their customers. Major upscale retailers want to be in places with major upscale shoppers but do not want to denigrate their brands by locating in places with down-market customers.

> There is a reason why there is no Walmart on Rodeo Drive.

Understanding the Implications of Below-Market Leases and the Time Frame for Those Leases

The Appraisal Institute specifically advises the use of discounted cash flow (DCF) analysis, rather than direct capitalization, for leased fee analyses. The driving force is the time frame of those below-market leases. The expiration of below-market leases does not always or even usually bring market rents. Below-market leases may have renewal clauses and options. Even in the absence of such options, existing tenants are in a favored position to negotiate new below-market leases. Landlords are reluctant to lose a happy tenant, even in "hot" markets, necessitating a period of vacancy, additional tenant up-fit, and commission and marketing expenses. This is even more pronounced with single-tenant properties or tenants with significant occupancy ("sign on the building" tenants). Market lease rates for new buildings may significantly exceed current and ongoing lease rates for competitive, fully leased buildings. Valuing a fully leased building would be a mistake if using new "going-in" lease rates on new buildings.

Understanding What Appraisers Mean When They Use the Word "Assumptions"

This is terrifically misunderstood, even within the profession itself. Every analysis is underpinned with a body of assumptions, and indeed the entire appraisal report can be viewed as a simple statement of the various assumptions made to reach a conclusion. Some assumptions are so critical to the final value determination that they are called *extraordinary assumptions*. These are assumptions that, individually, might affect the final value conclusion if found to be false.

Take, for example, comp rental rate evaluation. Each is researched and validated. If one is wrong, it may not have a material impact on the final value. If the rental rate is only slightly wrong, then it may only constitute a rounding error in the final determination. If it is significantly (and perhaps falsely) out of line with the others, then I would consider it to be an outlier and not use it in the final valuation conclusion. Thus, an error in a single assumption along the line, or even a few assumptions, may not make a major difference in the final outcome.

The highest and best use determination may be an extraordinary assumption. I determine that the highest and best use is for retail development, but it was actually for residential development. This single assumption has a very significant, material impact on the final valuation outcome. Thus, I need to delineate any assumption that is extraordinary.

I also need to delineate any hypothetical conditions. These are scenarios that are known to be false, but that I assume for appraisal purposes. I may be asked to value a hotel currently under construction (such as the example in the previous chapter). My appraisal would note the hypothetical condition that it was completed in a good "workmanlike" manner and was doing business at a sustainable level, similar to the comps used for valuation data.

3. Measuring Income—What Constitutes "Gross Rent"?

Consider the simplest rental property—a single family house or condominium, privately owned, and rented to a single tenant. The rental terms, including what is included in the gross rent payment, are outlined in a lease. As we move up the complexity scale, the delineation of gross rent becomes more and more detailed.

Commercial Buildings

One common delineation is *gross rent* versus *net rent* for tenant-occupied commercial buildings, such as offices, retail properties, and industrial properties. In most multitenant buildings, the tenant pays a single gross lease rate and the landlord is responsible for all taxes, maintenance, and insurance costs. Some gross leases include *escalation clauses* and *expense stops*. The former provide that the rent may increase over time in accordance with an acceptable index, such as the consumer price index. In lieu of that, the rent may be increased periodically based on a rent survey conducted by an appraiser. In a "rent stop" lease, the tenants pay a flat rent, but if certain expenses increase beyond a threshold level, the tenant is responsible for a portion.

Net leases are most common with single-tenant occupancy. The most common terminology is the *triple net lease,* abbreviated NNN in many documents. The tenant pays a flat fee and is also responsible for routine maintenance, utilities, taxes, insurance, and structural repairs. A somewhat less common lease is the *double net,* in which the landlord covers structural repairs. This latter lease form is occasionally seen in some kinds of retail establishments.

For many retail spaces, the lease calls for a *percentage rent.* These can be wildly complicated and difficult to audit. Nonetheless, retail landlords and tenants see favor with them. In this scenario, the lease calls for a base rent and then a percentage of gross sales above a certain threshold. Imagine a scenario in which a particular tenant in a shopping mall intends to do $1 million in gross sales per year. The landlord would normally expect to rent this space for $50,000 year. However, the landlord sets the rent at $25,000 per year plus 5% of anything over $500,000. This gives the tenant some breathing room to ramp up sales, and if the tenant is indeed successful, the landlord may enjoy a bonus rent (if the tenant's actual gross sales are above the $1 million pro forma). Landlords like this upside opportunity, and tenants enjoy the lower rent when the store is just starting.

Finally, in many high-demand areas in the United States, such as tourist resort shopping areas, retail landlords will demand a very long-term lease (five or more years) and a very large up-front, nonrefundable "key fee" equaling as much as half the total five-year rent. The most common locations are the "tourist trap" retail establishments frequented by cruise ship passengers. The landlord amortizes the key fee over the life of the lease. The term "key fee" generally comes from countries where leases are transferrable among tenants, which is usually not the case in America. A below-market lease in France could be "sold" to a new tenant via payment of a key fee determined by the net present value of the lease benefit. In some countries, such as South Korea, a very large up-front key fee for apartments is not uncommon in very desirable locations.

Apartment Buildings

Apartments seem straightforward in theory but get complicated in practice. Typical leases call for monthly rent, usually referred to as *gross rent* even though in practice some expenses are borne by the tenant. Typical apartment leases call for security deposits and the first and last month's rent in advance. Monthly rent payments are made in advance until the lease termination (usually with a one-month notice).

Tenants may pay some expenses, such as electricity, but rent will usually include water and sewer, garbage collection, and parking. Many nicer apartments will have washer/dryer hookups in apartments (and some may actually include these appliances in the rent), while other apartments, mostly B and C grade, will have central coin-operated laundry rooms. These coin-operated facilities, along with vending machines and other similar facilities, can constitute significant *other income* accounted separately on the income analysis. Some apartments include daycare centers, parking garages, central cable television systems, central Wi-Fi systems, and even membership arrangements at nearby country clubs, all of which constitute sources of other income. Complicating this is are rental concessions in hot markets. Most apartment owners tolerate a certain level of vacancy. Studies find that in most major markets, a vacancy of about 7% actually maximizes net income. At rates above this, the landlord is probably charging too much (and losing potential income), while lower vacancies suggest rents are too low. When vacancies increase, landlords are loath to cut rental rates, because existing tenants will demand concessions. To market properties, landlords grant move-in bonuses, such as a free month's rent, appliances (such as microwave ovens or televisions), or move-in assistance (free use of a truck). This complicates the income determination, because these concessions are accounted for as expenses, resulting in an actual but temporary NOI outcome very different from normal, sustained operations.

Hotels

Daily room rents are the basis for comparison, and hotels and markets are usually measured on a *revenue per available room* (RevPAR) basis. This metric combines aggregate average room rates with long-term occupancy rates, divided by the number of rooms available for occupancy, and constitutes a measure of effective net rent. As discussed previously, hotels famously earn income from other sources. Full-service and conference center hotels aggressively market to meetings and conventions. The catering, meeting room rental, restaurant and bar revenues, and even audiovisual services constitute important revenue channels. The marginal additional profit attached to renting each hotel room over and above the breakeven point is nearly 100% of the room rate. Valet or even self-parking, small concessions, and space rental to third-party vendors all add to the bottom line.

Hotel investors tell great stories of due diligence problems when acquiring hotel properties. A "400-room" hotel might not have 400 rooms available for rent on any given night, due to renovations, equipment and engineering failures, or other problems. Some skeptical investors actually go from floor to floor, during the due-diligence phase, and count doorknobs. Some have reported, anecdotally, that 400-room hotels may only have 390 doorknobs, with no particular explanation of what happened to the other 10 rooms! Some of those rooms may be missing television sets, beds, or even functional bathrooms. One might think these problems only occur with the acquisition of down-market hotels, but reports indicate that even upscale, major-brand, major-market hotels require significant due diligence at acquisition.

Determining PGI

The top line in any income analysis is *potential gross income* (PGI), the total rent that would be theoretically collected if every tenant paid rent on time and in full. Few properties ever achieve this, even single-tenant triple net lease buildings. As a matter of shorthand, the vacancy and collections losses (V&C) are usually combined into one line item, which is subtracted from PGI to arrive at *effective gross income* (EGI).

Determining PGI requires examination of competitive market rents and actual leases on the books. This exercise is complicated by the previous observation that current contract rents for comparable transactions may constitute below-market negotiations (thus those comparable transactions may be leased fee, rather than fee simple). For property types with rapidly changing tenancies, such as hotels and apartments, determining actual competitive market rents may be easier than for offices, industrial properties, and long-term land leases.

Reflecting back on the small apartment example used previously, Table 12-1 illustrates a competitive market analysis for competing two-bedroom apartments.

TABLE 12-1 Competitive Market Rents

Comparable	Location/Quality	Rent/Month	Avg SF	Rent/SF
1	Inferior	$845	937	0.90
2	Superior	$731	725	1.01
3	Superior	$950	930	1.02
4	Superior	$851	800	1.06
Averages		$844	848	1.00
Subject	Current rents	$867	900	0.96
Value Used		$867		

Most of the comps are superior in location and quality and have higher per-square-foot rents. The average market square footage is lower than the subject, and the superior comps have apartments that average nearly 10%

smaller (818 SF, not shown on the table). As such, the current rent for the subject, while slightly higher than the average for the comps, probably represents market value accounting for the difference in size.

Comparing PGI with Actual Income

I want to examine the actual income experience for this subject, as shown in Table 12-2. There is no factor for V&C losses, although there is an entry for late fees—not unusual for lower-end apartments. This market has an apartment shortage now, and competing apartments have long waiting lists with little current vacancy. This may not represent long-term stabilized income, and an investor may want consider supply/demand factors over a long-term horizon.

TABLE 12-2 Current Rent Summary

Current Rent	323,240
Other Income	10,034
Late Fees	923
Effective Gross Income	$334,197

PGI at current market rates would be considerably different—at $867 per month, each apartment should generate $10,404 in gross rent annually. Across 32 apartments, we get a PGI of $332,928. Why the difference? For one, there is a lag between contract rent and market rent. If rents are going up 5% annually, then a bundle of one-year leases will always lag the market by 2.5%. Second, in a medium-sized apartment complex like this, it is not unusual to grant rent concessions to long-term, trustworthy tenants in trade for one or more acting as a de facto on-site manager or manager's representative. Of course, this is handled gingerly, since actual third-party property management *for a fee* requires a license and significant regulation. Valuation using these reduced rents would result in the value of a leased fee interest, rather than a fee simple market value.

> An actual buyer should keep this point in mind—the market value of a fee simple interest assumes that the units will all be rented at the higher market-level rent, but actual results will almost always be lower.

Next, we reconsider V&C loss estimates. Actual history is V&C loss; the landlord has collected late payment fees, which only reimburse the landlord for the extra time taken to collect past-due rent and opportunity costs. In reality, there is a frictional loss with vacant units during transition from one tenant to another. If the local market is "hot," then the turnaround time may be very short, but units will almost always need to be cleaned, perhaps repainted, and readied for new tenants. Local experience and knowledge will be helpful, but generally one would expect to see V&C losses in the range of 5% to 15%. Recall that profit-maximizing vacancies are typically around 7%, although this may not be sustainable in "hot" or "cold" markets. Given the current demand, I might assume a 5% V&C loss, but a savvy investor will want to recognize that this is simply an average of the current reality (0%) versus the more probable long-term (10%) V&C losses.

Actual other income totaled $10,957, which included late fees, water reimbursements, and laundry income. Water reimbursements should be a set-aside against landlord-borne utility charges, but in practice, for small investments like this, it is easier to account for those as other income. This could slightly skew comparisons with other apartment investments that have separately metered water or other accounting methods, but the difference is negligible.

Comparing Actual Expense Experience with Market Averages

The next step is to compare actual expenses to market averages. This can be a real challenge. Comps rarely accurately report actual expenses. Indeed, for small, privately owned investments, the expense ledger can be a burial ground for a host of owner expenditures that would otherwise not be tax deductible.

> Reflect on the story of the college parents who buy a small apartment building for their student. One wonders how many such students are paid a tax sheltering "management fee" by Mom and Dad? Indeed, to the extent that rents on the other units will offset the cost of Junior's housing, this is a win-win for everyone as long as the investment breaks even. Readers are reminded this is *not* tax advice, but simply an observation based on more than a few years of experience in the field.

Theoretically, annual expenses should be fairly consistent, but in reality certain expenses will vary. There may be a legal issue necessitating the involvement of counsel, or an unusual repair one year not accounted for under the reserves for replacement. Table 12-3 shows the actual expense ledger for this property for the past two years, and then the projected expenses going forward.

TABLE 12-3 Expense Pro Forma

	2017		2018		Projected
	Total	Per Unit	Total	Per Unit	Per Unit
Property Taxes	28,456	889	28,454	889	890
Insurance	8,294	259	8,107	253	250
Management Fee	10,025	313	10,283	321	520
Utilities	25,182	787	18,220	569	800
General & Administrative	3,441	108	1,450	45	50
Maintenance & Repairs	5,563	174	11,832	370	500
Reserves	0	0	0	0	250
Total Expenses	$80,961	$2,530	$78,346	$2,447	$3,260

A few points should be made about these expense estimates. While accounting is on an aggregate basis, totals are then broken down on a per-unit basis. This is useful for comparison with industry norms and comps. Real estate taxes are not "manageable" in the short run but should be compared to the other competing properties in the long run. If the subject's property taxes are higher than comps, an appeal may be fruitful.

Insurance is difficult to manage in the short run. A new buyer will want to review the coverages and consider the potential for changes. Investors may have blanket coverage on a number of similar properties and may be able to get discounts from their broker. *Private investors will also consider this investment on their umbrella liability policy.*

For this property, management fees ranged from $313 to $321 per unit per year for the past two years. In practice, an investor in this market would pay 5% of EGI. Projected expenses are adjusted accordingly. Utility charges for this property included water, sewer, hot water, and trash collections. The actual, recorded expenses declined significantly in 2018, with no reason given. Actual practice in this market would be closer to $800 per unit. Also, for undisclosed reasons, general and administrative expenses ballooned in 2017 to $3,441, or $108 per unit, while market normal expenses would be more like $50 per unit (the experience in 2018). The landlord could have bought a new computer and expensed it to this investment.

> Indeed, the landlord's college student child could have bought a new computer to write Mom and Dad a note every time there was a broken hot water heater.

Maintenance and repairs vary not only from year to year but also from unit to unit. When there is a move-out, a unit will need to be cleaned, perhaps repainted, and maybe even repaired. A reserve for replacements should incorporate major repairs, such as new appliances or structural work. Year-to-year minor expenses will include:

- Appliance repairs
- Carpet/hardwood/vinyl flooring cleaning and repair
- Cleaning and painting
- Hot water heater and plumbing repairs
- Heating and cooling repairs
- Landscaping
- Maintenance parts and supplies
- Pest control
- General and minor structural repairs
- Trash removal
- Lock and key expenses
- Safety systems
- Maintenance supervision, salaries, and payroll taxes

Maintenance and repairs will be higher for older investments. This particular property has had below-average maintenance costs, compared to comps. Often, for smaller investments, the landlord performs maintenance labor, such as light plumbing, landscaping, changing locks, and cleaning and painting. For an investment valuation, the market normal expenses must be considered.

Reserves for replacement are generally not accounted with expenses, since these are typically not deductible for tax purposes. Depreciation should in some way proxy for such reserves—conceptually, an investor should consider that depreciation should be linked to a sinking fund for when things start breaking and large structural components need replacement. Investors need to consider categories of major uninsurable items that will need to be replaced periodically. These include, but are not limited to:

- Appliances
- Heating and air conditioning
- Hot water heaters
- Roof replacement
- Major floor covering
- Exterior repainting
- Major parking area repairs

These can actually be analyzed individually with an estimate based on the probable life of each and the sinking fund payments needed to fund such replacements. Consider a very simplified version as shown in Table 12-4.

TABLE 12-4 Sinking Fund Example

	Life Span	Cost	Sinking Fund
Refrigerator	15	800	37
Stove	15	500	23
Roof	20	1,500	45
Air Conditioning	10	1,000	80
Hot Water Heater	7	400	49
Total Annual			**$234**

This is consistent with the observation in the marketplace of $250 per year. This assumes, by the way, that the ongoing investor is actually accumulating a sinking fund, has been accumulating this for years, and thus will not experience a shock to the system when a roof needs to be replaced or every refrigerator breaks down the same year. When a new investor purchases this investment, a detailed sinking fund analysis is needed—usually as part of the cost approach—and if there are any reserves, these are transferred to the buyer. Alternatively, unfunded reserves become relevant in the purchase and sale negotiations.

Normally, the next step will be to combine the income and the expense estimates into a single pro forma of net operating income (NOI). Since this is expressed as a continuous stream of income, direct capitalization can be used to determine value. For simplicity sake, I will combine these two steps into one in the next section.

NOI and *before tax cash flows* (BTCF) are often confused. There are two important differences. First, NOI includes a reserve for replacements, which is often proxied by depreciation. This is a noncash item (even though it will eventually convert to a cash expenditure). Using reserves, even if the sinking fund is not accumulated in cash, allows the analyst to smooth out the annual estimate of cash flows and use the simpler direct capitalization method. Without this, cash flows would be irregular, since the actual timing of replacements is irregular. Second, BTCF includes debt service. This is investor-specific—some investors pay all cash, while others take advantage of leverage. Bankers are interested in BTCF because it is part of the debt service coverage (DSC) ratio calculation. This is a key element, along with loan-to-value (LTV) for evaluating the collateral for a commercial loan.

4. Determining the Capitalization Rate

I discussed this at length in Chapters 2 and 5, but it deserves further consideration. The three most common ways to determine this are:

- Market extraction
- Market surveys
- Band of investments (often called mortgage-equity analysis)

Market extraction is preferred when data is available. Surveys of investors are widely available from published sources, but these are broad, general averages that lag the market. Band of investments or mortgage-equity analysis depends on an array of assumptions about investor behavior and was explored at length in Chapter 5. It is important to understand which method or methods are being used by the appraiser. Each method has its strong suit and tells us something quite different about the value conclusion. For large, complex investments, investors should urge or even require their appraiser to use more than one method, and perhaps all three of these and more. Even small variations in the cap rate can have major, material impacts on the final valuation determination.

Market Extraction

As previously discussed, this depends on determining the NOI for comparable investments, inverting the market capitalization formula, and then taking an average or a weighted average of the results. Let's say that a comparable recently sold for $3 million and has an annual NOI estimated at $180,000. The overall cap rate (R_o) estimated from that comparable is:

$$R_o = \frac{180{,}000}{3{,}000{,}000} = 6\% \qquad \text{EQUATION 12-3}$$

This method depends on two critical assumptions. First, we assume that the selling price was for a bundle of rights similar to what we are valuing, and that all explicit assumptions of market value (or whatever value we are interested in) were met. If I am trying to value the fee simple interest, but this transaction was for a leased fee interest (arguably, a lesser bundle of rights), the cap rate may be very different from what I need.

Market Surveys

There are several national providers who survey market participants and report on cap rates, discount rates, expense ratios, market expectations, and other useful real estate investment metrics. Real estate investors, analysts, brokers, and appraisers usually subscribe to one or more services for general trends in the market and specific metrics. Some surveys are quite good and very detailed, while others are less exact. The surveys tend to lag the market. Also, some surveys focus on current acquisitions by institutional investors. These investors rarely use the same leverage as individual investors, have ROI goals set by income investors rather than capital gains investors, and have very different tax implications. Thus, the indications from these surveys may not specifically apply to individual investments under consideration. While measures of central tendency (means, medians) are reported in many surveys, the range of results can be quite wide.

> It is handy to think of the range of suggested cap rates in the same light as the range of returns on bonds—from the highest grade to "junk" quality. Indeed, at any point in time, the required returns (cap or discount rates) on problem real estate (e.g., brownfields) can be estimated by examining the basis point spread between investment grade bonds and junk bonds, and then adding that spread to the returns on investment grade real estate.

Band of Investments

The formula for this was presented in Chapter 5, but it is useful to reconsider it here. This is a weighted average of the annualized payment factor on a typical commercial loan (R_m) and the rate of return required by equity investors (equity dividend rate, or R_e). Weightings are determined by the typical loan-to-value (LTV) ratio currently prevalent for those types of loans. Assume that we can borrow a 60% LTV loan at 4% annually for 15 years, with monthly payments, and equity investors currently require a 10% return on real estate investments. The monthly payment factor (the amount of monthly payment for each dollar borrowed) is 0.007397. Annualizing this (simply multiplying by 12) we get 0.08876. The formula thus becomes:

$$R_o = 0.6 \times 0.08876 + 0.4 \times 0.1 = 9.3\% \qquad \text{EQUATION 12-4}$$

This assumes that we have been able to capture the true intentions of likely market participants. While the first half of this equation is pretty easily obtainable, the second half may be problematic. One principal criticism of this equation is actually unfounded. Market value presumes we have proxied the actions of most likely market participants. Some would critique this formulation because highly creditworthy investors may be able to get much better credit terms (say, 80% or better LTV) and institutional investors may have lower return requirements than private equity investors. This is perhaps true, but the difference in value obtained from some other set of metrics would probably constitute an *investment value* rather than a *market value*. This is actually very helpful information for a potential investor. If a project can be reevaluated with a cap rate that is more in keeping with the investor's specific return criteria, then any difference in price may constitute a windfall to the investor. Conversely, a seller who recognizes that institutional investors may be working under a different set of investment criteria may have an opportunity to reap enhanced benefits in a sale.

In our small apartment example, we have examined five recent comparable transactions to extract cap rates, as shown in Table 12-5.

TABLE 12-5 Cap Rate Market Extraction

Comparable	Location/ Quality	Date of Sale	Sale Price	NOI	R_o
1	Similar	June 2016	9,500,000	664,200	6.99%
2	Superior	Oct 2017	800,000	52,397	6.55%
3	Inferior	Jan 2018	1,160,000	84,082	7.25%
4	Similar	Apr 2017	855,000	59,940	7.01%
5	Much superior	Dec 2017	1,681,000	88,200	5.25%
Average					6.61%

As shown, the typical comparable apartment is superior to ours. This suggests our cap rate may be higher than the average of these five. We also examined reports from a major market survey reporting apartment cap rates, nationally, from 3.75% to 10%, with an average of 5.74%. Of course, these represent investment-grade properties reported by major investors, and our property is C grade, which will almost certainly be owned by a private individual or family. I would place more weight on the market extraction in this situation. The two properties that are similar to ours in terms of quality and location show cap rates of about 7%, so this appears to be a supportable conclusion.

Even with localized data, a cap rate as low as 5.25% is supportable for a property in the same general category. This suggests an evaluation of this subject property in terms of repairs, renovations, or even improvements in the location (ingress, egress, security, privacy, etc.). Shifts in cap rates will have significant and material impacts on value.

I can now develop a value indication with these factors, shown in Table 12-6.

TABLE 12-6 Value Indicated by Income Approach

	Monthly	Annual	Annual Total
Gross Income	867	10,404	$332,928
Less: V&C Losses @ 5%			(16,646)
Other Income			12,000
Effective Gross Income			328,282
Fixed Expenses			
Property Taxes		890	28,480
Insurance		250	8,000
Total Fixed Expenses			36,480
Variable Expenses:			
Management Fee @ 5%			16,414
Utilities		800	25,600
General & Administrative		50	1,600
Maintenance & Repairs		500	16,000
Total Variable Expenses			59,614
Reserves for Replacement		250	8,000
Total Expenses			104,094
Net Operating Income			224,188
Cap Rate			7.00%
Indicated Value			$3,202,679

I categorized expenses three ways: fixed, variable, and reserves. The first represents expenses over which we have little day-to-day influence. I may be able to affect some change in the long run, but in the short run these are simply bills I need to pay. The second category are items that will vary with occupancy levels and may actually be deferrable in the short run. Of course, reserves is a book entry, which should have a related sinking fund. Real estate appraisals generally do not attempt to compute breakeven rental rates, but this can be valuable information for the property investor. Recalling from basic finance, the formula for breakeven point is:

$$BEP = \frac{Fixed\ Costs}{Contribution\ Margin\ per\ Unit} = \qquad \text{EQUATION 12-5}$$

Contribution margin is simply the annual rental on one unit (12 × 867 = $10,404) minus the annual variable expense per unit, which in this case is the sum of management fees (5%), utilities, general and administrative (G&A) expenses, and maintenance. We can determine that the variable costs per unit total $1,863, so the annual contribution margin per unit is ($10,404 – $1,863 =) $8,541. We see that our annual fixed expenses are $36,480. Thus, the BEP for this investment, at least in the short run (ignoring reserves for replacement) is:

$$BEP = \frac{36,480}{8,541} = 4.27 \ units$$

EQUATION 12-6

This is pretty powerful information. This tells us that property breaks even if only 4+ units are rented on an annual basis. Of course, there is no debt service allowance and no reserves for replacement. This suggests a high degree of operating leverage.

Commercial real estate generally has a fairly high operating leverage. This is one reason that commercial real estate investments can support a high degree of financing leverage.

From a purely financial investment perspective these issues may be the most critical in this entire text. Institutional investors focus almost laser-like on cap rates, but all investors need to consider BEP as part of a sensitivity analysis. Marketing and pro forma materials available from brokers and principal sellers will usually headline the cap rate but rarely if ever pay any attention to breakeven occupancy.

Investors should also examine publicized cap rates with a critical eye. Are these cap rates current, forward-looking, aspirational, or even purely fictional?

By the way, novices to real estate investing may be confused by the term *FFO*, or *funds from operations*. It is analogous to EBITDA, and generally is NOI without regard to reserves for replacement. Increasingly, real estate analysts are also using *AFFO*, or *adjusted funds from operations*. This takes FFO and subtracts recurring expenditures that are capitalized and then amortized, such as periodic maintenance expenses. The goal of FFO is to measure the dividend-paying capacity of a real estate fund.

5. Cap Rates Versus Discount Rates

In real estate and some other fields, cap rates are a common way to express the relationship between the current income on a property and its value. The cap rate is a measure of how much an investor would pay for the current (usually first year) NOI. It is like a PE ratio for a stock except that it is earnings divided by the price instead of the price divided by the earnings. The cap rate will be lower the more investors expects the NOI to increase in the future just as PE ratios are higher for stocks where the first-year dividends are expected to increase in the future..

Discount rates, on the other hand, are useful when it is better to make the projected cash flows more explicit or the investment is discontinuous, such as a development deal or renovation project when there will be varying cash flows in certain years. The discount rate is a direct measure of the investor's required rate of return. Simple cap rates do not handle these situations very well. One solution to make the growth rate more explicit is the Gordon's Growth Model. There is significant academic research linking cap rates and discount rates. Over modest levels of growth, the Gordon's model does an adequate job adjusting cap rates for expected *and continuous* changes in NOI. Assume V is the value, d is the discount rate or rate of return investors require, NOI_1 is the NOI expected in year 1, and g is the expected annual growth rate in property value:

$$V = \frac{NOI_1}{d - g} \qquad \text{EQUATION 12-7}$$

Thus, if the market cap rate was 10%, and the NOI for the coming period was $1 million, then the flat-NOI value would simply be $10 million. If the NOI was expected to grow by 2% per year, then d minus g would equal 8%, and the value would be about $12.5 million. This intuitively makes some sense. Investors would be willing to pay more for an asset that had a continuously growing cash flow. This model begins to break down for large values of g. With the advent of cheap computers and computer spreadsheets, discounted cash flow (DCF) modeling works much better for discontinuous or growing cash flows.

6. The Internal Rate of Return

This is really more of a finance topic, but it bears discussing. Real estate appraisals are geared toward finding value, not finding the ROI. For the income analysis, the rate of return is assumed given either by the market or by the investor. If asked to determine the market value of property, an appraiser will seek out the returns demanded by the marketplace, either a cap rate or a discount rate, and apply that accordingly. If given a target rate of return, the appraiser can determine the investment value. Working this problem in reverse is usually not an appraisal's goal. Basic finance theory rejects simple internal rate of return (IRR) as a decision tool in favor of net present value (NPV) analysis.[1] Rank ordering potential investments by IRR can be problematic.

Determining IRR for a perpetuity is a simple inversion of the valuation equation, and is approximated by the cap rate. Once there is any variation in the periodic cash flows, then cap rate no longer equates to IRR. Modern spreadsheet programs and more robust statistical software make computing IRR trivial. There are a few caveats that are equally applicable to non–real estate investments:

IRR Presumes That Cash Flows Can Be Continuously Reinvested at the Same Rate of Return

This is a massive and frequently violated assumption. Given the variance in returns over time, there is no reason to believe cash flow in period 2 can be invested at the same IRR as in period 1. However, the math of IRR requires that.

When Comparing Projects, IRR Ignores Project Size

This is one main reasons why NPV analysis is preferred to IRR. Consider the potential investments in Table 12-7. You have a total of $12 million to invest this period. If you invest according to NPV ranking, then the office building investment is a clear winner. However, assume you also have two investments available that total exactly $12 million. By rank ordering by IRR, you would select the apartment investment. This leaves $4 million, and the only option available now is the retail project, also very short term but not very profitable. In the end, the apartment and retail projects together return $700,000 ($8.5 + $4.2 *minus* $12) which is far less than the NPV resulting from the office building project. Admittedly, the office building project leaves us with $2 million in uninvested assets, but the returns on the office compensate for that.

TABLE 12-7 IRR Versus NPV

Investment	Size	IRR	NPV
Office Building	$10,000,000	12%	$12,500,000
Apartments	$8,000,000	14%	$8,500,000
Retail	$4,000,000	4%	$4,200,000

Mathematical Problems with IRR

In short, highly volatile cash flows can result, mathematically, in multiple solutions to the IRR equation.

The IRR is a useful tool for evaluating a real estate project *as long as other investment criteria are used.* When comparing and choosing among investments of similar size and similar NPV, the IRR can help with rank ordering. A low IRR compared with a high NPV may illustrate timing issues in the return stream. Further, the IRR gives a sense of the true economic return on projects, which may not be revealed by the NPV. Also, investors are occasionally faced with making the "least worst" decision—two or more choices, one of which must be chosen, but all of which all have negative NPVs. The IRR can aid in figuring out which has the "least worst" outcome. By itself, though, the IRR it can lead to problematic results.

7. Sensitivity Analyses

The appraisal analysis makes some discrete and static assumptions about cash flows, rents, expenses, capitalization rates, and for that matter virtually everything to do with the investment. The general and somewhat heuristic assumption is that the estimates used are the central tendency of the range of likely outcomes. These ranges are often discussed, but in a very general sense, and rarely is any confidence level placed on those estimates. We saw that the expected rents were $867 per month (see Table 12-6) and comparable apartments rented for $845 to $950 per month (see Table 12-1). However, nowhere did we see language such as, "there is a 95% confidence that the gross monthly rent per apartment will be in the range of $845 to $950."

One great danger with any investment—not just real estate—is that risks are not symmetrical. Indeed, when investments are leveraged, as real estate often is, the investor shares the success of the investment but bears a disproportionate burden if the investment turns south, because the investor is responsible for any debt incurred.

> Development deals usually come with a rudimentary sensitivity analysis, which examines the investment, and particularly the risks and returns, under various scenarios. Unfortunately, these analyses are usually prepared by individuals who have a vested interest in the deal being done. This is analogous to taking driving lessons from a car salesperson. It is hard to imagine that anyone ever fails the test.

A thorough and complete discussion of sensitivity analyses is well beyond the scope of this chapter. However, any investment should rigorously consider the upside of expenses and the downside of revenues. Initially, you should model the most likely outcome, and then vary each input individually across a range of possibilities. Recognize that variables can change rapidly. An impending recession would cause companies to rapidly cut back on business travel. Hotel reservations would decline immediately, and hotels would quickly lower rates to keep occupancy levels high. Since business employees also stay in hotels on vacation, the recession would also lead to a cutback in vacation travel. Ironically, many business travelers accumulate "points" that they use for family vacations. Hotels would be in the situation of giving away rooms for free as business travelers used up their free points. All of this could happen quite quickly in the hotel industry, but offices, industrial properties, and even apartments could see cancellations in contract renewals.

A more aggressive sensitivity analysis would vary multiple items at the same time. What if expenses increased while rents declined? This is a fairly odd situation, but there are precedents. A property with major construction defects, contamination, water intrusion, or equipment problems would see expenses rise at the same time occupancy declined. While a reappraisal may not be needed every time situations change, the investor should understand the underlying analytical math and metrics and be able to conduct at least rudimentary shifts in the assumptions to see how those affect the bottom line.

8. Summary and Key Points

Understanding the income analysis is of critical importance for real estate investors. This chapter purposely dealt with top-level issues, and as usual tried to avoid being a tutorial on this subject. The goal was to isolate certain issues and ideas that are key to understanding the appraisal:

- For a market value, the income estimate will be a function of market rents not just contract rents. Contract rents may be below market, and the value estimated would be leased fee rather than a market value.
- If a fee simple acquisition can be made at leased fee prices, then there is an opportunity for an immediate value increase.
- Appraisals should be critically analyzed to see if the competitive market is correctly determined. Errors at this stage will be nearly incurable.

- Just because an investment is fully rented does not mean that it will always be fully rented. For most investments, some positive level of vacancy is income maximizing.
- Current expenses may not be representative of long-term stabilized expenses.
- Current expenses do not incorporate reserves for replacement.
- Cap rates are useful when NOI is stabilized over a long period. Discount rates and NPV analyses should be used when NOI is not expected to be stable.
- Internal rates of return are useful but should not be the investment selection criteria.
- Appraisals rarely contain sensitivity analyses. These should be separately engaged for any major investment decision.

9. A Final Note—Options Theory and Real Estate

When you hear about options in the real estate field, you are hearing about something different from what is meant in the securities field. Real options are the right to buy or utilize a particular asset, in this case real estate. The option can have a very specific delineation. A land option may give a developer the right to purchase a parcel of land at a particular price for a particular time. Pricing is extraordinarily idiosyncratic, and is basically "what the market will bear." Developers are able to tie up a parcel at a *de minimus* cost while conducting due diligence and exploring the development and entitlement options. Sellers are willing to take a parcel off the market for an extended period only upon payment of a significant fee, usually nonrefundable. Experienced developers have a good idea going into a situation as to the development potential, and so they are usually in a good position to price the option at or below their cost of capital. In other words, if a developer would normally pay $1 million for a parcel and has a cost of capital of 10%, then a one-year option at any price below $100,000 is a bargain, particularly if the likelihood of development is high.

Financial options span a wider array of nontangible situations. Derivatives, default swaps, insurance contracts, and actual stock options are all priced according to the Black and Scholes model. These models are stochastic but at their heart have relatively common statistical processes, such as normal distributions and the risk-free rate of return as an alternative investment.

Every real estate development is a bundle of real options. The investor is buying a tangible asset (the real property) and an intangible one (the option to develop the property). The two components are usually valued as one, but it is a handy exercise to view the two components separately. What if the development deal falls through? The underlying land is still valuable—and the same cannot be said for a financial option. Further, the two assets can be financed separately. Investors may be willing to finance raw land under favorable terms but are less likely to finance risky development deals. The financing can sometimes be bifurcated, with the development financed through mezzanine financing. Naturally, the mezzanine will be expensive, but since the land itself may be the most expensive part, bifurcating the financing may provide an overall cheaper way to do the deal. Even if this sort of bifurcation is not possible, visualizing the project in this way is a helpful tool to analyzing the project risks and returns.

13 Reproduction Cost Analysis

> No investment on earth is so safe, so sure, so certain to enrich its owner as undeveloped realty.
>
> —Grover Cleveland

OFTEN I VALUE a property based on the *cost approach*. Simply put, I estimate the cost of reproducing or replacing the property as is, including factors for depreciation.

Sales comparison and income analysis are more commonly used and better capture the thought processes of typical investors, lenders, and financiers. However, the cost approach emulates the developer's thought processes and patterns the cost flows and development flows of an actual project. There is a general axiom, although not altogether true, that the cost approach fails for older structures due to complexity estimating depreciation. That said, the cost approach is actually an excellent way to determine and allocate depreciation, since it directly measures the difference in value between a new building and a replacement structure.

Due to the complexity many appraisers avoid the cost approach, which can be a real mistake. This provides an investor with the opportunity to examine physical, functional, and locational flaws in the property, many of which may be curable and some of which may not be curable. There are significant investment opportunities buried in that analysis, and a careful examination of the cost approach details will yield vital information for prospective investments and properties already in the portfolio.

1. A Simple Primer on Construction

We could fill another volume with what sophisticated and successful real estate investors do *not* know about building construction. A detailed discussion of construction techniques and methods would not benefit the readers at this juncture. A few basic elements, though, will prove useful going forward.

Land First, Then Building

For purposes of valuation, I bifurcate the land and the building (Figure 13-1). The building can be depreciated for tax purposes. From an appraisal perspective, we want the site to be in "shovel-ready" condition, including all utilities, curb cuts, and entitlements (but not permits). Of course, in practice, raw land may be acquired for development. Whether the expenditures to get the land "shovel ready" are immediately expensed or capitalized and depreciated is a tax-specific problem.

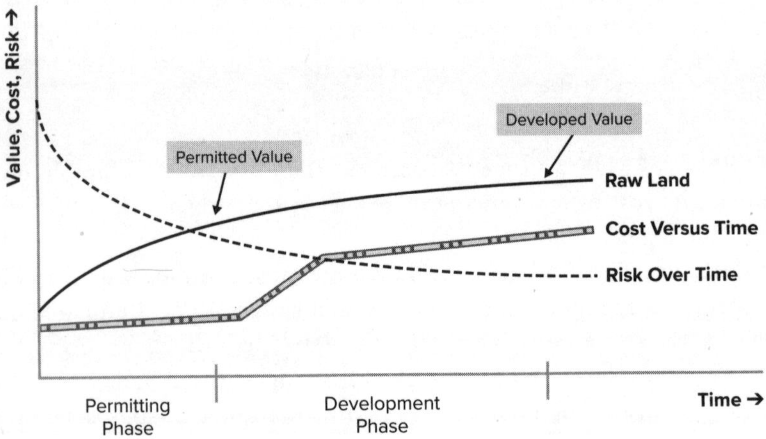

FIGURE 13-1 Land Development Timeline

Once the land is ready, a foundation is constructed. This varies in type, size, and composition depending on the nature of the planned buildings, soils, and other geological requirements. For a large office building, the foundation may be integral with a subterranean parking garage. In a location with poor soil conditions, the foundation may be supported by piers driven deep in the ground. While the building may be designed by an architect or designer, the foundation will usually be designed by an engineer, taking into account seismic issues, expansive soils, drainage and water intrusion, subterranean rights (subways, public utilities), and even wind loads. Extremely large or tall structures will require highly sophisticated foundations.

Structure

The building itself literally rests on the foundation. The properly constructed foundation will tie directly into the building's frame. This is true for the most basic residence and the tallest skyscraper. A modern structure depends on the integration of foundation supports with the building itself. Figure 13-2 shows a cutaway of a wall resting on a very simple concrete slab. This is not uncommon for a small building in areas where concrete slab foundations are used. The slab is only a few inches thick, but the footing at the edge will be much thicker with integrated reinforcing bars (*rebar*) and bolts tying the foundation to the wall above it. The general rule of tying the support walls to a supportive foundation is critical in all types of building.

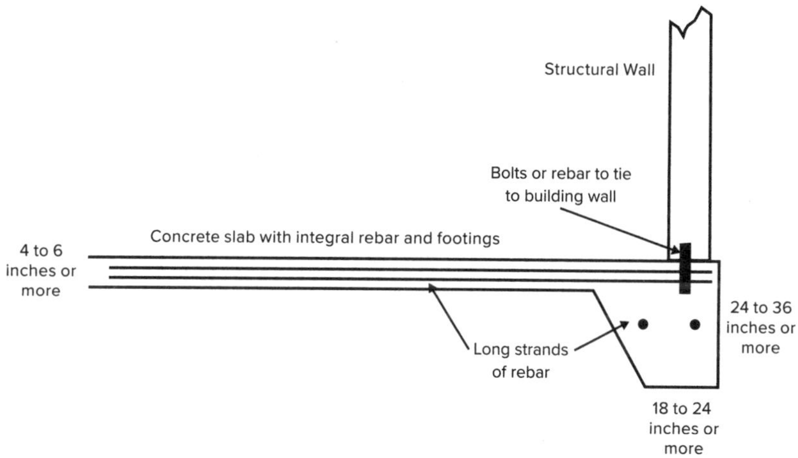

FIGURE 13-2 Wall Tied into Foundation

The types of structures can vary widely—high-rise and low-rise buildings, sheds and skyscrapers, and a nearly endless array of specialized structures. Nearly all share fundamental common themes of a supportive foundation integrated with a structure above.

Top It All Off with a Roof

Roofs are of particular concern to appraisers. The roof typically has a shorter physical and economic life than the building and is often the subject of constant maintenance. The cost and responsibility of roof maintenance and repair is a point of negotiation between gross, net, and triple net leases. Typically in the gross lease, the landlord is responsible for roof maintenance, and in the triple net lease the tenant bears responsibility. In between, it is a point of negotiation.

For any roof, the key design elements include material, construction, and expected durability. For an investment-grade building, the materials can vary widely, and while flat roofs are common for high-rise offices and apartments, the roof material may be metal, concrete, or even wood shakes and shingles. Most roofs in the United States have some *pitch* or angle between the highest point and the lowest point to carry off water. Thus, the "flat roof" is really a misnomer, since even a flat roof will have some slight slope and drainage system.

Visualizing the simplest roof system—a house roof with an attic—the horizontal structural members forming the ceiling system of rooms below are called *joists*. This term also refers to any horizontal structural member that supports a floor or ceiling. The angled structural members, to which the actual roof itself is attached, are called *rafters*. A vaulted ceiling may be constructed only of rafters, with additional supportive or tying members to provide rigidity to the rafter system. For a flat roof, by convention, the horizontal structural members are again called rafters. Again, these rafters and this roof only appear to be flat, but will usually have some slope needed to carry off water. In between the rafters and ceiling joists are supportive members that tie the joists and rafters together, generally called *lintels*. The use of rafters, joists, and lintels has been dated back to prehistoric times, and the Romans made extensive use of stone in constructing such roof systems. Attached to the outside of the rafters will be some type of roof decking, usually wood sheathing, plywood, or steel. For a flat roof, it is not uncommon to top this decking layer with a layer of insulation and then another decking layer. Above that there will be some impermeable membrane and a roofing cover itself. For the most common, simple roofs, this roof covering will be simple shingles. Within the roof structure, there will be some type of insulation. Of course, waterproofing is an absolute must.

Increasingly, commercial roofs are seen as either public spaces or spaces contributing to the building's energy needs. Many modern roofs have integrated decks, gardens, water catchments, solar panels, and an array of complex and useful tools for the building's utility. Even traditional buildings use roofs as handy places to store heating and air systems, water tanks, antenna, electrical connections, and booms and supports for window cleaning and maintenance. Roofs of high-rise buildings will often have utility structures providing access and equipment for elevators. All of this will be considered and designed from the inception of the building itself, since these features will integrate with the structure below.

This section is purposely short and incomplete. The investor who goes into development or who will buy a property for proposed construction will become considerably more familiar with the process. A real estate development investment is no small undertaking and is usually fraught with changes, amendments, and negotiations. The savvy investor will be adequately familiar with the process from the inception to knowledgably discuss critical issues with the professionals.

> Roofs protect against the elements, and the shape and design may be influenced by local climate conditions. In the 1890s, the US government settled on a federalist style for all national administrative buildings, with a very high-pitched, steep-slope roof to easily handle snow loads. Ironically, the Customs House in Key West, Florida, was thus constructed to handle heavy snow loads, even though there has never been a recorded snowfall in that island city.

2. Determining the Land Value

The beginning of my cost analysis is a land value estimate. This should be "shovel-ready" land, ready for construction of the improvements. As a practical matter I will view how land is purchased for construction of similar buildings. A lot for construction of a single family house may include sewer taps, water meters, curb cuts, and even some of what is usually considered yard landscaping, such as sidewalks. Conversely, a site for retail develop ment may have none of those amenities in place, and the cost will be part of the depreciable base.

The simplest way to find land cost is with a market survey. For the valuation of a single house, how much do vacant lots cost in this neighborhood? If the neighborhood is completely built out, then a new neighborhood with similar houses may proxy. For development of CBD commercial buildings, the prices of similarly located and zoned properties may prove useful. These are valued per square foot, but surplus and excess land issues now come into play. Imagine the construction of a building limited to 100,000 square feet. The local zoning rules require a 20,000-square-foot lot, but the only lot available that suits the development is 25,000 square feet. The unusable 5,000 square feet have no separable value. The 5,000 square feet extra do not carry the same marginal value as the 20,000 square feet needed for construction of the building. Thus, a simple market survey of available sites needs to include contributory value of surplus and excess lands.

Valuing property in any built-up area requires techniques to determine the contributory value of land. The *land extraction* technique is useful. I begin by estimating the replacement cost and depreciation of similar, recently sold property. I subtract the depreciated improvements value from the price to get the contributory value of the land. Table 13-1 illustrates a very simple example.

TABLE 13-1 Simple Land Extraction

Recent Selling Price		$13,500,000
Replacement Cost	*12,800,000*	
Less: Depreciation	*(4,200,000)*	
Contributory Value		(8,600,000)
Indicated Land Value		$4,900,000

Baked into this simplified analysis is the concept of *entrepreneurial incentive*, including the time value of money. Conceptually, a builder/developer would enjoy construction profits *and* the profits on the development project itself. Thus, if Table 13-1 represented a development deal, the land value would include entrepreneurial profit for buying and selling the land. This makes some sense. If the market extraction worked, and we could actually buy a subdivision lot for construction of a new house or other building, then buried in the market price of that lot would be an entrepreneurial profit to the developer of the subdivision—a reward for undertaking the costs and risks of development.

3. The Value of the Improvements

Next, I estimate the replacement cost of the improvements. This concept seems fairly simple on the surface but actually carries some fundamental confusion. The *Dictionary of Real Estate Appraisal* notes the following:

> ***Replacement cost.*** The estimated cost to construct, at current prices as of the effective appraisal date, a substitute for the building being appraised, using modern materials and current standards, design, and layout.

> ***Reproduction cost.*** The estimated cost to construct, at current prices . . . an exact duplicate or replica of the building being appraised, using the same materials, construction standards, design, layout, and quality of workmanship and embodying all the deficiencies, superadequacies, and obsolescence of the subject building.

Older or highly stylized buildings may contain construction techniques or materials that are difficult to reproduce today. Material in older buildings and the crafts needed to construct older buildings (such as stone masonry) simply do not exist today. The appraisal challenge is to value a property of equal *utility*, not necessarily equal structural design and technique. Sometimes, though, insurance policies, local regulations, or preservation agreements require the absolute reproduction of buildings as originally built. This can be horrendously expensive and should absolutely be a matter of consideration when acquiring or insuring a building with unique facets and features.

> In downtown New Orleans, before Hurricane Katrina, a developer acquired a historic building that had a preservable facade but a worthless interior. From an economic perspective, the building should have been torn down, but preservation rules dictated otherwise. The developer went to great lengths, and great expense, to preserve the exterior walls while gutting the interior. Then, Hurricane Katrina came along and blew down the carefully shored-up exterior facade.

There are several ways to determine replacement costs. For complex or expensive buildings, the most common and most accurate is some sort of building takeoff and costing. In other countries, the building cost business is a separate profession similar to appraisal or property management. In the United States, this is often done by an architect, general contractor, or engineer. This building estimate may not include the entrepreneurial profits and time value of funds previously discussed, and will have to be estimated. An extraction technique similar to that shown in Table 13-1 may prove useful for measuring the locally applicable factors. Entrepreneurial profits (and embedded building profits) may vary widely among markets and over time. When times are slow, builders and developers may be willing to sacrifice profits to stay busy. Similarly, subcontractors and even some tradespeople may be willing to shave their costs during slow periods. Equipment may be cheaper to rent, and even some building materials may be cheaper. This is a key reason to be mindful of market cycles and plan developments accordingly. As an example, construction profits often range from 10% to 20%, depending on the place in the market cycle. A compromise in that can make for a meaningful and material impact on the property price.

A very common way to estimate replacement costs is a per-square-foot method, which can be done by the appraiser, broker, or developer without the assistance of a professional cost estimator. Basically, this assumes that a building of a given type, structure, and construction quality will cost about the same to build throughout the local market. There are services available and software packages that take as input the various appraisal-type components (quality, desired materials, size, components) and output a value per square foot. These services are typically available on a localized basis, with a value component that takes into account the differences in costs among markets and an updated cost on a quarter-by-quarter basis. These services usually include construction profits in their estimates but not entrepreneurial profits.

Finally, there is a middle ground called the *segregated cost method*. This uses data and software from those same services but depends on very specific property characteristics. Sometimes, segregated costs can be used in conjunction with the per-square-foot method to value unique features, such as an elevator in a building that would not normally have an elevator. These segregated cost tools usually do not include builder overhead or profits, so these will need to be added in manually as line items based on local experience or surveys of local contractors.

An immediate use of cost analysis is determining the financial feasibility test in the highest-and-best-use analysis. I find that a vacant parcel can be legally and physically used for construction of a 10-unit apartment building. This building could be sold for $1 million. However, the construction costs would be $1.2 million. Hence, this use is not financially feasible for this site.

4. Depreciation—Physical, Functional, and External

In Chapter 9 we explored depreciation in a good bit of depth. At this juncture, we will integrate the depreciation estimates with land and building estimates to arrive at a value determination.

There are a few more issues regarding depreciation that begin to come to light at this point. Can depreciation be positive? Depreciation is the difference between the cost to construct a building and the cost to buy it in "as is" condition. In theory, depreciation should always be negative, since any structure begins to decline in value from the moment of first occupancy. What if a building sells for more than the reasonable cost to buy the land and build the improvements? Most likely, there are valuation issues that are not easily priced. Some properties, such as hotels and car dealerships, have a business component integral to the realty component. In the case of hotels, separating those components can be a real problem. What appears to be "positive" depreciation is actually masking a portion of enterprise value.

Another problem arises from measuring functional obsolescence using the segregated cost method. Certain key items, such as elevators, are usually required, but historic or otherwise desirable buildings may be deficient in elevators. Historic hotels are a prime example—many famous hotels have what would be considered deficient elevators, bathroom facilities, and public spaces by today's standards. However, market prices and values of these hotels do not reflect these obvious functional and physical deficiencies.

Buildings depreciate, but land does not, and this impacts the net effect of depreciation. Figure 13-3 reflects a simple value structure for a new building constructed with a 40-year life. The figure assumes that the land value is about 25% of the total value in the beginning, the land is expected to increase by about 5% per year, and the building is depreciated straight line

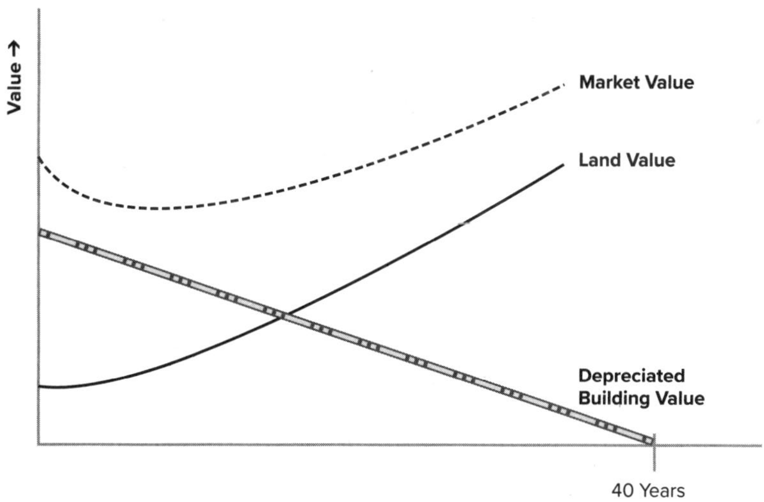

FIGURE 13-3 Physical Deterioration and Value Factors over Time

at the rate of 2.5% per year for 40 years. Notably, for the first quarter to third of the property's life, the total market value is declining, as measured by this cost analysis. However, the value begins to increase dramatically after that as increases in land value overwhelm decreases in the building value. The takeaway from this is that we tend to think of depreciation effects as being purely linear, when actually they are not. There are decisions that need to be made throughout the property's life, and even though value is increasing, the decision in year 10 may be very different from the decision in year 20.

Figure 13-3 assumes the building has a constant quality relative to other buildings (if it starts as a Class B, it stays a Class B), that land value growth rates are constant and continuous (which has been disproven in every market recently), and that the building receives average maintenance. These are issues that need to be revisited dynamically throughout the building life. This analysis provides action items for the building investors and can also provide investment opportunities when existing owners do not actively manage.

Technology can be a shock to the system. Some features can be easily retrofitted as part of a continuous maintenance process. Elevators are now programmable to optimize usage and energy costs. Class A and B buildings typically convert to these when elevator upgrades are scheduled. However, LEED and Energy Star ratings were not envisioned a few decades ago, and now many tenants demand those features.

What about dysfunctional buildings? Real estate is a very long-lived asset but constructed to serve fairly short-term purposes. A national retailer recently constructed a series of very large stores, only to realize a few years later that stores nearly twice that size were needed in some markets. It was quick to abandon the old buildings, since the cost of acquiring land and constructing new facilities was minor compared to the profits to be earned from the new facilities. The investors in those old buildings were left with structures that had no particular value after the lease end. Also, investors in out-parcels near those buildings were left holding the bag, having counted on the big retailer as an anchor "draw" for shoppers. These events, and the likelihood of these events occurring, cause significant difficulties in appraisals. By the way, the same problem arises with any sort of build-to-suit facility, particularly restaurants, specialty manufacturing, and even some custom-designed one-tenant offices. These issues raise some serious functional disutility issues that should not only be addressed in the appraisal, but should be anticipated in the sensitivity analysis for any specialized investment. A property without a broad market may suffer from functional disutility even when the market does not currently recognize that disutility.

External obsolescence can be locationally specific. One obvious case is airport proximity. For properties under or near the ends of the runways, airports can be a significant burden. Ironically, some of the most expensive real estate in Palm Beach, Florida, is directly under the glide path to the Palm Beach Airport. Consider proximity to shopping centers. The lighting, noise, and crowds of shopping centers are a burden to immediately adjacent properties, but once one moves a reasonable distance away, the shopping center converts from a negative to a positive. Proximity to public transportation can have a differential effect across property types and values.

Physical and functional obsolescence directly affect the structure, but in general do not affect the land value. The one exception to this rule is when the property's highest and best use is for continued albeit temporary use in its current condition, but eventual demolition and conversion to some other use. Obsolescence reduces the property's interim value and utility and may have an impact on the residual land value. Nonetheless, the value loss is generally ascribed totally to the building. Underlying land value may be masked by the disutility of the property as a whole while in its interim use. This has a very real opportunity for investors, since often such land can be acquired for less than it is really worth.

Appraisers often mistakenly confuse various sources of depreciation. This can happen when a market extraction is used and disutility from external sources is mistakenly ascribed to physical or functional sources, or vice versa. This mistake is important because external obsolescence actually does impact the land value, sometimes in unpredictable ways. Consider an apartment building that suddenly finds that a landfill or other noncompatible use is locating across the street. The value of the apartment building immediately declines, but is it a loss in value to the apartment building itself or to the land? It would be useful to find some market comps, improved and unimproved, adjacent to a similar landfill. Table 13-2 illustrates an approach to using somewhat similar market comps to tease out the disparate impact between the land value and the improvements value.

Delineating the impacts between the structure and the land is important. First, it helps us understand the value components when acquiring, managing, or disposing of a troubled asset. Second, it affects the highest and best use determination, particularly with respect to financial feasibility, Finally, it helps with adaptive reuse, with litigation over the impacts from the new landfill, or with tax appeals concerning the diminished value.

TABLE 13-2 Negative Externality Effects

	Subject	Comp 1	Comp 2	Comp 3	Comp 4
Property Type	Apartment	Apartment	Apartment	Vacant	Vacant
Zoning				Apartment	Apartment
Location		Similar	Unaffected	Similar	Unaffected
No. of Units	24	20	24		
No. of Units Approved				30	30
Sale Price		1,600,000	2,400,000	750,000	1,200,000
Price/Unit		80,000	100,000	25,000	40,000
Locational Effect		20,000			
(24 × $20,000)	480,000				
Land Impact				15,000	
(24 × $15,000)	360,000				
Building Impact					
(480,000 – 360,000)	120,000				

If such direct comparisons are unavailable, then an alternative method is the allocation of capitalized net income. First, the income loss due to the negative externality is determined and then capitalized to obtain the value to the property as a whole. This can be accomplished in two ways. First, if the actual loss in income is measurable, this should be capitalized or discounted using the same cap or discount rate applied if the property was not affected. If the income decrease is not knowable, an alternative would be to capitalize the "unaffected" income first by the "unaffected" cap rate and then by an "affected" cap rate. The difference between the two cap rates is often proxied by the difference between investment-grade and non-investment-grade bonds. The value impact is then allocated between land and building at the same ratio determined prior to the externality's discovery. Table 13-3 illustrates a simple example.

Determining the preimpact (unaffected or unimpaired) allocation between building and land can be achieved in several ways. Perhaps the simplest is to examine the local tax assessor's records. Most tax assessors allocate total taxable value between building and land. Even if the tax assessor's determination of market value is wrong, the ratio of land or building to total value may be reasonable. Another way to approach this is to simply re-create the cost approach "as if unimpaired" and either do a land extraction or find land values from a market survey. Again, this sort of allocation is extremely useful in making investment decisions, doing financial feasibility analyses, allocating damages in litigation, or in a tax appeal situation.

TABLE 13-3 Using Direct Capitalization to Allocate Damages

	Unimpaired	Impaired
Unaffected Value	5,000,000	
Land Component	1,000,000	
Building Component	4,000,000	
NOI	500,000	500,000
Cap Rate	10%	16%
Capitalized NOI	5,000,000	3,125,000
Land Component		625,000
Building Component		2,500,000

5. Above-Average Maintenance

The example presented in Figure 13-4 assumes normal, average maintenance. With this, the building has a predictable economic life span. By the end of this life span, the cost of maintenance and upkeep will exceed the financial feasibility, and the economically rational thing to do is tear the building down and convert it to something else.

Of course, no one bothered to tell this to the owners of Rockefeller Center, or the Empire State Building, or any one of thousands of landmark

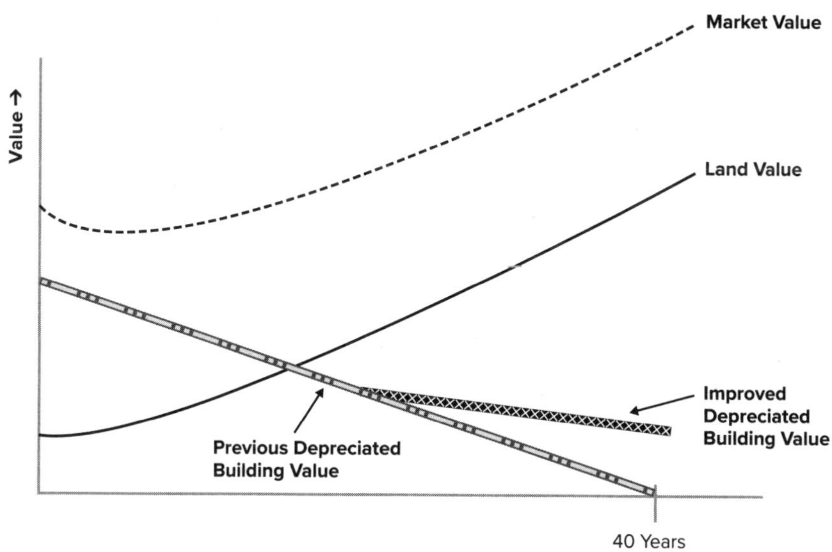

FIGURE 13-4 Physical Deterioration and Enhanced Maintenance

buildings dotting the landscape of America. Indeed, even small Class B and C buildings stand for decades beyond what would normally be considered the end of their economic lives. Often, these relics continue to stand as interim uses. An old Class C office building in a downtown business district may be owned and rented for breakeven rents (or sometimes even below breakeven) waiting for the right time in the market cycle, or waiting for permitting and entitlements, or simply waiting for financing. In the end, there are only so many wrecking balls to go around.

Conversely, though, there is a market for Class C office buildings, even in Class B locations. Indeed, the financial feasibility test must take into account the competitive landscape. An owner/developer might see that Class B rents are significantly higher, but carrying with that is a significant level of operational and marketing risk. Keeping a building as Class C but with enhanced maintenance sufficient for occupancy and health and safety requirements may be a financially optimal solution.

But, what happens to the property value? The income approach is the most direct measure of this. At any point in time, the owner can factor in the increased cost of maintenance versus the enhanced rents and see a resulting change in the value. Table 13-4 shows two comparative NOI estimates for an older Class C building. In one scenario, the building has about five years of "interim" life left, with demolition and sale of the lot (or use of the site for building a new structure) at the end of year 6. In the second scenario, the building owner enhances the maintenance over the coming years (as a permanent increase in the reserves for replacement) and is able to stretch the rents out to the financial horizon.

TABLE 13-4 Above Average Maintenance

	Demo in Five Years	Enhanced Maintenance
Annual Rents	400,000	400,000
Expenses (35%)	–140,000	–140,000
Increased Reserves (10% rents)	0	–40,000
NOI	260,000	220,000
Discount/Cap Rate	0.09	0.09
Discounted PV of Rents for Five Years	1,011,309	
PV of Land Reversion Year 6	549,615	
Total Current Value	1,560,924	2,444,444

In the first scenario, the building owner lets the property decline in value, with only average maintenance over the next five years. Of course, rents will probably decline during that time—tenants may see the handwriting on the unpainted walls and will not renew leases when they come due. We have built into this scenario the assumption that the land is worth about 25% of the total capitalized value today, and that this land value is increasing at about 5% per year. This is a fairly tempting scenario for a landlord—simply collect whatever rents remain for the next five years, which we determine to have a present value of just over $1 million, and then sell the land in year 6 after demolishing the building (we have not factored in any demo costs in this scenario, but that could be a very real and material number).

Conversely, in the second scenario, the landlord decides to increase maintenance by 10% of rents per year, or about $40,000 in extra maintenance per year. This may not seem like a huge increase, but given the size and value of this small property, such an increase in maintenance could nearly bring this building from Class C to Class B over a short period. In general, this changes the slope of the building's depreciated value, and thus changes the slope of the overall property value, as shown in Figure 13-4. As a very general rule of thumb, above-average maintenance, over an extended period, may be able to double a structure's economic life, and thus halve the depreciation slope.

The building value line slope changes significantly once the enhanced maintenance program goes into effect. Since the land value continues to increase (here assumed to be 5% per year, continuously), there is a commensurate improvement in the overall value of the investment itself.

6. Summary and Key Points

Unfortunately, investors pay little attention to cost analyses, except in development. Appraisers caution—often incorrectly—that estimates of depreciation are too specious to be trusted for older buildings, and hence the cost approach is often not used. Admittedly, good market data may be difficult to come by, and that may be a reasonable excuse for not using the cost approach under more pedestrian circumstances. For complex investment decision making, though, the cost approach can be a useful tool for identifying and analyzing a proposal's nuances.

For one, the simple ratio of land and building values to total value is extraordinarily illuminating. This can be compared with local and national norms to determine if the site is under- or overutilized. Indeed, there will be times when local zoning or land use regulations force an underutilization of land, and this can lead to powerful economic evidence of inverse condemnation. This can be further coupled with net ground lease information from the income analysis to apportion the net rents between the land and the building. If a significant portion of rents are really ascribed to the land rather than the improvements, this may call into question the determinations made in the financial feasibility portion of the highest and best use analysis.

Next, the physical depreciation curve for the building is subject to significant management influence. For one, the age-life method of calculating physical depreciation makes certain assumptions about the "average" level of maintenance. If maintenance can be enhanced, not only will this affect the overall value slope, but it can even be part of a program to change the building from one class (say, Class C) to a higher class. This sort of double-barreled approach to improving a property value may provide very real investment opportunities, particularly in down markets when current investors or competition may be ignoring a particular property.

Functional depreciation includes all of those issues that may not have been important in years past but are now of significance. Office size, ceiling heights, Americans with Disabilities Act (ADA) compliance, safety issues (e.g., fire suppression systems), hallways, the number of bathrooms, electrical systems, and internet connectivity are all key issues in commercial buildings that can enhance or detract from value. Eventually, these things pile up and render a Class B building into Class C status. Many investors will not even look at these buildings, and many tenants will also not consider them. This means there are investment opportunities here, and often the cost of bringing these buildings into the twenty-first century is less than the market value loss suffered.

External obsolescence derives from negative externalities, usually beyond the control of the property owner. The emergence of a negative externality may lead to a change in the highest and best use, forcing adaptive reuse. An apartment located across the street from a new waste dump may no longer be feasible as an apartment—declining rents will fall below the financially feasible level for rents. However, the site may still have value in some other use. Understanding the allocation of external obsolescence between the land and the improvements is a key step in maximizing value.

7. A Final Note—Replacement Versus Reproduction Cost Redux

Discussing cost analyses, I have relied on replacement costs as a basis. The *principle of substitution* points to the property's utility, rather than the exact physical characteristics, as the valuation kernel, and thus replacement cost. However, there are instances when reproduction costs need to be considered, and actually may be a bone of contention in the valuation process.

First—and somewhat trivially—insurance policies and appraisal methods usually use two different definitions of *replacement cost*. In an appraisal, the replacement cost includes a factor for depreciation. The insurance terminology for this would be *actual cash value*. Generally, property insurance policies with a replacement cost rider provide for the cost to replace "with materials of like kind and quality" without regard to depreciation. As shown, the difference can be significant, and can also be contentious. When an insurance policy calls for a value determination, this may also require an analysis of the loss of market value over and above the actual cost of repairs. A $1,000,000 property may suffer a water intrusion that only costs $100,000 to repair. The value of the property, though, has diminished to $800,000 even after the repairs are completed due to reputational losses.

Of more interest is the Federal Emergency Management Agency (FEMA) 50% rule. Flood insurance will fund property repairs, but somewhat contentiously, based on *reproduction* of whatever was there in the first place. Naturally, the thing that was there in the first place may be highly depreciated. What if the property was not in compliance with FEMA requirements? This lack of compliance, arguably, constitutes a significant level of functional disutility. Given the billions of dollars in natural disaster damages in America each year, these are not trivial issues. FEMA's 50% rule requires that if the repairs to the property cost more than 50% of the value of the structure, then the property will need to be replaced with something that conforms to FEMA's rules. Thus, while FEMA is basing the insurance reimbursement on the depreciated value, the restoration will have to comport to undepreciated quality. Studies show that construction costs and market values are often at odds with one another in high-demand but high-cost flood-prone areas (such as beachfront communities, which are targets for hurricanes). Clearly, terminology such as "replacement" and "reproduction" have new meaning in these situations. For high-value properties affected or potentially affected by such floods, a proactive approach, even including an analysis before storm season starts, may certainly be indicated.

Another potential situation—and certainly not the last one—arises from dedication of a historic or facade preservation easement. One basis for determining the value of the dedication is the present value cost of maintenance of the structure or the facade in its historic quality. The nature of this "maintenance" may vary from one situation to another. Some preservation ordinances simply require a historically accurate view, but with modern materials. Hence, a historically preserved building might have modern appliances, utilities, and other treatments. Other situations may require exacting craftspersons capable of replicating stonework, antique windows and doors, and interior features as they existed at the time of original construction. The difference between reproduction cost and replacement cost will be one of the measures used in this determination.

14
Reconciling the Various Approaches

A man complained that on his way home to dinner he had every day to pass through that long field of his neighbor's. I advised him to buy it, and it would never seem long again.

—Ralph Waldo Emerson

THIS CHAPTER WILL tie together much of what I have presented thus far, but first I want to put it all in perspective. Appraisal is usually heuristic. An appraisal report provides the appraiser's professional judgment, after analyzing very noisy data, to arrive at the property value. The quality and reliability of that point estimate—called a "reconciled opinion of value"—depends on the appraiser's experience, training, and expertise; the data quality; the methodological rigor; and ultimately the manner of performing the final reconciliation. This final reconciliation balances and evaluates all of the information fed into it.

An example that is not real estate–related illustrates this well. Consider two publicly traded equities, quoted with bid-ask spreads and a recent trade:

Security A—NYSE

Bid	98.50
Ask	98.60
Last	98.55

A reasonable inference might be made that 1,000 shares are worth $98,550, with a range of values of $98,500 to $98,600. This range is approximately 0.01%. Now, consider this actual quote, taken from the "pink sheets":

Security B—Over the Counter:

Bid: 2.50
Ask: 10.00
Last:. 4.60

Valuation of this thinly traded issue can be problematic indeed. Given the spread, this stock probably also has a very thin float and a low daily trading average. Entering a trade on one side or the other, even a small one, can have an undue influence on the share price. Notably, my trade (buy or sell) has almost no impact at all on the actual company value. Efficient markets and rational expectations imply that, for a highly traded security with substantial liquidity, the market price and intrinsic value should at least be in the same ballpark with one another. For illiquid holdings the price and value can be completely disassociated.

Further complicating this comparison are issues of control and marketability. When valuing a reasonably small holding in a publicly traded security, marketability may not be a big concern. Control is certainly not a problem if I have a small holding relative to the outstanding shares. But with the over-the-counter stock, even a small trade could influence the current share price, and the value of my holding may be subject to the whims of the bid-ask spread.

Real estate valuation deals with these problems in various ways. Most appraisals are for market value of the fee simple interest. If some other interest is valued, such as an undivided cotenancy, then some discount for lack of control or marketability would be appropriate. Imagine a $10 million building owned by four partners, each with a tenancy in common, a partnership interest, or some other undivided cotenancy, of 25%. One partner asks me to appraise her interest separate from the other partners. Her share is worth something less than one-fourth of $10 million, due to lack of control and lack of marketability. Most well-written partnership agreements have some restrictions on sale of interests that have implications for my valuation.

We have explored the inner workings of sales comparisons, income capitalization, and cost analyses. Each technique has implications for investors that are critically important when property is acquired, owned and managed, and disposed or converted into some other use. Up to this point I have focused on the inner workings of approaches rather than the end results. The end results of three different approaches to value may be three materially different numbers. At the appraisal conclusion, I need to *reconcile* these findings into a single point estimate of value.

Understanding reconciliation is vitally important. While the market value of a parcel may be almost totally explained by sales comparison, the investor may be more interested in the income capitalization. For an office building, the discounted present value of income may be the most useful for the appraisal, but the buyer may be more interested in the cost analyses, particularly when investing in older properties.

Hence, the ability to unpack—reverse engineer—the final determination of value may be a key element in the understanding and usefulness of a property's valuation report. The remainder of this chapter will explore that reverse engineering in some detail to point the reader toward some useful appraisal aspects.

1. How Reasonable and Reliable Are the Alternative Approaches?

Unfortunately, there is no hard-and-fast methodology for determining an appraisal's statistical reliability. This is a matter of some concern in the industry, particularly in litigation and appraisals in support of securities, where real estate valuation has to stand up against statistically explained securities valuation methods. In the absence of quantitative metrics, each alternative approach, and the appraisal as a whole, needs to be evaluated on a set of qualitative standards. Common questions that should be asked include the following:

How Old Is the Underlying Data?

The sales comparison approach relies on recent comp sales. The income analysis relies on market rents, expenses, and investor rate-of-return expectations. Cost analyses depend on land values, construction estimates, and various means of extracting depreciation. In a perfect world, this data would be current, but as a practical matter the data is probably many months old. In rapidly changing markets, inferences may be misleading. Appraisers may assume linear trends when in actuality data follows a nonlinear path. This leads naturally to the next question:

How Volatile Is the Market?

Assume I am faced with the pricing data shown in Figure 14-1.

The inference made from these three sales is not unreasonable. The most recent sale, from three months ago, is perhaps the most informative, and the other two sales seem to support it. A linear trend through this data gives a reasonable value indication of the property. Consider Figures 14-2 and 14-3, using the same data.

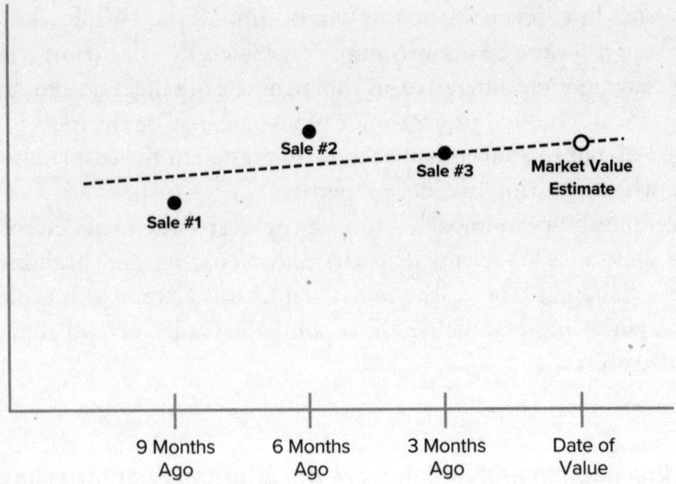

FIGURE 14-1 Market Pricing Data

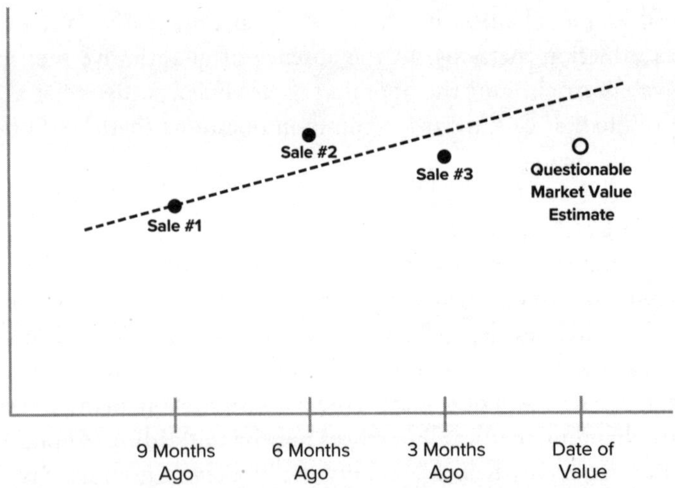

FIGURE 14-2 Alternative Linear Extrapolation of Market Pricing Data

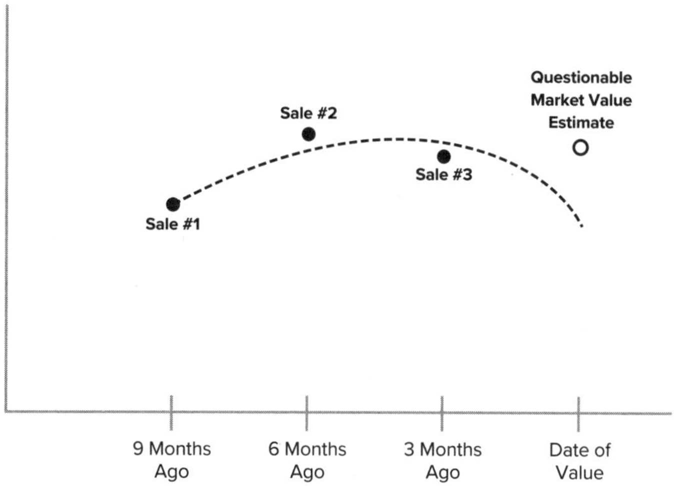

FIGURE 14-3 Nonlinear Market Pricing Data Trend

Figure 14-2 takes a slightly different view. Perhaps the first sale (nine months ago) is most valid, and the other two are slight outliers. This means my current value estimate is widely *undervalued*. Figure 14-3 shows a nonlinear fit, suggesting local prices peaked somewhere between three and six months ago and are now on a trend back where they were nine months ago. This means a significant *overvaluation*. The use of old data in a volatile market begs for the use of more than just a few data points.

How Available Is Market-Rate Financing?

Even if the investor buys for cash, or has exclusive access to favorable financing, the availability of market-rate financing influences the marketability of the subject and the comps. If the current market offers limited financing, then comps may have suffered from a buyer shortage. In tight markets, choice property owners may stay put and weather the storm. Comp sales may represent distress sales or sales to bottom feeders. This suggests that my appraisal may understate value. This also suggests bargain opportunities for cash buyers.

How Well Has Obsolescence Been Measured?

Poor maintenance, inattention to functional issues, or the emergence of negative externalities all have an influence on the subject property, particularly if these are difficult to measure and adjust against comps. Conversely, above-average attention to these factors may not be properly accounted for in the appraisal. The same can be said for zoning changes, which can have varying influences not readily apparent from comp prices. An adverse zoning change for a commercial building with long-term leases may not have an immediate impact on the income capitalization. The leased fee valuation may not be affected immediately. But the adverse zoning may have a long-term impact on the surrounding neighborhood, on the adaptive reuse, or on the ability to rebuild if damaged. These increase the risk of ownership and should be reflected in the cap or discount rates.

Are Neighborhood Trends Flat, Constant, or Accelerating?

Most appraisals look at supply-and-demand factors and neighborhood trends as "snapshots in time." Whatever is going on right now must be the long-term reality. Of course, markets are dynamic. An excellent downtown commercial district this year may be next year's depressed area, and a disadvantaged neighborhood may see gentrification by year's end. Tickling out these "truths" about markets can be difficult, and yet property ownership is a long-term proposition. Neither the owner nor the potential buyer is really interested in the market today, but rather the market a year, or 5 years, or 10 years from now. Finding those trends can be like soothsaying, yet these are critically important to determine pricing and purchase or sale decisions.

Local trends should be taken in the context of national trends. The national market dictates return on investment and financing expectations, while local cycles may signal buying opportunities. Local movement—positive or negative—greater than suggested by national cycles may signal dangerous roiling in the local investment market.

The reconciliation includes a deep dive into the methodologies used. The data quality and the trend analysis timeline must be examined with a keen eye to reliability. In a perfect world, this data and these analyses could be examined quantitatively, and even in the not-so-perfect world, sensitivity analysis is always a good idea. Incorrect assumptions about the methodological quality in the final reconciliation can lead to significant errors in the valuation product.

> By the way, the savvy investor will look for flaws in the data and underlying assumptions to find undervalued gems in the market.

2. How Reasonable and Valid Are the Alternative Findings?

Somewhere out there, some appraiser has produced a theoretically and empirically perfect appraisal. Cost, income, and sales comparison analyses are all used, with few adjustments. Each valuation conclusion agrees perfectly. The final conclusion of value is just a rounding error difference among the alternative value conclusions.

Here are two danger signals when looking at the alternative value conclusions:

> Problem 1: The two or three alternative approaches agree almost perfectly.
> Problem 2: The two or three alternative approaches do not agree.

Well, that makes it simple, doesn't it! In the first situation, there is a very real suspicion that the appraiser cherry-picked the data to develop that perfect-looking appraisal. Indeed, the value conclusions may be correct, but who knows? Even the original analyst has no idea, since he or she was too busy validating preconceived notions about the value to really conduct a serious examination. These sorts of problems may seem far-fetched, but consider residential appraisals submitted during the housing bubble, used to support billions of dollars in residential mortgage-backed securities. Many only served to validate overly inflated prices rather than make a skeptical examination of the validity of those prices. If such analytical errors could occur in simple residential appraisals, then consider the potential problems in more complex commercial valuations.

In the second situation, the data is simply all over the map. Each approach to value is a set of methodologies replete with embedded assumptions. Slight errors in these assumptions can lead to major differences in value conclusions. Consider two scenarios for valuation of a small commercial property investment (Table 14-1). Effective gross rent (EGI) for each has been determined to be $1 million. In the first, the expense ratio is 35%, and the cap rate is 6.5%. In the second scenario, the expense ratio is 40%, and the cap rate is estimated at 7%. Neither change seems to be a very significant shift in assumptions, but see how these differences in assumptions impact the value conclusions.

TABLE 14-1 Alternative Income Valuations

	First Scenario	Second Scenario
Effective Gross Income	1,000,000	1,000,000
Expenses	(350,000)	(400,000)
Net Operating Income	650,000	600,000
Capitalization Rate	6.50%	7.00%
Capitalized Value	$10,000,000	$8,571,429
Difference	16.67%	

Slight differences in the expense estimates and in the forecast of investor expectations can result in very significant differences (in this case, over 16%) in the determination of value. The previous section showed that such value differences should be closely inspected, perhaps with a sensitivity analysis. This section is more about the validity of the final estimate. Which number is actually correct, $10 million or $8.5 million? Internally, the appraisal may give some clues. If the sales comparison and cost estimates come in at or near $10 million, then it would appear that the assumptions imbedded in the first estimate may be closer to the truth. If the alternative approaches are inconclusive, or based on flawed or inconsistent data, then some outside sanity check may be useful.

There are methods that fall far short of the quality of an appraisal but nonetheless add value to the appraisal review process. One is a *broker price opinion*, or BPO for short. State laws vary widely on just when and how a broker may issue a nonappraisal opinion regarding value. In many states, a broker may only issue a BPO for a listing or purchasing client in anticipation of setting an asking or offer price. Nonetheless, if a BPO is available, it can serve as a somewhat noisy but useful cross-check on the appraisal determination.

Another sanity check on the value conclusion can come from an *automated valuation model* (AVM). These are most commonly associated with residential valuation, and the quality of AVMs vary widely. Some of the popular AVMs have ironically been shown to be the least accurate. Further, AVMs are black boxes, and while they produce a value determination and some statistical tools for evaluating that estimate, the methodology is almost always proprietary. Some firms are now tentatively offering AVMs for commercial properties. While these are mostly untested as of this writing, an AVM value may at least help with the appraisal review.

Finally, if prior subject sales are available, then a simple trend analysis is extremely useful. If nearby comparable properties have repeat sales over a similar time frame, then a simple extrapolation of trends may prove useful (Figure 14.4). The caveats noted earlier still apply, but if more than one repeat sale is available, a useful check figure may be found.

Comp 2 had the most recent sales, and so naturally the subject property trend line is somewhat closer to the trend line for that comp. Nonetheless, the two trend lines provide a nice bracketing for the subject and may give additional quantitative support for one or more indications of value.

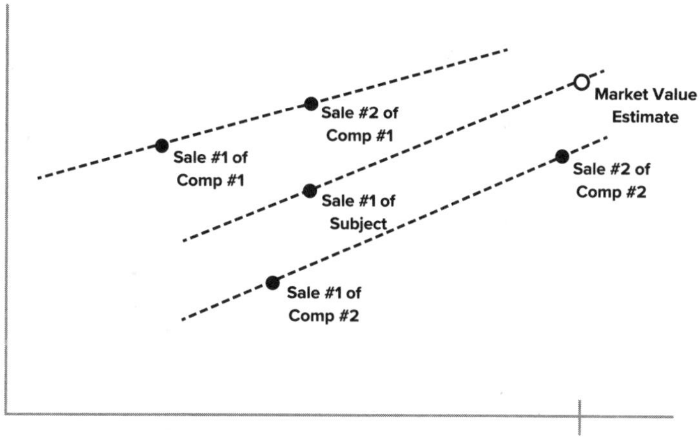

FIGURE 14-4 Repeat Sales of Two Comparable Properties

> The reliability and credibility of an appraisal rests more on the validity of methods, data, and underlying assumptions. Poor analytical or methodological determinations may not be evident in a review of the appraisal itself, but may have to be detected using outside valuation metrics. If these quantitative sanity checks reveal value conclusions that do not seem to stand up to real-world comparisons, then the underlying appraisal itself should be revisited. In the end, these quantitative checks at best reveal whether or not the appraisal may have some undetected flaw that needs to be fixed, and *not* whether the appraisal should be tossed out with the trash.

3. Is the Data Reasonable?

Both prior sections invited a reevaluation of underlying data. It is helpful at this juncture to summarize the data being used:

Sales Comparison Approach Data

- Recent comp prices, and:
  - Sale dates (to measure market conditions trends)
  - Financing terms and conditions (market rate or other)
  - Locations (proximity, quality, ingress and egress, topography)
  - Legal characteristics (fee simple, arm's-length, etc.)
  - Physical characteristics

Cost Approach Data

- Recent sales of comparable sites *or*
- Recent comp sales to extract land values
- Construction cost estimates
- Measures of physical, functional, and economic depreciation

Income Approach Data

- Estimates of:
  - Market rents (for fee simple valuations)
  - Current contract rents (for leased fee valuations)
  - Forward-looking expenses
- Discount or capitalization rates
- Timing of cash flows

A thorough and rigorous appraisal of a complex commercial property will contain some or all three approaches. One notable problem is that all three approaches rely on recent comparable transactions. The sales comparison approach is centered on an adjustment grid made up of those comps. The cost approach uses either land comps or an extraction process with sales comps. The income approach requires recent market rent comps and extractions of market normal expenses and cap/discount rates. All too often, the same set of comps are used for all data sets. This raises some serious empirical problems:

- A data error, such as a simple transcription error in any individual comp, will migrate throughout all three approaches.
- Systematic errors in comp selection are difficult to detect.
- Assumptions such as market conditions adjustments become common to all three approaches.
- Basic assumptions about highest and best use are embedded in the comparable selection process. If these assumptions are flawed, so are the comps selected.
- The appraiser may invoke hypothetical conditions or the client may require certain conditions for the assignment, such as fee simple interest versus leased fee. These choices permeate throughout the appraisal.
- Assumptions about the impact of external obsolescence are buried in all approaches. In the cost approach, this is a direct deduction. In the sales adjustment grid, it constitutes a location adjustment. In the income approach, it affects the discount or cap rate. Generally, the same level of impact is used in all three approaches, and the error becomes undetectable.

The reconciliation depends in large part on reconciling the quality of the underlying data. Data should be authentic, pertinent, and sufficient to the process at hand. Indeed, the user may want to test the data, at least by having a conversation with the appraiser on how critical data points were verified and validated. Approaches that use excellent data and require few assumptions or adjustments are preferred to approaches and methods that are replete with empirical shortcomings. A review of any appraisal will include a serious stress test on the data, the assumptions, and adjustments made to that data. If it is found that common data is used throughout various approaches and methods, then a particularly skeptical view should be taken to decisions based on that data.

> At one time, the IRS required that preference be given to the single comparable that required the fewest adjustments in the sales adjustment grid.

4. Why Is the Appraisal a Point Estimate Rather Than a Range?

The short answer is, "it simply is."

The long answer goes to the heart of what an appraisal really is and does. It is a professional opinion of value. It is based on a very stylized and methodologically fastidious analysis of real estate data, but it is a professional judgment call. This can be difficult for investors to swallow, particularly those who are used to valuation metrics expressed as a range or as a confidence interval. There are no such statistical metrics in an appraisal report. Further, the span of comps does not constitute a potential range of values. Take, for example, the very simple reconciliation shown below:

Value indicated by the sales comparison approach: .$10,000,000
Value indicated by the cost approach: $11,000,000
Value indicated by income capitalization: $12,000,000
Reconciled indication of value: $10,500,000

The following language appears in the report:

> The data supporting the sales comparison approach was considered to be the most valid, and this approach required the fewest assumptions and adjustments. The cost approach, while supportive of the value indication, was the least reliable of the three. I weighted the income approach 25% and the sales comparison approach 75% in the final reconciliation of value.

So, what does that mean? The naive reader may view the reconciled indication of value as something like a mean or median, and thus the other three approaches provide a range of potential values. However, this is not at all the way to read this. That "range of values" take on the results suggests that $12,000,000 has an equal chance of being the true value as does $10,000,000. The appraiser, though, made it clear that the sales comparison approach, at $10,000,000, is the most reliable and his or her value determination is influenced only slightly by the much higher value determined in the income analysis. Indeed, the value at the midpoint of this range—provided by the cost approach—is given no weight at all.

Imagine going to your physician and receiving a diagnosis that you have an ulcer. You ask the physician for a range of values, and he says, "OK, you have an ulcer, but it's in the range of appendicitis to gallstones." This would be a nonsensical diagnosis. That does not mean that physicians are not occasionally wrong. However, the diagnosis is the professional judgment of the physician, who has analyzed data, conducted acceptable tests and methodologies, and weighed the various results to make a determination. The same is true with an appraisal.

Appraisal standards do provide for an appraiser proffering a value range rather than a point estimate. The same standards and methodological constructs apply. However, these are fairly rare. Lending institutions, courts of law, municipalities, the IRS, and local tax collectors all look for point estimates of value, and most appraisers are actually uncomfortable proffering a range of values. When such a range is produced, it almost always comes with no distributional characteristics. The likelihood of a value falling at the edges of a range varies widely depending on the shape of the distribution of those values. See Figures 14-5a and 14-5b, which illustrate the problem.

Prices are actually somewhat skewed. Prices cannot be negative, but they can go positive up to (theoretically) infinity and tend to be lumped near the lower part of the range. Depending on the exact distribution characteristics, about two-thirds of outcomes fall within plus or minus one standard deviation of the midpoint (medians are usually preferred ways to describe the central tendency of real estate prices). About 95% will fall within plus or minus two standard deviations. Mathematically, this tells us that the likelihood of an outcome occurring between plus-one and plus-two standard deviations, or between minus-one and minus-two, is considerably less likely than something happening in the middle.

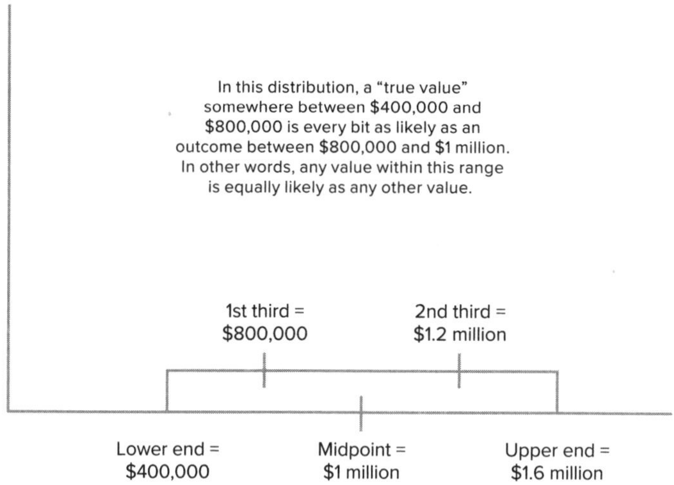

FIGURE 14-5A Two Different Distributions of Value—a Uniform Distribution

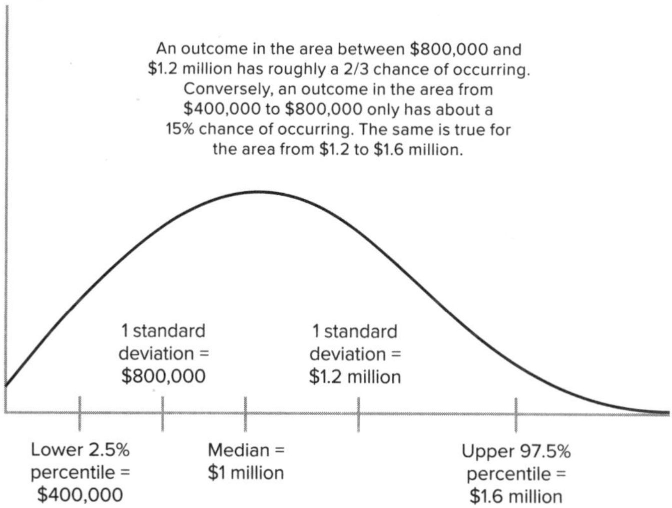

FIGURE 14-5B Two Different Distributions of Value—a Skewed Distribution

This is far outside of the range of expertise for most appraisers, and the data is rarely sufficient to support this sort of description of possible or likely outcomes. While appraisals may, from time to time, express the outcome as a potential range of values, only with some advanced analytical tools can we determine the probabilities within that range.

5. How Does the Appraiser Actually Assign Weights?

The point estimate summarizing the appraisal is more properly called an "opinion of value." As noted, this determination is a professional opinion and is often a weighted average of various methodologies applied. Some approaches and methods may actually be weighted zero. Rarely is the outcome a simple average, since the reliability of various approaches and methods will vary.

There is more than one reconciliation embedded in an appraisal. For starters, the sales comparison outcome is a reconciliation of the adjusted values of a set of comps. Some comps tell a more compelling story than others and may require fewer adjustments or operate more closely to the subject in the marketplace. When an income evaluation is useful and necessary, it may actually be performed several times, as a sensitivity analysis or as for purposes of comparing different methodologies (i.e., discounted cash flow versus direct capitalization). At the end of each approach, some reconciliation is appropriate.

The overarching challenge in the appraisal is to mimic the behavior of market participants, given a set of market characteristics. This is not always as straightforward as it might seem. Consider a situation in which location—the specific neighborhood, and indeed the street on which a building fronts—is the most deciding factor among investors. One recent study of a downtown central business district found that a certain set of main north-south arteries were preferred for high-end retail, and only then within a few blocks. A location on an east-west "side street," or a location on a north-south artery several blocks away, has a significantly different value for a retailer. The value may still be strong—say, for an office building—but not for a property determined to have a highest and best use as retail.

Now, consider two comps—one right next door to the subject, in that "hot" retail zone, but requires a significant number of adjustments. The other is several blocks away, but the only adjustment is for location. Since the two properties have different highest and best uses, the location adjustment may be inconsequential, since one property may be very valuable as an office and the other, more nearby property more valuable as a retail site.

Under the old IRS guidelines, for example, the distant property, with few adjustments, would be the one given the most consideration. However, this comparable fails to mimic the actual investment consideration of retail location buyers, given the facts in the marketplace. Hence, the actual reconciliation process has to take qualitative factors into account, and not just quantitative ones.

The first step in any reconciliation is usually a rank ordering of choices. This reflects the mindset of market participants, since buyers tend to consider the "best" property at the top of the list. There is certainly an argument that no two investors have exactly the same rank ordering, but the concept of rational expectations suggests that the prices of properties should somehow equate the utility preferences among investors. Thus, after adjustments, these differences in utility preferences should be endemic to the reconciled data. In the end, appraisal standards require that the reconciliation address "applicability and relevance" of data and methodologies. Logic and professional judgment are the keys to a successful and useful reconciliation.

A generation ago, rational expectations was taught as dogma in business schools. Today, it is recognized as an interesting hypothesis. Behavioral economics now recognizes that decision making among choices can be much more complex. Hence, the heuristic aspects of an appraisal, when conducted properly, may be superior to the more quantitative ones in many circumstances.

6. Caveats, Assumptions, and Conditions

The final reconciled value is always subject to a bundle of conditions, generally falling into five categories:

- Assignment conditions
- Assumptions
- Limiting conditions
- Extraordinary assumptions
- Hypothetical conditions

Each can have a major impact on the final reconciled value and needs to be understood in interpreting and using the appraisal findings.

Assignment Conditions

These are established between the client and the appraiser at the project inception. In complex projects, such as development analyses or litigation, these may evolve over time. A client cannot force an appraiser to use flawed judgment, violate appraisal standards, or issue a misleading report. The client can, though, set down a set of conditions under which the appraisal is being performed.

I have discussed the difference between a fee simple valuation versus leased fee. The two appraisals may result in materially different findings because of comp data used and analytical techniques employed. If two parties in a litigation are at odds over the property value, one may proffer one appraisal and the other proffer a different one, each based on different conditions.

The basis of value is another assignment condition. Most appraisals are to determine the market value. Investment value, though, may be more significant in some situations. Distressed sale value, aggregation value, or some other basis of value may tell a more fulsome story about the property. These are key elements to be discussed at the onset.

For that matter, who are the clients and the intended users of the final report? These are two separate but intertwined questions. For a financing appraisal, the client is generally the lender, despite who may or may not pay for the appraisal. This has some important bearing on the *confidentiality* rule, which requires that information gleaned in the assignment be kept confidential unless and until the client says otherwise. Thus, the building's owner may be given a copy of the appraisal report (a decision left to the lender) but may not have access to the underlying workfile. The report needs to stand on its own legs and present a fulsome synopsis of the appraisal analysis. This leads to the notion of intended users. The property owner may be an intended user, as might be other investors in a loan syndication, the government (in a takings matter), or tenants in the property (when setting rental rates based on an appraisal). The determination of intended users has important implications for the nature of the report. If the intended users are limited to highly knowledgeable "insiders," then the report may be fairly brief and concise. If the intended users are less sophisticated, then the report may need to be longer and more detailed.

Applicable standards are a condition of the assignment. State licensed and certified appraisers agree to abide by the Uniform Standards of Professional Appraisal Practice (USPAP) as a condition of their licensure, and many situations (such as federally regulated lending) also specify USPAP as governing standards. Other standards may include:

Uniform Appraisal Standards for Federal Land Acquisitions. Applicable whenever federal money is being used for any portion of a project that includes a property acquisition.

Federal National Mortgage Association (Fannie Mae) Selling Guide. Constitutes supplemental standards for any loan that may be sold to that agency.

IRS Real Property Valuation Guidelines (Section 4.48.6). These are the primary standards for any appraisal to be submitted to the IRS.

Of course, it is highly unlikely that the typical user will be familiar with these supplemental standards, or how and when they apply. The appraisal should reference any additional standards that apply and explain how those impact the valuation exercise, the methodology, analysis, and final outcomes.

Another key element is the effective date of valuation. This may seem perfunctory, since most appraisals are done "as of right now." In litigation, proposed development projects, or takings matters, determining the effective date of the value is a key and sometimes contentious element. This is not the same as the date of the appraisal itself—valuations may be retrospective or prospective. Very specific methodologies and guidelines exist for determining a value at some point in the past or future. Implicit in this are assumptions and perhaps hypothetical conditions, as described below.

Assumptions

Valuation of anything is based on a set of assumptions. An obvious assumption in any market value appraisal is that there is actually a market for the thing being valued. In the absence of a market for the property, it may have a value-in-use or even an investment value to a particular user. Market value usually depends on the competitive market of multiple buyers and sellers. Anything short of this will have some severe implications on the viability and reliability of the value estimate.

Other assumptions include issues surrounding the title, the correctness of information received from the client and/or third parties, latent defects in the property itself, and legality of the current or prospective uses of the property, including encroachments or easements:

- Appraisers generally have some expertise in title matters, but are not attorneys or licensed title agents and therefore not legally empowered to render opinions about the title. This is true about the subject property and about comps being used.

- Appraisers are required to make efforts to verify data being used. Indeed, under the Federal Land Acquisition standards, there are specific requirements set out for verification of comparable data used. Faulty or invalid information can have a material impact on the appraisal, particularly given that only a few comps are being used. Large-scale valuation exercises, such as automated valuation models, use hundreds or thousands of data points, and so a few individual errors typically cancel out. With only a few comps, the law of large numbers does not, unfortunately, apply. The user of an appraisal report will want to examine carefully the methodologies used to validate data, particularly data received from the client with a direct impact on the final valuation.
- Latent defects, and particularly environmental contamination, may be difficult if not impossible to spot with a normal and reasonable appraisal inspection. Appraisers are usually required to perform some level of inspection or verification of subject and comparable properties, but there are no specifications as to the nature and extent of this effort. Appraisers usually inspect property to ascertain the utility for its highest and best use, to examine for functional or external depreciation issues, and to observe the obvious level of construction quality and/or upkeep. Many years ago, appraisers were expected to perform detailed construction examinations, such as are currently performed by licensed and trained building inspectors. Today, though, a property buyer relying on an appraisal report would be well advised to also engage a building inspector and other such due diligence investigators as may be warranted in the situation.
- Appraisers are also not land surveyors and must make certain assumptions about the site size by depending on public records or surveys provided by the owner. Generally, such surveys and public records will disclose known encroachments, either by the subject property or by neighboring properties. Easements that run with the land, called *easements in gross*, are also usually disclosed. Some prescriptive easements may not be fully disclosed on older surveys. Surveys and other public records may not make clear delineation of *accretion* and *reliction* of properties bordering waterways. The former happens when the waterway migrates away from the land, increasing the size of the holding. The latter is the opposite phenomenon. Sometimes there are legal prescriptions to cure such problems, but often that is not the case. Changes in tidal runs or erosion of waterfront banks can also change land sizes, shapes, and even locations.

The airport in St. Joseph, Missouri, is not directly accessible from the city itself due to movement of the Missouri River. City residents have to drive thru Kansas to access their airport. Movements of the Ohio River shifted portions of Kentucky north into the Indiana side of the river. Newport County, Rhode Island, is only accessible to the rest of the state by driving thru Massachusetts, thanks to the Taunton River. Finally, thanks to movements of the Mississippi River, Illinois's Kaskaskia Island lies on the Missouri side, and Missouri's Grand Tower Island lies on the Illinois side.

Limiting Conditions

These are generally issued to protect the appraiser but may have some bearing on the usefulness of the analysis and findings. Typically, appraisers will explicitly prohibit users—including the client—from publishing the appraisal report. This may have bearing if the appraisal and the report itself are being used to support a securities offering. The appraiser usually has some language reserving the right to amend the findings and the report if new facts come to light that have a material impact on the appraisal. Finally, most appraisers will have some language in the report specifying that there is no implication of follow-up work, such as testimony or public presentation, and that the report delivery itself constitutes the finality of the project unless other arrangements are made.

Extraordinary Assumptions

The inside joke among appraisers is that some assumptions are better than others. The reality is that many ordinary assumptions may be proved false, or perhaps less than perfectly accurate, but might not have a material impact on the appraisal findings. An extraordinary assumption is some fact that is assumed to be true, and necessary for the appraisal analysis, but has a material impact on the results if found to be false. Appraisal standards require that any such extraordinary assumption be clearly laid out in the report.

An appraisal of a site for a new office building may depend on the extraordinary assumption that the permits, entitlements, and other requirements can be readily obtained in the normal course of business. One recent appraisal was for a shopping center site, and the land needed for the shopping center was only a small portion of a larger parcel. The appraisal was only for that portion of the land needed for the retail development, and it rested on the extraordinary assumption that the site could be easily and readily subdivided (and, of course, that permits and entitlements could be obtained!). A prospective appraisal of raw land designated for a residential subdivision, with a prospective value after full build-out, may depend on the extraordinary assumption that the development actually occurs. Appraisals of apartment developments often hinge on the extraordinary assumption that stabilized occupancy can be obtained within the requisite time frame.

As shown, there are a host of important assumptions on which the appraisal rests. The appraisal report user is well advised to pay close attention to these. Many assumptions are buried in the appraisal report, and so a careful reading is often needed to pick out which assumptions are pivotal to the final determinations.

Hypothetical Conditions

These are the brothers and sisters of extraordinary assumptions. The extraordinary assumptions (EAs) are assumed to be true, while the hypothetical conditions (HCs) are known to be false but assumed for purposes of the appraisal. The most common example is the appraisal of a contaminated site in litigation. The basis for damages is usually the value "as if unimpaired." The land is thus appraised under the hypothetical condition that the property is not, and never was, impacted by the environmental disamenity.

An often overlooked HC derives from the eminent domain "taking" of commercial property. Most commercial properties are rented with long-term leases, and as such any appraisal using those leases is a leased fee appraisal. Recall, the basis for a "taking" is the fee simple market value, and so the appraiser has to invoke the hypothetical condition that the property was leased at market rates on the official taking date.

Relaxing or changing assumptions or conditions may have a material impact on the value conclusions. Readers may be used to conducting sensitivity analyses in a more quantitative fashion, but most assumptions and conditions have a qualitative impact on the valuation equation. For that reason, simply relaxing certain factors may or may not produce a valid set of alternative results to analyze.

In the end, though, these assumptions and conditions are the core of the analysis. They dictate which comparable data is used, how that comparable data is analyzed, and how the results are interpreted. Readers and users of appraisals must develop a working familiarity not only with the conditions and assumptions themselves but how they are used in the analysis. Actual clients are at an advantage because they can be engaged with the appraiser at the front end to influence, and perhaps even determine, which assumptions and conditions will be used and how they will apply. Non-client users of appraisals may not have that luxury, and so may need to engage separate *review appraisers* to examine the analysis at a granular level.

7. Summary and Key Points

The appraisal is a combination of quantitative and qualitative factors. While quantitative adjustments and weightings may be applied in the analytical portions and at the reconciliation, these quantifications are often driven by qualitative factors and decisions. The appraisal report reader is frequently left to reverse engineer the logic behind these decisions. A well-written appraisal report should clearly and compellingly lay out the qualitative basis for these decisions.

Unfortunately, that sort of clarification is rare. The reader is stuck with a conundrum—how to make sense of reconciled findings in the absence of an understanding of qualitative processes underpinning the weightings that led to those findings. The casual reader may take this the wrong way—that the whole appraisal process, and the report itself, are worthless. Far from it! The focus of this text thus far has been to uncover the hidden gems buried in the appraisal analysis and report. Even failing to understand how the appraiser reached the final conclusion, or even failing to agree with that final conclusion, the reader will find immense usefulness in the appraisal and the appraisal report.

Thus, understanding the reconciled appraisal results will require a bit more in-depth study by the user, and particularly if that user is an investor trying to make an acquisition or development decision, or a property owner making a reversion or disposal decision. The user will want to thoroughly enumerate the assumptions and conditions that underpin the final results. Three questions should be answered at this juncture:

How Do the Results Change If Key Assumptions and Conditions Are Relaxed?

Consider a litigation, in which one party—for example, you—have proffered a leased fee value, while the other side—for example, the people suing you—are hinged on a fee simple value. It would be handy at the onset to observe the difference in valuation outcomes if this set of assumptions is relaxed. All too often, the "other side" may actually be asking for damages that are not even supported by their own theory of the case!

What Assumptions and Conditions Were Ignored?

One common hypothetical condition concerns environmentally impaired property. Appraisers will often invoke the HC that the property is *not* contaminated to proffer an unimpaired value. Most appraisers, like it or not, have little or no expertise, training, and experience in valuing such property. Thus, what if one were to value the property in the not-so-hypothetical "as-is" condition? In many situations, this value, coupled with the HC value, can be an important decision tool. By the way, this also comes into play in any sort of easement, encroachment, takings, or damages situation.

How Do the Results Change If the "Second Best" Is Considered Instead?

If the "best comp" or "best method" has the most powerful weighting in the final reconciliation, how do the results change if the "second best" is considered instead? Often, the choice really isn't that clear. Of three comparables, it is not uncommon to see one weighted 50%, one 40%, and one perhaps 10%. Of three approaches to value, it is common to see most or nearly all weight placed on one (say, the sales comparison approach) and no weight at all on one. Most often in practice, the cost approach is given little or no weight, due in no small part to its complexity and array of underlying assumptions. But, what if the ratios were flipped? What if indeed the third comparable or the cost approach had the most key truth about value buried in it?

With millions of dollars at stake, this is worth some investigation and review.

8. A Final Note—How Will This Look on the Accident Report?

Pilots do dumb things occasionally. Don't worry, though, most of the time, the guys and gals who fly the "big tin" are inoculated from making dumb decisions. They religiously follow checklists. In the United States, there is little or no "rank" in the cockpit, and three-stripe copilots feel free to call out the four-striper if he or she is doing something marginally dumb. Nearly constant visits to the simulator, constant oversight from instructor pilots, and the requirement of regular flight reviews makes flying the safest form of transportation on planet Earth. Nonetheless, pilots still occasionally do dumb things.

In flight training, there is a great adage, "How will this look on the accident report?" Given the choice between two options, which one will the accident investigators think was a bad idea? Sadly, appraisers do not ask that question often enough. Appraisers are required to adhere to sets of standards, USPAP and supplemental standards. These standards are very broad and sometimes do not specify exact methodological decisions. Yes, the standards constitute a checklist, but not nearly as detailed as the volumes of checklists carried in the average cockpit.

So, with that in mind, appraisers often do dumb things. Further, they generally do not have "copilots" in the cockpit to call them out if something is going awry. Sure, many appraisal reports are cosigned by two appraisers, but one is often a trainee or apprentice, and the equality of opinion that exists in the cockpit is not available when the appraisal is being conducted and the report written.

In addition, appraisal reports, while necessary and important, are not the easiest things to read. Appraisal reports tend to be fairly stylized. Regardless of the intended use, the report generally comports to the format expected by other appraisers and lenders. Equity investors, buyers, sellers, or property owner/managers may be frustrated by the convoluted style, scope, and content of an appraisal report. “Why aren’t the reconciliation and explanation on page one?” is a common refrain.

One cost-effective and efficient way to cut through the clutter is to engage a review appraiser. The content and format of appraisal review reports is typically much less stylized. “Tell me, in plain English what this thing says and if the results are valid!” is not an unreasonable scope of work for a review appraiser. (And you could add, “Oh, and by the way, make sure there weren’t any dumb mistakes in this thing.”) Engaging a review appraiser can be a simple and relatively inexpensive way to ameliorate risk in the appraisal process. In the simplest situation, hiring a second appraiser to read through the report and make comments can be surprisingly inexpensive. For more complex and critical situations, seek out a top-tier appraiser, someone who is known in litigation or consulting circles. That appraiser may not normally take on this sort of assignment itself, but can offer insights from a simple read-through of the report. If the client has specific, targeted concerns, then the review appraiser can test those areas and provide either some comfort or some ideas for future research and analysis.

15
Valuing Raw Land for Income or Development

Find out where the people are going and
buy the land before they get there.

—William Penn Adair

EARLIER IN THE book, we discussed land valuation from a purely investment perspective. This chapter and the one that follows expand on this topic in some detail. Land valuation would seem straightforward enough. It is a simple asset, with no improvements, no depreciation, and fairly easy-to-understand income. When purchased for income, the cap or discount rates should be relatively effortless to extract from local data, and thus the valuation should be a fairly ordinary exercise.

In reality, the subtlety of land valuation causes very real confusion, even among experienced appraisers. As has been shown, some specialized types of land, such as agricultural land and timberland, have very specific, focused valuation formulas. Most other investments, such as net ground leases, development sites, or even collectible real estate, also have deeper complexities. This chapter will focus on those tracts that are acquired for current or future income, and the next chapter will discuss land acquired purely for collectible purposes. Even collectible or trophy lands have certain income or development implications. Such lands may be leased to third parties, may be the source of transferrable development rights in some jurisdictions, may be used for open space preservation tax credits, or at the least will have tax and insurance implications. All of that will be discussed in the next chapter.

For now, though, we will be concerned with land that is acquired for net ground leases, for immediate development, or perhaps both. Such investments are extremely common—every parcel of developed land in America, and many undeveloped sites, were at some time acquired with an eye to leasing or development. We have already discussed agricultural land and timberland in a previous chapter, so we already recognize that land can be valued as a function of capitalized or discounted future cash flows. As we will also see, some components of sales comparison and even the cost approach may be applicable to investment-grade raw land.

1. Collectible, Income, Development, or What?

Most parcels of collectible real estate have alternative uses that may be financially feasible (Figure 15-1). Determining feasible alternative uses will have bearing on the subsequent preservation, as the value of development rights dictates the tax credits that can be enjoyed by the donor. The Hearst Family dedicated California's famed Castle at San Simeon to the state about a century ago, but only recently contributed a conservation easement. Determining the intersection of collectible values and development values was key to this transaction.

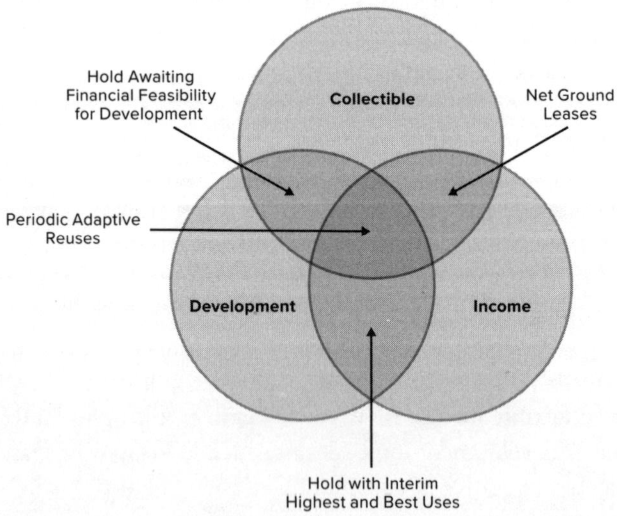

FIGURE 15-1 Overlapping Motivations for Investing in Raw Land

Even for the more typical investor, collectible lands can provide income from mining, oil and gas, timber, and other natural resources. Lands can be leased for various purposes as either an interim use (until some other development is feasible) or as a permanent use. Holding a remainder interest in land while leasing it to a commercial user can be an excellent bifurcation of values. The landowner retains the capital gains, while the commercial user enjoys the current feasible use and pays rent accordingly. Later in this chapter, we will discuss determination of market rents and how land investors can benefit from the combined values.

An interesting situation in the United States, showing how collectible land also enjoys income, arises from the 1971 Alaska Native Claims Settlement Act. This legislation transferred ownership of 44 million acres to a set of 12 regional corporations (owning the subterranean rights) and village corporations (owning the surface rights), along with nearly $1 billion in cash payments. Natives still living on the land received shares of stock in their village corporation and in the applicable regional corporation. Other Natives only received stock in the regionals. The land was collectible and available for income, much of this coming from either mineral rights (including oil) or logging and timber. Parallel legislation preserved another 100 million acres as federal lands. An example of this is Admiralty Island, off the coast of Juneau, Alaska, one of the largest islands in the Unites States. Most of the island, about 1 million acres, constitutes a national monument. Several native corporations have profitable inholdings on the island, about 10% of the total. One Native corporation continues to live there in the village of Angoon, a traditional Tlingit community home to 572 people. The island is reportedly also the home to the world's largest concentrations of brown and grizzly bears.

Conceptually, the value of an asset is a function of the discounted present value (DCF) of expected income and the DCF of expected capital gains:

$$Value = DCF(income) + DCF(gains) \qquad \textbf{EQUATION 15-1}$$

Of course, this gets interesting in that current "income" can be either *rents* or *speculative income* (ignoring for a moment that even an estimate of contract rent going forward has a speculative aspect to it). In a practical sense, the value of any income-producing holding—and this is true of land and improved properties—is a function of the prospective year-to-year income and the eventual capital gains upon resale. Consider the formula for valuation via direct capitalization and think that perhaps something is missing:

$$Value = \frac{NOI}{R_o} \quad \text{EQUATION 15-2}$$

Huh, you say! This formula has a factor for the capitalization of current income (NOI), but none for the capitalization of the eventual resale. The eventual resale is buried in the NOI capitalization itself. The value at resale would simply be the capitalization of *future* cash flows as that time. Ignoring all selling costs, payoff of financing, and such, we could say that for a project with constant NOI and an expected resale in year *n*, the value today is:

$$\frac{NOI}{R_o} = DCF\left(NOI_{1\ to\ n-1}\right) + DCF\left(\frac{NOI_n}{R_o}\right) \quad \text{EQUATION 15-3}$$

Without getting too deep into the math, this means that:

$$Value = DCF\left(income\right) + DCF\left(gains\right) = \frac{NOI}{R_o} \quad \text{EQUATION 15-4}$$

This all may seem patently obvious, but it illustrates an important point about valuation in general and valuation of land holdings in particular. Assuming a constant cap rate, R_o, and the same discount factor for current income and eventual gains, the method used for valuation is irrelevant. The value should turn out the same, mathematically, regardless of which method is used.

This all falls apart in the real world. For one, the cap rate is simply the ratio between expected, constant, NOI and what current investors are willing to pay for that endless NOI stream. Of course, expected NOI and R_o change regularly and rapidly as a result of actual property results impacting and changing investor expectations. Second, even in a world where NOI and investor expectations are changeless—a dream world, of course—the cap rate for highly speculative future gains will be different from the cap rate for much less speculative current income.

Consequently, the expected present value may be significantly impacted by an investor's future intentions for the property. To illustrate, assume a net ground lease on a property under two different scenarios. In the first scenario, the land is expected to be rented in perpetuity with an NOI to the investor of $140,000 per year. Investors in the current market expect a 7% cap rate on such perpetuities, and so the value of this investment is:

$$Value = \frac{140{,}000}{.07} = \$2\ million \qquad \text{EQUATION 15-5}$$

Now, assume that the lease is expected to run out after five years. The investor/landlord expects to sell at that time for the capitalized value *at that time*. For purposes of simplicity, the NOI and cap rates are treated as constants. The discount rate on current income is also 7%, but the discount rate on future, somewhat speculative capital gains is 9%. Now, the valuation equation looks more like this:

$$DCF_{7\%,\ 5\,yrs}\left(140{,}000\right) + DCF_{9\%,\ yr\ 5}\left(\frac{140{,}000}{.07}\right) = \$1{,}873{,}890 \qquad \text{EQUATION 15-6}$$

Thus, the impact of converting otherwise expected annual rents—a somewhat less speculative cash flow—into a more speculative capital gain at the end of year 5 has some materially large impacts on the expected value today. Of course, this does not take into account any tax implications in year 5 (capital gains versus ordinary income) nor does it take into account the usefulness of being able to reinvest into other projects. Some investors have "buy and hold" strategies, while others profit from value-added situations resulting in capital gains.

> Investors familiar with financial analysis will quickly recognize that options valuation would help reconcile this appraisal conundrum. For now, though, we will stick with the real estate appraisal methodology.

One other example provides additional illustration into this problem. Consider the situation of holding the investment for 20 years and then selling. Many net ground leases are structured this way, and indeed 99-year net ground leases are not altogether uncommon. In addition, we employ the same scenario, but with the exception that the property will now be sold at the end of year 2:

$$DCF_{7\%,\ 20\,yrs}\left(140{,}000\right) + DCF_{9\%,\ yr\ 20}\left(\frac{140{,}000}{.07}\right) = \$1{,}840{,}024 \qquad \text{EQUATION 15-7}$$

$$DCF_{7\%,\ 2\,yrs}\left(140{,}000\right) + DCF_{9\%,\ yr\ 2}\left(\frac{140{,}000}{.07}\right) = \$1{,}936{,}483 \qquad \text{EQUATION 15-8}$$

Since the more speculative portion of this investment occurs at the end, then logically the shortening the time frame until that speculative event occurs increases the value. Ironically, though, the proportion of value contributed by the speculative resale changes dramatically. In those two scenarios, the total value is the sum of two DCFs. In the 20-year scenario, the actual numbers summed are:

$$1,483,162 + 356,862 = \$1,840,024 \quad \text{EQUATION 15-9}$$

While in the two-year scenario, the components of value are:

$$253,123 + 1,683,360 = \$1,936,483 \quad \text{EQUATION 15-10}$$

In the 20-year scenario, the present value of the expected gain on sale constitutes 19% of total value, while in the 2-year scenario, the gain is 87% of total value. This exercise is a form of *partitioning the internal rate of return* and is an extremely useful tool to examine the relative proportions of the investment coming from the alternative strategies (cash flow versus eventual resale). In another form of this partitioning, one can determine the actual IRR on the investment itself, and then partition the cash flows based on that constant IRR. Either way gives an important perspective on the investment.

Most land investment appraisals will not go this deep into the analysis. Value will be determined with a sales comparison model and a simple discount or cap analysis based on comparable transactions and contract NOI. Investment decision making requires a somewhat deeper dive into the numbers presented in the appraisal. In the end, the choice between "buy and hold" or "short-term flip" may be situationally dependent, may be a function of individual investment philosophy, or may even be left up to chance. Some eventual gain-on-sale scenarios depend on some outcomes, such as a zoning change or recovery from a recession, that cannot be predicted with precision. Thus, this analysis should be revisited periodically to see how the values may have changed with changing conditions.

2. Highest and Best Use of Vacant Land

We have already visited the concept of highest and best use. For a developed site, we also consider the highest and best use (HBU) as if vacant, taking into consideration the cost of demolishing the present improvements and readying the site for reuse. For an already vacant site, the HBU actually requires a reverse determination—what is the value *as if developed*. Any use that is legally permissible, physically possible, and financially feasible might be a candidate for HBU. With an already developed site, there is often a bias in favor of continued use "as is." With a vacant site, the HBU is a blank slate, limited only by the various potential uses. Consider a commercially zoned site that could be used for one of four developments: light retail, apartments, an office building, or a stand-alone restaurant. Development is reflected in Table 15-1.

TABLE 15-1 Alternative HBU Calculations

	Development Costs	Value upon Development	Net Profit
Light Retail	8,000,000	9,600,000	1,600,000
Apartments	6,000,000	7,000,000	1,000,000
Office Building	10,000,000	11,100,000	1,100,000
Restaurant	5,000,000	5,800,000	800,000

Interestingly enough, the highest value for the site is not the highest value for the project overall. Development of an office building will result in an $11.1 million value for the project, but only $1,100,000 in profits. Conversely, developing light retail will have a smaller completion value but results in the highest profit at $1,600,000. Hence, the HBU under this scenario is for light retail development.

Consider alternative scenarios for a net ground lease. In the previous section, we estimated that a net ground lease of $140,000 per year for 20 years, and then a reversion at the end, would yield $1.84 million. If that scenario was on the table, then it would be a preferred option. However, 20 years is a long time, and our DCF presumes a fairly creditworthy tenant. Such tenants might be large, stable grocery or drugstore chains. Recently, though, many large big-box chains with net ground leases have proven to be troublesome tenants. With that, perhaps a reanalysis of the net ground lease value may be useful. If we reevaluate the 20-year lease with a discount rate of 9% (rather than 7%) on the annual cash flows, and 11% (up from 9%) on the reversion in year 20, the value drops to about $1.53 million. Now, the present development looks much better than the long-term net ground lease income.

More and more often today, mixed-use developments are common. For one, in densely populated urban areas, mixed use may be required under zoning and land use ordinances. Conversely, even in suburban or less densely populated areas, mixed use may enhance rents and provide synergies for land uses. Thus, the HBU for a vacant site may not be a simple solution, but rather an optimization of a variety of uses. This will usually require a two-step process. First, we will consider the maximum amount of space the market will absorb, usually in terms of square footage. Along with this we will also consider the minimum square footage that can be feasibly built and managed. An apartment complex of 100 units may be feasible, or even 50 units. But managing a small building of 10 units may not be financially useful or even sellable to an investor.

Second, consider the costs and profits on a per-square-foot basis. This will also need to take into account common areas, such as green space, gathering space, community use space, or other recreational space that may be required under ordinance or contribute to the overall site salability. Table 15-2 revisits this scenario based on those parameters:

TABLE 15-2 Mixed Use HBU Inputs

	Maximum Market Absorption	Development Costs / SF	Value / SF	Profit / SF
Light Retail	120,000 SF	128	160	32
Apartments	100,000 SF	120	140	20
Office Building	250,000 SF	200	222	22
Restaurant	200,000 SF	125	145	20
Common Space		80		(80)

Readers may recognize this as a linear programming problem, to optimize the mix of space, given the constraints of market absorption, so as to maximize profits. There are a number of statistical tools available to streamline this computation. Table 15-3 shows the typical output, in terms of optimized square footage.

> This level of detail will rarely, if ever, appear in a real estate appraisal. However, the appraisal will have the inputs for this model and this will provide an effective springboard to finding the optimized mix, and hence the site's true HBU.

3. Apples, Oranges, and Other Elements of Comparison

How do we measure the vacant site size? Acreage? Square footage? Or something else entirely?

TABLE 15-3 Optimized Mixed Use Model

	Max Market Absorption	Development Costs / SF	Value / SF	Profit / SF	Optimized SF	Net Profit
Light Retail	120,000 SF	165	192	27	60,000	1,600,000
Apartments	100,000 SF	120	140	20	50,000	1,000,000
Office Building	250,000 SF	256	278	22	50,000	1,100,000
Restaurant	200,000 SF	560	580	20	40,000	800,000
Common Space		80		(80)	10,000	(800,000)
Total Value of Project						$3,700,000

First, it is helpful to reflect on the concepts of surplus and excess land, as discussed previously. Surplus land is any portion of the property not currently needed to support the existing improvement, and that does not have a separate highest and best use. Surplus land may not have any independent value. A factory may require a 10-acre site to build the structure, provide worker parking, and provide ramps for trucks and outdoor fixtures. If the site is actually 12 acres, then the excess 2 acres provide little additional value (Figure 15-2). No one buying this factory will pay more because there is an extra two acres there. Conversely, excess land may have a separate highest and best use and value. Take that same example, but now assume that the site is 22 acres rather than 12. The extra 10 acres could be separately sold off as a site for another similar factory, and thus has contributory value.

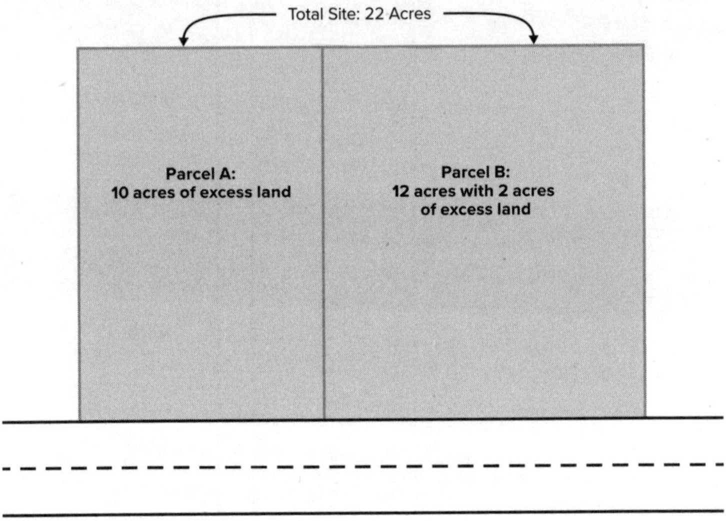

FIGURE 15-2 Surplus and Excess Land

Imagine a lot in a standard, ordinary, middle-of-the-road subdivision. When the subdivision was first platted, the lots were generally planned to be about the same size and sell for about the same price, more or less. Topography, street layout, protection of trees and other foliage, local land use provisions, and the desire for an aesthetically pleasing neighborhood will usually obviate the urge to cookie-cut the lots. Indeed, some lots will end up being substantially bigger than others, and some, particularly at the ends of cul-de-sacs, may be much larger and much more private. The typical lot in a reasonably upscale suburban subdivision may have a gross acreage of 8,000 square feet, but a few may be closer to 10,000 or even 12,000 feet. The textbook would tell us that the extra acreage is surplus, and thus has no contributory value. Marketing consultants would beg to differ, though. The 12,000-square-foot lot might not sell for 50% more than the 8,000-square-foot lot, but certainly should sell for more. Is this extra land surplus, excess, or something else entirely?

But, this does not directly address the question. Why do some appraisals report land size in acreage and some in square feet? (And, of course, appraisals of properties in other countries may report the land in hectares.)

Appraisers acknowledge in the report's assumptions and limiting conditions that they are not skilled surveyors and typically rely on land measurements from surveys or public information. Thus, the accuracy level and units of measure are a direct function of the quality of underlying data sources. If the survey or tax assessment map was in square footage, then so too is the appraisal report. Complicating the matter is the fact that some surveys and public reports will provide land dimensions but not size. In some jurisdictions, there are legal reasons for this. Appraisers are left to perform their own calculations. While some handy and cheap computer-based measuring tools are available, the quality of measurement varies widely.

Some reports imply a level of accuracy that is simply not rational. An appraisal reporting that a particular tract is 42.837 acres implies that the size is known to the thousandth of an acre. One one-thousandth of an acre is about 44 square feet, or roughly the size of a powder room. This level of accuracy begs credulity.

Property size should be considered in the context of topography. A 10-acre site on the side of a mountain has less utility than a similar-sized but relatively flat site. Sites for residential subdivision development are benefitted by gently rolling terrain, while commercial sites need to be flat, with a slight slope for drainage. Add to this questions of shape, road frontage, and visibility. Consider two different 10-acre sites as shown in Figure 15-3 (see next page).

Clearly, the size alone does not tell the full story about site utility. For commercial development, particularly a factory with significant in-and-out truck traffic, Site B may be significantly inferior to Site A, and in fact Site B may be woefully inadequate for a factory. In theory, this sort of comparison should be clear in the HBU analysis, but usually this is only apparent upon deeper and more careful property inspection.

This only scratches the surface of detail about a raw site that needs to be considered by the user of an appraisal report. Is the road on which the site is located adequate for the site? If the site will be used as a factory or

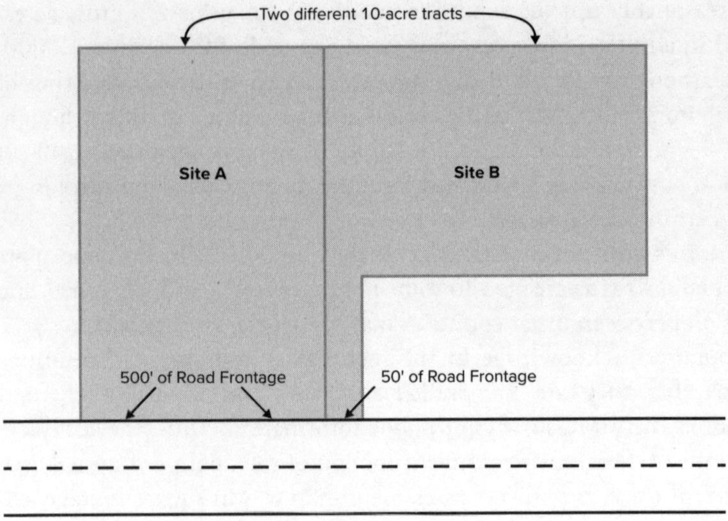

FIGURE 15-3 Two Comparable 10-Acre Tracts

warehouse, can the road support the turning radius of large tandem trucks? If the site will be used for retail, does the roadway provide for both left and right turns into the site? Does the site have wetlands, protected lands, or nondevelopable portions? Is the soil adequate for the planned development? Loamy, clay-based soils are superior for construction footings, while expansive soils or glacial fill are problematic for the same construction. Is there adequate supportive utility infrastructure to the site, such as storm drainage, sewerage, water, and electricity?

In short, the site size tells only part of the story. The size has to be taken into account along with other physical features to properly assess the value and evaluate the value determination. The users of appraisal reports will need to carefully investigate the accuracy and adequacy of the site description to determine if the value estimates are valid, and to determine if the development or rental value is sustainable.

4. Tests of Feasibility

The *Dictionary of Real Estate Appraisal*, in defining *economic feasibility*, notes that:

> An investment property is economically feasible if its prospective earning power is sufficient to pay a fair rate of return on its complete cost (including indirect costs), i.e., the estimated value at completion equals or exceeds the estimated cost.

This is actually not far removed from most financial tests of economic feasibility. For any other nonrealty investment, economic feasibility is achieved if the project breaks even. One implicit cost for a project is the weighted average cost of capital (WACC), which includes a return on the equity investment. For real estate analysis, the "fair return" is usually broken out as a separate line item. This is because different alternative site uses may have different required rates of return. Consider again the profits on proposed alternative uses shown in Tables 15-1 and 15-4. In all four alternative uses, there is a value upon completion that can be determined by a capitalization of expected future NOI. There is no reason to believe that the cap rates are equivalent for each possible use. Cap rates for restaurants are usually somewhat higher than cap rates for apartments, given the differential risks attached to the two property uses.

TABLE 15-4 Changing Feasibility Assumptions

	First Set of Assumptions			Significantly Lower Development Costs	
	Value Upon Development	Development Costs	Net Profit	Development Costs	Net Profit
Light Retail	9,600,000	8,000,000	1,600,000	5,600,000	4,000,000
Apartments	7,000,000	6,000,000	1,000,000	4,200,000	2,800,000
Office Building	11,100,000	10,000,000	1,100,000	7,000,000	4,100,000
Restaurant	5,800,000	5,000,000	800,000	3,500,000	2,300,000

Slight variations in the underlying assumptions can have a dramatic impact on the rank ordering of various potential uses. Take the scenario outlined in Table 15-1. In the prior example, the light retail was the dominant use under the single-use proposal. Now, we find a materially significant decrease in construction costs using a new technology. The development costs are lowered across the board by 30%. This has a dramatic impact on the rank ordering of proposed uses for the site, and now the office building is the most profitable single use.

Thus, for any given proposed site use, the feasibility analysis should be coupled with sensitivity analyses. Key variables should be modified across an array of potential outcomes to determine alternative valuations. If possible, probabilities can be assigned to these potential outcomes to construct a true Monte Carlo simulation. Lenders are increasingly looking for such simulations and often refer to them as stress tests.

There are several key elements to feasibility analysis that bear careful examination. These include:

Conduct market research first. Market demand for various property types and competitive market analysis should precede any feasibility test. Indeed, the maximum market absorption numbers are key and critical inputs to the next step.

Determine an optimized mix of tenants or an optimized set of uses for a mixed-use proposal. The linear programming model discussed earlier, or any sort of constrained optimization, should be the next step in the feasibility test. All too often, appraisers, analysts, and investors use broad assumptions about property uses as the starting point for the feasibility analysis.

Clearly identify assumptions. Too many analyses treat inputted assumptions as if they were empirical determinations. Clarifying these in the beginning and delineating them separately from the feasibility analysis makes it easier to determine which things are inputs into the model and which are outputs from the model.

Determine the reasonable range of those assumptions. Even market-determined inputs, such as absorption and competitive market supply, are subject to some measurement error or invalid assumptions about property uses. A feasibility model assuming that there are already 1 million square feet of occupied office space in the central business district will look very different if suddenly a large tenant leaves a competing building, changing the competitive landscape to 1.2 million square feet.

Keep it simple. All too many analysts and appraisers try to dazzle the reader with brilliant models. Given that this is all based on assumptions, the more complex calculations will only add a layer of unnecessary fragility to the outcome.

Delineate control variables from variables outside the investor's control. This is where a feasibility analysis goes from being a simple valuation tool to being an operational control tool. The investor may have little or no control over inflation, competitive market supply, property tax rates, or the T-bill rate. These variables are important to the feasibility model but should not be conflated with design elements, construction costs, tenant mix, and development timing. These latter variables are also important, but they can be controlled by the investor/developer. These will transcend the investment decision process and will prove useful after the project is underway.

> In an appraisal, the feasibility analysis should tell us two things. First, is the proposed use financially viable? Second, which potential use is better than others? A truly excellent feasibility study will give the investor some rank-ordered choices and measure the value difference between the best choice and the other choices. If the feasibility study delineates the impact of control variables, separate from external variables, then the investor has a tool that can be used and revisited during the project's management phase. An investor should require these in an appraisal, but too often these are lacking in depth and detail.

5. Net Ground Leases

Up to this point, we have examined the site use, value, and investment without discriminating between development uses and net ground lease uses. The former imply some development and operational risks for the investor/owner. The latter become more passive investments but also carry certain aspects of ongoing risk. This section will explore net ground leases in a bit more detail for appraisal aspects important to the investor.

For the totally uninitiated, a net ground lease allows a tenant to develop a parcel for a specific period of time. After the completion of the lease, subject to any renewal or option clauses, the land and any improvements revert to the landlord (although there may be stipulated exceptions). During the lease period, the tenant is responsible for taxes, insurance, and maintenance costs, although the landlord will probably carry general liability insurance and will have legal, monitoring, and accounting expenses. Typical lease periods are 20 years or more, and it is rare to see a net ground lease less than 10 years. Ground leases are very common among major chain retail tenants.

Net ground leases differ from traditional triple net leases in that the landlord is not responsible for the structure in any way. In a traditional triple net lease, the structure itself is usually built by the landlord, and the tenant is leasing both the land and the improvements. Maintenance may be stipulated in the lease, and usually the tenant is responsible. In a net ground lease, the tenant builds the structure (subject sometimes to landlord approval) and is responsible for all expenses during the lease.

> Anecdotally, appraisers often see net ground leases trading at a cap rate 100 to 200 basis points below triple net leases on comparable properties.

Ground leases usually come in two flavors—subordinated and unsubordinated. In the former the ground owner agrees to take a lower priority to construction or permanent lenders so that the tenant can finance the development. Effectively, the landlord becomes a junior lender on the project. Usually this subordination comes with a cost—the landlord is able to extract a higher rent and other concessions. In an unsubordinated lease, lenders will often still lend to highly creditworthy tenants, and will simply take the lease into account when determining the maximum loan amount.

In theory, valuing a net ground lease is no different from valuing any other contractual cash flow with a remainder interest at the contract's conclusion. Of course, the complexity with ground leases is that the remainder value is a matter of significant conjecture. Many ground leases are simply appraised as raw land, without consideration of the lease. The issue of the ground lease or leases becomes more of a consideration for the investors. Table 15-5 shows a typical array of comps drawn from an actual appraisal of land leased for wind turbines in Nevada.

Each parcel has another potential use, although two (comps 1 and 4) are simply classified as "rural land." The valuation is very straightforward (Table 15-6, in pages following.).

Some adjustments are quite large, and while there is underlying quantification (matched pairs, trend lines), these adjustments are rife with assumptions. Any reconciled value from such an appraisal will simply be the starting point for any negotiations, and true investment value may be very different.

Key elements to examine in any net ground lease appraisal include the clear delineation of:

- Contract rent, net effective rent, and market rent
- Remaining period in the lease
- How improvements will revert to the landlord
- Shortfalls between contract and market rent
- The time horizon

If I appraise a site using market rents and market cap rates, the income analysis should be straightforward. However, the valuation of a leased fee interest, using contract rents, implies a different layer of complexity, including:

TABLE 15-5 Land Characteristics for Ground Lease Example

	Subject	Comp 1	Comp 2	Comp 3	Comp 4	Comp 5	Comp 6
Location	NW of Tonopah, NV	S of Laughlin, NV	W of Kingman, AZ	S of Gila Bend, AZ	N of Gila Bend, AZ	S of Eureka, NV	W of Carson City, NV
Distance		308 mi SE	314 mi SE	533 mi SE	525 mi SE	164 mi NE	200 mi NW
Sale Date		2/12/2018	4/15/2018	1/1/2017	6/30/2017	9/30/2017	12/15/2017
Price		$2,800,000	$1,640,000	$1,930,000	$2,400,000	$2,600,000	$1,745,000
Size (Acres)		835.82	182.22	259.06	813.56	472.73	183.68
Price/Acre		$3,350	$9,000	$7,450	$2,950	$5,500	$9,500
Zoning		Rural land	Residential, 5 acres/dwelling	PUD	Rural land	Industrial	Planned community
Flood Zone		X	X	A	X	Partial	Partial
Shape		Rectangular	L-Shaped	Irregular	Rectangular	Irregular	Irregular
Property Rights		Fee simple	Fee simple	Fee simple	Fee simple	Fee simple	Fee simple

TABLE 15-6 Adjustment Grid for Land Example

	Subject	Comp 1	Comp 2	Comp 3	Comp 4	Comp 5	Comp 6
Location	NW of Tonopah, NV	S of Laughlin, NV	W of Kingman, AZ	S of Gila Bend, AZ	N of Gila Bend, AZ	S of Eureka, NV	W of Carson City, NV
Distance		308 mi SE	314 mi SE	533 mi SE	525 mi SE	164 mi NE	200 mi NW
Sale Date		2/12/2018	4/15/2018	1/1/2017	6/30/2017	9/30/2017	12/15/2017
Price		$2,800,000	$1,640,000	$1,930,000	$2,400,000	$2,600,000	$1,745,000
Size (Acres)		835.82	182.22	259.06	813.56	472.73	183.68
Price/Acre		$3,350	$9,000	$7,450	$2,950	$5,500	$9,500
Zoning		Rural land	Residential, 5 acres/dwelling	PUD	Rural land	Industrial	Planned Community
Market Condition		100	300	500	200	200	300
Location		0	–1,500	0	0	–2,000	–1,500
Topography		0	0	–500	0	–200	–200
Zoning/Use		0	–3,500	–4,500	0	–1,000	–4,500
Total Adjustments		100	–4,700	–4,500	200	–3,000	–5,900
Adjusted Price		3,450	4,300	2,950	3,150	2,500	3,600

- What is the payment schedule?
- Is the buyer/owner anticipated to hold the investment until lease conclusion?
- What is the tenant-specific risk?
- Are the lease terms comparable to market normal leases?
- Is the lease transferrable?
- What are the assumptions regarding the reversion value?
- How are discount rates determined?

When the appraisal relies solely on a sales comparison, these questions may not be fully addressed. These are critically important to assess the net ground lease feasibility from an investment perspective.

Here is an example of how these issues come into play in the real world, adapted from a recent appraisal:

> In 2010, a tenant leased a commercial lot in Vancouver, BC, for a term of 45 years with an initial lease payment of CDN$8.00/SF. The tenant constructed a retail facility subleased to two tenants, one of which was a large, creditworthy national tenant and the other a locally owned business. Rent was to be adjusted every five years. The basis for the rental adjustment would be the average annual change in the All-Items Consumer Price Index for Vancouver, BC, for the preceding period. As of January 1, 2015, the adjusted contract rent had increased to CDN$9.50/SF. However, local market comparable rents were CDN$11.00/SF. As a result, the basis for appraising the leasehold interest would be CDN$1.50 plus any future gains if real estate rents were projected to CPI. Further consideration would also have to include the present value of the impact on the remainder interest.

In short, the appraisal of a net ground lease property should treat the site like other fee simple land appraisal, using recent comps and adjusting them accordingly. Large net ground lease sites, often leased for big industrial or commercial purposes, may end up being valued with fairly large and heuristic adjustments.

> In the appraisal, the investor should find necessary elements to fully evaluate cash flows and to value the investment. These are not just "value and forget" scenarios, since periodic rent changes built into the lease may not actually match market rent changes. Thus, periodic revaluation is a necessity.

6. Valuing Land Subject to an Improvement

You want to buy a tract of land for investment or redevelopment, but it already has a building there. There is some significant dispute over value—the seller has a "value in use" or "investment value" idea about the property, but you believe the HBU is for teardown and redevelopment. You hire an appraiser to value the tract "as if vacant." If there are adequate nearby vacant land comps, this is straightforward. If local land comps do not exist, or do not adequately aid in the valuation, then the appraiser will resort to a *land extraction*. This is a cost approach in reverse—we value the entire site and then subtract everything that is not the vacant parcel.

Since there is a disagreement about that HBU, finding sales or rent comps can be fraught with complexity. When analyzing and using the appraisal, the reader may mistakenly focus on the land value without paying adequate attention to the underlying assumption. A property that is a candidate for an HBU shift may evidence significant depreciation. Indeed, depreciation may equal all or nearly all the replacement cost. Note the paradox—the "fully depreciated" structure may still enjoy rents or other utility. In many cases, the rents are not financially feasible but still sufficient to warrant a "value in use."

Several other methods are found in appraisals, with varying degrees of accuracy. These include:

Land Allocation

This leverages off of tax assessments. In most jurisdictions, the tax assessor allocates the fair market value (FMV) between land and improvements. Even if the total FMV is inaccurate,[1] the allocation ratio may itself be reasonable. Thus, an examination of allocations of similar properties applied to sales prices of nearby properties with similar sites (albeit without necessarily similar improvements) may give some indication of site value. This is a very useful tool, and Equation 15-11 illustrates it further. Assume that we have examined the tax assessments of several recent comp sales and found that the county typically allocates 75% of the assessment to the building and 25% to the land. Comp A is our most similar comp and recently sold for $1,600,000. We then simply allocate the value as shown:

$$1{,}600{,}000 = .75(1{,}600{,}000) + .25(1{,}600{,}000) \qquad \text{EQUATION 15-11}$$

Subdivision Development

The appraisal may examine raw land and the cost of development into improved tracts. This is particularly useful when there are nearby raw land sales but very few improved site sales.

Depth and Frontage Factor Analysis

Particularly in some urban settings, site depth may be a controlling factor, as long as the site width is sufficient to satisfy the "physically possible" and "legally permissible" rules of HBU. In some high-amenity situations (such as lakefront property), frontage may be the controlling factor. Both may be useful in identifying values when there is some delinkage between value and site size.

> A direct valuation of land, either through income analysis or sales comparison, is preferred over indirect methods. Anytime an indirect method is used it will be fraught with assumptions and shortcuts. Indirect methods, however, may be the only ways available. Readers and users of appraisal reports are cautioned to examine such analyses carefully. The use of alternative methods may prove useful as an adjunct to the main valuation method. A land allocation arriving at a significantly different number than a land extraction may suggest flaws in the extraction assumptions.

7. Subdivision Analysis

Many parcels are acquired to be developed and/or subdivided. When the word "subdivision" is used, it usually implies a residential neighborhood, although land is subdivided for many purposes, residential and commercial. Two common nonresidential subdivision investments are industrial parks and shopping center out-parcels.

When the appraisal is for lending purposes, it usually focuses on the sales comparison approach. The land is valued at four stages:

- Raw land, ready for development (the "as-is" condition)
- Land with the entitlements, permits, and all legal conditions to break ground
- The developed lots as if sold to wholesale (such as a builder buying bulk lots)
- The value of finished lots, accounting for marketing time (a DCF model)

Even when a developer is also the end user, such as a homebuilder or a shopping center developer, the land development analysis is bifurcated from whatever subsequent use is made of the land. Thus, the land development ROI, feasibility, and valuation need to stand on their own.

It may be handy to review how raw land is turned into a residential or commercial subdivision. This is almost always a multiyear process. Land development takes time, and subdivision projects are "phased in" over a period of many years. A developer may want to build 1,000 homes on a tract of 250 acres and determines that the market will absorb 200 homes per year. Some infrastructure (master permits, entrance roads, main sewer and water lines, main storm drainage trunk lines) will need to be installed at the beginning, but much of this may wait. It is not unusual for final plans to change over time. The market demand may shift, and subsequent phases may shift to larger or smaller lots or even some other use (such as condominiums rather than single family homes). This allows some flexibility for the developer, and it also means the developer need not tie up funds at the front end.

Like any project with discontinuous cash flows, the analysis will involve discounted cash flows. The DCF for a project like this will be far different from a simple textbook DCF. Cash inflows and outflows will vary widely from month to month, and risks attached to cash inflows may be very different from cash outflow risks. Hence, different discount rates may apply. Finally, it is rare to undertake a project like this without complex financing. The capital structure needs to be integrated with the valuation analysis even in the planning stages.

The developer either buys (less likely) or options (more likely) a tract targeted for a specific development. Developers tend to be specialists—people who develop residential subdivisions rarely dabble in shopping centers. But there are exceptions. (Old saying: All generalizations, including this one, are false.) Before optioning or acquiring the tract, the developer has probably conducted some preliminary market research and is aware of demand level and timing. Perhaps the developer plans to construct a shopping center in a particular part of town and searches for a suitable site. Once a potential tract is identified, the developer will finalize the market analysis. It may be that while the east side of town needs a new shopping center, the particular tract identified on the east side may have access or locational negatives that vote against it. In the residential subdivision business, access to mass transportation, shopping, and good schools can be extremely localized amenities. All of this will need to be considered before moving forward.

After the land is optioned, the developer may move forward with initial permitting and entitlements. This process will vary from location to location. At a minimum, the developer will ensure that necessary utilities, access roads, and other neighborhood amenities exist. The developer will check zoning and permitting and will probably have detailed discussions with local permitting authorities. The developer will be assisted by land planners, architects, engineers, and attorneys experienced in the nuances of permitting and development in this locale.

Once it is apparent that permitting, entitlements, and zoning requirements can be met, the developer will exercise the option and purchase the land. In some cases, the landowner may come in as a partner and subordinate the fee simple interest to development or construction financing. From a cash-flow perspective, this can be a win-win for the developer and the land seller.

Groundbreaking will be handled by a general contracting firm, usually supervised by an architect and/or engineering firm. General contractors who specialize in land development will grade the site, lay out roads, install some underground utilities (particularly sewer, water, and storm drainage) and coordinate other utilities (gas, electric, and technology such as telephone, television, and internet). After the underground utilities are in place, curbs and sidewalks are poured and final paving is finished. (Curbs and sidewalks typically go in before final pavement because the heavy equipment needed for the concrete work will damage road paving.) All of this work will be periodically inspected by public authorities, and a surveyor will record a final plat.

> This is a massive oversimplification, and no two subdivision developments are alike. The actual process will also take into account local practices, climate, topography, and regulatory issues. Developing a subdivision in a rural area is far different from developing an urban infill in a major city.

Early in the process, the developer will have decided about the disposition of developed lots. When developing a shopping center, we may sell the main shopping center pad and parking and retain out-parcels. A residential subdivision may be developed by the homebuilder, or more likely large swaths of lots will be sold in bulk to builders. This bulk sale may have been committed before the subdivision was even started, and such commitments may have been a prerequisite for financing. Conversely, a developer may hold all the lots and retail them over a period of years (the scenario discussed earlier—1,000 lots over a five-year period). Typically, these sales will not occur in a nice, neat order. There may be a few sales in early months, building to a crescendo, and then sales will taper off near the five-year mark. These projections will need to be built into the pro formas and DCF, and of course this is all ripe for sensitivity analyses. By the way, the likelihood of all lots selling for the same price is rare, and the analysis will need to take into account the differential pricing and price changes over time.

It should be obvious that this entire project resembles a very large spreadsheet. The five-year residential subdivision build-out may require a year of permitting and a year of general contracting at the front end, plus continued general contracting in phases for two or three more years. From inception—from the first day that a dollar is spent on any sort of analysis—until the very last sale, seven years may pass. Since seven years translates into 84 months, a detailed analysis starts resembling a spreadsheet with 84 columns.

This huge spreadsheet is the starting point for two related analyses—the valuation (a DCF of all revenue and expense flows) and the investment. Since monthly net revenue—positive or negative—drives the investment cash needs, these two analyses are dependent on one another and should reconcile with one another.

> This leads to a big mistake investors make valuing subdivision development deals. Investors are often likely to begin with the investment analysis and then provide those spreadsheets as a fait accompli to the appraiser as the basis for the valuation. Since the investor is going to have to pay for both analyses, why not have them done *simultaneously and independently*? Clearly, there will be some basic information that will be provided to both analysts, but how the two analyses proceed with that data can be extremely informative. Since both the investment analysis and the appraisal will need to be performed at some point, having them done at the same time by different analysts is a costless way to sanity-check the development finances!

8. Special Issues in Condemnation

Is it a business, or is it real estate? For hotels, restaurants, and car dealerships, the price may incorporate both, and the valuation may be muddied by enterprise, franchise, and investment values. Large shopping centers are bundles of contractual relationships, and there are arguments among appraisers about enterprise value versus real estate value. There are actually multiple schools of thought about this appraisal problem, particularly in hotels, and different allocations may land the appraisal in different places.

In Figure 15-4, two different appraisal methodologies may arrive at the same total value but a different basis for allocating value among various subcomponents. For tax purposes, an investor may prefer one allocation over another. Note that when faced with a condemnation proceeding, real estate (land and structure) are typically compensable but business values (everything else) are not.

This often hits auto dealers, who typically build on high-traffic (and growing traffic) arterial roads. Those sorts of roads are frequent candidates for road widenings, and the road widenings often impact the road frontage enjoyed by the dealer. Some courts have held that the "street" side of a car dealership is much more valuable than the back side. Thus, taking a slice of the dealership from the road frontage may have a disproportionally high impact on the site value.

Hotels are often faced with the same problem. The loss of parking can have a huge impact on hotel value, particularly a convention hotel that depends on parking. Some methodologies may allocate that loss to noncompensable business value, while other methodologies will recognize it as a disproportionate impact to the overall hotel real estate value.

> Investment-grade real estate is often subject to physical condemnations and inverse (regulatory) condemnation actions. Investors—and particularly their attorneys—often fail to think strategically about these actions when they arise.

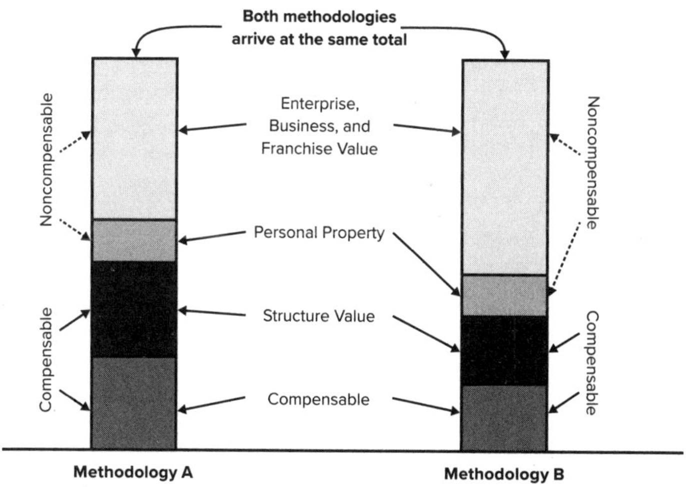

FIGURE 15-4 Different Approaches to Allocating Value

9. Summary and Key Points

Investing in vacant land can be exceptionally profitable, particularly on a risk-adjusted basis. Knowledgeable and experienced developers understand the nuances of researching a vacant site, contracting with the various service and material providers, and ending up with an improved property or a subdivision ready for construction. Many wealthy families who invest in development land focus on one particular use. However, larger and more valuable tracts are often slated for complex mixed uses. Understanding the valuation variants of different uses may be necessary. Vacant sites ready for a net ground lease can provide decades of reliable and sometimes inflation-hedged cash flows.

These are usually long-term propositions. Even the most straightforward and simple land development project may take a few years, and net ground leases are usually structured for the life of the building—often many decades. Add to this the complexity of mixed-use projects, as developments and as ground leases. Various components carry differential levels of risk, and thus overall IRRs and present values may not reflect shifts in component weighting. A project that was 50-50 apartments and retail may have a higher cash flow if shifted to 90% retail (and 10% apartments). However, the higher risk may reduce the value on a risk-discounted basis.

Given the long-term commitments of land projects, these investments should be subjected to serious scrutiny—sensitivity analyses and feasibility studies. These should carefully delineate the real estate valuation from the overall investment value. The appraisal is a great starting point for this analysis, and should be ordered independently of the investment feasibility study and capital structure analysis. The appraisal scope of work should clarify that cash flow analyses are needed to feed subsequent analyses at the investor level.

Even a simple sales comparison can be fraught with assumptions, particularly if reliance is placed on allocation or extraction. This is another reason why DCF or capitalization may be preferred in the appraisal of any vacant site.

10. A Final Note—More on the Yellow Book

Investors in the western United States will likely have dealings with a federal agency. Federal agencies own about 28% of US land—640 million acres of a total 2.27 billion in this country. About 92% of this is in 12 western states (Table 15-7). Of all land in Nevada, 84.9% is federally owned. Compare this with 0.3% of Iowa or Connecticut, and you can see why this may be more significant in the western United States.

TABLE 15-7 Federal Land Holdings in 12 Western States

State	Federal Ownership
Nevada	84.9%
Utah	64.9%
Idaho	61.6%
Alaska	61.2%
Oregon	52.9%
California	45.8%
Arizona	38.6%
Washington	38.5%
Colorado	35.9%
New Mexico	34.7%
Montana	29.0%
Wyoming	27.4%

Several times in this book we have mentioned the "Yellow Book," which governs valuation of property when either a federal agency is the acquirer or federal funds are being used (such as a federally funded highway project). Property owners may be surprised to find situations where these rules apply. As discussed in an earlier chapter, about 2,200 miles of abandoned railroad lines in America are converted to hiking trails each year. Thanks to a Supreme Court ruling a few decades ago and congressional mandates, many such conversions are treated as right-of-way acquisitions with compensation to the adjacent property owner. In those cases, the valuation, including the damage to any adjacent property, is determined with an appraisal using Yellow Book standards.

Even though the Yellow Book states that it is congruent with USPAP, there are some significant differences. Notably, there are significant reporting requirement differences. While USPAP provides for a fairly broad and customizable level of depth for reports, the Yellow Book is not so generous. Another significant difference is that the Yellow Book, and Yellow Book compliant appraisals, have a very important role under US law. Specifically, the Fifth Amendment provides for the payment of just compensation whenever property is acquired, and a host of federal court rulings have fleshed that out. Appraisals performed under the Yellow Book are frequently used as evidence in an adjudication. This tends to color data gathering, analysis, and reporting requirements.

The Yellow Book is filled with subtle nuances. For example (and this list is far from complete):

The appraiser has an obligation to invite the property owner on any property inspection. This may seem trivial, but the Yellow Book takes very seriously the notion that owners may have special insights into the property value. Hence, the appraiser must offer a face-to-face meeting, at the property itself, so that the features can be discussed in person.

Only properties with "economic" highest and best uses may be used as comps. This has been a matter of some contention. Much land acquired in the West was "collectible"—preservation, parks, forests, national monuments, or other protected lands. Often, the federal government paid amounts with no relationship to financial feasibility. If several such properties are used as comps for a subsequent acquisition, the newly acquired property would also have no financial feasibility basis for value. Conversely, there are schools of thought that hold that collection and preservation of trophy land should itself be a highest and best use of a valuable site. Nonetheless, the federal government sees it the other way, and any comp used must have a sale price based on a financially feasible use.

Appraisers must personally verify comparable data. This can be an onerous and expensive task. Many land sales, particularly in rural areas, may be very old. Courthouse records may not provide clear evidence of transactions, and some states do not disclose full transaction details on public records (Table 15-8). Further, in most situations, the appraiser must personally inspect all comps used in the appraisal.

TABLE 15-8 Nondisclosure States

Nondisclosure States
Idaho
Indiana
Kansas
Mississippi
Missouri
Montana
New Mexico
North Dakota
South Dakota
Texas
Utah
Wyoming

Yellow Book appraisals are based on the federal definition of market value. Even if a partial interest is valued, it will be the market value of that partial interest. Investment value, liquidation value, value-in-use, or some other basis for value are not allowed. Further, only market rents can be considered, even if the property is currently subject to below- or above-market leases.

Any influence of the government-funded project must be ignored in the appraisal. Thus, if the government is acquiring the land to build a power plant, the plant's influence must be ignored. This may seem unfair—assume that a power plant will be a benefit to the property in a given county. Thus, all of other properties in the county will go up in value. The property actually being taken for the power plant, though, will be valued and purchased without this benefit.

The appraisal must include a 10-year history of ownership, uses, and occupancies of the subject property. Conversely, USPAP only requires a three-year sales history plus any current options or contracts.

Subdivision development methodology is only used if direct sales comparisons are unavailable. Thus, even if the site has a highest and best use for development, and even if that is the way an investor would look the site and test financial feasibility, the Yellow Book imposes a preference for a direct sales comparison with other similarly situated parcels.

Owners of parcels subject to such an acquisition may hear the phrases "federal rule" and "state rule" bantered about. These are two different approaches to determining the just compensation in an eminent domain matter. In the federal rule, the basis for just compensation is the value *before* the acquisition minus the value *after* the acquisition. This naturally takes into account all damages to the remainder (the portion being valued *after*) and may, depending on the circumstances, take into account certain benefits accruing to the property. The benefits are usually divided into two categories:

> ***General.*** The benefits enjoyed by all properties in the market, such as the enhanced values that may come from a road being paved into a neighborhood that previously only had a dirt road
>
> ***Special.*** The benefits accruing only to the property being impacted by the taking, such as a new retaining wall being built when a road is widened into a hillside.

Whether or not these benefits offset any damages or the value of a portion taken may be a matter of some negotiation or even litigation.

The *state rule* should end up in the same place, dollarwise, but gets there in a different fashion. A state rule appraisal directly measures the value of the portion taken (irrespective of larger parcel impacts), then directly adds any damages and subtracts any special benefits. In theory, these two approaches should arrive at the same value, but often they do not. Any valuation performed under the Yellow Book will use the federal rule. If the property owners find that the state rule ends up with a favorable determination, this may be a matter presented to the court.

Often, the acquisition involves lands with natural resources such as minerals or oil and gas. Notably, the ownership of subsurface natural resources may be a matter of state law rather than federal. The Yellow Book cautions appraisers to draw a distinction between operating rights and royalty rights, and to consider the differential impact on the property value. Similar issues apply to forested lands.

If a federal agency endeavors to acquire property, either in whole or in part, either through a physical taking or an inverse taking (legal restrictions), either temporarily or permanently, then it will be the agency's responsibility to hire an appraiser and perform a Yellow Book compliant valuation. The investor/owner—and often this means the attorneys representing the investor/owner—will be well advised to engage the services of a Yellow Book expert *who does not regularly work for the government*. This ensures an independent review of the government's valuation, and may perhaps indicate the need for an alternative valuation if the matter becomes contentious.

16
Valuing Raw Land for Collectible or Personal Use

The best investment on earth is earth.

—Louis Glickman

IN THE PRECEDING chapter, I discussed appraisals of land acquired for development, leases, or other income. In this chapter, I want to focus on how to appraise a tract acquired simply for collectible purposes. These investors can have their cake and eat it too—some collectible lands also throw off income. Income generation, though, is usually not the principal reason for the acquisition.

Purely collectible real estate may be held for intergenerational transfers, for preservation, or for personal or public use. In a famous situation on the South Island of New Zealand, the Canadian singer Shania Twain acquired nearly 62,000 acres (about 100 square miles!) to build a small personal vacation residence. Coupled with the acquisition was an agreement to make significant preservation and conservation investments and provide for access trails for casual hikers and for Maori to visit culturally significant sites.

Art, gems, and even stamps and coins are collected with an eye to storing wealth and enhanced value over time. Automobiles are usually thought to be a depreciating asset, but a well-curated collection of autos is expected to increase in value over time. The late billionaire Paul Allen was a competitive player in the hypercompetitive—and hyperexpensive—world of historic airplane collecting, and the very act of curating and collecting such historic aircraft lent value to otherwise fully depreciated investments.

The same is doubly true about collectible land. Even when land appears to be acquired solely for personal enjoyment, properly curated investments in raw land should be an excellent store of value, a countercyclical hedge against high inflation or other economic distress, a synergy to other for-profit investments, and a very real source of capital gains.

Some real examples came out of the 1997 Kyoto Protocol on climate change. Many countries—albeit not the United States—agreed to explore a variety of methods to reduce atmospheric greenhouse gas. Whether or not these protocols were successful or even effective is another subject. One very real outcome was a commitment to market-based solutions. This evolved into the pricing of carbon credits, which could be generated by owning and preserving forest lands.

While existing forest owners reaped a windfall from selling carbon credits on the global market, other investors found that they could invest in collectible forests in out-of-the-way places. Credits could be sold or profitably used to offset tax burdens in countries recognizing the Kyoto accords. Environmentally important investments were available in places like Tierra del Fuego, the Philippines, and New Zealand. Forest lands used for carbon credits were preserved or put into active harvest programs.

In an earlier chapter, I reviewed some basics for valuing timberland. This demonstrates that there are layers of investment opportunities on a tract of collectible land. Some uses may be mutually incompatible or may have negative social or political ramifications. A tract of collectible land may have valuable timber tracts as well as endangered or threatened species that depend on those forests. In the United States, such species may be protected, but in other countries such legal protections may not exist. The same can be true of petroleum or mineral rights. A parcel of collectible land may have a variety of potential competing uses, some of which are long-term (forest production, carbon credits, long-term holdings or gains) and some of which may be short term (petroleum or minerals, preservation credits, near-term development, farming leases). An investor faced with the valuation of such a tract may mistakenly make the assumption that the true value is the simple sum of all these appraisals. This confusion is exacerbated by the fact that the various appraisers (land, minerals, timber cruise) may not coordinate, and so may not consider that one valuable use may obviate another value.

This is situationally dependent. A particular collectible tract may be subject to several different types of appraisals, and sorting through these is confounding. The true value will be some optimized combination and will be colored by the investment criteria and preferences of the investor. Tracts with competing uses and hence competing values will ultimately have an investment value that may be far different from the market value. This investment value may actually be higher than the market value, if synergies exist. The investor is well advised to engage a separate consultant with expertise in these facets and an understanding of individual investor expectations.

The remainder of this chapter will focus on interpreting and understanding simple collectible land valuations. The goal is to provide some insights into the appraisal process to aid in investment decisions. As a practical matter these appraisals focus on a limited facet of market value and assume away some complexities that actually make collectible land interesting and valuable.

1. Personal and Collectible Land

Up to this point, I have treated land as a function of its productive use. It may be acquired for timber, agriculture, a net ground lease, subdivision, or development. Market value usually anticipates the highest and best use. If a parcel is best used for timber production, then sales, rentals, or income data from competing, comparable timberlands are used to appraise. This section, and the rest of this chapter, will focus on the appraisal of land as an investment holding rather than for its economically productive use.

Reflecting back on the previous chapter, this may run counter to the Yellow Book edicts if a party to the transaction is a federal agency or if the Yellow Book is somehow invoked as an appraisal condition. In the western United States in particular, this can be confusing since many land appraisers are steeped in Yellow Book methodology and may fail to understand that a tract of land may be purchased, valued, or sold with an intrinsic value outside of what the Yellow Book calls an *economic use.*

Take the Headwaters Preserve acquisition in Humboldt County, California. In 1996, the State of California and the federal government agreed in principle to acquire about 7,472 acres of old-growth timber, including some second-growth buffer land. The total price was $380 million, or about $51,000 per acre, not including some local economic mitigation funds spent to compensate the logging community for removing this land from production. The deal was tied to a state acquisition of two smaller tracts for $100 million and certain agreements by the seller for restrictions on logging surrounding lands. The purchase price was disconnected from any logging value and was a function of collectible value, the value of natural habitat, and the public interest value attached to preserving the habitat of numerous endangered and threatened species.

During that period, there were numerous notable collectible land acquisitions, particularly in California, that leveraged off of such lofty valuations. Valuation considerations included:

- Natural habitats, such as endangered species or old-growth forest habitats
- Historic features, such as petroglyphs, cemeteries, or village sites
- Archaeological or paleontological features
- Views, particularly waterfront, forests, or grasslands
- Recreation, such as fishing, hunting, horseback riding, or skiing

Each amenity contributes to site value but not necessarily in predictable or linear fashion. Consider a tract of lakefront land in Michigan, in an area of high-amenity recreational land. Water frontage was naturally and obviously a factor in the valuation. Land *depth* was also key, since a long, narrow strip of water frontage may have amenity value but lacked utility for enjoyment.

The appraiser has a very real obligation to discuss the scope of work before undertaking data gathering or analysis. The nature of the property and perceptions about value should be discussed in depth. This is one area where collectible real estate practice is in full agreement with the Yellow Book dictates. Owners and sellers, in particular, are probably the most familiar with the land features and nuances. Buyer-investors will want to ensure that the appraiser has considered the important and salient issues, such as:

What is the property's highest and best use from a market value perspective? Recall that investment value may differ from market value, although market value is usually going to be a consideration in purchase and sale negotiations. One key element of highest and best use (HBU) is the zoning or land use restriction. Even unzoned rural land may have restrictions from easements, covenants, environmental regulations, or legislative mandates. All of this is key to land value.

Does the appraiser fully understand the topography? For development land, this is critical, but for collectible land, the topography may have unexpected implications. The most obvious is access, particularly for recreational enjoyment, firefighting, or access to valuable sites (historic, archaeological, or paleontological). The topography may have environmental implications, such as water frontage (beaches, cliffs), runoffs to neighboring properties, and erosion control. In some places, exposure to earthquakes and volcanic activity is noteworthy.

How is the property taxed, and how will the sale impact the property taxation? Some states such as California have significant property tax resets upon sale.

Are utilities available, and are there any latent easements? Utilities may be important for recreational enjoyment, but the trade-off is often an overhead power line. There may be pipeline easements or easements that have been recorded but not yet used. Easements that are actually in use may be apparent, but latent easements may come as a surprise when and if the dominant easement elects to exercise the rights. Abandoned, overgrown railroad rights-of-way may be claimed by the federal government for railbanking and converted to hiking/biking trails for public use. While the landowner must be paid for the taking, the difference between market value and investment value—and particularly the impact on the investment value of the remainder—may be significant. Further, the seller may have previously adjudicated this issue, yet the easement itself is not apparent to the casual observer until the local government decides to build a trail through the middle of a collectible land holding.

Even in the absence of public utilities, the appraisal should address the availability of water rights and the allowances for sewerage disposal. Water rights may have been sold by a prior owner, and so the land use may be restricted. Sewerage disposal may be restricted by environmental concerns, further limiting the site's usefulness even for recreational purposes.

Are there flood zone issues? The Federal Emergency Management Agency (FEMA) makes the headlines when disasters strike, but a lesser known role is the publication of nationwide flood risk maps. These are easy to check, and this determination is a normal and expected appraisal component. Because FEMA's flood zone determinations change periodically, risk is a matter of some complexity. In the dry Southwest, soil conditions do not allow for immediate rain absorption. When the occasional storm occurs, floodways, such as arroyos, can become treacherous.

Is there ready access to the property? I appraised a small but highly valuable island off the Alaska coast only accessible via boat or via a causeway and an easement through an adjacent property. The island's owner and the adjacent property owner disagreed over the use of this easement, leading to years of contentious, expensive litigation. During the litigation, the value of the island was in serious doubt.

What are the property's physical dimensions? Some collectible sites are very large, and dimensions are irregular. Others can be fairly small, or portions of a site can be oddly shaped. This may or may not have implications for the use and enjoyment.

Are there wetlands, habitats, or endangered species on the property? One investor acquired a large tract of desert land as a recreational holding with an eye to eventual development of a golf course community. A highly endangered species was discovered on the site, and all vehicular access to the property was immediately ended. Naturally, development was now out of the question, and a long, complex negotiation was needed to swap this land to a land trust for a more suitable parcel.

Wetlands may impact the use and enjoyment of a collectible parcel. Some property may be acquired specifically because of wetlands. Wetlands are acquired and preserved to provide mitigation for development sites. Some wetlands are preserved—with attendant tax credits or other compensation—as habitats. The existence of a wetland may not be visibly apparent. Wetlands may be ephemeral or seasonal. Something that appears to be a small drainage ditch may turn out to be a salmon habitat in the spawning season (as was discovered by an investor near Seattle) necessitating habitat conservation expenditures. Usually, determining the presence of a wetland or habitat will require a specialist.

Are there environmental contaminants on or near the property? One investor acquired a long-abandoned military base as open space mitigation for a residential development. Later, it was determined that buildings had been constructed with asbestos siding in the 1930s. When the buildings were demolished following World War II, proper environmental controls were unknown. The site was highly polluted with asbestos dust blowing into homes in the surrounding neighborhood. This economic disaster could have been averted with proper environmental investigations. Even apparently pristine waterfront properties may be at risk. Some lands that have never been developed may nonetheless have been exposed to migration of contaminants from other sites. In the 1990s, Avila Beach, a small waterfront community near San Luis Obispo, California, discovered that oil leaks from uphill had been systematically migrating onto waterfront and village lands. Remediation took years, and property values were frozen during that period.

What were previous property uses? This is a concern in the environmental review, but examining prior uses may indicate subtle problems not normally apparent in that review. Agricultural use may not trigger any environmental suspicions. If a farm used pesticides that were legal when used but are now banned, the farm might not be detected as a problem in an environmental audit. Latent pesticide in the soil or groundwater may become a matter of concern. Land with abandoned mines may have subsidence problems or air quality issues.

A highway was being widened in the rural South, and the adjacent landowner had agreed to sell an easement for the widening. The landowner noted to the highway department that there was a small, untended cemetery on the property with just a few grave sites. The highway department engineers planned to simply move the cemetery—the highway widening was critically important for a new factory. After acquiring 14 miles of right-of-way, the highway department discovered that one of the graves in the cemetery belonged to a signer of the Declaration of Independence. The entire roadway had to be realigned and the cemetery preserved as a historically important site.

Are surrounding properties also collectible? A valuable site also gains value from its neighborhood and other surroundings. Collectible land should generally not be surrounded by factories or other nonconforming uses. Pristine views contribute to the value of high-amenity sites, but views can be negated in any direction. Having a wonderful ocean view to the west can be virtually canceled by views of smokestacks to the east. The appraiser should conduct an assessment of intended or permissible uses of surrounding lands. Even if a factory is not presently located within sight of the collectible parcel, is one allowed or planned? This is important information.

Finally, and somewhat in summary, why is this land vacant in the first place? It may be that this parcel is out in the middle of nowhere and has no economically interesting use other than as a collectible site. That fact has some important implications for value and marketability. Even if the site is highly desirable for its amenity value, the investor should be made aware that resale may not be easy. On the other hand, a collectible vacant site near a high-density area ripe for development is odd. In some parts of Florida, many collectible sites are valuable simply because development authorization will not be obtainable for many years. A patient investor may be able to acquire such a site and find it to be very valuable down the road. A careful analysis from a net-present-value perspective should underscore the purchase price.

2. Appraisals of Trophy Lands

I discussed "trophy property" earlier and now want to address problems with trophy property appraisals in more detail. Recall, the appraisal literature classifies trophy properties as the top 2.5% of that particular category. Hence, out of every 200 office buildings in the world, or in any particular market for that matter, only the top 5 would be considered trophy buildings. Naturally, most Class A building owners want to classify their buildings as "trophy." Indeed, in downtown Philadelphia, there is a building called the "Trophy Office Building," at 1735 Market Street. Most investors would recognize examples of trophy buildings around the world, such as Rockefeller Center or the Empire State Building in New York, the Wedbush Center in Los Angeles, or the Lloyd's building in London. Investors pay top dollar to have their names associated with apartment buildings such as La Pedrera in Barcelona or hotels like the Dancing House in Prague. These are all landmark properties with highly desirable addresses and coveted ownership. In short, these buildings carry with them a certain "collectible" value over and above the intrinsic economic value.

Notably, each building, and in general most trophy buildings and trophy houses, have a story to tell. They may be architecturally significant, such as La Pedrera, designed by the famed Gaudi, or have a significant place in history, such as the Empire State Building. The appraisal challenge is to isolate and properly adjust comp trophy sales. Trophy lands are a bit more difficult. Consider again the ratio of 5 trophy properties out of every 200. A typical 5% turnover rate means only one trophy sale every four years. Computing market conditions adjustments over such a long period, particularly for a property subset as fickle as trophy sales, is almost pure guesswork. As shown earlier, brokers often test the market with asking prices that have no basis in reality and recognize that very long marketing horizons are expected. Of course, hardly anyone is ever in a rush to sell a trophy property because their job just transferred them to another city.

As an example, Table 16-1 is adapted from an appraisal of a preservation ranch community in the western United States. Recent tax law changes have weakened their popularity, but there is still interest, and they are a common form of land investment throughout the United States by wealthy investors. Common features include a homesite with a limited building envelope specified on a plot plan, a common natural preservation area shared by all property owners as tenants in common, some community amenities shared as tenants in common, and some nearby or on-site recreation. Fee-owned land is usually deeded, while other preserved lands or buffer lands may be leased from the Forest Service, Bureau of Land Management, state agencies, or private land trusts.

TABLE 16-1 Comparables for a Preservation Ranch Community

	Comp 1	Comp 2	Comp 3	Comp 4	Comp 5	Comp 6	Comp 7	Comp 8	Comp 9	Comp 10
Deeded Acres	4,530	1,360	1,800	3,600	10,520	4,200	8,200	12,500	1,700	1,900
Leased Acres	0	1,200	0	1,500	2,550	3,000	0	15,000	0	1,800
Total Acres	4,530	2,560	1,800	5,100	13,070	7,200	8,200	27,500	1,700	3,700
Common/Preserved Acres	1,200	0	850	1,300	4,000	0	5,830	15,000	0	2,000
No. of Homesteads	18	85	12	22	150	24	55	122	12	44
Typical Homestead (Acres)	190	30	80	170	60	300	40	100	140	40
Building Envelope (Acres)	None	3	8	17	None	30	None	10	14	4
Common Facilities	None	Guest house	None	None	Equestrian center	None	Limited	Guest house	None	None
Recreational Amenities										
Hunting	X		X	X		X			X	X
Fishing	X	X	X	X						X
Winter Sports		X				X	X	X		X
Other	Aviation				Riding trails					
Residential Amenities										
Equestrian					X					
Guest Lodge		X			Limited			X		
Pool and/or Tennis			X	X	X			X		X
Golf Course		X					X	X		
Management Services										
On-Site Manager		X			X			X		
On-Site Concierge		X			X					
Housecleaning Services		X		X	X		X	X		X
Typical Price	$2,450,000	12,500,000	6,000,000	7,500,000	14,500,000	6,800,000	3,000,000	9,000,000	1,200,000	3,500,000
Association Fees (Annual)	$24,500	$25,000	15,000	16,000	90,000	9,000	15,000	45,000	5,000	17,000
Sales Prior 12 Months	6	25	12	12	45	12	20	65	4	28

Specific forms may include, but certainly are not limited to:

- Equestrian communities (with or without shared stables and on-site 24/7 care)
- Hunting lodge–type communities
- Skiing communities, either slope-front or with easy slope access
- Fishing lodges, with limited access to world-class fishing
- Aviation communities, with a private airstrip
- Water amenity communities, such as marina access or simply beachfront access

While these may seem to be a very specialized niche of collectible and personal land acquisitions by wealthy families and investors, this sort of trophy acquisition is surprisingly common. Even when an individual investor acquires a trophy collectible holding, many of the same features and analyses are considered.

The lack of timely data and the difficulty drawing any quantitative comparisons among comps may leave the appraiser with the unenviable task of performing a qualitative comparison among comparable trophy sales. Table 16-2 is adapted from a recent appraisal of trophy property in the western United States.

TABLE 16-2 Qualitative Ranking of Comparables

	Colorado	Colorado	Montana	Montana	Montana
Date of Sale	Jan 2016	April 2016	Aug 2017	Dec 2017	2015
Sale Price	4,436,000	34,000,000	16,650,000	11,349,200	33,600,000
Size (Acres)	1,230	6,600	3,509	1,100	14,400
Price/Acre	3,610	5,150	4,740	10,320	2,330
Overall Comparability	Inferior	Superior	Comparable	Superior	Inferior

The appraiser should provide a significant narrative in the report explaining the rank ordering system and how these sales compare to the subject being valued. In the end, the appraiser is left with the sort of bracketing shown in Table 16-3.

TABLE 16-3 Summary of Comparable Rankings

Inferior	Comparable	Superior
Comp 1 @ $3,610	Comp 3 @ $4,740	Comp 2 @ $5,150
Comp 5 @ $2,330		Comp 4 @ $10,320

In this case, the range of likely value is from $3,610 to $5,150, a range of over 40%. Clearly, some qualitative ranking is needed. Table 16-4 (see next page), taken from an appraisal of a large waterfront tract, further illustrates the problem.

On the surface, there is no rhyme nor reason behind these prices. They are all from the same county (Santa Barbara, California), but waterfront properties and non-waterfront properties seem to sell for the same range of prices. Also, large and small tracts seem to sell at about the same range of prices, suggesting little or no clear size adjustment. All of this tells us that the appraisal will need to focus on a variety of amenities, and judgmental determinations will be necessary.

A special note of caution is warranted. Trophy land appraisals may seem, on the surface, to be the simplest situation. Granted, there will be some disagreements on the contributory value of certain amenities, and comps may be older than desired, but consider the problem's simplicity:

- There are no improvements.
- The lack of improvements means no cost approach.
- The lack of a cost approach means no depreciation to estimate.
- Access, ingress and egress, and road frontage are important, but not as critical as with an office building or apartment complex.
- Environmental issues should be obvious.
- Measurements should be easy.

And the list goes on. And so investors are often tempted to engage a less-expensive, less-experienced appraiser, believing even a rookie can handle such a straightforward job. The reality is far from being so simple. The user of a vacant land appraisal may find a host of unpredictable and surprising problems. The following are taken from actual files on vacant land appraisals from appraiser errors and omissions insurance carriers:

- The appraiser inspected, valued, and reported on the wrong parcel, which can happen with any parcel but is more common with trophy sites because they are less likely to be clearly delineated.
- The appraiser was unable to uncover unrecorded easements, which may be latent or difficult to discern due to topography or ground cover.
- The land appears to have access but is actually legally landlocked.
- A site that appears to be flat and buildable actually has soil erosion or subterranean problems preventing any future construction.
- Environmental problems are anything but obvious.

TABLE 16-4 Large Tract Sales

Comp No.	Location	Gross Price	Size (Acres)	Price/Acre	Date
1	Coastal Santa Barbara County, CA	$110,000,000	8,500	$12,941	Jan 2016
2	Coastal Santa Barbara County, CA	$45,000,000	15,500	$2,903	June 2017
3	Coastal Santa Barbara County, CA	$13,750,000	3,300	$4,167	Listing
4	Northern Santa Barbara County, CA	$23,000,000	3,470	$6,628	June 2017
5	Central Santa Barbara County, CA	$6,250,000	1,430	$4,371	Jan 2018
6	Central Santa Barbara County, CA	$6,000,000	680	$8,824	Jan 2018
7	Central Santa Barbara County, CA	$140,000,000	25,000	$5,600	Jan 2017
8	Northern Santa Barbara County, CA	$24,000,000	1,178	$20,374	Listing
9	North Santa Barbara County, CA	$8,000,000	2,090	$3,828	Listing

Consistently, insurers find that inexperienced appraisers are engaged on these projects and make rookie mistakes that cost everyone time and money. The cure, of course, is for the investor to be properly advised by an experienced team that focuses on trophy property valuation.

3. The Special Case of Trophy Ranches

Trophy ranches are a special case of vacant land valuation. Trophy lands may be acquired for a variety of purposes but are usually valued as a function of location, size, and recreational amenities. Trophy ranches couple all of that with actual ranching and often trophy hunting and/or fishing rights as well. Trophy ranches are usually very large tracts, mostly in the western United States, although some are available in the Southeast as well. Trophy ranches may or may not feature residences, and these residences may range from rustic log cabins to extensive mansions. Ted Turner, one of the most famous ranchers in America, has a 25,000-square-foot "ranch house" built by famed industrialist William H. Bartlett at the turn of the twentieth century. Casa Grande, as it is known, was designed by Joseph Lyman, a student of Frank Lloyd Wright, and features Italianate mosaic floors and a refurbished 1905 Steinway. (The eight bedrooms are currently available for guest rental, not that Mr. Turner needs the money.) Many residences are much plainer, and some trophy ranches have no residence at all.

The market for trophy ranches—and hence the comps used to value a trophy ranch—may be international. Most large trophy ranches are in the United States, New Zealand, Australia, and Argentina. There are occasionally sales in Costa Rica, but those tend to be much smaller and not very good comps for larger trophy ranch appraisals.

Notably, New Zealand has recently cracked down on foreign ownership of real estate. One unintended consequence is that appraisers can no longer consider an unfettered global market for New Zealand ranch sales. However, Table 16-5 (see next page) shows some sales used to value a New Zealand ranch about a decade ago before the more restrictive laws went into place. These comps were from all over the Pacific Rim, recognizing that the market for New Zealand real estate at the time was global. Not withstanding that country's restrictions, this example shows the typical methodology and span of data used for a trophy ranch valuation.

Most trophy ranches are found here in the United States. At any given time, there may be hundreds of such ranches on the market. Sales are infrequent, and so ranch sellers, brokers, and appraisers recognize that the exposure time may be in the years. Table 16-6 (in pages following) shows a representative list of recent ranches on the market.

TABLE 16-5 Trophy Ranch Sales

Comp No.	Sale Date	Size (acres)	Price US$	US$/Acre	Buyer	Location	Use/Intent
1	Sept 2007	3,611.14	$10,300,259	$2,852	Australian	Australia	Beef farming
2	Aug 2005	132,058.55	$296,583,000	$2,246	USA	Australia	Timber and hiking
3	Jan 2002	1,363.44	$2,496,000	$1,831	USA	USA	Farming and conservation
4	Oct 2006	424.84	$2,090,560	$4,921	Tahiti	Tahiti	Farming and vineyard
5	Dec 2007	2,862.73	$6,222,761	$2,174	UK	UK	Sheep and cattle

TABLE 16-6 American Trophy Ranch Market

State	Size (Acres)	Price	Price/Acre	Features
Colorado	138.85	$12,500,000	$90,025	Cattle ranching; equestrian; 10,304-SF trophy compound; stock pond; big game hunting; winter sports
South Dakota	3,060.00	$9,752,422	$3,187	Cattle ranching; equestrian; hunting; mineral rights; barn/shed
New Mexico	17,529.00	$12,950,000	$739	10,590 deeded acres, remainder leased, BLM, and uncontrolled acreage; 2 residences total 3,800 SF + outbuildings; cattle ranching; fishing; big-game hunting; mineral rights
Nebraska	7,880.00	$13,100,000	$1,662	Cattle ranch rated for 1,400 head; hunting; mineral rights; 620 acres irrigated
Wyoming	6,713.00	$16,950,000	$2,525	Stream through property; cattle ranching; up to 3,500 elk in the area; water rights, pond; large log cabin; heliport
California	26,600.00	$31,000,000	$1,165	Dwelling and several outbuildings; dog kennel; barn; 800 head of cattle; 16 miles of river frontage
California	788.00	$10,000,000	$12,690	Ocean frontage; 2 dwellings; agriculture; big-game hunting
Nevada	240.00	$6,500,000	$27,083	9,625-SF brick mansion + caretaker home + outbuildings; 4-acre private lake
Utah	12,740.00	$39,000,000	$3,061	Continuous ridgeline with 24 peaks and 15 bowls; 1.75 miles of fly-fishing river; 50 miles of trails; numerous ponds, creeks, and meadows; 45 minutes to Park City and 35 minutes to Salt Lake Airport
Florida	6,255.80	$35,000,000	$5,595	Cattle ranching; hunting; 525 acres improved pasture; 1,016 acres wetlands; surrounded by protected lands; half mile from river
Tennessee	1,600.00	$32,500,000	$20,313	6,750-SF main house with 2 safe rooms & escape tunnel and 1,250-SF garage; swimming pool; kennel; equestrian barn with 1,000-SF apartment; farm manager home; 2 fenced paddocks/pastures; hardwood acreage; wildlife; ATV trails; 2 spring-fed lakes
New Mexico	16,309.00	$32,000,000	$1,962	Cattle ranch supporting 1,600 yearlings; 112 landowner elk tags; all deeded acreage; numerous creeks, ponds, and springs; mineral rights

Ranch homes and structures have some impact on value, but so do water frontage, equestrian and other facilities, and hunting rights. In general, trophy ranches tend to be a bit bigger than other trophy land holdings but with a somewhat more narrow set of amenities. Most trophy ranches on the market with cattle or other grazing rights advertise those rights as an attraction to ownership. In reality, though, the values of ranching and grazing rights rarely match up to the prices paid for these properties. Investors buy and hold the properties as collectible investments, and the ranch rights provide additional income or even support for the caretaker and staff.

In the New Zealand appraisal, the property was 5,000+ acres with a 3,000-square-foot, fairly plain log home and several other outbuildings, including a visitors' lodge/office building, manager's residence, and dorm-like buildings for other ranch hands and visiting sheep shearers. The property has about 15 miles of pristine shoreline. The ranch had about 6,000 head of sheep, and the sheep business was losing about a quarter million US dollars per year. The ultimate value of US$22 million had little to do with the sheep farming and everything to do with the collectible, trophy caliber of the property.

Oh, and by the way, in New Zealand, a property owner may have *use* of shoreline, but not ownership. The entire New Zealand shoreline is considered the personal property of the Queen and may only be used with the permission of her agent. As for the sheep farm, shoreline use was necessary to build a dock for barge and boat traffic.

4. Land with Historic, Archaeological, or Paleontologist Importance

Sue, mentioned earlier, is the most complete T. rex skeleton ever discovered. Found in August 1990 in the Black Hills of South Dakota, she has been featured extensively in the media and now resides at the Field Museum in Chicago. After discovery, though, Sue became a point of significant contention. Sue was discovered on Indian Trust Land—a complex arrangement whereby land is held in trust by the Interior Department, in this case for benefit of a member of the Sioux nation. The complex ownership interests eventually involved not only the FBI but also the South Dakota National Guard. Ultimately, the beneficiary was paid over $7 million for Sue.

Additionally, other paleontologists wanted to lease rights to explore on the property. This is a common situation when owners find valuable interests on their property that scientists and others wish to study or even excavate. The remains themselves have value, and the land containing those remains has a very special value that can be monetized for access rights and lease rights.

Typical findings include:

- Paleontological remains, such as dinosaur bones
- Archaeological and historic artifacts (historic residences, native artifacts, remains of prehistoric villages)
- Petroglyphs (ancient cave paintings with historic, religious, and artistic value)
- Geological formations
- Religious and cultural sites
- Open space and view easements

These carry rights and obligations as well as valuation implications. These can be confused with the valuation implications of historic or architecturally preserved homes or the tax credit valuation of preservation easements. Here, the issues are more like compensation for an eminent domain taking or the granting of an easement. On one hand, a valuable artifact discovery makes the property more valuable. Conversely, there are now significant obligations—some of which may turn litigious—to provide access to the artifacts. A proactive stance is usually in the property owner's best interests, since courts generally hold that the public has an interest in artifacts discovered on private property.

The appraisal needs to address these two problems simultaneously, but for very different reasons. In the case of a paleontological find, such as Sue, the artifacts themselves have a value much like mineral rights. The artifact can then be valued in place or "as if removed." Once this is accounted for, the real estate may be considered as a source of other potential finds. Even when Sue was removed to the Field Museum, the remaining property could contain more such artifacts. In the case of historic property or property with geological formations or petroglyphs, the artifacts remain in place. The value of such sites takes into account the artifact value itself.

This raises some interesting ownership issues. For religious artifacts, the ownership may pass to the cultural group associated with those artifacts, while the surrounding land continues to be owned by someone else. In the case of removable objects, such as archaeological or paleontological finds, the property owner may negotiate with a single party or a consortium of parties for discovery and removal rights, much like mineral rights may be negotiated.

Access will be valued and/or negotiated separately, considering the value of artifact(s) found or thought to be on the site. This is different from an investor who elects to monetize the asset, such as turning a historic building into a tourist destination. This is more an easement negotiation. One large ranch owner in Wyoming found a veritable dinosaur burial ground on his active cattle ranch. The ranch owner desired to continue grazing cattle, and proactively worked out a complex easement agreement allowing access to university paleontologists along with a preservation/conservation tax credit. It was a win-win for the various parties but required complex appraisals of the property before the easement and the remainder rights after the access agreement. Notably, sitting by and doing nothing was not an option for the rancher—courts have generally held that once found, the public has an interest in such artifacts.

Easement/access rights may be specific to a particular site on the property or may span the entire property. The remainder rights retained by the property owner may run continuously with the access rights. These will need to be carefully negotiated so that the easement grantor and holder can conduct operations simultaneously. Since the appraisal needs to account for these simultaneous rights, and the pricing of rights takes into account the appraisal, it is apparent that the negotiations and the appraisal are best conducted simultaneously and dynamically. This sort of dynamic valuation may not be familiar to most appraisers. The end result may prevent hard feelings and potential litigation and will help ensure that value is optimized now and in the future.

5. Land with Environmental Concerns

At the other end of the spectrum, brownfield land can be and often is bought as an investment for rehabilitation and resale. A land holding may suddenly be found to be either a point source of contamination or impacted by an adjacent or proximate environmental disamenity. The two situations have somewhat different economic and financial motivations and different legal implications, but from an appraisal perspective they are very similar.

One group of investors purchased an industrial plant as a business investment. Unbeknownst to them, the land was severely contaminated (this was before the days of mandatory environmental audits). The local authorities required that the plant be shut down and the contamination remediated. Afterward, the investors found that the remediated site—with a changed highest and best use—was worth more than they had invested, including the original plant cost, remediation cost, and financial costs. Leveraging off of that experience, they changed their investment business model to seek out brownfield remediation deals.

From an appraisal perspective, an environmental disamenity may take one of three forms:

- On-site
- Adjacent
- Proximate

The legal term "point source" addresses potential liabilities for remediation as well as to third parties. This appraisal list is agnostic to legal liabilities and focuses entirely on the selection and analysis of data for the valuation exercise. Notably, if a property is contamination source, there may be legal liabilities that travel with the land or the landowners. From an appraisal perspective, on-site contamination may result from the property itself being the source of the pollution (potentially the "point source" under the law) and one where the property has been contaminated by a pollutant migrating from off-site.

The differences among these forms of environmental disamenity may be misunderstood, even by appraisers who work on these projects. Figure 16-1 (see next page) shows very rough examples of how a given pollutant, in this case a plume of groundwater contamination, may emerge and migrate.

For appraisers, "environmental contamination" is a loaded term in the law and appraisal guidance. Obviously—and this should be common sense—a property that has never been subjected to an environmental disamenity is worth more than a property that has suffered any kind of negative environmental impact. It has been argued that on-site contamination at levels below regulatory levels should not be a factor in valuation. However, studies have found otherwise, and properties with on-site contamination, even below regulatory levels, are at least as badly affected as properties stigmatized by nearby negative externalities, if not more so.

In a perfect world, the appraisal would rely on some sort of matched pairs (or even a rudimentary statistical analysis) to glean the discount. Of course, such data is rare, and usually not very informative. Actual valuation data will include:

- Surveys of market participants—eliciting discount information from potential buyers, brokers, lenders, and others
- Case studies of similar situations
- Published academic and practitioner literature
- Quantitative surveys or analyses of pricing trends

The value of environmentally affected property may be impacted by the remediation status (pre-remediation, remediation underway, or post-remediation). Values may be affected by changes in expected costs, in allowable property uses, or in risks attached to the property. Even post-remediation, there are expected costs, such as monitoring, insurance, and management costs. Even if a commercial property enjoys a full level of rent, the net operating income will generally be discounted at a higher cap rate by investors. The simple fact is that the potential universe of investors for a post-remediation contaminated property is smaller than the universe of potential investors for a never-contaminated site. Risks are very real, since some types of contamination are hard if not impossible to cure. Risks may cause problems with financing, interruptions in use, and marketability.

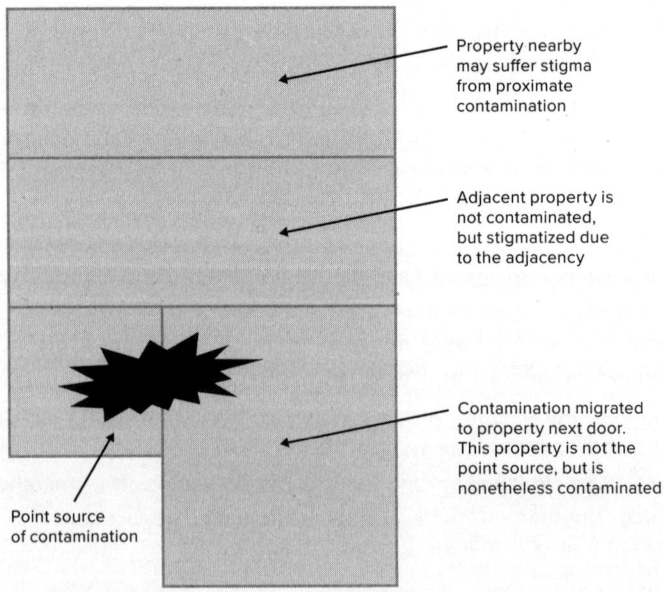

FIGURE 16-1 Impact of Environmental Disamenity

One common impact of environmental contamination is a change in the highest and best use (HBU). Consider the components of HBU and how they may be affected by an environmental disamenity:

Legal permissibility. This is the most obvious potential impact. Allowable uses of "clean" property may no longer be permitted if the property is impacted. Even after remediation, some prior uses may no longer be permittable. Consider a site approved for residential development and then discovered to be environmentally contaminated. The remediation brings the contamination level down to industrial standards but not to standards allowing residential occupancy.

Physically adaptability. Another impact will be physical limits placed by contamination. One 10-acre site was perfectly suitable for a large suburban office campus until it was found that one corner—less than one acre—was contaminated. The immediate consideration was to cleave off the one-acre portion and develop the nine-acre portion. However, the contamination site was in the only permittable ingress and egress location for the development (see Figure 16-2). Since this portion of the site had to be reserved for remediation facilities, the development of the entire 10 acres was held up until a suitable solution could be negotiated.

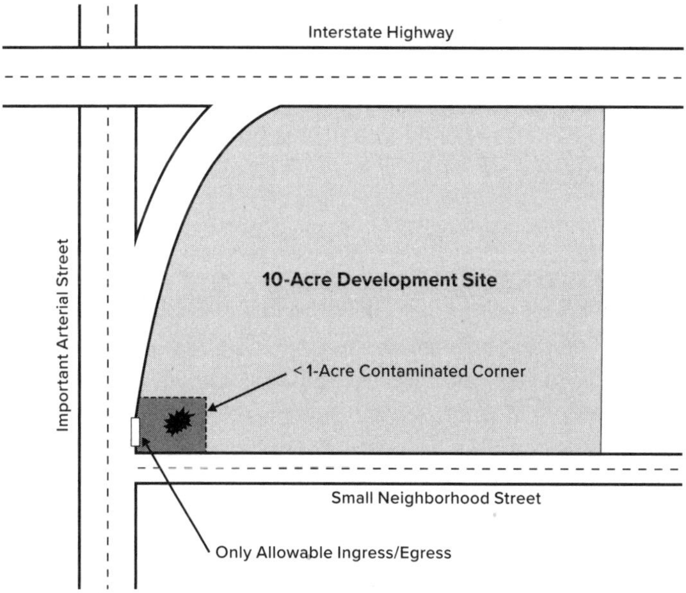

FIGURE 16-2 Contamination Impact on a Development Site

Financial feasibility. Consider the impacts on the NOI (increased costs) and the capitalization or discount rate (increased ROI demanded by risky-property investors). Can the property be purchased at any positive price which results in a positive return to the developer/investor? If not, then the project is no longer financially feasible. If the investor would be responsible for the environmental remediation, then it is often the case that there are few if any financially feasible uses for the property. At this juncture, the investor who is "stuck" with a brownfield may consider the government partnerships, specialized funding, or even litigation against responsible parties in an attempt to restore feasibility.

Maximally productive use. Even if several uses are still financially feasible, the mix of rents and returns may change dramatically, in the "as-is contaminated" and in the "as if remediated" condition. Imagine a property previously suitable for residential or commercial development. In the "as if uncontaminated" condition, the residential development was most profitable. After remediation, there is market reluctance for residential use, and as such commercial development is the preferred outcome.

In summary, the appraisal of impacted property will take into account factors such as the contamination location relative to the property itself, the contamination life cycle, the changes in highest and best use, and the data and analysis to measure the impacts. The key element is to understand market reaction, and particularly the reaction when all facts are known and appreciated by market participants. Most appraisers have little experience or expertise in this sort of problem, and environmental experts (engineers, hydrologists, etc.) have little or no understanding of real estate valuation. Hence, the investor/owner will be challenged to carefully manage and monitor the appraisal process.

"Stigma" is a common term tossed around by appraisers, attorneys, brokers, and others when dealing with environmentally damaged property. Of course, stigma has a common usage meaning, but "environmental stigma" has been inculcated into the appraisal lexicon. It was first introduced by appraisal scholars shortly after the advent of federal brownfield legislation, when appraisers began noticing that contaminated property, even after remediation, sold for less than could be explained by simple engineering costs to cure the problem. This unexplained reduction in market value became labeled as stigma, and it is a measure of market pushback against the price and value of environmentally affected property.

6. Accretion and Reliction

With modern-day erosion and flood control, these issues are not as important as they were a generation ago. However, this does still occasionally arise. More significantly, old surveys and maps, on which appraisers sometimes rely, may be inaccurate as a result of this.

Accretion (see Figure 16-3) is the process of a site growing in size due to the deposit of soil, usually from a river or a shoreline. Related terms include avulsion and erosion. Accretion implies that a site grows in size slowly and nearly imperceptibly. Erosion is exactly the opposite—the site slowly and imperceptible shrinks in size. Avulsion is a sudden and noticeable change in the parcel size or shape, usually due to water action. Legal doctrine varies from state to state, but in general slow and imperceptible changes may impact legal size (and hence value), but avulsion has no legal impact on the property boundary. The challenge is understanding which doctrine applies in a given situation, and this may require a legal opinion supporting the appraisal.

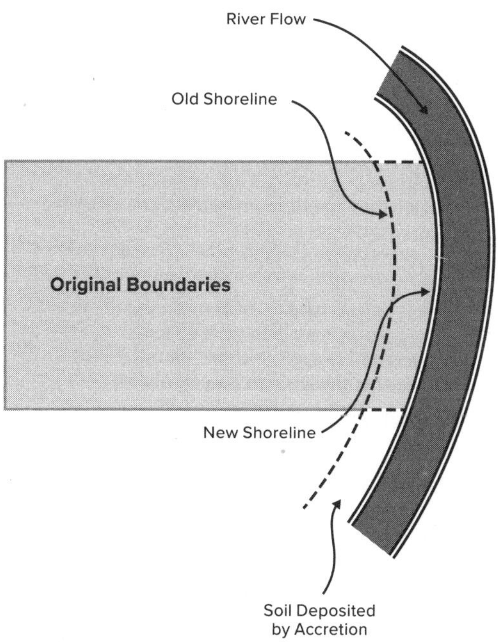

FIGURE 16-3 Accretion

Reliction (see Figure 16-4) is a site growing in size due to the water level receding. Generally, title to additional land is gained, but this again varies according to local doctrine and legal precedent. The opposite of reliction is submergence or subsidence, and title is generally not lost in those cases, although the value of newly submerged lands may be very different from the value of uplands.

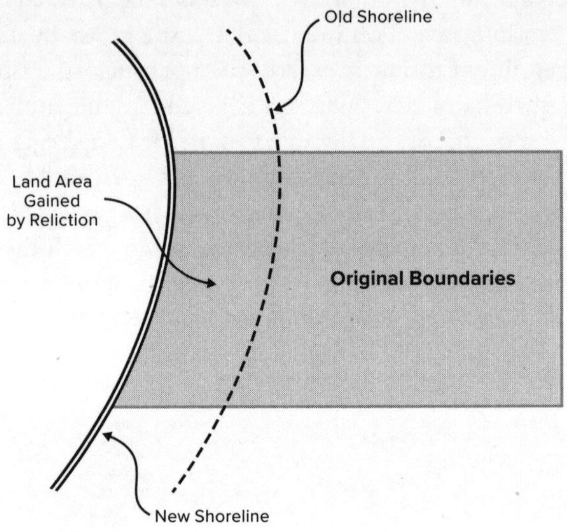

FIGURE 16-4 Reliction

Any site that fronts on a body of water may be impacted by these forces over time, and there may be significant valuation issues. Assumptions implicit in an appraisal, and particularly assumptions about older, poor-quality surveys, will need to be tested and questioned. Related to this, of course, are long-term sea level changes that are evident in parts of the world. Investors with an eye to very long-term, multigenerational holdings will seriously consider these implications.

7. Prescriptive Easements, Adverse Possession, and Encroachments

Easements are usually granted through contract and recorded in a place of public access, such as the county clerk's office, along with a survey. A *prescriptive easement* arises if someone uses a portion of a property openly, notoriously, and without the owner's permission. A prescriptive easement usually involves only part of a property, such as a pathway or driveway (Figure 16-5).

Prescriptive easements can either be *appurtenant* or *in gross*. An appurtenant easement travels with the land, and so can be transferred when the dominant property is sold. This easement will continue in force even if the servient easement is sold.

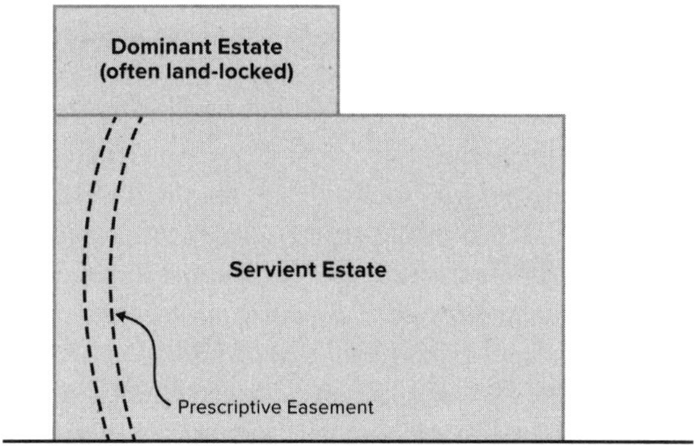

FIGURE 16-5 Example of a Prescriptive Easement

State law should be consulted for the exact statutory requirement for a prescriptive easement. Law varies, and it may define a time period required for a prescriptive easement to take effect. These easements may be difficult for an appraiser to discern since they do not show up on title reports. The actual location or use of the easement may actually move from time to time.

While the most common prescriptive easements are pathways and driveways, the courts have upheld a variety of uses that have created such rights. In one 2004 California case, restaurant delivery trucks regularly drove through an adjacent bank parking lot for years. The court held that the owner of the restaurant parcel had established an easement. In a famous 1977 case, *MacDonald Properties v Bel-Air Country Club*, some badly hit golf balls landed on nearby property each day for over five years. The court held that the club had acquired a prescriptive easement to use this adjacent property as a rough. In 1991, also in California, a court ruled that a public reservoir that encroached 20 feet onto an adjacent property had created a prescriptive easement. (Subsequent court rulings have supported the end result but have cast some doubt on the underlying theory of law.)

Again, a prescriptive easement may not be publicly recorded and may not even be known by the seller. This encourages an appraiser to conduct a thorough and complete inspection, looking for potential easements and encroachments that disagree with public documents. State law generally requires that a prescriptive easement be "open and notorious." In a 1959 California case, an irrigation pipeline was hidden underground. The court held, though, that the fixtures coming off the pipeline were sufficiently visible to satisfy this open and notorious requirement, and hence upheld the prescriptive easement.

An *encroachment* is like an easement, but has one significant difference. First, in most states, a prescriptive easement cannot exclude the owner's right to use the land. In the restaurant truck case, the bank continued to have full and unfettered use of the parking lot, albeit with the occasional delivery truck passing through. In the Bel Air Country Club matter, the only easement was as a golf course rough. The servient property owner could continue to use the land, again with the slight exception of an occasional errant golf ball.

With an encroachment, though, the owner may have been excluded from using a portion of the land. Examples include a fence extending over a property line, misplaced landscaping, or a structure extending onto an adjacent property. Encroachments typically occur right at a property line and may be difficult for an appraiser to discern. Generally, if an investor suspects an encroachment, then a survey is needed because the encroachment may impact the value.

Adverse possession is a somewhat rarer situation, although it does occasionally occur. The actual legal basis for adverse possession varies from state to state. In general, while a prescriptive easement does not exclude the servient property owner, adverse possession must typically be exclusive to the possessor. Further, the time frame for adverse possession is usually somewhat longer than for a simple prescriptive easement. Finally, adverse possession typically implies a whole property being used exclusively by the possessor, rather than just a driveway or pathway that is occasionally used. A common example is a misplaced fence, which over time may establish actual ownership if not challenged. Adverse possession should usually be evident to the appraiser when conducting a site inspection. A properly defined scope of work for the appraisal should generally include some discussion of current or proposed property use. The client should arrange access, and if the appraiser discovers that the current use or user is something very different, there may be an issue of adverse possession.

This raises an interesting issue about intended use under a lease versus actual use. Landlords or their agents are expected to inspect a property from time to time, if for no other reason than to ascertain that the property is being used as anticipated and provided under the lease. Oftentimes, misuse of property can lead to adverse zoning actions, damage to the property, or even environmental issues.

8. Curating Property Holdings and Values over Time

Many years ago, I was consulting with a client who had acquired several hundred acres from a timber company. He had a long-range plan to develop a residential community and let the land just "sit" for a while, letting the market mature and arranging financing. When time came to actually develop the site, he asked me to provide some assistance. We went on a walk through the forest one day—a lovely hike through a beautiful, hilly site. Not very far in from the main road, along an old logging trail, we stumbled on a not-long-abandoned liquor still!

Monitoring and managing trophy real estate holdings does not need to be a full-time job, but a certain amount of *curation* is needed to preserve and enhance value. Selecting investments is a careful task and carries similar implications to selecting any other investment. Properties should be inspected periodically, and nowadays, much of this is being done with drones and small airplanes. Taxes need to be paid, insurance reviewed occasionally, and values monitored.

This raises an interesting question—what should happen to values over time? One investment manager, who specializes in dot-com millionaires, told me that his clients don't look to him to "make them money." They just don't want him to "lose their money." This is a delightful sentiment, but in a world with positive inflation and very real financial risks, simply maintaining value is the same as "losing them money." Buying low and selling high (or not selling at all!) continues to be an important adage.

9. Summary and Key Points

In contrast to the prior chapter, this chapter focuses on land being purchased for "hold" rather than development or immediate income. The phrase "land banking" is often used to describe buying land without immediate plans for its use. Reasons for buying and holding land vary, but often include recreational value or trophy land collection. Many issues facing a land-banking investor also apply to a buy-and-develop situation, such as considerations of easements, encroachments, lands with unique and publicly valuable amenities, and lands with environmental considerations.

Landholdings may be large, complex, and of varying size, shape, and topography. Since vacant land is not continuously occupied by an owner or a tenant, it is ripe for encroachments, prescriptive easements, environmental damage, and other changes that may impact value. When acquiring such a property, and periodically during the property ownership, a thorough and complete due diligence inspection is appropriate. This may include, but not be limited to, an appraisal with a rigorous site inspection, a survey, and an environmental audit. Public records should be examined regularly, but given the various opportunities for untoward things to happen, public records should not be considered as the last authority.

10. A Final Note—Wealthy Investors and the Hobby Farm

There is an old saw in the wine business. "Do you know how to make a small fortune in wine?" "Start out with a large fortune and work your way down." The same, by the way, is true about horses. There are magazines, websites, and brokerage firms dedicated to the care and feeding of hobby farmers. A surprisingly large number of successful executives and wealthy investors find their weekend relaxation riding a tractor, tending grapes, feeding horses, or even gathering eggs.

There is a relatively famous Tax Court case, dating from the 1970s, involving a hobby farm owned by a physician in Manhattan. Every weekend he would tend his "farm." He had an on-site farm manager to handle the details during the week and, among other things, a fair-sized chicken coop. Since the chickens produced far more eggs than the farm could consume, the manager sold the excess at the local farmers market. Since this was revenue to the farm, the physician dutifully wrote off the farm expenses against egg revenue. The IRS protested that there was never an intention for the farm to make a profit, and in Tax Court, it was uncovered that his farming deduction for the year was over $12,000 . . . per egg.

Sigh . . . this is not a book about tax advice, and this story gave rise to some very specific rules and regulations about deducting losses from hobby farms, probably written by attorneys and members of Congress who, themselves, own hobby farms. Rather, this is a book about valuation, and there are some very special considerations when examining the appraisal of a hobby farm.

First, and this is key—the appraiser doesn't know whether you intend to be a hobby farmer or an actual for-profit, full-time farmer. The difference can be important to understand the appraisal. For one, there are certain economies of scale in farming. A 10-acre grape orchard may have very different valuation metrics than a 100-acre orchard. The same will be true for any type or scale of farming.

> One hobby farm we visited grew a healthy crop of corn each year. In that part of the country, corn was no longer a viable cash crop, and certainly not at the scale being grown by this family. Upon closer inspection, it turns out their 98-year-old aunt lived in the farmhouse, and still thought the farm was being operated as a for-profit venture. She had very little appreciation at all that the daughters and sons who had grown up on that farm were now attorneys, stockbrokers, and physicians. Nonetheless, the family had a nice corn crop planted every season, and gave away the corn to friends and charities at harvest time.

Next, finding comps for a hobby farm tends to be complicated. The biggest, and somewhat surprising, difference is the number and quality of buildings. The main house will usually be very nice, even if this is a weekend cottage, and the outbuildings are usually in excellent repair and larger in number. One hobby grape orchard in the Russian River Valley had a 1,000-square-foot, nicely constructed and maintained building dedicated to the owner's model train collection. A hobby farm in the South had two well-stocked ponds and a garage to maintain the owner's classic, collectible European sports car. This particular owner actually forgot to plant a crop one year. He was too busy as a political officeholder. A bank president was fond of holding weekend meetings while sitting atop his antique—but well-maintained and still functional—tractor. The tractor was kept in a barn much nicer than many surrounding houses. An insurance executive hired a university architecture professor to design a 12-horse stable, with spacious tack room and office, for his 14-year-old daughter. These are not the usual trappings of a full-time, for-profit agricultural enterprise.

Most hobby farms will be purchased for cash, so an appraisal for a mortgage is typically not needed. However, it is significant that Freddie Mac, one of the nation's largest mortgage securitizers, analyzes appraisals of "for-profit" farms and "hobby" farms quite differently. Interestingly enough, Freddie Mac does not purchase purely agricultural loans, but only residential ones. Thus, a "hobby" farm would qualify for a Freddie Mac conforming loan if it was primarily residential (yes, even weekend residential) with farming as an ancillary activity. Freddie Mac publishes the following guidance:

> Hobby farms are typically small farms where the homeowner engages in farming activity for personal use and are eligible properties [for lending]. In this case the primary use of the property is residential and the secondary use is for insignificant farming activity. Therefore, the existence of a small roadside stand used for selling fruits and vegetables does not result in the property being ineligible. Ineligible properties include properties used primarily for farming or ranching.[1]

Some hobby farms actually generate positive income. In Walla Walla, Washington, there is a huge demand for the locally produced sweet onions. There are also problems gaining water rights for farms greater than five acres. As a solution, many hobby farms grow less than five acres of onions profitably and consolidate marketing through local co-ops. Many hobby farms grow organic crops sold through farmers markets. Thus, the simple fact that a farm is small may not render it financially infeasible. Also, there has been an upsurge in demand for hobby farms in recent years, and the hobby farm—even when unprofitable as an agricultural venture—may have a market all to itself, just like trophy land or other collectible properties. Many traditional appraisers are just catching on to this conundrum. They will need to recognize that the comps that may be useful for valuing a more traditional farm may not be useful for valuing a weekend hobby farm, even if that hobby farm is producing a small for-profit crop.

17
Real Estate and the Family Business

Land monopoly is not the only monopoly, but it is by far the greatest of monopolies; it is a perpetual monopoly, and it is the mother of all other forms of monopoly.

—Winston Churchill

THERE ARE TWO kinds of families with substantial for-profit real estate holdings. One is the wealthy family whose business is primarily real estate. A great example is the descendants of Sol Goldman, former owner of the Chrysler Building in Manhattan, who was purportedly New York's biggest landlord when he died in 1987. His family has continued in the tradition and grown their real estate–based wealth, owning at least 400 New York City properties as of this writing. *Forbes* magazine estimated the family's net holdings in excess of $12 billion as of 2016. For a professional real estate family such as theirs, understanding valuation, appraisals, and the nuances of finding value are almost second nature.

In this business, you make money slowly. The main point is not to sell anything.

—Sol Goldman, as quoted in *Forbes* magazine, 1985

This chapter is focused on the second family—the one that owns lots of real estate, but as an ancillary to its core business. The most obvious example is the Walton family, with substantial holdings in Walmart stock, that also owns many buildings housing Walmart stores, warehouses, and distribution centers. The Walton family spends a significant amount of time and energy managing that real estate, recognizing it is a separate and distinct conduit for maintaining and growing wealth.

Consider the family-owned business, such as a manufacturing firm or car dealership, housed in one or two facilities. The family's focus, naturally, is on the business itself. It is often overlooked that a substantial portion of family wealth is tied up in real estate, and sometimes this real estate is not used to its highest and best use.

Several years ago the Chrysler Corporation opted to "pull" the franchises from over 800 allegedly marginal dealers around the United States. The ensuing uproar from the dealers—many of whom had been in the car business at the same location for generations—masked one irony of this episode. Often, the land on which the dealership sat was worth more than the dealership as a going concern. Repositioning the property to a higher and better use—such as apartments or retail—leaves the family better off financially with significantly less business management effort.

> In downtown Seattle, a major road widening threatened a car dealership that had been housed for decades in an old, historically valuable building. The building was so very valuable that an investor purchased it, had it carefully dismantled, and then moved it just a few feet away to accommodate the road widening. The old car dealership building was then used as the anchor for a much larger building and has become an architectural objet d'art.

This chapter will address several common valuation issues facing families with real estate holdings supporting their business holdings. Each issue probably deserves a book all to itself. The next section, on estate planning issues, can only be fully addressed by including legal and tax accounting issues. From a real estate valuation perspective, though, there are issues that are often overlooked when addressing estate planning as a purely legal or tax phenomenon. Hopefully, this chapter will provide some food for further thought.

1. Real Estate as a Residual Value

In the Chrysler example, the real estate was assumed to have a highest and best use independent of the business. There was no particular assumption as to what that highest and best use (HBU) might be.

What if the real estate in question has no particular HBU independent of the business operated there? There are two common phenomena that give rise to this. The first is an extractive business, such as a quarry, a mine, or an oilfield. Once the minerals are extracted from the subsurface, then the surface rights may have little or no value. This may seem odd to readers who are mostly familiar with urban or suburban areas. In parts of the West or in Alaska, this is not an uncommon phenomenon. The cost of maintaining the land (insurance, taxes) may actually exceed the present value of holding the land.

The second situation comes from activities that pollute the property. There may be an ongoing "value in use" for the property, but the contamination, even if contained or remediated to regulatory standards, may have rendered the property unmarketable. This may occur with factory sites, warehouses, or even residences if some polluting activity occurred there.

The key way to value such real estate is a land extraction. The market value of similarly situated comps are compared to the value equation in the cost approach. Table 17-1 shows a simplified version of this.

TABLE 17-1 Land Residual with Negative Land Value

Reconciled Value from Comparables		$10,000,000
Reproduction Cost of Improvements	$12,500,000	
Less: Physical Depreciation	($9,600,000)	
Replacement Cost of Improvements	$2,900,000	
Value of Minerals On-Site	$7,200,000	
Indicated Value		$10,100,000
Residual Value of Land		($100,000)

This is not an uncommon situation in a mining or extraction situation, where there are significantly depreciated assets in place (value of the improvements) and minerals remaining to be extracted. The residual land value is actually negative. This suggests that there may be some contamination residual on the site, and comparable properties are picking up this stigma problem.

2. Land Versus Improvements

Have you seen "for sale" signs on vacant commercial and industrial tracts that advertise "Build to Suit"? These usually fall into two categories. In the first, albeit less common case, a merchant builder or developer owns the land (or controls via an option) and will build and lease a custom facility to a business. Of more interest is the common situation of a landowner who will construct a custom facility for a buyer and sell the entire package to the end user. This package deal allows the seller to reap the profits on the land and the development and construction profits. From the buyer's perspective, the financing is simplified and the construction risk is contained.

Whether built by a third-party seller or constructed by the family business owners, the custom-built facility has both benefits and limitations. Obviously, any custom-designed facility will fit the exact end user needs. The alternative would be to acquire a generic building that may not have the proper facilities, utilities, dimensions, or mix of components. For retail facilities, even the orientation to the street and setbacks for parking and deliveries can be user-specific.

The principal detriment to a custom-built facility is the lack of marketability. In the same way that a family business wanted a custom facility, subsequent buyers may also disdain the property in favor of their own design. At the extreme, a highly unique facility may be utterly unmarketable without economically infeasible modifications. It is not uncommon for such a facility to be a complete teardown when adaptive reuse is in order.

The starting point for the appraisal should be the cost approach, and specifically a determination of functional obsolescence. This will be based on the cost (plus entrepreneurial profit to the builder) of adapting the existing structure to a market-acceptable condition. Functional obsolescence usually stems from two conditions—a deficiency or a superadequacy. The former are typically considered to be curable, while the latter are usually, although not always, incurable. A superadequacy may not negatively impact value (unless the cost of maintenance is unusual) but will constitute an investment that cannot be recaptured upon resale, and thus makes no contribution to market value.

These distinctions are important. If the business use of the newly constructed facility will exceed the expected economic life of the improvements, then the issue may be moot. Indeed, there will be little residual facility value at the end of the economic life, but little value was expected. Conversely, if we expect to use the improvements less time than the expected life of the improvements, then there will be a trade-off at construction. Will the benefits from building a unique facility outweigh the anticipated cost-to-cure at the project conclusion?

Common family businesses include car dealerships, factories, and retail establishments. A grocery store probably has little risk of either deficiency or superadequacy, but factories are often highly customized. Factories usually have a long business life span, transcending the economic life span of the structure, and as such this is usually not an issue. Car dealerships, though, can be troublesome to appraise. The structures are often built with a very short economic life. While some portions (service bays, parts departments) can be adapted for other use, showrooms and offices are often superadequacies from the onset.

This leaves land value. In earlier discussions of highest and best use, we noted that if real estate—land plus improvements—had a different HBU than the current use, then the land value had to take into account the cost of demolishing the improvements and restoring the land to "buildable" condition. Factories can prove to be a unique problem. Factories are often built in locations with very cheap land. Demolition costs and environmental remediation may actually exceed vacant land value. Adaptive reuse of such a facility may require additional funds and often will not be accomplished in the absence of a public or legal mandate.

> The family business often focuses entirely on the business needs and ignores the real estate implications. Appraisals may or may not do an adequate job of noting deficiencies or superadequacies of the proposed development compared to the needs and expectations of other market participants. As a result, the family may dissipate the benefits from the business by investing in a real estate asset that has little or no residual market value.

3. Real Estate Versus Plant and Equipment

On the surface, this seems simple enough. Some appraisers specialize in plant and equipment (P&E) valuation. The appraisal of a factory may require two specialties—one for the real estate and one for the P&E. This is not unlike the timber stand discussed in an earlier chapter, requiring a timber cruise and a real estate valuation.

This situation gets interesting when some real estate components are developed or modified to accommodate specialized equipment. A factory building itself may actually be an integral component of P&E, and so has no stand-alone real estate value. Even when the building has a stand-alone residual value, such as a warehouse adapted for manufacturing, then some components may have little or no contributory market value. As discussed previously, these are superadequacies, which may be useful in the present but for which the typical buyer will pay very little, if anything.

Typical superadequacies related to P&E include:

- Thick concrete pads or footings for specialized equipment
- Additional height (specialized roof structures) for tall equipment
- Electrical or water services over and above the norm
- Holding ponds and tanks
- Unusual parking requirements for specialized vehicles
- Truck wash pits
- Waste treatment facilities

Differentiating between real estate and non-realty components (P&E) is necessary for three important reasons. First, from an appraisal perspective, the P&E is depreciated over a shorter period than the real estate. This leads to the second important reason—the tax implications of shorter depreciation. Finally, upon resale, there is an expectation that the realty will stay but that the P&E needs to be separately contracted, or else it will leave with the seller.

In real estate jargon, "fixtures" are anything not permanently affixed to the real estate. To use a simple residential example, a stand-alone stove would not be part of the real estate, but a built-in stove would be. In a factory or a restaurant, the question gets murky. Some pieces of equipment are affixed in a fashion that appears to be permanent. Consider kitchen equipment in a restaurant versus kitchen equipment in a typical home. When developing a scope of work for a real estate appraisal, there will need to be a delineation of what is considered to be part of the realty and what is not. An experienced appraiser with expertise in that particular property type will be of great assistance in delineating normal market expectations. Guidance may also come from the tax accounting arena, who can help with current expectations under the IRS regulations.

Consider a hotel appraisal. Beds, televisions, and stand-alone furniture are fixtures rather than realty. However, there is increasing use of built-in furniture in limited service hotels. Are these items personal or real property? Usually, these will be classified as personal property, regardless of how attached to the structure. Guidance should be sought from tax advisors.

> Family-owned businesses with realty holdings may have some control over the delineation between equipment—with shorter depreciation schedules—and realty components. If there are disparate ownership interests between the business and the realty, then this allocation may impact the allocation of rents and returns to the various interests.

4. Family Business and Realty Organizational Issues

The family business organizational structure is a legal matter and will be influenced by a number of factors. The real estate ownership structure may impact the valuation. One business was owned jointly between two married couples. The underlying real estate was owned as a tenancy in common among the four of them. When one died, the probate interests were complex, but so was the valuation aspect. The valuation of the realty assets required a marketability discount and a lack of control discount. These are fairly straightforward and are provided for under IRS guidance and salient Tax Court rulings. There is a good bit of guidance on these issues for the appraiser to follow.

Many investors became owners of real estate assets as tenant in common (TIC) investments resulting from 1031 exchanges. For the uninitiated, 1031 exchanges allow investors to defer capital gains stemming from the sale of real estate if a like-kind acquisition occurs within a fixed period. There are a variety of rules, but essentially partnership and LLC assets can be problematic for these exchanges. However, TICs are allowed. As it happens, TICs may have operational and liquidity issues that make them very tough to value.

As of this writing, investments in "opportunity zones" are attracting significant attention. These have very real tax benefits but may be done via comingled funds. The fund value—just like any private equity investment—will depend on liquidity provisions in the investment agreements. LLCs and LPs have the same issues. These are great tools for managing real estate, but in the absence of liquidity provisions, the valuation is dependent on a secondary market for ownership interests.

The ownership structure should be carefully considered with an eye to the best legal and tax situation and also to the optimum valuation solution. Ideally, these ownership structures are revisited regularly to review changes in the tax laws, probate laws, and valuation metrics.

5. Tax Issues

Again—and this bears repeating—not only should wealthy investors consider the implications of real estate valuation with their tax advisors, they should do this on a regular basis. It may be handy to reflect on the various tax implications experienced by privately held businesses:

- Income taxes, which may be pass-through depending on the ownership structure

- Property taxes, which are often at a different rate and basis for real versus personal (or business) property
- State and local business and occupation taxes (such as licenses, fees, and permits)
- Employment-based taxes
- Mandated fees, such as workers' compensation and other withholdings

Also, recall that business assets (such as P&E), real estate improvements (buildings), and land have differential depreciation factors and thus differential sheltering and long-term-gains implications.

Privately held businesses have some control, within reason, as to the asset allocation among various categories of holdings. Land cannot be depreciated, and minimizing the allocation to land as opposed to buildings and equipment will have a tax implication for a long-term hold situation. Depreciation may need to be recaptured at sale, so an owner anticipating a sale may want to allocate business interests to real estate for estate planning or tax purposes.

There are cautionary tales to be told when making arbitrary allocations. One seller of a privately held business asked that the sale be mainly allocated to real estate, but for a token amount allocated to the business. Later, the buyer found that the seller was interfering with the conduct of the business (stealing clients and employees, mischaracterization of certain assets, etc.) and sued. One defense raised was that there was very little allocated to the *business*, and no claim that there was interference with the use and enjoyment of the *real estate*. Fortunately for the buyer, the court saw through the ruse.

Separating the business from the real estate, or even the land from the improvements, may allow a closely held family business to allocate profits to the family member or family trust entity with the most favorable tax treatment. As an example—and please check with your tax accountant on this—say that Sister Susan lives in Florida, with no income tax, while Brother Bob lives in New York with high rates of income taxation. If there is a way to allocate ordinary income to Susan but long-term gains to Bob, all the better.

One very successful business developer owned a vast amount of real estate and business assets. Unfortunately, he was very poorly advised on organizational structures, and apparently never thought he would ever die. It took years and teams of lawyers scattered around the United States to unravel his holdings. One very valuable business was situated on a parcel of land leased from the local city government. Upon his death, it was discovered that the lease was far below market (he was a masterful negotiator) and *in his name personally.* Negotiations with the city delayed the business sale for several years.

Finally, studies have shown that holdings shared among family members are perhaps more prone to disputes and litigation than holdings shared by disparate, unrelated owners. Simply put, business litigation is an all-too-easy way to air family grudges and grievances. One brother and sister spent years in litigation over a large and very profitable family real estate management company. Splitting up the holdings and letting everyone go their merry way turned out to be simple. The complexity emerged when it was discovered that the brother had never been paid by the company for managing the family holdings—he had simply managed the family trust as an ancillary of his own successful company. Once the arbitration panel decided to break up the family trust, the brother was then forced to sue to be paid a fair compensation for years of his professional management. In a bit of irony, the sister's legal fees far exceeded what the court ended up awarding the brother. The lesson in this—and countless related stories—is that family holdings should be structured carefully and with an eye to the countless issues that can transcend a family through the years.

6. Even More Complex Issues

Thus far in this chapter, I have focused on fairly simple examples—an enterprise including a business and underlying real estate. The real estate may be composed of land plus improvements. The business will have personal property, such as factory equipment or furnishings.

Many wealthy families are invested in businesses that have complex asset structures. For example:

Car dealerships. The business value is heavily dependent on the franchise relationship. Newer dealerships may be located in "auto malls" or other high-traffic areas, and may be very valuable for sale to other dealers. Older dealerships may be in less desirable parts of town, in towns with declining economics, or on real estate with environmental issues from decades of auto repairs. The HBU may even be indeterminable.

Hotels. Much like the car dealer, the hotel may be dependent on the relationship with the franchisor, or "flag" as it is called. This relationship is particularly pronounced in lower-end or business hotels and drives occupancy through the reservation system, brand awareness, and customer loyalty. Upscale hotels often do not have such brand dependency. The underlying real estate for branded hotels will generally have an HBU for a hotel, and hotels may shift brands without changing ownership. The HBU for the real estate for unbranded hotels may or may not be for continued use as a hotel and is heavily dependent on location and financial feasibility. Also, many large hotels, particularly in downtown locations, have significant sublet space or even a shopping court adjacent to the lobby area. Bar and restaurant income may be substantial, and often that area is subcontracted or joint-ventured. Parking is a substantial revenue source for large, downtown hotels, as is catering, conference, and meeting income. Many hotels are just adjuncts to large, profitable conference centers.

Retail. If a shopping mall can be thought of as an agglomeration of different stores with different names, then a large retailer can be thought of as an agglomeration of different stores with the same name. Often, the large retailer will sublease portions of the store, such as shoes, jewelry, or perfume, to specialty enterprises. These subcontract relationships may be under the same name as the parent store or even as stand-alone kiosk-type stores-within-a-store.

Eldercare. This includes a host of for-profit and not-for-profit enterprises and includes the real estate and the business within the real estate. Complicating this is the availability of exceptional financing and the desirability for these investments by offshore investors (especially EB-5 investors[1]). The investment valuation is complicated by layers of ownership.

Such facilities are usually bought as going concerns. Appraisers often need to value separate components for eminent domain or tax assessment. This would also be needed for a family trying to separate realty from business assets to establish or settle an estate. Unfortunately, there are actually different schools of thought within the appraisal community about exactly how to do that. The answer to the question, "what is the real estate worth?" may be different depending on whom you ask. Investors are well advised to understand this issue when interviewing appraisers.

* * *

One defining characteristic of complex investments is the role real estate plays in the overall value. Rather than a real estate investment with a minor business component (such as an apartment, with ancillary income from vending, laundry, and parking), these are primarily viewed and traded as enterprises within which the real estate plays a lesser role. Appraisers with expertise in these properties view the real estate as a *residual* value, rather than the starting point for the valuation. The normal approaches to value (cost, income, and sales comparison) cannot be directly applied in the usual fashion.

The cost approach may be preferred in some situations. Developing a complex enterprise requires a long time frame, mainly for permitting and design, and so the cost approach may do the best job accounting for holding period costs. Further, such properties are frequently subject to complex functional obsolescence issues, and this is best explained in the cost approach (although often best computed using the other approaches).

The income analysis generally treats the real estate income as a residual after accounting for the business NOI and a normal return to the business investors. Thus if a hotel had a total NOI of $10 million, but $5 million was allocated to pay a normal ROI to the business portion, then the remaining $5 million would be capitalized as realty value. The controversy arises when determining exactly which assets and expenses are business and which are not. An eldercare facility is intensively managed, but some cost of management needs to be allocated to the real estate. How much of management's time is real estate, and how much is something else? Second, what is a fair allocation of returns? It is widely recognized and agreed that the skills and talents of managers are more important than the real estate itself, but how much more?

An alternate approach is to value the real estate, determine the portion of income needed to support market feasible returns, and then capitalize the remainder as a business value. One school of thought uses the capitalization or discount rates applicable to simple assets, such as using apartment cap rates to value the realty component of an eldercare facility. This approach is not widely used, but does appear occasionally even in scholarly works. The problem is that these complex assets are just that—complex. No one would take on the complicated problem of developing a hotel property for the same expected rate of return from a simple seasoned apartment complex. Nonetheless, this approach is benefitted by being simple and easy for the appraiser to apply.

The sales comparison approach is widely recognized as nearly worthless for allocation of a complex enterprise between business and realty components. The situations are simply too unique and idiosyncratic to be compared and adjusted. While the sales comparison approach is useful for valuing the entire enterprise (e.g., the price per room of a large hotel), the different components of hotels are usually difficult if not impossible to value in such a fashion.

7. Estate Planning for the Family Business

Consider the simple example of a family farm. Two hypotheticals illustrate the significant potential implications of land-versus-business transition. Both stem from the fact that many farm family "offspring" simply do not want to continue the family business into the next generation. Sometimes this is based on the complexity and marginal profits of the business. Sometimes, it is simply a lifestyle choice. Often, it stems from the fact that the land holding has a higher and better use as something else.

Let's say a farmer died, leaving a considerable, profitable family farm to his two daughters. They moved away, married, raised families, and had little interest in returning to the family farm. The land was in the pathway of suburban growth and had great prospects as a simple "hold" investment. Indeed, there were ample tax benefits to such a hold, and the land could eventually be sold to pay for their children's education or their own eventual retirements. Either way, the potential benefits of farming the land—or even the complexity of leasing the land to another farmer—simply paled compared to doing nothing with the tract and holding it vacant for a suitable buyer.

A suitable buyer eventually emerged. The sisters could have held out for more, but the sight of the seven-figure check sliding across a closing table mollified desires to play hardball. Several years later, the county was installing underground utilities, a necessary precursor to development of the site. The backhoe hit an underground rivulet of discolored soil that turned out to be seepage from an otherwise undisclosed leaking underground storage tank—the tank where the farmer had stored tractor fuel. This happened several years after closing, but the sisters—living in another state—were surprised one morning by process servers. Expensive, lengthy, and time-consuming litigation ensued.

> The key mistake made by the sisters was failing to realize that they had transitioned from being in the farming business to being in the merchant

landholding business. The investment implications, including insurance, due diligence, and environmental concerns are somewhat different and require more than a simple "for sale" sign in the front yard.

An example is typical to the auto dealership business. Mom and Dad started the family auto dealership after World War II. In the second generation, two kids want to stay in the family business, but some brothers and sisters want to move on to other fields. This needed to be arranged with a simple family trust, but the inner workings of that trust were complicated. Any such trust will have to accommodate the normal employment of family members who continue to manage the business, the share of business profits accruing to the nonparticipating family members, and the rents on the family real estate. Bifurcating these last two can be critically important. First, the entire business (land and enterprise) needs to be valued and a fair return on those assets agreed to by all family members. Imagine the very simple example in Tables 17-2 and 17-3.

TABLE 17-2 Simple Annual Business Profits Example

Annual Profits	$1,000,000
Reasonable Manager's Salary	($250,000)
Return on Enterprise Investment	$750,000

TABLE 17-3 Valuation of the Enterprise

Expected Return	$750,000
Cap Rate for Enterprise Value	10.0%
Enterprise Valuation	$7,500,000

This is a grossly oversimplified example, but it is a good basis for understanding the valuation implications. The annual return on the business gets distributed by a formula to the business owners—probably brothers and sisters. In practice, this distribution may also reward the managing sibling in some fashion to better align his or her interests with those of other family members, but that is a consideration for the estate attorneys rather than the valuation people. Part of this annual return—and with valuation implications—is a return on the real estate, and part of it is a return on the business. In Table 17-4, I use a simple allocation method to determine that one-third of value is to the real estate and two-thirds to business. As previously discussed, there are possibly better ways of doing this, but this method will prove satisfactory for now. The common return on land in this market—a net ground lease rate—is 7%. Hence, the returns can now be bifurcated between the land and the business itself.

TABLE 17-4 Bifurcation of Business and Land Values and Returns

Total Enterprise Value	$7,500,000
Land Value	$2,500,000
Total Business Value (B)	$5,000,000
Net Ground Lease Rate	7.0%
Rent to the Land	$175,000
Remaining Return on the Business (A)	$575,000
Total Return on Enterprise	$750,000
Rate of Return on Business (A/B)	11.5%

Clearly, the investment in the business is considered riskier than the land. If these tables constitute a pro forma for the business, a later bifurcation of business and the real estate based on these assumptions would transfer the portion of expected return allocated to real estate to a fixed expense (rent). Many family businesses do just that—by bifurcating the real estate and the business, the rent is now a business fixed cost, but paid to a holding with very different tax and estate implications. This is one way of transferring land to a separate trust. This may have implications for the estate, but the valuation, if done correctly, should still be the same.

Consider the same situation. In this second example, the owners decide to have an actual appraisal performed before the creation of this bifurcated trust. The appraisal comes back with a much higher land value—$5 million rather than $2.5 million. How can this be? Simply put, the earlier land value was based on a simple allocation, and in turn based on the overall return on the business investment. If the business is not the highest and best use of the land, then the return to the land will be less than the appraised value. Consider the income and balance sheet for this enterprise, taken from a land perspective, as shown in Table 17-5.

Now, this is where it gets a little confusing. The recognized value of the *land* appears to increase by $2.5 million—doubling from the former implicit value up to a now appraisal-determined value of $5 million. However, the total enterprise value—the value of the land plus the implicit value of the business which uses this land—only increased by about a million dollars, up to $8.5 million. The cash flows are still the same—the total paid out on the land and on the business is still $750,000 per year. This is a key, critical element—the market "caps" the land rents at 7%, but caps the more risky business value at 11.5%. Because we're allocating more profit to

TABLE 17-5 Value of the Business After Bifurcating the Ownership

Land Value	$5,000,000
Net Ground Lease Rate	7.0%
Rent to the Land	$350,000
Expected Return on Business Investment	$750,000
Rent to the Land	–$350,000
Remaining Return on the Business	$400,000
Implicit Rate of Return on the Business	0.115
Implicit Value of the Business	$3,478,261
Land Value	$5,000,000
Total Enterprise Value	$8,478,261

the land, which has a lower required rate of return, the overall valuation is higher. This is a function of lower risk (and thus lower cap rate) for land and the higher risk for the business. In the earlier implicit value, the business was actually taking advantage of lower contract rents on the land. This gave a false picture of the implicit business value, when the business value was much lower.

The lesson in all of this is that when carefully crafting the structure of the estate holdings, it is important to *explicitly* value the land and improvements separately from the business assets. Otherwise, the business can be misvalued, and there can be a misallocation of value between the business and the real estate. Further, if there is an allocation of business and real estate among the heirs, it is critically important to get that straightened out ahead of time so there is no question as to the proper allocation of rents to the various claimants.

8. Summary and Key Points

Probably the biggest problem observed with real estate as an ancillary to the family-owned business is that the family focuses on the business but not on the real estate. All too often, the real estate is an afterthought. This may lead to two very significant oversights.

First, over time, the real estate may actually have a higher and better use than the current business. Indeed, there are situations where the real estate value exceeds the business value. The family may not realize this in situations where there is little or no implicit rent allocated to the real estate, thus masking the true value (or lack thereof) of the business. Consider the scenario in Table 17-6.

TABLE 17-6 Land Rent as a Portion of EBITDA

	Market Optimal	Actual
Total EBITDA	$1,000,000	$1,000,000
Land Value, at HBU	$20,000,000	$20,000,000
Implicit Rent, @ 7%	$1,400,000	
Actual Rent Paid		-0-
Business share of EBITDA	($400,000)	$1,000,000

If a fair market-optimal rent was paid, the business would actually show a loss. In this scenario, no allocation is made to land rent, masking the fact that the land is suboptimally used.

Another problem arises when the land is, for lack of a better phrase, mistreated. The most common problem comes from environmental issues. Many businesses, particularly in manufacturing or warehousing, will generate wastes that may be mishandled. Many family business operators attempt to sell their holdings only to find that the contingent liabilities associated with the land exceed the value of the business they are trying to sell.

One cure for this is to treat the land as if the business was a rental tenant. Put up the same property management structure that would exist if the land was being rented to a third party, and in turn pay a market-determined rent from the business to the land. There may be legitimate family estate planning reasons to actually bifurcate the business and the land into separately owned entities with a different mix of family member ownership.

Owning the real estate that supports a family business is a natural investment, and one that provides a high degree of security and control for the long-term business interests. That real estate must be carefully managed, and the value monitored regularly, recognizing that it is an important source and storehouse of family wealth.

9. A Final Note—Real Estate as a Family Business

Brokerage, investment, finance, development, construction, and property management are all facets of a successful family business in real estate. Indeed, understanding these topics is a key requisite, and rare is the successful family real estate investment business that does not incorporate most of these core areas. At least one major university business school now offers a graduate course in the topic of managing the family real estate business. Since real estate is so very long-lived, and investment decisions are made over long time frames, real estate begs for a multigenerational approach.

While the structure, nature, and focus of the family real estate business will be unique to each family, there are some patterns that successful family real estate businesses seem to follow. For land investments, these patterns include:

Specializing. For the family that casually invests in real estate, some careful diversification is usually appropriate. This is not to suggest a haphazard approach. Many types of real estate, or ownership forms, require extensive specialized knowledge. Properly managed, curated, and vetted, a diversified portfolio of real estate is not only internally healthy but also important for the rest of the investment portfolio. But families actually focused on real estate as a business usually take a more focused approach. There is an old saying in marketing, "to dominate, concentrate." Thus, a family that invests exclusively in agricultural land usually buys a lot of land. Families that buy land to develop into residential subdivisions, or shopping centers, or suburban office complexes are rarely interested in diversification. They usually take a very long-term investment approach, and indeed optimum real estate investing demands a long-term investment horizon. Since gains are compounded, the impact of a small investment today reaps huge rewards over a long time horizon. Indeed, the deadweight costs of transactions make it nothing short of amazing that anyone makes money in short-term real estate deals. However, this leads to an interesting conundrum.

Different generations have different interests. Successful families know that each succeeding generation has to be encouraged to find its own path to success in the business. While Grandma and Granddad may have earned their wealth in agriculture or timber, the second and third generations may look to suburban development or complex infrastructure projects. Intriguingly, a single tract of land through the generations may have each of these highest and best uses, and perhaps even more. A timber tract in the early twentieth century may now be in the path of suburban growth, and indeed there will be complex transit problems associated with moving those dwellers to their jobs every day.

One successful family with whom we consulted had earned their money in textile manufacturing in the United States several generations ago. Today, the fourth and fifth generations of that family are grappling with problems and opportunities. The plants are no longer viable, but they are on large tracts near profitable suburban growth. Great-Great Granddad and Grandma could never have imagined bustling interstate highways, suburban communities, shopping, and even millions of square feet of suburban offices on the same fields where cotton used to grow.

Successful families make judicious use of debt. There is an old saying, "neither a borrower nor a lender be." Whoever wrote this probably never worked for a bank. But part of the adage is true. Families who specialize in real estate investment are very careful about leverage. This is ironic, since these families often have access to highly preferential sources and could make significant use of leverage. Land accumulation, particularly as a business, is a very long-term proposition and fraught with countercyclical decisions. In short, a family buying land may have to hold that land through an economic downturn or an interest rate bubble. For these reasons, the short-term attractiveness of leverage may be overwhelmed by the long-term downsides.

Real estate families rarely diversify out of real estate. While wealthy families from a host of fields usually view real estate as a great place to store money, wealthy real estate families rarely look outside of property as a place to store money. Certainly, many have cash, and many end up in businesses that are related to real estate. Families that are focused on land acquisition as a primary source of wealth do not seem to be interested in much else: those wealthy holdings seem to grow and prosper through the generations.

18
Brownfields

> Before you start trying to work out which direction the property market is headed, you should be aware that there are markets within markets.
>
> —Paul Clitheroe

THERE ARE HUNDREDS of thousands of brownfields in America, mostly commercial investment properties. The likelihood that an investor has one or more brownfields in the portfolio, either by accident or on purpose, is surprisingly high. Often this comes as a surprise.

There are myriad legal, tax, and regulatory issues relating to brownfields. Usually, state regulations will predominate since the US Environmental Protection Agency (EPA) has delegated most property-specific issues to state regulators. In some cases, such as properties on the National Priorities List or true Superfund sites, federal regulations may come into play. Also, when federal waterways or tribal lands or fisheries become impacted, the EPA may step in even if state regulators are already handling the problem.

Many investors tackle these opportunities on purpose. An appraisal, as a component of a thorough financial analysis, should come early in the process. This chapter will explore the actual fundamentals of developing the brownfield appraisal.

1. So, You're Stuck with a Brownfield—a Few Things to Consider

Obvious brownfields are old factories or warehouses. Even retail stores used as dry cleaners, paint stores, or liquor warehouses can be affected. Finding that a site was thought to be clean but is somehow impacted by environmental contamination is never a good thing. It can be less of a bad thing if investors are proactive. Indeed, there are investors and investment funds specializing in acquiring, remediating, and adaptively reusing brownfields. There is a fair amount of regulation that provides legal safe harbors for investors who follow the right steps.

Valuation is tricky. General practice appraisers lack the expertise to even try. To paraphrase John Kenneth Galbraith's comments about economists, "There are two kinds, those who don't know, and those who don't know they don't know." Most appraisers fall into one of those two categories. For the few who specialize in the topic, the data and methodology can be analytically challenging. Generally, a brownfield will be appraised in a manner similar to an eminent domain "taking"—the property will be valued in the "as if unimpaired" state, and then valued again in the "as-is impaired" state. The difference between these two constitutes the discount ascribed to the brownfield status. Importantly, that difference should be further broken down into two categories: cost and use impacts, and risk impacts.

Cost and Use Impacts

The literature breaks these into two separate subcategories, but in practice that division is fairly arbitrary. These impacts represent the out-of-pocket reductions in net cash flows resulting from the brownfield situation. Note the formula for net cash flow in a real estate investment in Table 18-1.

TABLE 18-1 Net Cash Flow Snapshot

Gross Revenue	$1,000,000
Less: Vacancy and Collection Losses	(100,000)
Net Revenue	900,000
Operating Expenses*	(300,000)
Net Operating Income (NOI)	600,000
Add Back Reserves	50,000
Debt Service (Principle and Interest)	(200,000)
Before Tax Cash Flow (BTCF)	450,000
Income Taxes	(90,000)
Net Cash Flow	$360,000

* *Includes noncash reserves for replacement*

Net operating income can be impacted by reductions in net rents (primarily through vacancy and collection losses) or increases in operating expenses. At a minimum, increased operating expenses will likely include legal and engineering costs to monitor the problem, additional accounting (and yes, appraisal) costs, and perhaps some increases in insurance, maintenance, and repair costs. As an offset, property taxes may be reduced if it can be shown that the property has decreased in value. Many jurisdictions tax commercial property at a "value in use" level, and so actual reductions in market value, without a change in property use, may not result in a reduction in property taxes. All of these constitute "use" impacts. If the property owner is the responsible party, this may include remediation costs, which would be "cost" impacts. Interest costs (the difference between NOI and BTCF) may increase if less favorable financing becomes necessary. Offsetting this may be a reduction in tax burdens, particularly if depreciation increases or taxable basis is otherwise decreased.

Risk Impacts

These usually manifest as increases in the cap or discount rate and represent the increase in return demanded by brownfield investors in trade for increased risk associated with holding, remediating, and repositioning a brownfield. Directly measuring this increase is difficult. Many scholars suggest a good proxy would be to examine the difference in returns between investment grade bonds and subprime or "junk" bonds. This methodology has some empirical merit. For one, the basis-point difference may vary from time to time, as market-average risk aversion changes over time. For another, the junk bond rate at any given time includes a direct measure of the very real prospect that the investor will receive zero return. Consider the components of a junk bond rate at any given point in time:

$$R = R_f + R_i + R_r \qquad \text{EQUATION 18-1}$$

In this formulation, R_f is the risk-free rate of return, R_i is the expected rate of inflation over time, and R_r is the risk premium on the bonds in question. This sort of formulation can, at least theoretically, be applied to a brownfield valuation if there is some guess as to the likelihood of success or failure. Indeed, this formulation is quite good for a sensitivity analysis if measures of success or failure, albeit subjective, can be estimated. Presume, for this example, that the required return is 18%, based on the following formulation:

$$R = 2\% + 2\% + 14\% = 18\% \qquad \text{EQUATION 18-2}$$

Further presume that the likelihoods of total loss, expected outcome, or double the expected outcome are 10%, 60%, and 30%, respectively. This sensitivity analysis can now be applied to the ex ante expected returns:

$$R = 10\%(0\%) + 60\%(18\%) + 30\%(36\%) = 21.6\% \quad \text{EQUATION 18-3}$$

Thus, the expected returns under this scenario exceed the required returns, even after accounting for the 10% likelihood that the project will be a total failure.

The highest and best use (HBU) of a distressed property may be different from the HBU under normal circumstances, and the HBU may change over time. Recall that the HBU for any investment property should be considered in the "as if vacant" and "as-is improved" states (Figure 18-1). The difference between these two HBUs takes into account the cost/benefit of demolishing or adaptively reusing the current improvements. For a brownfield, these two HBUs can change during a remediation process or even after adaptively reused. The cost/benefit relationship between "as-if vacant" and "as-is improved" may vary throughout the life of the brownfield.

	As-Is Improved	As-If Vacant
Pre Remediation	HBU 1	HBU 2
During Remediation	HBU 3	HBU 4
Post Remediation	HBU 5	HBU 6

FIGURE 18-1 Various Highest and Best Uses Depending on Remediation Situation

Thus, as shown in Figure 18-1, the HBU may take on as many as six different identities during the remediation life cycle. Of course, that remediation life cycle itself may follow a number of different paths. There are many theoretical representations of this in the literature, and Figure 18-2 shows just a few relative to time and the expected value of a property over time.

The valuation exercise should be an ongoing component of monitoring and remediation. The appraisal should continuously take into account the competitive market for an "as-is" property versus one that is remediated, and should chart the value such that the investor can make an optimum decision about remediation versus disposal at various points in time. The HBU may change over time, with changing market conditions, updated costs of remediation (affecting the ongoing financial feasibility of various remediation alternatives) and as such the terminal value may—and likely will—change over time.

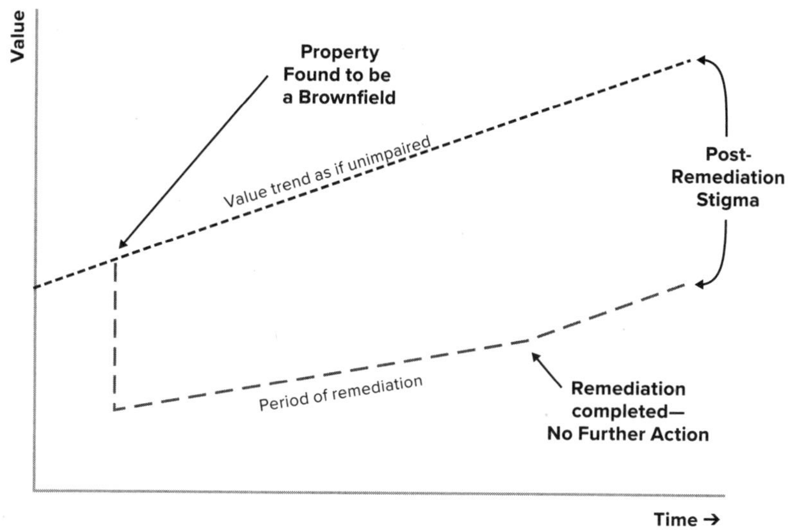

FIGURE 18-2 Brownfield Timeline

One brownfield in the Midwest involved a very large (over 2,000 acres) manufacturing facility that, for many reasons (mostly political), needed to be adaptively reused as both commercial and residential. The ultimate mix of uses would dictate the remediation processes and levels. Ultimately, the ongoing appraisal process needed to take into account urban planning issues, optimum commercial/residential land use mixes, traffic patterns, population growth, and even—somewhat surprisingly—congressional district boundaries. Viewing the appraisal as a dynamic exercise rather than a static document ended up netting the developers quite a few millions of extra dollars on the project by optimizing the final remediation solution.

2. Point Source, Adjacent, and Proximate Contamination Issues

These issues usually arise in litigation, but should be considered for every property discovered to be a brownfield.

Most brownfields are the contamination point source. This is a legacy of federal (and most state) brownfield laws and regulations, which approach brownfield remediation from the perspective of the responsible party. "Responsible party" may have a meaning under law that is quite different from the economic or layperson definition. From an appraisal perspective, a point source may have two different implications:

Point Source Valuation

The literature and most empirical data differentiate properties that are *on-site contaminated* versus those that are *adjacent or proximate* to contamination. The on-site contamination properties will have a use and risk effect and a cost effect. The adjacent or proximate properties may not have a cost effect, save for avoidance costs that arise in the use and enjoyment of the property. The contamination may have originated with the site or may have migrated onto the site. In the former situation, the property owner is probably responsible for any remediation costs (the "cost effects"). In the latter situation, the property owner may or may not be responsible for remediation costs, depending on third-party liability determinations and litigation outcomes.

Point Source Liabilities

If the property is actually responsible for the on-site contamination, then the property owner may (or sometimes may not!) be responsible for on-site remediation and off-site, third-party remediation. Adjacent properties find themselves to be next-door neighbors to brownfields. Some investors seek out these situations, acquiring these adjacent properties at a deep discount. The resultant return on investment is significantly greater than would be suggested by a discounted cash flow or capitalization rate model where the discount or cap rate includes a risk factor. Indeed, sellers may often lowball prices just to dump these adjacent properties, to the benefit of the acquiring investor.

There are two valuation issues here. First, any buyer should take thorough steps to ensure that the adjacent property being acquired has no on-site contamination. There is some guidance from the EPA on this, called "all appropriate inquiry," which derives from the 2002 Brownfield Amendments. Buyers should be thorough and careful, and well advised by appropriate legal counsel. Some sort of indemnity may be demanded from the adjacent point source responsible party, since a currently clean property may suffer migration of contaminants from the adjacent dirty property at a later date.

Second, the appraisal should take into account increased borrowing costs in the discount rate. Many brownfield investors will eschew debt to avoid these increased obligations. Debt costs, however, may be lower than the ROI required by equity investors. Hence, the overall discount rate decision may impact the investment value, but not the true market value. Table 18-2 shows three hypothetical valuation scenarios demonstrating the difference between market value and investment value for a property adjacent to a brownfield. In each case, the market value is a function of market-derived cap rates and the band-of-investments analysis (including investor ROI and typical borrowing costs). In the investment value model, it is assumed that the cap rate is dictated totally by the investor required ROI.

TABLE 18-2 Value Under Various Scenarios

	Clean Property	Brownfield Discovered	Post Remediation
Estimated Annual NOI	$1,000,000	$200,000	$800,000
Market Cap Rate	7%	14%	12%
Market Value (rounded)	$14,300,000	$1,400,000	$6,700,000
Investor ROI	8%	18%	14%
Investment Value (rounded)	$12,500,000	$1,100,000	$5,700,000

Finally, proximate properties are those in a brownfield neighborhood that are impacted by a nearby contaminated site as a negative externality. These properties frequently have substantial changes in the highest and best use, with attendant valuation implications. These cost and use implications may be negligible. Consider a property discovered to be near a brownfield, zoned residential with an HBU for multifamily. Afterward, market rents for the proposed apartment complex are lower, and the project *as planned* is no longer financially feasible. The developer may be left with two choices. If the property can be rezoned, then some other project, such as retail, office, or even industrial may be substituted. If the property cannot be rezoned, then the property may need to be revalued at the lower rent level to determine if any financially feasible multifamily use can emerge. If this means that the land value is now lower, then there may be a basis to pursue legal action against the responsible party.

While "brownfield" will normally refer to the property that is actually a point source of contamination, there are also brownfield valuation implications for adjacent and neighboring properties. Properties legally defined as brownfields number in the hundreds of thousands in the United States, but including these proximate and adjacent properties into the mix expands the universe of affected real estate parcels significantly. Commercial property investors regularly get environmental audits in the acquisition or financing process, but these audits are often limited to the property itself. Savvy investors will demand that the investigation expand to adjacent and nearby sites as well. Those same savvy investors, if risk tolerant, may use this exercise to seek out properties with investment potential.

3. Cleanup Versus Remediation

The literature—and particularly the valuation guidance—is sloppy with the use of *cleanup* versus *remediation*. The two terms have very different implications, and these implications are important for understanding the valuation exercise.

First, consider the property *as if never impacted by contamination*. We can consider that to be "clean" from an appraisal perspective. One might posit that any property may have some sort of contaminants on it. What if a lawn mower leaks gas from the tank? Is the yard now contaminated with petroleum? Theoretically, perhaps, but practically no. Arguably, some state laws (notably New York) would require that one drop of contaminant be reported to regulators and become public record. From a practical perspective, the contaminants on the property would likely not be detectable, reportable, nor potentially a hazard to health.

Next, consider a brownfield that has been affected by a contaminant such that the contaminant is detectable and perhaps even reportable. Does the property need to be remediated? This may be a matter of regulatory coverage. California, as recently as 2006, had no regulatory limits for perchlorate (essentially, rocket fuel) in drinking water. Hence, while the presence of perchlorate may be reportable and may certainly be a hazard to health, there may be no requirement for remediation or even liability for third-party, off-site migration.

Further, consider that the contaminant has to be remediated, but the remediation is required to a level below some regulatory limit. These limits may be scientifically derived or even arbitrary, but nonetheless are at some level above "non-detect." The fact of the contamination is certainly still reportable and disclosable to potential investors, and monitoring may be required into the future. Many contaminants, such as the gasoline additive MTBE, are famously ephemeral and may be detected below regulatory limits one day and yet measure above those same limits the next.

Can this property that has been contaminated but below regulatory levels, or the other property that has been contaminated and remediated to below regulatory levels, be considered "clean"? Probably not, yet the term "cleanup" is used in a fairly sloppy fashion in the real estate and even legal circles. Even if the property has been remediated to levels below detection, the original contamination event or discovery may still be a disclosable or discoverable condition well into the future. The regulations in the United States about environmental contamination and brownfield remediation are still fairly new, and as such there is little experience with the passage of sufficient time that such events or conditions are no longer reportable.

The upshot of this is that a brownfield property, even if remediated, should not be referred to as "cleaned up" or "clean." Those can be wildly misleading characterizations. Property investors should be on the careful lookout for sites that are advertised as "cleaned up." *Remediated* is the more appropriate term. Even valuation professionals fail to understand this and may incorrectly appraise a remediated property as "clean" when it is really not. From an investment perspective, the difference can be quite meaningful.

4. Consent Decrees—State Versus Federal

While this is more a legal topic than a valuation one, the issue has some very real appraisal implications. Probably the best known and understood consent decrees involve the EPA, but some state environmental agencies also used such agreements to bring finality to brownfield problems.

From a valuation perspective, the consent decree has three components. The first, which is of little appraisal interest, is some sort of settlement of legal liability issues. This may or may not include an admission of guilt or acknowledgment of responsibility, a stipulation of some facts (which may continue to be disputed by some parties), and perhaps a fine. While all of this is interesting, and provides important informational background for the appraisal, it has little to do with the valuation itself.

Second, the consent decree will usually have an agreed-upon or stipulated remediation, which may have time limits, budgets, benchmarks, or specific deliverables. This outlines the remediation efforts being undertaken, and until benchmarks are achieved the property is considered to be "in remediation" from a valuation perspective. In many cases, the property may continue to be used, and may even be used at its highest and best use, during the period of remediation. Nonetheless, the "in remediation" state, and the liability attached to that remediation, may have severe implications for the valuation.

Finally, the consent decree may have one of two endgames. In the first, some sort of "no further action" letter will be issued. As some environmental officials have put it, "no further action" means "no further action for right now." This does not mean that the property is now "clean" or "exempt from monitoring or further action." Indeed, a reoccurrence of contamination above certain benchmark levels (which may be different from regulatory levels) may bring cancellation of protections under the consent decree. Additionally, if the responsible party fails to perform under the consent decree, then all bets are off.

For appraisers, a consent decree provides a road map for valuation. The property under remediation has one set of valuation metrics, and the consent decree also provides for an endgame when the property may be valued "as if remediated." If there are time frames allotted to these scenarios, then a discounted cash flow model can properly account for the varying degrees of risk and marketability. The appraisal has to invoke the extraordinary assumption that the consent decree is followed and that the benchmarks are met on time and in full.

Consent decrees can include a variety of restrictions on the current or future property use, including:

- Easements
- Covenants
- Zoning restrictions
- Well drilling prohibitions
- Special building permit requirements
- Deed restrictions and hazard notices
- State or local ordinances
- State registries of contaminated properties
- Restrictions on groundwater use

Each individually can have a materially large impact on value. Easements to the access or monitoring site(s) may be required. We consulted to an automobile dealership wishing to pay top dollar to acquire an adjacent site for expansion. The site was a former gas station and had an easement for remediation equipment, rendering the site utterly unusable for the auto dealer. Since the dealer was the only prospective buyer, the site sat unused and unmarketable for many years.

Covenants or zoning restrictions can prohibit some financially superior uses, such as residential or other occupancy, where latent problems (such as air quality) may prove hazardous. Well drilling or special building restrictions can severely limit the site's physical adaptability. One manufacturing property I examined sat on a large, shallow plume of oil spilled from a nearby refinery. The industry was moving toward larger, heavier equipment requiring thicker, stronger concrete footings. Unfortunately, building restrictions prohibited the plant owners from piercing the ground for such new footings. Eventually, the plant owners had to abandon the site and build a new plant several miles away.

Notices, registries, and deed restrictions all affect marketability, putting buyers on notice that the site is problematic. The duration of such notices is presently not a well-tested issue, with legal implications. Does the brownfield seller have to give notice for 10 years? 20 years? 100 years? Indeed, even if there is a time limit on the consent decree itself, the prior existence of such restrictions may impact the property marketability long after any hypothetical expiration of the decree. Given the relative recentness of brownfield legislations (e.g., the Brownfield Amendments of 2002, which gave rise to some safe harbor provisions for buyers), none of this has played out over time, and all these issues still have valuation implications.

Finally, limitations on groundwater usage can have severe implications for a variety of developments. One vinyl chloride problem we studied had direct implications for the sourcing of a city's drinking water. At a somewhat more granular level, a local golf course, which was a valuable amenity to a residential development, was drawing irrigation water from wells polluted by that brownfield. The golf course had to find more alternative, and more expensive, sources of irrigation water as a result of regulatory limitations.

The best and desired "endgame" for a brownfield is a *no further action* letter issued from a regulatory body. Typically this allows the investor to move forward, with the caveats outlined in the consent decree. However, *no further action* is not a "get out of jail free" card. Continued monitoring may be required, and regulators may step in if there is a consent decree violation or if there is evidence of changes in the contamination levels. Changes in the regulatory scheme may imply changes in the agreements. A contaminant that is remediated to a previously agreed-upon level may require subsequent, further remediation if more stringent regulations are established.

5. Third-Party Liability Issues

The golf course story provides a salient segue into the issues of third-party liability. Naturally, the brownfield owners—or any buyers not protected under safe harbor provisions—may face liability issues stemming from such costs and risk and marketability problems borne by innocent neighbors. Attorneys and appraisers with expertise in these matters can be invaluable in proactively identifying potential liabilities.

This has very real valuation implications. An investor may acquire a property with off-site contamination migration impacting a nearby neighborhood. Proactive attention to the problem may be a useful strategy, and investors may face some sort of mass tort or class action from these innocent third parties. Appraisers should work with attorneys and physical science experts determining the problem's physical and economic extent and the potential aggregate damages. Simple metrics such as automated valuation models and references to prior, similar cases may give the responsible investor a broad idea of the order of magnitude of claims. Armed with this, an investor can make informed decisions about the brownfield investment.

6. The Brownfield Remediation Timeline

Clearly, a brownfield value will probably shift over time. This phenomenon has been explored in the literature at length and studied empirically by academics and practitioners. It is often called the "contamination life cycle" or "remediation life cycle," although both terms are incorrect. This implies the property will cycle back to its original states. Indeed, most empirical studies confirm that just the opposite is true—even after remediation, the property value will be impacted.

There are a host of models trying to explain different types of property impairment. These models are basically theoretical and generalize the movement of values over time. Figure 18-2, a few pages back, shows one such generalized model of how the value of a brownfield is expected to react to different actions over time. Naturally, the specifics of any particular brownfield may be different, but this model provides a handy conceptualization.

Begin with the assumption that the property is thought to be clean and free of environmental problems. This requires a suspension of disbelief. We have such a significant level of experience dealing with industrial properties that we know to expect—or at least suspect—some problems. However, the value "as if clean" provides an appropriate baseline against which all other values can be measured.

Next, the property is discovered to have environmental issues and is labeled a brownfield. No remediation is undertaken, and it takes time to fully characterize the problem. A "Phase I" environmental assessment may pick up the fact that the property is likely to have problems but will tell us nothing about the nature or extent of those problems. In general, environmental audits fall into three categories:

Phase I assessments. These may either be preliminary assessments (PA) or full due diligence Phase I audits. In general, these take the form of a public record search and may identify areas of concern (AOCs) or recognized environmental conditions (RECs). Either way, if something is detected, it will almost certainly lead to the next phase.

Phase II assessments. This will usually necessitate actual physical sampling and analysis. The goal is to determine the degree or extent of contamination or other problems.

Phase III assessments. These are usually referred to as assessments, but are really the development of an action plan based on the findings in Phase II. Actions may include, but may not be limited to, excavation and removal of underground storage tanks, asbestos, lead, mold or soil, elimination and remediation of chemical contaminants, "pump and treat" system installations for groundwater contamination, bioremediation, ventilation, coating/encapsulation, enclosure, or other engineering solutions, and development of any needed institutional controls.

In some situations, an "in situ" solution is recommended. The problem is simply left in place and allowed to dissipate over time. If there is no intention to sell, and no regulatory enforcement actions or litigation forcing the issue, this may be the optimal solution from a cost/benefit perspective.

Once the problem is characterized and remediation begins, the site value may improve over time. If the remediation is ever completed, then the property valuation may improve to some final value level or trend.

> The terms "brownfields" and "contaminated sites" are frequently used interchangeably. A contaminated site is known to have some on-site or point source environmental damage. The term "brownfields" is generally used in the literature and in legislation to characterize industrial or commercial sites that have become contaminated due to activities on those properties. Hence, a residential property could be a contaminated site but would usually not be referred to as a brownfield.

7. Valuation—Various Approaches

Environmental contamination may constitute a physical, functional, or external disamenity. Thus, the cost approach is at the appraisal's core. The cost approach is frequently preferred for unique properties, such as industrial buildings and sites. As discussed previously, the cost approach has problems when applied to older buildings, and brownfields are often old and worn out. Thus, identifying the age-life deterioration in value and separating this from the loss of value attached to an on-site contaminant may yield spurious results. Interestingly, many cities, particularly those with active urban restoration activities, find that remediated brownfield buildings can be adapted to commercial or even residential use. It is not uncommon in old mill cities to see these well-constructed old manufacturing buildings remediated and converted into housing or other higher and better uses. On paper, though, the economics of this adaptive reuse may not be immediately evident via a strictly applied cost approach.

In practice, the "as-is" property value will consider sales prices of similar properties adjusted for the present value of expected remediation costs and the present value of the post-remediation discount. If the site is proposed for redevelopment, then some sort of discounted cash flow may be more useful. Of course, the redevelopment plans may be generated organically in the Phase III assessment, and so might not be understood sufficiently to put a value on the site in the early stage.

A preferred valuation analysis is a combination of direct capitalization and a discounted cash flow model. This allows for direct consideration of changing valuation metrics over time. The cumulative effect can be measured at any given point, or from the present looking forward. Consider a simple brownfield project that will require three years of remediation until a "no further action" letter can be obtained. Due to permitting and other issues, the remediation cannot start for a year. Prior to remediation, the property has a limited usefulness. During the remediation period, the property will probably not be useable. Rental values, vacancy and collection problems, and management expenses will all change. Table 18-3 illustrates a simplified summary of methodology and findings.

At the beginning of year 3, with two more years of remediation required, the owners receive a purchase offer from a brownfield aggregator. This template allows the owners to evaluate that offer, as shown in Table 18-4.

Thus, any cash offer above $16.2 million would be a win for the current owners. In practice, such offers are rarely so straightforward, and they come with a host of caveats, conditions, and contingent liabilities. Putting a price tag on all of those contingencies can require painstaking and time-consuming analysis. Nonetheless, there are few shortcuts available. The complexity of selling a brownfield is often so problematic that many investors simply cannot wrap their heads around the situation. This valuation requires specialized skills and knowledge, but the returns can be worthwhile.

The sales comparison approach is frequently used, but it makes certain "static" assumptions about the brownfield problem. Typically, the sales comparison model will begin with a value "as if unimpaired," then will derive the adjustment for the brownfield status by finding matched pairs or by determining the discounted present value associated with the reduced cash flow from with the problem. While this can be useful for valuing the property at a given point in time, this model derives the adjustment from other models, and has to be reevaluated completely with the passage of time and with any changes in the brownfield status.

TABLE 18-3 Discounted Cash Flow Model

	Time 0: Brownfield Determination	Year 1: Limited Use. Negative NOI	Year 2: Remediation Begins. NOI negative	Year 3: Remediation Underway. NOI negative	Year 4: Remediation Finalized. NOI negative	Year 5: Post-Remediation. NOI positive
NOI		(500,000)	(2,000,000)	(2,000,000)	(2,000,000)	4,000,000
Cap Rate						14%
Capitalized Value						28,571,429
Discount Rate		18%	18%	18%	18%	14%
Discounted Value		(423,729)	(1,436,369)	(1,217,262)	(1,031,578)	14,839,105
Value as of Time 0	10,730,168					

TABLE 18-4 Value at the Beginning of Year 3

	Time 0: Brownfield Determination	Year 1: Limited Use. Negative NOI	Year 2: Remediation Begins. NOI negative	Year 3: Remediation Underway. NOI negative	Year 4: Remediation Finalized. NOI negative	Year 5: Post-Remediation. NOI positive
NOI			(2,000,000)	(2,000,000)	(2,000,000)	4,000,000
Cap Rate						14%
Capitalized Value						28,571,429
Discount Rate				18%	18%	14%
Discounted Value				(1,694,915)	(1,436,369)	19,284,900
Value as of Year 3				16,153,616		

8. Strategic Brownfield Investing

Some strategic investors and even some specialized funds acquire and redevelop brownfield sites. This usually begins with the remediation process, after the site has been characterized and a plan of action outlined. The goal is the rezoning to a higher and better use. Investors generally fall into two categories. Some complete the remediation and sell the restored site to an end user, who in turn completes the planned development. Other investors retain and develop the remediate site themselves.

This requires a team of experienced brownfield specialists, including engineering, risk management, real estate planning, finance, and, of course, valuation. Many brownfield developers take advantage of tax credits, public brownfield funds, and a variety of local, state, and federal incentives. Insurance research is an important component to this—if older general liability policies indemnified the site during a period before contamination exclusions were in vogue, then these may add important sources of capital. (And yes, there are consultants who specialize in that research!) As of this writing, there are even newly minted opportunity zone funds that are focused on brownfield redevelopment.

Investors are often attracted to brownfield projects for the potential returns and societal contributions of remediating dirty sites. Often these sites are in urban areas, and brownfield remediation and adaptive reuse help with inner-city restoration. Investors are encouraged to engage third-party advisors before selecting a fund or a joint venture partner. Not only does brownfield restoration require specific expertise, but even the vetting process requires expertise.

> Brownfield legislation in the United States has long had more of a punitive reputation, rather than a restorative one. As one wag said, "It's more important to blame someone, rather than to fix the problem!" In other countries, brownfield restoration is more the focus. For that reason, it is not uncommon to see more advanced brownfield restoration investment in Canada or Europe.

9. Summary and Key Points

Investors engage in brownfield redevelopment for two reasons. First, and this is probably the most common, they own a property that is suddenly found to be a brownfield. There may be some latent and undiscovered contamination from a prior use, or the current use may be contaminating the site. In the second situation, investors strategically invest in brownfields, looking for profits from remediation and adaptive reuse opportunities.

Strategic investors tend to be experienced and knowledgeable about valuation and have key metrics at their fingertips. They often, indeed usually have access to specialized sources of funds at favorable rates. Their experience in the field allows them to deal with the massive layers of red tape associated with these projects.

Accidental investors are often well advised to joint venture with these strategic investors. The playing field is far from level, and the accidental investors need to duplicate the analytical and valuation work to be effective partners in the enterprises. Adaptive reuse is a desirable endgame and can provide substantial quantitative and even qualitative opportunities.

Taking bad property and turning it into good property is a way to do well by doing good, and it has community benefits that provide halo effects to other investments. A family fund that is focused in a particular region, state, or even municipality can garner substantial goodwill among local regulators by turning a brownfield eyesore into a productive community asset. These qualitative benefits are hard to quantify but have very real value to the investor.

Whether a strategic or accidental investor, the brownfield owner is well advised to monitor and even manage the valuation at key stages in the process. At a minimum, revaluations should occur when the brownfield status is discovered (or at ownership inception), at the beginning and key points in the remediation, and at the end of the remediation.

> A defining characteristic of brownfield appraisal is the dynamic nature. These valuations change over time in manners far different from simple market conditions adjustments. Investors need to reconsider the valuation throughout the ownership and remediation cycle.

10. A Final Note—Brownfields and the Family Business

In our practice, it is very common to see real estate neglected by family-owned businesses. In truth, this is not just a problem with privately held enterprises. Even large corporations frequently neglect real estate holdings and are thus surprised to find that a property has become an environmental problem. This even happens to corporations that should know better—ones that are in businesses that are environmentally problematic.

> I am shocked—shocked—to find that gambling is going on in here!
>
> —Captain Renault in *Casablanca*

In the family business, the real estate should be managed separately from the business and periodically valued accordingly. These periodic valuations, by the way, serve to help allocate business returns between the enterprise and the underlying real estate. Environmental preliminary assessments and Phase I audits are comparatively inexpensive and can serve as an outside monitor on property activities, current regulatory and licensing issues, and areas of concern. The audit or assessment should be coupled with this periodic valuation. If environmental issues can be caught in time, they can often be handled comparatively inexpensively—much like catching a disease before it turns into something fatal. State regulators are often overworked and are positively inclined toward voluntary reporting and voluntary actions in lieu of a mandatory compliance order. Thus, the terms of an agreed settlement can be favorable to the family business if the problem is caught in time and dealt with proactively.

Thus, the periodic valuation exercise serves several functions and should be a trigger to periodically reassess any potential brownfield issues. This is particularly acute for family businesses that are involved in industrial, manufacturing, transportation, or other environmentally sensitive lines of business.

19

REITs, 1031s, Limited Partnership Interests, and Tenancy in Common

A funny thing happens in real estate. When it comes back, it comes back up like gangbusters.

—Barbara Corcoran

MOST SUCCESSFUL FAMILY offices choose direct investments in real estate. When joint ventures or partnerships are proposed, they prefer to be in a controlling or at least "sidecar" position.

Family offices may occasionally encounter securitized, syndicated, or limited partnership opportunities. While these may appear to offer important advantages, particularly tax advantages in some circumstances, these investments are not without pitfalls and should only be taken on when appropriate in the context of the bigger investment picture.

In these situations, how does the family office correctly interpret the valuation provided? In the simplest case, the publicly traded real estate investment trust, the market value should be easy to ascertain. That said, why do some carefully curated REIT funds significantly outperform the market as a whole? Could it be that REIT valuation is misunderstood, or at least not informationally efficient? Understanding the nuances of valuing these asset types, and indeed the subclasses within these types, can provide valuable insights for managing the successful portfolio.

1. Public REITs—What Are They, and How Are They Valued?

REITs are securities and may be publicly traded or private. The REIT is a tax code manifestation. If a trust derives most of its income from operating real estate (as opposed to real estate development or trading gains) and pays out nearly all of the otherwise taxable net income in the form of dividends, it may be classified as a pass-through for tax purposes. The phrase "otherwise taxable net income" takes into account depreciation and other sheltering. Investors in qualified REITs can have their cake and eat it, too, with respect to tax advantages.

Further, since shares are classified as securities, they can be publicly traded. Indeed, most publicly traded US REITs are on the NYSE. Since REITs derive from the tax code,[1] REITs are not as well known in other countries, although some other countries have enacted similar codes providing for similar vehicles. The tax sheltering associated with US REITs may or may not be available to US investors owning shares of non-US REITs.

Public REITs offer a high degree of liquidity and transparency. Private REITs have liquidity and transparency problems. Private REITs behave more like limited partnership or private equity investments.

In the early days, until the mid-1990s, REITs tended to be small and narrowly focused—usually geographically concentrated. Often, a REIT was formed by a single company, perhaps a retailer, wanting to remove deadweight real estate, with its accompanying debt load, off the balance sheet. By selling REIT shares, the real estate could be financed with equity without impacting core firm metrics. These were *captive REITs* and were often allegedly fraught with problems since the management was beholden to the parent company and not to the REIT shareholders. Many advantages of captive REITs dissipated in the 1980s, particularly with certain tax law changes. In the 1990s, REITs came into their own as an investment class as investors discovered the diversification and liquidity benefits. In the mid-1990s, there was an order of magnitude increase in the size of REIT IPOs. Modern equity REITs are generally type-concentrated but geographically diversified. While there continue to be a few captive REITs in the field, the market recognizes those and prices them accordingly, given the quality of the real estate management.

One client, in the 1970s and early 1980s, was a developer of suburban office parks. He controlled three different interlocked companies. His development company was traded on the NYSE and made most of the taxable profits. The developments were financed with private equity tax shelters. After the properties were heavily depreciated, they were sold to a NASDAQ-traded REIT. The funds from those sales went back to the private equity shareholders. It was a great business, taking full advantage of the growth in suburban offices and the then-available tax shelter laws, and a good example of how REITs can be useful in conjunction with other real estate strategies.

Operationally, the key financial metric for a REIT is *funds from operations* (FFO). This is analogous to EBIDTA for other securities, or NOI with an add-back for noncash reserves. FFO is usually reported on an enterprise-level basis. Getting from net income to FFO requires adding back not only interest, depreciation, taxes, and amortization, but also any gains or losses on real estate transactions. Recent rulings by the IRS have significantly broadened the definition of real estate for purposes of REIT certification. For example, a billboard fund may now be classified as a REIT, even if a majority of the income comes from rental of personal property (billboards) and not the actual real estate itself. Since depreciation shelters a significant portion of cash flow, actual payouts may *exceed* nominal taxable income, with the REIT still retaining significant funds for reinvestment. See Table 19-1 as an example.

TABLE 19-1 Typical Summary REIT Balance Sheet

Nationwide Apartment REIT Balance Sheet		
	Year Ended December 31	
	2018	**2017**
Net Rental Revenue	$27,854,054	$26,182,811
Misc Unallocated Income	142,827	74,042
Total Revenues	27,996,881	26,256,853
Maintenance	5,570,811	5,236,562
Property Tax & Insurance	3,063,946	2,880,109
Direct Management	1,030,600	968,764
General Administration	501,373	471,291
Depreciation	6,963,514	6,545,703
Total Expenses	17,130,243	16,102,429
Net Operating Income	$10,866,638	$10,154,424
Funds from Operations	$17,830,151	$16,700,127

Key valuation metrics are *market value* and *net asset value* (NAV). NAV is the simple sum of the periodic appraisals of properties. REITs are rarely passive owners of real estate. Hospitality REITs have NAVs that are a function of real estate value, personal and intangible values, franchise values, and management acumen. Healthcare REITs are even more complex, with significant business income buried inside real estate returns. Even simple office REITs compete to efficiently manage properties, thus enhancing FFO and dividends.

REIT investors will rarely get the chance to evaluate the underlying appraisals, so NAV and its relationship to market value (MV) is a proxy. Recent accounting changes have called this into question. Many simplistic investment advisory models look to the ratio between NAV and MV as well as trends over time and/or the moving average. Most are fairly shortsighted. If the market perceives that the underlying REIT is well managed and FFO is expected to grow, then MV should and probably will systematically exceed NAV. Conversely, if the REIT is not well managed, and assets are expected to dissipate over time, then the opposite is true. Thus, a model that suggests that a particular REIT is undervalued because the MV is less than NAV is ignoring the fundamentals of REIT management.

Investors need to understand fundamentals of real estate market sectors. While REITs are a specific asset class, they can be subdivided into sectors due to the purposeful lack of type diversification by individual REITs. There is no particular reason to believe that hotel REITs, in general, will perform in concert with apartment REITs, or healthcare REITs, or any other subcategory. Additionally, some REITs within a sector will be better managed than others. While the largest REITs tend to be well diversified geographically, smaller REITs may have local concentrations or be particularly susceptible to the performance of a new acquisition. From time to time, REITs become takeover candidates, since this is a famous way for large REITs to become even larger.

In short, the valuation metrics—FFO, NAV, MV—can be extremely useful when taken in the context of trends in those metrics, industry movements, subsector movements, and underlying REIT fundamentals.

2. Private REITs

Without sounding too jaded, many private REITs have gained popularity among some marketers because they pay large commissions. Indeed, prior to 2017, when FINRA instituted new rules, the up-front costs of many private REITs reached 15%.

Private REITs behave much like private equity funds. They are rarely or thinly traded, and the only liquidity event is a promised liquidation after a fixed period of time. So, why do people invest in these? Ironically, the REIT model envisions an investment in income properties, which may improve over time if properties are well positioned or well managed. Private equity, conversely, is better suited for development, turnaround, or capital gains deals.

There are some limited liquidity channels available under some circumstances, but usually these are at deep discounts (20% or more, as of this writing), for limited share disposal (usually emergencies or other crises), and not widely obvious. One big advantage of REITs is the opportunity to invest in real estate with almost immediate liquidity. Private REITs violate that fundamental premise.

From a valuation perspective, private REITs also often lack the transparency of exchange or NASDAQ-traded funds. Under SEC limited offering safe harbors, Regulation D and Rule 144A, the same level of reporting may not be available. Even fundamental analytics, such as the calculation of FFO, may not be readily apparent. Thus, at any given point in time, the underlying value is some discounted present value of expected cash flows, discounted at a rate that captures the illiquidity, lack of transparency, and risk. Of course, it is rare that the investor will acquire such shares in an open market transaction after the initial offering. Typically, these secondary market acquisitions occur as the result of a gift, bequeath, or merger.

> Two clients were university endowments that had been gifted shares in a private REIT. The controlling, inside shareholders owned very favorable stock options that would trigger if the NAV exceeded a certain threshold. Exercising these options would significantly dilute the endowments' shares. The NAV was established via a private appraisal of underlying properties, and arguably the appraisal overvalued the properties, to the benefit of the insiders. The matter turned litigious, with litigation costs disproportionate to the values of the gifts. As one endowment manager said, the university funds would never have acquired the private REIT shares had they not been gifted by a major alumni.

FINRA notes that there are two principal ways in which private REITs report per-share estimates of value:[2]

Net Investment Methodology. The private REIT must disclose whether a part of the distribution includes a return of capital, which reduces the estimated per share value. This methodology may only be used until 150 days following the second anniversary of breaking escrow in the public offering, after which the REIT is required to use . . .

Appraised Value Methodology. This methodology uses an appraisal that is also disclosed in the most recent SEC filing. FINRA requires that the appraisal is performed annually (or more often), that it be conducted by a third-party valuation expert or service (or at least confirmed by such a third-party expert), and that the appraisal methodology conforms to acceptable industry practice.

The Net Investment Methodology acknowledges that some returns to investors may come from principle. The SEC notes that, "Non-Traded REITs may use offering proceeds . . . and borrowings to pay distributions."[3]

FINRA also notes that most nontraded REITs start out as blind pools. Many wealthy families will structure an investment as a "sidecar," having some specificity regarding the investments made with their portion of the pooled investment.

If this discussion about private REITs sounds very negative, it is meant to be. The disclosure problems in this sector are well known. That said, there are some bright lights on the horizon. Some private REITs are voluntarily joining the National Association of Real Estate Investments Trusts (NAREIT) and adhering to their standards. But the bottom line is, family offices should be wary of private REIT opportunities.

3. The 1031 Exchange

The tax benefits of 1031 exchanges are so important that the valuation aspects are often overlooked until the last minute, leaving a tax trap for the otherwise successful investor.

Under Revenue Code Section 1031, an investor can defer capital gains and other federal income tax liabilities from the sale of real estate if the proceeds are immediately (or soon thereafter) invested in a similar investment. A big focus of this book is the accumulation of real estate, rather than the sale. However, there are situations when investors dispose of a particular piece of real estate but simply do not need the cash. In those cases, a 1031 exchange will solve a lot of tax problems.

> One client had accumulated a significant fortune in real estate over many years, primarily as the general partner of several limited partnerships. Reaching retirement, he wanted to streamline his investments by cashing out his various partners and consolidating his holdings—from a *lot* of properties he partially owned to a smaller set of properties he owned exclusively. Naturally, this generated a lot of complex tax issues, and it eventually led to acquiring new properties as 1031 exchanges.

The tax regulations are fairly liberal in their definition of "similar investment." In general (and again, only a qualified tax advisor can answer this for a particular investor), any US-located parcel of real estate can be exchanged for any other US-located parcel. Whether it is improved or unimproved is irrelevant. The only principal exception is taxpayer-based—if the taxpayer is a dealer in real estate (the real estate is held as inventory for sale, such as for a homebuilder), then the 1031 exchange does not apply. The exchange period begins on the earliest of the date of the deed records or the date that possession of the property is transferred to the buyer, and ends after 180 days or the date the exchangers' tax return is due, including extensions, for the taxable year for which the relinquished property is transferred. These deadlines may only be extended in the case of a presidentially declared disaster. Intriguingly, the rule about filing taxes on the first business day after the calendar due date does not apply. If April 15 falls on a Saturday, then the 1040 doesn't have to be filed until Monday, the 17th. The expiration date for the exchange, though, would be Friday the 14th. If multiple properties are involved in an exchange, then the window begins with the sale of the very first property.

The term "boot" does not appear in the IRS Code, but it is commonly used in valuing 1031 exchanges. It refers to something either received or given to facilitate a 1031 exchange. Boot can include cash or cash equivalents, debts, liabilities (including mortgages), and other property such as personal property. In a simple exchange, with no "boot," the investor must acquire one or more properties of equal or greater value to what was sold. Cash received may spoil the 1031 treatment. There are specialized intermediaries who handle 1031 exchanges, and they receive and hold any cash proceeds until both sides of the 1031 are consummated.

A key issue is value, and many investors get tripped up on the issue of value versus cash proceeds. Table 19-2 illustrates three similar 1031 exchanges with very different tax implications.

TABLE 19-2 Comparisons of Three 1031 Exchanges

	Exchange 1	Exchange 2	Exchange 3
Property A Sold	22,000,000	22,000,000	22,000,000
Cash Proceeds	11,000,000	11,000,000	11,000,000
Debt Paid Off	11,000,000	11,000,000	11,000,000
Property B Purchased	22,000,000	22,000,000	20,000,000
Cash Down Payment	11,000,000	10,000,000	11,000,000
New Debt	11,000,000	12,000,000	9,000,000
Cash Proceeds	-0-	1,000,000	-0-
Tax Exposure	-0-	1,000,000	2,000,000

In the first example, the properties exchanged have similar values and there are no cash proceeds taken out and no tax exposure. In the second example, the properties have the same value, but by taking on extra debt, the investor is able to take out $1 million in cash "boot." This creates a tax exposure. Another trap occurs in the third example. Here, the investor undershoots the value threshold, and even though no cash is taken out, the exchange creates a tax exposure. Had the investor put additional cash into a deal (to buy a larger property, or to pay down debt), this may have avoided a tax exposure.

The biggest problem with 1031 exchange appraisals is the trap that the appraiser is influenced by the transaction price or by comp from another 1031 exchange transaction. The tax and investment decisions being made in 1031 deals mean that these are rarely true arm's-length transactions. Prices are often overstated to cover transaction costs, which are not trivial. Typically, these transaction costs are considered *exchange expenses* and may be paid out of sale proceeds or subsequent borrowing. While there is no canonical list of IRS-approved expenses, most often Revenue Ruling 72-456 is cited, which says that exchange funds may be used to pay broker commissions. In general, the following are usually lumped under "broker commissions":

- Actual commissions paid
- Exchange fees paid to qualified intermediaries, including attorney fees

- Owners' title insurance fees (but not lenders)
- Escrow fees
- Appraisal fees required for the exchange (but not if required by the lender)
- Transfer taxes
- Recording fees

There are many other expenses that may not be paid with exchange funds, even though these are typically paid at closing with the proceeds of a sale. These include such things as security deposits and prorated rents, which are common and not trivial items in commercial property transactions, and financing costs. Prorated property taxes would not be covered as acceptable expenses from exchange funds.

In short, all of this means that the conditions of sale in a 1031 are not requisite to the conditions assumed in a market value appraisal. Indeed, the arm's-length problem probably means that 1031s cannot even be used as comps in any real estate appraisal, much less an appraisal for another 1031. Further, since 1031 consultants usually combine the marketing (brokerage) aspects with the intermediation function, sales prices tend to be a "take it or leave it" situation, rather than a negotiation informed by well-performed appraisals.

For larger transactions—the sort that may be seen in a wealthy family office portfolio—most issues can be negotiated. In other words, the fees charged and "price taker" limitations imposed by 1031 exchange firms for smaller transactions would clearly not apply to larger transactions initiated by family offices. For that reason, a strong appraisal of target properties would be an important part of due diligence during the property identification period.

4. Limited Partnership Interests

Limited partnership interests have lack of marketability, minority interest, and lack of control features impacting the appraisal. Of course, investors in a limited partnership are usually interested in the financial metrics. The actual investment value at any given point in time may be irrelevant. However, families may need to appraise these interests for tax purposes, transfers, or probate. The appraisal takes into account the net asset value (a simple market value appraisal) plus the limitations imposed by the fact that the ownership is something other than fee simple.

This begins with a standard appraisal of the underlying assets. Two discounts are then usually applied:

Minority/noncontrolling interest discount. Usually a function of the degree of control or influence in the transferred interest.

Lack of marketability discount. A function of investment illiquidity.

These are inherently interrelated. A minority interest is harder to sell and thus less marketable. The delineated and legal rights of limited partners dictate the extent and applicability of discounts. A provision in the partnership agreement restricting transfers and withdrawals by limited partners has a bearing on the degree of discount. These discounts, which can be quite large, are typically measured via comparable case studies from other appraisals. For that reason, appraisers with some experience in these projects are typically needed to have access to acceptable data. There are some services that provide data on actual sales and resales of limited partnership interests. Private REITs have marketability discounts similar to those experienced by limited partnership shares, and that data also proves useful in such valuations.

For family offices, a common tool is the family limited partnership (FLP). Senior family members contribute assets to the FLP in exchange for general and limited partnership shares. Usually there is no gain or loss recognized by the senior member when appreciated assets are contributed, although there are exceptions that can be avoided with careful planning.

The senior members retain the general/managing partner shares and transfer limited partnership interests to other family members or trusts. The general partner retains control over the partnership assets and thus controls cash flows to the limited partners.

The IRS has ruled that family limited partnerships must be established for valid underlying business reasons, such as enhancing the management of a family-owned enterprise, promoting family involvement in decision making, or ensuring sound decisions over multigenerational assets.

This vehicle has many advantages but has significant appraisal challenges. All the above—including discounts used in appraisals—are highly dependent on the moving target of tax laws, regulations, and interpretations. The underlying assets are best valued by appraisers, and the discounts are usually determined by tax advisors. All members need to work as a team in the case of large, complex assets and FLPs.

5. Tenancy in Common Investments

These are time-shares for upscale investors. Tenancy in common investments, or TICs, as they are commonly known, are undivided co-interests in a real estate investment managed by a third party. They are tempting, and on the surface provide lots of apparent benefits in terms of hands-off management and simplified cash flows. Indeed, TICs are suitable for 1031 exchanges and can be custom tailored to fit the needs of the 1031 exit strategy. On the other hand, TIC investments have the same shortcomings as private equity or private REITs, along with the lack of centralized control by a managing partner. TICs have come under significant regulatory fire of late, principally suitability claims arbitrated by FINRA. (TICs are considered a security under *SEC v. Howey*, 328 U.S. 293, 1946.) From a valuation perspective, a TIC can be onerous to appraise.

It has not been uncommon for TICs to be offered with implicit up-front fees amounting to 30% of actual value of underlying real estate. In short, a TIC organizer may take $1 million in real estate equity (say, a small commercial building) and divide it into 12 TIC units each sold for $100,000. The total of the units obviously exceeds the equity being subdivided. Why would knowledgeable investors agree to such a thing? First, many TICs were sold to satisfy 1031 exchange needs. In addition, many investors were nearing retirement and disposing of management-intensive properties. They wanted to clean up their portfolios and enjoy the net rents without the management hassle. With eyes wide open, they were willing to pay a premium to be relieved of management burdens. The fair value of a one-twelfth ownership in that $1 million TIC is $80,000. A similar management-intensive investment might throw off $8,000 per year for a 10% return, but with lots of headaches. The investor, nearing retirement, is happy to enjoy tax benefits and only an 8% return (that same $8,000 divided by $100,000) but with no management responsibilities.

At this point in the chapter, it may be useful to introduce a fairly famous Tax Court ruling, *Ludwick v. Commissioner* (TC Memo 2010-104) (May 10, 2010). Ludwig does not always apply in these complex real estate holdings, but appraisers looking at private REITs, private equity, and TICs would be well advised to consider its implications. Investors attempting to understand those appraisals would also do well to consider Ludwick.

The Ludwicks (a husband and wife) each transferred a 50% undivided interest in their Hawaiian vacation home to their individual qualified personal residence trusts (QRPT). For many years, the IRS had held the position that the only discount available for valuing undivided interests was the cost of partitioning. A number of cases have come up in which minority interest and marketability discounts were applied, somewhat haphazardly. *LeFrak v. Commissioner* (TC Memo 1993-526) applied a 20% minority interest discount and a 10% marketability discount. In a more complex case, in the *Estate of Ellie Williams* (TC Memo 1998-59), the IRS offered no expert testimony. The court rejected the simple partitioning approach and allowed a discount of 20% for marketability and an additional 30% of the remaining 80% for lack of control. The *Estate of Baird* (TC Memo 2001-258) had a whopping 60% undivided interest discount for timberland.

The court, weighing the evidence and the testimony of two different experts, found that the property could probably be sold in one year if not partitioned at a 16.2% time-value-of-money discount. Further, the court determined that the property could be sold in two years if partitioned, resulting in a cumulative loss of 26.5%. The court held that the property would probably not need to be partitioned to be sold (a 90% likelihood), and thus concluded a weighted discount of 17.2%.

This is a friendly TIC between two related parties with a TIC agreement in place. Thus, arguably, the Tax Court decision perhaps sets a floor for the expected discount for an undivided TIC share, and indeed for any illiquid minority interest in real estate.

Wealthy families may not encounter TIC opportunities very often. But there is a very special type of TIC called a *space assignment co-ownership* (SACO) that even wealthy families may find in their portfolios. These have been referred to as "time-shares for the rich," and indeed there is some truth to that. These have the look and feel of a condominium, but with a caveat that there is a time-interval ownership.

One common SACO is a vacation rental at a high-end resort, such as a ski resort. The developer may construct a large condominium tower, say 100 units in a high-rise, with the expected amenities (restaurant, concierge, parking garage, other services). The developer will sell five eight-week ownership slices in each condominium, for a total of 500 units sold. Each unit will have exclusive use of the condo for four different two-week sessions during the year, ensuring that there is a roughly equal distribution of use throughout the various seasons. Of course, five units times 8 weeks is 40 weeks. The developer will retain the remaining 12 weeks to rent out the condo to the general public or for maintenance and upgrades. The developer will also typically retain control of the restaurant, parking, and other services. The condo agreements will include some language about profit sharing on the unit rentals and other services, but rare is the circumstance when the unit owners actually have any positive cash flow.

Given the restrictions on development slope-side in places like Whistler or Vail, it is not surprising that even very wealthy families would invest in SACOs. Indeed, the pricing and financing are completely out of the realm of affordability for middle-class investors. Resales and valuations are complex. Many are built and sold at the height of some special demand (e.g., many were built in Whistler, BC, in anticipation of the Winter Olympics), but then demand wanes. Like any family investment, valuation for estate and probate can be required. These investments are, in the end, a TIC and need to be valued as such, with the same sort of marketability and lack of control discounts. The original sales prices often bear no relationship to the subsequent value.

6. Summary and Key Points

Wealthy families tend to invest as lead players in joint ventures or funds, or at least have *sidecar* positions in comingled funds. There are, though, some valid reasons why a wealthy investor or family may have a minority or limited interest in a larger real estate holding. Publicly traded REITs, when properly understood and well managed, can offer significant diversification and above-average returns. REIT shares offer the income of a bond coupled with the very real potential of capital growth.

Minority and illiquid interests in untraded real estate holdings are appraisal challenges. Investments promise long-term returns, but at the cost of liquidity and transparency. There are occasions when these investments need to be valued before maturity. Determining the underlying undivided value at those intermediate points can itself be a problem, since such investments are sold at prices unrelated to actual market value. TICs or 1031 exchanges may be priced as a function of the investment value, the relief from management responsibilities, or the tax sheltering. SACO-type investments may be priced as a function of the "hot market" in which they are sold. Subsequent resales may give some evidence of current values, but valuation in the absence of any competing sales may have to rely on secondhand evidence of discounts.

Court cases and comparable case studies may give some great evidence of discounts applicable in these matters. Tax Court rulings can be particularly helpful, although the data is constantly evolving.

7. A Final Note—How Do You Get Rid of This Stuff?

Valuation of private holdings is usually associated with intermediate events, such as gifting or estate settlement. Most wealthy families will not be faced with disposing of minority interest, or the value consequences of such disposal. However, these things happen. These disposal events all have valuation implications. First, someone needs to set a probable selling price, and as has been shown, this will be a function of the true underlying NAV minus a discount. In a perfect world, the sort of valuations and discounts estimated for nontransaction appraisals (such as gifts and probate) should be great proxies for the actual net value to be received when trying to liquidate. The secondary market for these holdings is far from efficient, and as such the spreads between actual value and realized value may be very noisy.

A first place to look is the internet, which has become a great equalizer in the private equity world. Recent federal legislation has loosened up the opportunities for secondary marketing of private shares. There are currently several web-based auction platforms that provide, in essence, a listing opportunity for investors trying to sell private equity shares. There are also specialized platforms that focus on private REIT shares. These companies are typically FINRA-regulated broker-dealers, and there will be auction costs (bid-ask spreads), potential fees, and commissions. Some firms actually list the private REITs in which they attempt to make a market, although that market is far from being as efficient as NASDAQ or even the pink sheets.

One recent private REIT had a quoted NAV of $5.55 per share. The highest bid on one of the private REIT platforms was $4.25 less any dividends paid after an arbitrary ex-dividend date (set by the platform as part of the bid process, not the actual ex-date set by the REIT). There was also an "administrative fee" of $100 per investor account. Thus, ignoring the admin fee and dividend clawback, the discount from NAV *for the best bid* was about 25%. The next best bid for those same shares was $3, which amounts to a discount of about 46%.

Intriguingly, for savvy investors, there may be a reason to be on the buy-side of these auctions. More often than not, the investors seeking liquidity are doing so for reasons wholly unrelated to the performance of the investment itself. Not withstanding the lack of transparency in many private REITs and private funds, if the underlying investment pool is still in good shape, the acquisition value in the secondary market can have two significant benefits. First, the investment is being purchased at a steep discount, which is obvious. Second, and less obvious, is the fact that most private REITs and private funds have maturity or exit-strategy dates. Valuation in the secondary market not only lowers the entrance price, but may significantly shorten the period over which future cash flows are discounted. Consider Table 19-3, which shows the true valuation of a private equity holding at the IPO and later on in the secondary market.

The annual preferred returns and the anticipated return upon liquidation are the same. However, the internal rate of return for the secondary market acquisition is nearly double, and the investor's money is only exposed for half the time. Further, consider what happens if the investment does

TABLE 19-3 Comparison of a Private Equity Offering at IPO and in the Secondary Market

	IPO	Secondary
Purchase Price	10,000	7,000
Years to Maturity	10	5
Annual Preferred Return	700	700
Value at Maturity	20,000	20,000
Internal Rate of Return	12.55%	30.38%

not play out as planned. Rather than receiving the proposed $20,000, the investor only receives the initial IPO share value of $10,000. In that case, the original investment becomes a bond and the only return to the IPO shareholder is the dividend rate of 7%. The secondary market investor is in an analogous position to having acquired a bond at discount. Table 19-4 illustrates this.

TABLE 19-4 Private Equity Comparisons with Return of Capital

	IPO	Secondary
Purchase Price	10,000	7,000
Years to Maturity	10	5
Annual Preferred Return	700	700
Value at Maturity	20,000	10,000
Internal Rate of Return	7.00%	16.21%

Further, if the underlying investments are performing according to plan, then the underlying NAV in year 5 is probably higher than it was at the IPO. Of course, all risks and caveats associated with minority interests in private real estate continue to apply, but it is noteworthy that the valuation metrics change materially in the secondary market.

Obviously investing in non-listed private REITs is not a strategy many family offices will pursue. But for the experienced and savvy investor, there is no shortage of opportunities available.

20
Special Topics Frequently Encountered by Family Offices

In my experience, in the real estate business past success stories are generally not applicable to new situations. We must continually reinvent ourselves, responding to changing times with innovative new business models.

—Akira Mori

EACH OF THESE next topics could have had at least its own chapter, and indeed some very fine books are devoted to these topics. Unfortunately, lengthier expositions on these would be beyond this already-weighty book. Also, I have already touched on many of these topics, directly or peripherally. These topics come up so very often in consultation with family offices and real estate businesses that it seems useful to at least synopsize each of them here, and perhaps stimulate further inquiries by the readers.

This book is about how to *understand* and properly utilize appraisals. The typical family buying a condominium will naturally rely on an appraisal to give some indication of the retail value. Wealthy investors look at condominiums as investment opportunities and may want to buy a block of them "wholesale" rather than "retail." How can a normal appraisal be used to provide some indication of the discount when buying condos for investment? Co-op valuation is another frequently encountered issue as an inherited asset.

Spectacular views, clean water, and clean air all have implications for real estate development. Eminent domain situations often arise when owning commercial real estate. Leveraging off the last chapter, the differences between REITs and REOCs are widely misunderstood. As will be shown, the former are a fairly constrained and liquid investment. The latter really fall into their own category, without the tax advantages but with very different risk/reward profiles.

Finally, automated valuation models (AVMs) are currently supplanting individual appraisals in a host of functions, including banking due diligence, home equity lending, and residential investment. This section is really of more interest to families with significant investments in banks and lending pools, and it may provide some interesting information for increasing returns and decreasing risk in real estate lending.

1. Valuing Condominiums

Many wealthy families own condominiums. Grandma and Grandpa may retire to one, leaving the estate to be managed by the next generation. Condos are great ways to own property in key cities where business may be regularly conducted, in recreational areas (ski slopes, marina-side) or in foreign cities where a higher degree of security is needed than can usually be accorded in a hotel. Many wealthy families buy condominiums in college towns for junior. In addition, investors often buy condominiums—individually or in wholesale bundles—as rental investments. Understanding how the condominium appraisal works can be key in unlocking bidding values.

Several key elements should be considered to understand the condo appraisal:

Condo appraisals are typically reported on a brief form, similar to the single family detached form. Condos are usually valued with a very straightforward sales comparison approach, although an income analysis (gross rent multiplier) can be very useful in condominium situations where rental is a common property use. The lack of a cost approach is of little consequence for a buyer of an individual unit, but what about a wholesale buyer who is acquiring a distressed development? There have been occasions when a large condominium project suffered from physical or structural problems such that an investor purchased the entire project and simply started over. The value of underlying land can be an important piece of information.

While little is written on the subject, some studies indicate that the "finished land value" underlying a condominium may approximate 12% of the total condo value. Thus, a 100-unit condominium complex selling for $500,000 each has an aggregate value of $50 million, and an implied land value of about $6 million. Proportionally, each condo has about $60,000 worth of land.

Newer condos should use comps from both within and without the same complex. Indeed, Fannie Mae and Freddie Mac require this. Even older condo appraisals would benefit from using comps outside the same complex. Why? Developers may set artificially high prices in "hot" markets, and stimulate sales with marketing tools that pass by the wayside in future years. Investors would be well advised to consider the valuation indicated by comps that are competitive in the same market but *not* in the same complex. Investors should also be aware that condo development and new condo sales can really catch fire in hot markets, but then subside when external stimulus retreats. Since appraisals feed off of recent comps, these appraisals can sometimes simply serve to confirm developer prices rather than actually independently examine long-term value trends.

Retail condo appraisal are a starting point for wholesale values. Many investors look to failed condo complexes as potential investments in rental properties. Additionally, a developer may presell a batch of condos at a wholesale price to jump-start the marketing. The discount is typically a function of the discounted present value to market these plus the risk attached to this sort of investment. Table 20-1 (see next page) illustrates the typical analysis.

Beware of gross rent multipliers. Many investors buy condos as rental investments, relying on gross rent multipliers generated from nearby apartments. Condos are often (usually?) built with more amenities than rental apartments, such as in-unit laundry rooms; covered, indoor, attached, or even security-protected parking; somewhat more room; and nicer appliances and fixtures. Conversely, apartments may be built with more utilitarian fixtures and features, cognizant of the regular tenant turnover. Thus, values suggested by gross rent multipliers may not pencil out. Typically, an investor looking for a condo as a rental investment will look in the secondary market, and perhaps even for distressed sales.

TABLE 20-1 Typical Condo Wholesale Analysis (Synopsis)

Retail Selling Price	$250,000
Annual Price Appreciation	4%
Units to Be Purchased	40
Expected Annual Absorption	10
Required Rate of Return	20%

	Price	No. Sold	P/V Factor	Total
Year 1	250,000	10	0.83333	2,083,333
Year 2	260,000	10	0.69444	1,805,556
Year 3	270,400	10	0.57870	1,564,815
Year 4	281,216	10	0.48225	1,356,173
Aggregate Acquisition Price				$6,809,877
Per Unit Acquisition Price				$170,247
Per Unit Average Discount				31.90%

This cannot be stressed too strongly—too many condo appraisals simply validate the sales price rather than critically analyze that price and the market pricing trends. Not surprisingly, many condo purchases (particularly new condo units) fall into distress. Savvy investors who are looking for deals in this market will track those distress sales.

Be careful of underfunded condo associations. The common areas, exterior walls, and often the roofs are the association's responsibility. If these are underfunded, if reserves for replacement are lacking, or if insurance was bought "on the cheap," then the long-term viability of the association may be questionable. Further, be careful of trigger dates for transfer of common amenities from the developer to the association. Often, condo developers will spend extra money to maintain these in first-class condition as part of their marketing budget. Many condo associations are surprised when a transfer trigger date (usually based on sales of a specified number of units) leaves the association holding the bag for significant unbudgeted costs. These nuances will rarely be picked up in an appraisal, and so the well-informed and well-advised investor will want to look deeper into the finances.

2. Cooperatives

Most states do not have enabling legislation for cooperative apartments, although in some areas, such as Manhattan, the co-op is common, particularly in upscale markets. For that reason, surprisingly few appraisers have skills or training in co-op valuation.

Upscale co-ops may be purchase directly for cash, with little or no leverage. An appraisal consistent with FNMA-FHLMC standards may be very useful to help inform the investor of the market, comparable transactions, and property values. The FNMA Selling Guide Section B4-1.4-04 (2014) provides the guidance for appraisers on this subject. The issues applicable to these sorts of appraisals is good reading for investors.

FNMA's guidance includes consideration of:

- The number of co-op shares attributable to the unit under consideration
- The total number of shares issued and outstanding for the co-op corporation
- The name of any lienholder, the lien position, and the amount and repayment terms of all project blanket financing
- The *pro rata* share of blanket mortgage payments that are attributable to the unit, as determined by dividing the number of shares attributable to the unit by the total number of project shares
- The *pro rata* share of each lien attributable to the unit
- Any tax abatements or exemptions that are attributable to the unit
- The remaining term for any tax abatements or exemptions and provisions for escalation of real estate taxes, which is the dollar amount by which the taxes will increase and the year in which the increase will occur
- Any monthly maintenance fees, including:
  - Utility charges, if they are part of these fees
  - Monthly special assessments
  - Ground rent
  - Other fees for the use of facilities that are attributable to the unit
  - The fee type, amount, and term (if applicable) of those other fees[1]

Appraisers can request this information on a standard FNMA Form, *Request for Cooperative Project Information* (FHMA Form 1074). Indeed, gathering and systematizing this information may be a good use for a co-op real estate appraiser, and may be a good reason for hiring an appraiser in these situations even when financing is not a question.

3. Real Estate Operating Company (REOC)

For a whole lot of very bad reasons, REOCs and REITs (real estate investment trusts) are often taught in the same breath in MBA school. Indeed, there are common threads and themes, but the two entities are very different.

REITs typically—although not always—focus toward generating cash flow from through the rent or leases. For a REIT, a new construction project will aim at a "develop and hold" strategy.

Conversely, a REOC will typically consider new development from a capital gains perspective. REOCs are also often in the rehab-and-flip business or even in the property management arena. While REIT returns must be paid out in the form of dividends, REOC returns can be reinvested. Thus, a REOC can populate a portfolio quickly with internally generated projects.

The confusion lies in the fact that many REITs are actually real estate–oriented businesses that masquerade as passive real estate holding companies. Consider a hotel REIT, which owns the underlying real estate and enjoys rents. Some other operating company overlays this and extracts profits from the various businesses that occupy the real estate. The real estate rents and the business profits ultimately drive the performance. Further, the allocation of rents to real estate (and thus residual profits to the business) can be somewhat arbitrary and based on a host of other factors (income taxes, local property taxes, franchise values, etc.). A REIT and a REOC may be tied to one another, and some REOCs use REITs as an endgame for developed real estate.

REIT valuation takes a somewhat long-term approach to capitalization of net rents. Net rents (net operating income, or NOI) may cycle with the general economy, and the underlying business acumen of REIT managers may be measurable by comparing the REIT profitability trends to other similar REITs. Hence, a properly curated portfolio of REITs can outperform the market and attenuate risk.

Conversely, REOCs may take on other types of risk—leverage, market, and operational, to name a few. Consider a REIT in the business of buying single family rental houses versus a REOC in the business of building such houses. The REIT bears some market risk in the occupancy of these properties. The REOC bears operational risk (delivering the properties on budget), leverage risk (predictable acquisition, development, and construction financing), and market risk (success of the REIT acquisition contract being closed per the agreement).

REOCs will be valued with fairly traditional equity valuation tools and techniques. Publicly traded REOCs (such as homebuilding or commercial real estate development businesses) are evaluated the same way as any other publicly traded stock. Private REOCs will require more intense analyses, since SEC-mandated transparency and the market's collective pricing wisdom market are absent. However—and this is the key issue for family offices—the underlying assets are in the real estate space. To value a REOC it is necessary to understand something about that real estate, in the same way that to value an automobile manufacturing company, it is handy to know something about cars and trucks. A traditional real estate appraisal *may or may not* be useful, but the advice of experts in the appraisal space can be invaluable. Remember—companies in the buggy whip business had great-looking financials right up until the end of the buggy whip market. Engaging a real estate expert on these issues, in conjunction with other financial analysts, can be money well spent.

4. Preservation, Conservation, Historic, and Architectural Easements

Before the recent recession, these were very popular among investors looking to shelter income while at the same time making a contribution toward preserving the environment. At the upper tier, investors bought large tracts of forest land (Tierra del Fuego was very popular) to enjoy carbon sequestration credits against income taxable in countries that recognized the Kyoto accords. At a more basic level, investors donated the development rights on vacant tracts to a qualified land trust, while retaining land ownership for nondevelopment purposes (largely recreational). Investors who owned or acquired historically or architecturally valuable sites would donate a preservation covenant to an appropriate trust, thus agreeing to ensure that the property would be maintained in its valuable condition forever. Often these credits would be taken together with open space or new market tax credits, depending on situational specifics.

Most commonly, the value of the tax credit for a preservation or conservation easement is the marginal value of forgone development rights or options. Thus, if a vacant parcel is worth $1 million considering its highest and best use (e.g., as a commercial development site), but the value without the development rights (say, as an agricultural tract) might only be $300,000, the basis for the tax credit is $700,000.

For a historic or architecturally valuable site, the credit is a bit more complex. Arguably, the value of many historic properties is actually enhanced by preservation easements or ordinances. The basis for the tax credit is usually determined by the present value of increased costs of maintaining the property in its preservable state, of course taking into account the impacts of any functional obsolescence.

We recently consulted on a historically interesting home (albeit not one listed on any federal register). The owners had added a garage, apparently not original to the structure but built "architecturally" consistent with the original home (but with more modern materials). The question arose as to whether the property value was impacted with the removal of the garage. The final determination was "yes, but not by much" since the garage added some functionality to the home but was clearly not part of the original structure.

In prior years, when these credits were very popular, the IRS instituted some new—and some would say draconian—rules regarding the appraisals. This was in response to a very few appraisers, and appraisals, that went over the line in the valuations. The IRS determined that if an IRS review found the appraisal to be flawed, both the taxpayer and the valuer (as the IRS calls them) would be subject to fairly stiff penalties. Again, this was aimed at a handful of appraisers, but the end result was to drive many respected firms out of the business.

Today, the process is usually that a tax advisor (CPA or attorney) contracts with a local appraiser with sufficient and specific expertise to perform the appraisal in accordance with IRS regulations. The appraisal is then reviewed by a second firm, usually one with more gray hair and general, nationally recognized expertise. This is not only more cost-effective (since these nationally renowned appraisal experts tend to be pricey) but also puts a lot of ammunition in the workfile if the IRS ever raises an issue. There are currently several private funds available that directly invest in tax credit projects. In our experience, these funds should require comprehensive reviews of 100% of the appraisals used for tax credits.

Few appraisers fully understand the market value impacts of historic or architectural preservation. This is particularly acute with the enactment of historic neighborhood preservation ordinances. Many years ago there were some studies—not very good ones—that historic preservation was actually linked to *decreases* in market value. These studies used historically preserved properties and tax assessed values. As it happens, such properties do not transact as often as nonhistoric properties, and so tax assessors are left relying on the cost approach (particularly with nonresidential properties, as was the case in these studies). Since tax assessors treat physical depreciation as a linear function, with a theoretically finite economic life for the structure, these older, historic properties naturally had lower tax assessed values than their nonhistoric, newer brothers and sisters in the marketplace. Aha, these flawed studies said, this is support for the notion that historic designation is connected with property devaluation! Of course, nothing could be further from the truth, and those studies were eventually debunked. Nonetheless, opponents (and there are some) of historic district preservation continue to cite such studies in their arguments. Indeed, the bulk of studies in the literature support the notion that historic preservation, historic district designation, or historic preservation ordinances actually *enhance* market values.

As long as we are on the subject, the historic preservation community has often shot itself in the foot by using arguments in favor of historic preservation that fail to connect with property owners and investors. The general argument posed by the preservation community over the years has been that there are certain *community values* attached to the value of a property, and thus if a property is worthy of preservation, it is the community obligation of the property owner to facilitate that preservation. Sadly, that argument ignores rational expectations and the profit motive, and so often falls on deaf ears. The fact is, preservation is actually good for the investors' pocketbooks. However, a full and fulsome analysis of this, at a property-specific level, requires some understanding of how these markets work.

5. Automated Valuation Models

Generally, there is little that an individual investor needs to know or understand about automated valuation models (AVMs). Behind the scenes, at banks, mortgage lenders, and agencies that securitize mortgage loans, AVMs have become the benchmark against which residential appraisals are measured. For that reason, investors with significant interests in mortgage lending or securitization will inevitably run into AVMs and may need to know a bit about them.

An AVM is a statistical program, usually a regression model, to value large numbers of properties simultaneously. The output is a property-specific valuation, and when used as a tool by an appraiser can be an acceptable methodology for a residential appraisal. There are substantial fixed costs to operate an AVM, including the cost of a large data set, statistical oversight, and model operation. However, when used for a large number of properties, the per-unit cost falls rapidly. For very large numbers of properties, the cost per property can be surprisingly low. Couple with this, the AVM usually has a statistical characterization, a confidence interval, and a host of information about the market in which the individual property will compete.

Investors in mortgage-backed securities or in banks (or other lenders) that originate mortgage loans will ultimately rely on AVMs for loan-level underwriting support. While current legislation and regulations require that a mortgage loan be supported by an appraisal (although there are some exceptions), residential appraisals will most likely be compared to the more statistically defendable output of an AVM. If that review process indicates any valuation problems, a full review may be useful.

AVMs are used in a host of other situations. Tax assessors use AVMs or other computer-assisted valuation models to ascertain tax values. Federal and state agencies use AVMs to measure the accuracy and efficacy of the appraisal process. Large-scale real estate developers use AVMs to help price building lots and final sales prices on new homes. In the years since the mortgage meltdown, AVMs have proven their worth in the courts, helping adjudicate billions of dollars in failed mortgage-backed securities.

The upshot is that any investment in the debt side of the residential lending business, or for that matter in the equity side of residential development, may ultimately rely on an AVM for value determination. Some AVMs are better than others, and investors may want to pick and probe a bit to determine the quality of AVM being used to secure their investments.

6. Eminent Domain Situations

Real estate investments are very likely to encounter eminent domain situations. Roads are widened, new interchanges are installed, or property is simply "taken" for locally beneficial use. Normal real estate appraisal rules apply. The taking authority will typically hire an appraiser, and if a large number of properties are being acquired, one appraisal firm may win the contract to appraise all properties fronting on a road to be widened. The property owners may or may not hire their own appraiser, but it is often difficult to fight city hall on this one.

Investors *must* be proactive about these things. Most eminent domain "takings" are aimed at the market value of the fee simple interest in the real estate, and are adjudicated against the fee owner. Commercial real estate can be a complex nexus of contracts, relationships, options, and expectations.

Large "chain" tenants have experts and sometimes whole departments devoted to negotiating contracts, and they frequently take into account the expectation that an eminent domain action may impact the leasehold estate gained over time. Most eminent domain actions are silent as to these leasehold estates and leave it up to the landlord to negotiate lease terminations with the tenant.

It is not uncommon for commercial leases to have clauses that favor one party or the other in the face of an eminent domain actions. In one recent eminent domain action, the tenant claimed that nearly half the award should be paid to them as compensation for loss of the leasehold estate in a long-term lease. The tenant sued the landlord, and the litigation costs to the landlord to defend this action were exorbitant. In another recent situation, the retail tenant—experienced in these matters—included a clause in the lease that if any eminent domain action ever required their sign to be moved, there would be an exorbitant decrease in the lease payment.

Despite having good legal contract advice, many investors find themselves surprised when an eminent domain action occurs. One way to minimize the surprise is a regular appraisal, which addresses the market value of the fee simple interest and any other claims against the property (contractual below-market leases being high on the list). At the time contracts are renewed, an audit by a competent valuation expert should be a key element of the renewal process. Indeed, an investor who owns a significant portfolio of real estate should have a competent appraiser on retainer at all times to help manage these valuation issues.

7. The Valuation of a Spectacular View, Clean Water, and Clean Air

On the surface, these issues seem to be valuable components of a trophy real estate holding. These values often contribute to the tax credits when a conservation or preservation easement is donated. An even more interesting issue arises when the property in question is accused of violating some other property's spectacular view, clean water, or clean air.

The dominant property (the term usually reserved for a property subject to an easement) may have a highest and best use for some sort of development. However, the effect of that development will encroach on a neighboring property's view, clean water, or perhaps even clean air. Of course, the better the view (air, water, etc.) and the greater the burden, the greater the valuation issue.

A proactive negotiation is always in order, but that negotiation should be informed by some valuation metrics. Of course, the proposed development will be supported by an appraisal, but what are the valuation issues surrounding the property that will be burdened (again, using easement jargon, the servient estate)? The key element is the value with and without the amenity in question. In the case of an undeveloped site, the appraiser should also take into account the likelihood of development or use of the amenity by the dominant estate. Indeed, if the dominant estate has very little likelihood of ever benefitting from the amenity in question, then the value should take that into account.

This actually raises a somewhat bigger question about the impact of real estate ownership and development on surrounding and neighboring parcels. Rational expectations theory requires that we include the likelihood and potential outcomes of protests and litigation from neighbors. That does not necessarily require that we agree with their premises, only that we recognize that there is a cost associated with such protests. Appraisers who assist with the development of a site should be required, as a condition of the assignment, to make some learned assays into the likelihood of such protests, their potential costs, and the effect of delays on the site development.

> A homeowner was an Air Force reserve pilot called up for active duty during a recent conflagration in the Middle East. Prior to his call-up, he had constructed a home on a beautiful site with a spectacular view. During his call-up, his family went to live with relatives and their new home sat vacant. Upon his return from active duty, he found that the next-door neighbor had constructed a new home that completely blocked his view. He protested, and litigation ensued. The use and enjoyment of his home—the dominant estate, in this case—was severely impacted. The occupancy of the servient estate—the one newly built—was put on hold for an extended and expensive period until the litigation could be completed.

8. Summary and Key Points

If there is a prevailing theme in this chapter, it is that there are subtle and nuanced needs for appraisal expertise in a variety of situations. Condominiums, co-ops, REOCs, and tax easement properties all have complex appraisal needs. Wealthy investors (and for that matter, most market participants) often consider the appraisal issues on an "as-needed" basis, but successful investors understand the need to be proactively informed about valuation issues. Taken in the context of the values in question, such advice is fairly cheap insurance.

Condominiums and co-ops are fairly common in the wealth family portfolio. Condos are useful ways to get some return on junior's expenses while he or she is in college, or to have a family "place" at the slope or the shore. Pricing is all too often a secondary concern, leaving a family with an overpriced asset and no good exit strategies. (In most circumstances, taking a loss on junior's college condo is not tax deductible, unless you planned ahead!) Co-ops have the same problem—a family may want an apartment in a particular building or location, and the price is simply the cost of joining that club. For estate management or tax purposes, these need to be valued from time to time, and specialized appraisal tools and techniques are required.

REOCs, even publicly traded ones, are distinct from publicly traded REITs. From a liquidity perspective, they are more like private equity funds or even private REITs. Under some circumstances, REOCs can be useful investments, but the valuation requires real estate appraisal techniques and security valuation.

AVMs are increasingly common components of mortgage lending, and investors with debt-instrument investments that have mortgage ties will ultimately be dependent on the quality and use of such AVMs in the underwriting process.

Eminent domain issues are fraught with litigious challenges. Commercial property owners can insure themselves against these issues by taking a proactive stance at the contracting stage. Every commercial property owned in a portfolio should be periodically reviewed for potential eminent domain issues. This leads inexorably to the fact that investors should be proactive in the litigation front. Evaluating how our development will be subject to potential litigation (i.e., eminent domain, adjudication with tenants) or the cause of litigation (impacts on neighboring or surrounding properties) should be an ongoing inquiry in a well-managed portfolio. The cost of such an inquiry pales against the benefits.

9. A Final Note—What Happened in 2007–2008?

Texts and PhD dissertations will kill countless trees and empty vats of ink in the coming decades studying the causes and impacts of the most recent recession. So my take on the real estate valuation component is clearly going to be just a drop in an ocean of words. Naturally, the various components were interactive, and to try to separate just one will be problematic. Nonetheless, we will try. There is an important reason for trying—to the extent there are lessons to be learned from that debacle, we should benefit from those lessons.

Going back to World War II, residential values actually increased at a fairly steady pace year after year. Indeed, studies have indicated that from 1946 until the mid-1990s, residences increased in value on average about 2% above the year-end inflation rate. In short, residential property owners and lenders could count on a slow but steady increase in value *and* a hedge against inflation or other economic travails. Figure 20-1 shows some of this data, dating back to the mid-1970s.

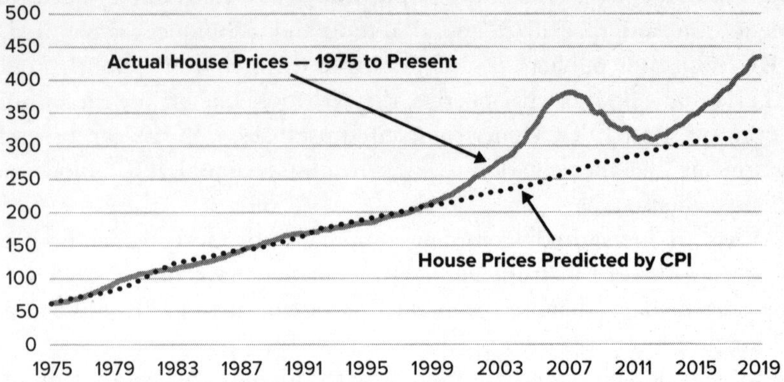

FIGURE 20-1 The House Price Bubble

Then, in the mid-1990s, the housing bubble began. There are a variety of reasons proposed, not the least of which was liberal lending policies encouraged by the federal government. Inflated valuation often became a self-fulfilling prophesy. In acutely hot neighborhoods, every property was assumed to be at the top of its market. These markets essentially fed on themselves, and lenders believed that the markets could never collapse, or at least behaved that way.

Historically, real estate loans were made by local lenders and retained in the portfolios of those lenders. These local lenders had a very strong vested interest in the quality of loans being made. The secondary market cast all of that aside. A local lender could sell a loan into a securitization pool and have more money to lend nearly the next day. While there were theoretical penalties for making a bad loan, no one ever thought such penalties would actually be paid. Indeed, rather than the secondary market contributing to local liquidity, as it has been designed to do, the secondary market was actually driving that lending. Since mortgage loans were considered to be ironclad, the securities were generally AAA rated regardless of the quality of the underlying loans.

Also historically, home buyers either made a substantial down payment or bought mortgage insurance. Typically, the down payment to avoid a mortgage insurance premium was 20%. Studies showed that a home-owner with that sort of equity in a deal was a good risk. If a buyer had less than 20%, then some sort of insurance—such as the FHA insurance offered thru HUD or the VA guarantee program—would be required. Since mortgage loans were thought to be ironclad, why worry? 90%, 95%, and even 100% loan-to-value (LTV) loans were made. Indeed, the flawed appraisals supporting these loans meant that many were actually well above the 100% theoretically impossible threshold. A home with an appraisal of $100,000, but an actually value of $90,000, may get a $95,000 loan. On paper, the loan has a 95% LTV. In actuality the LTV is greater than 100%, and thus the lender will be left holding the bag if and as the loan goes bad.

Many residential mortgage-backed securities (RMBS) had a built-in assumption that about 2% or so of the loans would go bad, and historically this was not a bad estimate. That estimate failed to take into account the increased liberalization of lending, the emergence of subprime, "ALT-A," "low doc" and other non-prime loans. This failure rate assumed 20% down payments (or adequate insurance), adequate underwriting, and legitimate appraisals. Instead, many RMBS tranches were bought with leverage. Thus, investors (many of whom had no clue what was happening), borrowed money to invest in bad loans. Looking back, the moral hazard problems are obvious. At the time, no one seemed to notice.

Intriguingly, this was not the first time. Bad appraisals were cited as a core component of the 1980s lending crisis, which destroyed the savings and loan industry. The 1989 Financial Institutions Reform, Recovery, and Enforcement Act was supposed to address these and other concerns, and Title XI of that act provided for a nationwide set of appraisal standards and licensure. Amazingly, it took less than two decades to get back into a worse situation than before.

So, how has the industry addressed this, and how can investors be wary? First, the appraisal industry has doubled down on regulation, education, and enforcement. Lenders recognize that appraisals are not supposed to simply validate a loan, but instead take a critical look at the value of the underlying collateral. This has led to appraisal management companies (AMCs). These intermediate between lenders and appraisers, insulating appraisers from undue pressure and moral hazard issues. Second, the underwriting industry—the lenders and securitizers—are placing increasing reliance on statistical tools, such as AVMs, to assess the valuations supporting mortgage (and mortgage security) collateral.

Data suggests that home prices are on a tear again. Figure 20-1 shows that after the housing bubble burst, prices reverted back to long-term trends. A number of forces are at work in the economy today that may change house price metrics, at least in the short run. For one, purchases of "starter" homes (homes bought by first-time buyers) are at a very low level. Because of this, statistics on house pricing today are more influenced by upscale homes than in previous years. Homebuilders suggest that the current market mix (first-timers versus subsequent buyers) is not sustainable, and the market will need to figure out a way to accommodate these buyers in the future.

Also, interest rates have been remarkably low for quite a few years, stimulating affordability. This is somewhat ironic—normally low interest rates would favor first-time buyers. Increases in interest rates may dampen the demand. Finally, the remarkably strong economy since the recession has fueled a strong housing demand.

From an appraisal perspective, this is all very interesting stuff. Appraisals incorporate the notion that yesterday's market will continue into the future. Appraisals in general are backward looking. Thus, an economy for the past 10 years that supported a value of $1 million for a property will continue to sustain that value into the foreseeable future. As practitioners know, property values actually cycle with the economy. Well-heeled investors take advantage of this, buying choice properties in recessions (or making plans for development in anticipation of cheaper costs during a recession), and holding properties off the market until the cycle turns back up. Thus, the sellers in a recession are often those who are least able to withstand economic travail, and as such the real estate troughs can overstate the severity of the recession itself. Users of real estate appraisals understand this—an appraisal is a snapshot at a point in time, and a baseline for consideration of what values will do with changing economic conditions. Thus, while appraisals did not predict the last recession, and will not predict the next one, those same appraisals provide a launch point to uncover actual, long-term sustained value trends.

21
Some Final Points to Ponder

Buy land—they're not making any more of it.

—Mark Twain

THIS BOOK IS organized around investment topics rather than appraisal topics. A fulsome understanding of how best to use appraisals might also consider the history, structure, organization, and fundamental first principles of the appraisal profession. Just as filing a tax return or an audited financial statement does not require a full understanding of how the AICPA or the Financial Accounting Standards Board actually operate—but it's handy to understand the accountant's references to "generally accepted accounting principles" or "FASB 118"[1]—the same is true for the use of appraisals and the appraisal profession. Throughout the text, we have referenced USPAP, the Yellow Book, and a variety of regulatory and professional bodies without discussing the origin of these in any detail. While investors may not generally *need* to know these things, this can be critically important in litigation or in regulatory issues, just to name a couple of examples.

In addition, often investors (and their accountants and attorneys) don't really know whether they have a problem unless they have at least a cursory understanding of how the appraisal profession works. Hopefully this information will help point the reader in the right direction if and as the need arises.

1. The Organization of Real Estate Appraisal in the US and in the World

Real estate valuation derives from the bundles of rights possessed by a property owner. Indeed, it could be said (and often is, in legal tomes and at cocktail parties) that real estate itself is not actually owned, but rather the so-called "owner" simply possesses a bundle of rights to use, enjoy, and transfer the property. Since the legal bundle of rights in the United States may be very different from the legal bundle of rights in another country, it comes as no surprise that the appraisal profession is taught, licensed, and organized nationally.

Since the practice of appraisal is subject to licensure, which in the United States is generally a state-granted function (with some exceptions), then it should also come as no surprise that the core licensure of appraisers is at a state level. This licensure carries with it state-level discipline, which varies widely from state to state. It also carries with it a state-mandated set of standards. For a variety of reasons, most states have adopted the Uniform Standards for Professional Appraisal Practice (USPAP). There are some exceptions, but in those states in which USPAP is not adopted directly, a set of standards similar to USPAP is required.

USPAP actually predates appraisal licensure in the United States. A group of various appraisal organizations, led by the preeminent Appraisal Institute, came together in the mid-1980s to develop a common set of standards, which became USPAP. At the same time, there was concern in the United States about the quality of appraisals, particularly given the rampant failure of the savings and loan industry. In 1989, Congress passed the Financial Institutions Reform, Recovery, and Enforcement Act (FIRREA). Title XI of that act required that states adopt appraisal licensure and that lenders require that appraisals adhere to a common set of standards. Those same appraisal organizations came together to create the Appraisal Foundation, a not-for-profit organization headquartered in Washington, DC, which promulgates minimum licensure standards. The Appraisal Institute, which owned the copyright for USPAP, donated it to the Foundation, and since that time the Foundation has maintained, updated, and published USPAP. While the Foundation is a private organization, congressionally mandated oversight is provided by the Appraisal Subcommittee, consisting of representatives of various federal agencies involved in mortgage lending. The Foundation is not at all involved with appraiser discipline—that is a state function. However, the Subcommittee, on its website, maintains a nationwide roster of licensed appraisers for the benefit of consumers.

States license and discipline appraisers. Discipline strictures vary from state to state. Generally, but not always, if an appraiser is found to have committed egregious violations of USPAP, or a series of lesser violations that in the aggregate call into question the credibility or believability of an appraisal, a state may fine the appraiser (up to some statutory limits), require additional education, admonish or reprimand publicly or privately, suspend or revoke a license, or some combination. In some cases, when an appraiser's conduct is particularly egregious, the state licensing board may refer the matter for prosecution. Appraisers are occasionally prosecuted for fraud and have regularly been caught up in investigations of mortgage fraud. As of this writing, there is increasing interest in third-party tort cases against appraisers who may have contributed to investors losing money.

As mentioned, the Appraisal Institute (AI) is the preeminent professional society for appraisers in America, over 85 years old. It also has very active publication and education arms, managed and operated by members, and its classes and publications are increasingly attractive in countries that have emerging valuation professions. The AI, as currently constituted, was formed in 1991 from the merger of the American Institute of Real Estate Appraisers (formed in 1932 out of the National Association of Realtors) and the Society of Real Estate Appraisers (which dated from 1935, out of the U.S. Building and Loan League).

About a quarter of US real estate appraisers are members of AI, either "designated" (having earned the coveted MAI or SRA designations) or candidates for those designations. The MAI designation is awarded to appraisers who demonstrate top-tier expertise in commercial appraisal, while the SRA is granted to appraisers demonstrating similar levels of expertise in residential valuation. The coursework, experience requirements, and examinations needed to earn these designations are considered functionally equivalent to a master's degree in real estate.

This is important, because valuations of commercial buildings or upscale residences should almost always involve an AI designee. While there are other professional organizations in the valuation field in the United States, and some of them award honorifics to members, the AI's designations are so deeply welded into the fabric of American real estate that it is not uncommon to see a commercial lease contract require that renewal options be valued, at the time of renewal, by an MAI-designated appraiser.

The AI does not regulate appraisers, and has no authority to grant licenses or discipline appraisers, but does have the authority to evaluate and sanction its members. The certification for any narrative appraisal report signed by an AI member affirms that the AI reserves the right to review the report.

In other countries, the Appraisal Institute designations are highly regarded, particularly in countries with rudimentary regulatory and licensure structures. The AI designations provide a significant level of credibility when working abroad.

Appraisal regulation does exist in varying degrees outside of the United States. Since other countries did not go through our savings and loan crisis, appraiser regulation tends to vary. For example, the Canadian Appraisal Institute was an original member of the panel that developed USPAP, and for many years was a member of the Appraisal Foundation. Since then, Canada has adopted its own standards, regulated by the Canadian Appraisal Institute. Canadian standards are similar to those in the United States, but recognize that Canadian valuation is not aimed toward FIRREA-compliant mortgage lending.

In the United Kingdom, property experts are called "surveyors." In 1868, a number of them formed the Institute of Surveyors, which has since been redesignated the Royal Institution of Chartered Surveyors (RICS). This organization spans valuation (real estate, personal property, etc.), property management, insurance, cost estimating, and other property-related fields. At the top of the ladder, RICS awards "Fellow" status to experts in the field after a minimum of 10 years of membership. RICS designations are recognized in the United Kingdom, Australia, Hong Kong, and much of Europe. RICS promulgates the "Red Book," which is essentially an amalgam of appraisal standards and a code of conduct.

It is not uncommon for investors to own properties in many countries. Local knowledge and experience is essential for a useful valuation. Since valuation is conducted under different regulatory paradigms in different countries, appraisal reports may not look alike, nor will they necessarily comport to US expectations. Conversely, a British investor with US holdings may be confused at the FIRREA-influenced requirements in a US appraisal. At some point, aggregating valuations into a meaningful, cohesive portfolio valuation may require some significant review and understanding of these variations.

2. Appraisal Standards and Methods

USPAP was developed in the 1980s, and with FIRREA became the governing standards for appraisals conducted for federally regulated mortgages. Most states have adopted USPAP as the standard governing appraisals. States that have not formally adopted USPAP still require that appraisers be schooled in it, and that appraisers adhere to a set of enumerated standards that are similar in tone and content to USPAP.

Much like the accounting profession has generally accepted accounting principles (GAAP) as well as stated rules and standards (AICPA and FASB pronouncements), the appraisal field has generally accepted methodology. Indeed, USPAP Standards Rule 1-1(a) requires that appraisers be familiar with and correctly employ such generally recognized methods. The fact that USPAP only came into existence in the 1980s does not mean there were no recognized methods for appraisals before then. Indeed, the AI has produced the *Appraisal Journal* for almost nine decades and *The Appraisal of Real Estate* in 14 editions since 1951. These, and the other teaching and continuing education materials produced by AI and its predecessor organizations, provided the core of the appraisal body of knowledge for decades. One major strength of AI's process is that these materials are authored and edited by members or other highly regarded experts in the field, rather than AI staff. For that reason, this body of knowledge carries with it an authority inherent in the widespread agreement of peers in the field. Indeed, USPAP's Scope of Work rule requires that appraisers adhere to methodology that would be expected by peers in the field who perform the same sorts of appraisal assignments.

So, an appraiser is required to be familiar with and apply USPAP and the broadly accepted methodology in the field. It would be simple if it stopped right there, but valuations are done for a variety of reasons. Valuation of land that is being transferred to the federal government (in a sale, a swap, or a condemnation, among other ways) must adhere to the Uniform Appraisal Standards for Federal Land Acquisition. Appraisers who undertake these projects must also be familiar with those rules and regulations. Appraisals for Fannie Mae or Freddie Mac must adhere to their standards, and generally this means the requirements outlined in the FNMA Selling Guide. While most FNMA/FHLMC issues arise from simple, single family or condo valuations for mortgage, loans, the FNMA/FHLMC standards also apply to land being subdivided and financed by FNMA/FHLMC, for nursing homes or assisted living facilities, for many multifamily projects (particularly workforce housing), and a host of other situations. Eminent domain or tax appeal appraisals must adhere to any locally developed standards. The definition of market value commonly used in appraisals in the United States is the one promulgated for federal lending purposes (often called the "federal definition").[2] Locally adjudicated matters may require adherence to definitions of market value contained in case law or model jury instructions. If something other than fee simple interest or market value is the goal of the valuation, then more intense scrutiny needs to be paid to the conditions and definitions imbedded in the appraiser's scope of work. Any time a valuation is being performed for IRS-related issues, the appraiser needs to be familiar with and adhere to IRS regulations.

When the property is outside the United States, a different set of standards may or may not apply. What if the property is in another country but being valued for a US client in a US matter (such as probate of a US estate)? While USPAP governs an appraiser working in the United States, the Canadian USPAP, produced by the Canadian Appraisal Institute, is different in significant ways. In the United Kingdom and many other British Commonwealth areas, the Red Book will apply. Similar differences arise in nearly every country around the world.

These all have implications for valuation of real property under varying scenarios. It is not sufficient for the appraiser to simply be asked to produce a "USPAP-compliant appraisal" because that may not be adequate to the task. Indeed, most appraisal assignments for wealthy families will involve complexities outside the normal scope of a mortgage appraisal or a simple eminent domain issue. Property owners, their agents, attorneys, and accountants are highly advised to have serious conversations with the appraiser about the use of the appraisal report, other potential users, and the assignment goals.

3. Appraisal Licensure and Regulation

In a recent state court case, the plaintiffs proffered an MAI-designated appraiser to opine about property values. The defendants, a municipal agency, proffered a CPA to rebut the appraiser. The plaintiffs moved to strike the CPA's testimony, noting (among other things) that state law required real estate valuation be proffered by a state-certified appraiser. The court concurred, and it directed that the CPA could offer testimony about simple math (any errors in the MAI's mathematical computations) but could not offer an opinion of value.

In another recent court case, also in a state court, an MAI appraiser offered opinions regarding the value of a business sale, opining as to the allocation between real property and business property. The opposing side objected, arguing that the real estate appraiser should be limited to opining about the market value of real property, not business property. The court disagreed, noting that appraisers regularly value business interests. The appraiser was allowed to testify.

FIRREA mandated that the states enact licensure and certification of appraisers, and the Appraisal Foundation, through its Appraisal Qualifications Board (AQB), promulgates minimum standards for such licensure.

Unfortunately, as they say, the devil is in the details, and over the years the various states have interpreted these edicts somewhat differently.

The one thing they all have in common—even the states that have not adopted USPAP as the governing standard for appraisals—is that appraisers themselves must be trained in USPAP prior to acquiring a license, and must update their knowledge with a biennial continuing education (CE) course in USPAP. Further, in the early 2000s, the states asked the Foundation to provide some uniformity in USPAP instruction across the United States. Following that request, the AQB developed a rigorous certification course for USPAP instructors. As of this writing, only about 500 appraisal educators around the United States are certified to teach these courses. To maintain licensure, appraisers must take an approved USPAP CE course every two years, plus typically about a week's worth of classroom hours every two years in other CE courses. Many states have also inaugurated specific courses in appraisal law and regulations pertinent to that state.

Of somewhat greater interest, there is a very real disagreement among the states as to exactly who needs to be a licensed or certified appraiser in that state. In every state, an appraiser must be licensed or certified to appraise properties for loans envisioned under FIRREA (generally, mortgage loans issued by a federally regulated lender when the loan amount is above a *de minimis* level). After that, though, the states are a mixed bag. Some states are "mandatory" states, which means that any person holding him- or herself out to be an appraiser must be licensed or certified in that state. Typically, appraisers are regulated by their home states and may get a temporary practice permit in any state that requires such for a one-time project. Further, the appraiser may get a permanent license, via reciprocity, in any state in which he or she will have continuing business. However, the various states have widely varying reciprocity laws and regulations. In some states, reciprocity may be granted by simply demonstrating good standing in all the other states in which the appraiser practices (no outstanding disciplinary matters). Other states may have somewhat more onerous requirements, and may even require that the appraiser travel to that state and be examined or tested.

Why is this important? An investor may hold properties in multiple states and may need valuations for estate planning purposes. If the appraiser is certified in Florida but the property is in Washington, there is probably no need for a Washington reciprocal license, since Washington is not a "mandatory" state. Conversely, if a Washington appraiser wants to value a property in Florida, even for nonmortgage purposes, a Florida reciprocal license is probably required.

This also affects the ability to review appraisals performed by other appraisers. Assume that an investor, a resident of New York, owns a property in Arizona. The investor hires an Arizona appraiser to value a property, and then asked a New York appraiser to "review" the appraisal in accordance with USPAP. The New York appraiser finds problems with the value, and instead recommends a different value. The New York appraiser needs to have a reciprocal license in Arizona, even if he or she never sets foot in Arizona!

By the way, we have used the terms "licensed" and "certified" somewhat interchangeably. These terms actually have very different meanings in appraisal regulation. Top-tier appraisers in each state are considered certified. They may either be certified "general" or certified "residential." The former may appraise any property, commercial or residential, while the latter may appraise any residence (one- to four-family residences). Certification requires a significant level of education, experience, and testing. In the early days of regulations, the states grappled with how to deal with appraisers who only value simple residences. They arrived at a solution—issue appraisal "licenses" that severely limit the bounds of a residential appraiser. Over the years, most states have also enacted "trainee" or "apprentice" licenses for beginners in the industry who are working directly under the supervision of a certified appraiser (either general or residential). Some states are now dropping the "licensed" category, with some grandfathering available. (The Appraisal Institute requires that a person be a certified general appraiser to become a candidate for the MAI designation, and a certified residential appraiser to become a candidate for the SRA.)

Most of this is utterly transparent to the investor or other client or user, but the one takeaway is that a "licensed" appraiser is almost certainly not qualified to appraise investment-grade property. The safe harbor for investors is to require an Appraisal Institute designee (either MAI or SRA, depending on the circumstances) for any serious project.

4. Tax Assessment Appeals

This is a common area where investors engage appraisers and appraisal consultants. Indeed, large REITs and real estate–oriented private equity funds often have full-time tax management departments, headed by appraisers who are experts in the field. Naturally, there is an enormous return to the property owner. Consider a $50 million building in a large metropolitan area. The annual taxes may approximate 1% or more of the property value, or $500,000 per year. A 10% savings in the annual tax bill amounts to $50,000, not a paltry sum by any estimation. However, this is an *annual* savings, and so, capitalized at 5%, the present value of this perpetuity savings is actually about $1,000,000. Admittedly, this savings will need to be nurtured, and it may come as no surprise that this tax appeal may have to be renewed in the coming years, much the same way any $1,000,000 investment may need to be maintained. Surprisingly, this is a frequently overlooked source of value enhancement. Part of the problem is that investors are frequently trying to *maximize* the apparent property value, rather than establish that the value is *lower* than the tax assessor thinks. If an investor wants to sell that $50 million building in the next few years, then encouraging the tax assessor to think it is only worth $45 million may be counterintuitive.

When properties are in a "long hold" position, held by families or trusts that are cash flow maximizers (rather than paper value maximizers), the tax appeal is, well, appealing. It is not without controversy and complexity, however. Appraisal standards and the AI's requirements prohibit an appraiser from acting as an advocate for a client *when also acting as an appraiser*. There are many appraisers in the field who double as tax advocates with significant success. The actual property appraisal for the appeal, though, needs to be performed by a separate appraiser (albeit coordinated by the appraiser who will argue the tax appeal) to avoid the conflict of interest problems.

Also, the basis for property tax valuation may be very different from the basis for sale or portfolio valuation. Some jurisdictions allow property taxes to be assessed based on a "value in use." In appraisal lingo, this may mean a leased fee value rather than a fee simple value. Of course, sale of a property may or may not be based on the leasehold value. To reflect on some earlier discussions, a brand-new office building (or any commercial building, for that matter) may be valued assuming that the space will be rented at market-rate rents. This produces a market value of the fee simple interest. Three or four years later, if contract rents are below market rents, the value of the cash inflows is somewhat less than the market value—it is the leased fee value, and is based on the discounted present value of contract rents rather than higher market rents. In property tax jargon in some states, this is also referred to as the "value in use."

Consider a warehouse currently used by a family-owned business. If the family vacated the warehouse and rented it to a market-rate tenant, the discounted present value of that net cash flow would approximate the market value of the fee simple interest. That would be the asking price if the property was put up for sale (or, for that matter, the "book" value for internal recordkeeping or allocation of rents among family members). However, the *contributory* value of the warehouse to the family business may be somewhat lower than market value. This constitutes a value in use.

Naturally, tax assessors want to collect property taxes at the market value, which assumes highest and best use. Property owners (and their tax appeal consultants) will argue that the highest and best use assumes some sort of market transaction (willing buyer, etc.). Would a willing buyer pay full market value for a property encumbered with long-term, below-market leases?

In the appraisal world, this problem manifests in four different questions, which may have four different answers:

1. What is the value of the property for internal portfolio purposes?
2. What is the value for tax assessment?
3. What if the property was put up for sale or acquired via eminent domain?
4. How does the value (particularly for a family-owned business) get allocated for IRS tax purposes?

The property owner and his or her appraisers, accountants, and lawyers may need to be ready to defend different values for the property under different circumstances. It would be handy if the case law supported one and only one procedure in these very common situations, but of course the case law is all over the map.

In short, a tax appeal is a useful tool to maximize cash flows for a portfolio property for which there is a long-term hold strategy. The value proffered under the tax appeal should be congruent with other valuations used for other purposes. Understanding the nomenclature (market value, value in use, leased fee value, etc.) will be important to be consistent with local tax laws and other valuations that may be proffered for other uses.

5. Inverse Condemnation

Rezonings, new local ordinances, building code changes, and other municipal or state actions, or even some federal actions, may manifest in a reduction in value to the property. Consider a situation in which a property was acquired for development. During the feasibility phase, someone discovered an endangered desert tortoise on the property. (We know it was endangered because they only found one.) The property is no longer suitable for development, and indeed the property owner is prohibited from driving his own SUV on the land.

Is this legally an inverse condemnation? Certainly, the property owner is now prohibited from enjoying the previously intended highest and best use. Whether this is legally a "taking" or not is a matter for the courts. From an appraisal perspective, though, there is no question that the property value is impacted.

This is a common situation—the legal damage to a property due to some action or inaction may or may not be recoverable. Nonetheless, the loss in value is an economic reality. This frequently occurs in environmentally damaged property. In recent years, the Federal Emergency Management Agency has had to address flooding in places that were not predicted by flood maps. As such, flood maps have been updated to reflect new data. Two very interesting things have happened here. First, some property owners have faced damages for which there is simply no recovery without adequate insurance. Second, though, a property previously not thought to be in a flood zone, but now determined to be in one, has probably declined in value (all things being equal). Is there a responsible party? Sure. Can the property owner recover any losses? Maybe not. These are legal questions outside the purview of an appraiser. Nonetheless, an appraisal will probably be a first step in the argument, since the decrease in value is real.

This leads to a more interesting conundrum: many appraisers will have a problem with such an assignment in the absence of clear and compelling case law and courtroom examples. Consider a tract of raw land suitable for development. It is now in a newly determined flood zone. There are ways of dealing with this problem from a development perspective—elevation changes (which come at a cost) or changes in the use (which come with a decrease in prospective income). The valuation questions can be challenging. The economic damages to property distressed with zoning changes, flood zone changes, or other negative municipal or regulatory decisions can be very real and difficult to measure.

Actual physical condemnations are fairly easy to measure, but inverse condemnations are much more difficult. For one, there is always an argument that a property owner is not due the "highest and best use," only some lesser value measured by current or some more probable use. Also, municipalities will often posit that zoning ordinances or building restrictions actually enhance a neighborhood, thus arguably improving the property's value. Property investors will need to work carefully with appraisers to outline the issues at hand and to properly measure the economically measurable impacts.

6. A Final Note—Did George Washington Really Sleep Here?

I went to school at a small, at the time all-male college in Annapolis, Maryland. The town was veritably littered with historic properties, including a tavern down on the main square, overlooking the harbor, that dutifully had a plaque noting that George Washington had slept there. The tavern did a land-office tourist business way back then, not because George had ever darkened the door but because it was a handy spot to enjoy a cold beer on a warm summer day.

All too often, property owners, their agents, and their appraisers fall in love with a property because of some unique, idiosyncratic factor. In many years of litigating property issues, we have heard amazing arguments about heterogenous, idiosyncratic property characteristics that supposedly contribute to value. One of our favorites was a pair of trust fund babies who were pursuing PhDs in something ("Advanced Sanskrit" or something like that) at a well-respected university. They were heavily devoted to the notion of the blue-collar experience and dutifully bought a home in a working-class neighborhood in transition. From the outside, the house resembled every other home in the neighborhood—two or three bedrooms, story-and-a-half, wood clapboard, screened porch, old wooden detached garage. It was probably built in the 1920s or '30s. I grew up in a house like that. The value was in contention due to a contamination spill in the backyard, and it befell to me to visit them, inspect their house, and opine about the value in litigation.

Everything about the inspection was normal, except for the kitchen. It is difficult to imagine a first-class, top-of-the-line appliance that had not been installed in this kitchen. This house, worth $150,000 on a good day, had a $100,000 kitchen (and probably a $50,000 wine collection in the custom-built cooler, but that's another story). Appraisers often refer to these situations as "gold-plated bathroom fixtures." The idiosyncratic features may be nice, and may be of value to the current owners, but may not contribute to market value.

But back to the George Washington tavern. Many years ago, when historic preservation was becoming the rage, many properties in the mid-Atlantic states advertised that "George Washington Slept Here." This was ironic, since some of those properties had not even been built in Washington's lifetime, but that's another story. The real question was, did such advertisement contribute to the property's value? Earlier in this text, I discussed the value of historic properties and how an appraisal needs to address that. Admittedly, owning a historic property makes for great cocktail party conversation, but does it really have a value over and above what another, newer property might have?

These idiosyncrasies are neat and interesting and may contribute to the world around us. Market values, though, are a function of market norms. The most architecturally beautiful building in town will still be valued on its net rents. If the building costs 20% more than its competitors to build but only achieves a 5% bump in rents, then the expenditure was mostly affectation.

Probably the main lesson from this book is that value is a function of situation-specific underlying economics. Appraisers need to be informed of those economics, and the complexity pertinent to a particular situation, for the appraisal to be useful. Investors need to understand the nuances of valuation—the assumptions, limiting conditions, data collection problems, analytical constructs, standards of practice, and economic realities—to fully appreciate the value conclusions. Generally, idiosyncratic issues have little bearing on the property value—the property is being compared to other properties that provide the same utility in the marketplace. Defining exactly what that utility is can be a challenging proposition. Appraisals are supposed to take into account what atomistic market participants would value. Property owners frequently resent the fact that appraisers may gloss over intriguing facets of the property that, unfortunately, carry little value in the marketplace.

For the little tavern in Annapolis overlooking the harbor, the fact that George Washington may have slept there is only interesting if it drives up the rent or the contributory value to the business being operated there. That may very well be a tough premise to sell to a potential buyer.

> Of course, appraisers may be swayed by just such ancillary issues in reaching a value conclusion. The real usefulness of an appraisal is the mound of information contained in the analysis and presented in the report. Sifting through that information and gleaning useful decision tools from the appraisal is an art and a science, but the leverage and advantage it provides the investor makes the exercise worth the effort.

Notes

Chapter 1

1. *Great Expectations* (Ethan Hawke, Gwyneth Paltrow, Anne Bancroft) used the prerestoration Ca' d'Zan as a centerpiece to the film. The restoration was begun shortly after that filming, and fund-raising was in no small part stimulated by that movie.
2. Back in 1995, in the journal *Real Estate Finance*, Dr. Glenn Mueller published an insightful paper titled "Understanding Real Estate's Physical and Financial Market Cycles." For the non-PhD, the paper is fairly complex, but extraordinarily useful. I have attempted to simplify, with apologies to Dr. Mueller for any errors. Dr. Mueller is currently a professor at Denver University and the real estate strategist at Black Creek Group. He promulgates his market cycle monitor quarterly.

Chapter 3

1. In 2018, Robert Marchand's physicians told him to quit competitive bicycle racing. He was 106 years old. He responded to them by competing in a 4,000-meter indoor race in France.
2. KathleenKowal.com.
3. Leopold, T., and T. Schneider, "Family Events and the Timing of Intergenerational Transfers," *Social Forces* 90-2, 2011, 595–616.
4. De Nardi, Mariacristina, "Wealth Inequality and Intergenerational Links," *Review of Economic Studies* 71-3, 2004, 743–768.
5. Hansen, Marianne, "Self-Made Wealth or Family Wealth? Changes in Intergenerational Wealth Mobility," *Social Forces* 93-1, 2014, 457–481.
6. For a thorough and excellent discussion of these issues, see Williams, Roy, and Amy Castoro, *Bridging Generations* (Orlando: Higher Life Development Services, 2017).
7. www.nextfinance.net, as of 2015.

8. Mundy, Bill, "Defining a Trophy Property," *The Appraisal Journal* 70-4, October 2002, 377–379; Mundy, Bill, "Trophy Property Valuation: A Ranch Case Study," *The Appraisal Journal* 71-1, January 2003, 68–74.
9. At one time the largest industrial building in the world, famed for having the roof camouflaged with faux city streets and houses during World War II.
10. My firm advised the owner of the ranch on the complex valuation issues attached to this historic find. The find is chronicled in *A Dinosaur Named Sue* by Fay Robinson with the SUE Science Team of The Field Museum.
11. I consulted on this project to a group of investors who had planned to donate the property to the Chicago Art Museum.
12. My firm consulted on this preservation project.
13. Including my sister, who graduated from Honolulu High School.
14. This sort of ratio is common for many types of properties and tends to be constant across a broad geography. For example, net ground leases—leasing the land on which a commercial building is constructed—tend to average about 7% for most creditworthy tenants in most markets. That way, an investor interested in net ground leases can invest without fear of an arbitrage problem.
15. *Author's note:* This was literally written at 4:00 p.m., sitting by the docks at Friday Harbor, Washington, watching a billion dollars in boats return from a day on the water.

Chapter 4

1. This question was addressed in a series of journal articles in the 1980s—does historic preservation diminish the value of historic homes due to the deadweight cost of maintenance, or does the value increase even with those costs due to the "trophy" or "collectible" quality? Evidence shows that historic designation increases the value, and designating an entire neighborhood as historic increases the value even further.
2. Santa Monica Airport (California) has been required to reduce traffic as a result of petitions by local property owners.
3. For the totally uninitiated, the Western model of equity investment holds that the equity investor enjoys upside benefits out to infinity, but his or her losses are capped at the amount of the investment. Thus, if I invest $1 in each of two games, and one of them makes a million but the other loses a million, I enjoy the entire million on the upside one, but my losses on the downside one are capped at $1.

4. Some counties have multiple tax assessment jurisdictions, but rules governing tax assessment are typically common on a county-by-county basis. Tax assessment is regulated at the state level.
5. The Uniform Standards of Professional Appraisal Practice, or USPAP, discussed later in the text.
6. This is actually a complex technicality, and not well understood even by practicing appraisers and regulators. Many appraisers have different lines of business, such as appraisal, brokerage, and consulting. Appraisers are prohibited from charging contingency fees *when acting as an appraiser.* Thus, technically, if an appraiser acts as a broker or consultant (who has no such contingency prohibition), disclaims that he or she is acting as an appraiser, and relies on an appraisal performed *by another appraiser for a fixed fee*, then generally that satisfies the requirements.
7. *Insurance Serv. Co. v. Brodie*, 337 S.W.2d 414, 415.
8. "Arm's length" implies the buyer and seller are acting in their own self-interest and not subject to any pressure from the other party.

Chapter 5

1. Of course there are occasional bubbles, but our research at Greenfield indicates that post–World War II, housing prices in America have moved steadily upward averaging 2 percentage points above CPI inflation year after year.
2. We Buy Ugly Houses is a registered trademark of HomeVestors of America, Inc.
3. No, I am not in the employ of either city's Chamber of Commerce.
4. We acknowledge that sales prices do not always equal value. Indeed, in our experience, sales prices deviate from true market value at the most inopportune times.
5. Math purists will recognize that this is not quite correct, but the difference is less than a rounding error. To try this yourself, use a spreadsheet or a financial calculator and find the payment for amortizing a loan of $1 for 180 periods at an interest rate of .05/12, then multiply the result by 12. You should get the same result you see in Equation 5-4. If you don't, drop me a line.
6. Appraisers use the term "opinion of value" with good reason. They are expressing a professional opinion, based not just on the mathematics of the exercise but also on a professional evaluation of the quality and quantity of data. The difference is important.
7. See, for example, Kilpatrick, John A., "Real Estate Investments of the Rich and Famous," *Journal of Wealth Management*, 2007.

Chapter 6

1. IRS Publication 561.
2. ASC 820, formerly Financial Accounting Standards Board Statement of Financial Accounting Standard 157.
3. This is sometimes referred to as the federal definition, and often mistakenly referred to as the Fannie Mae definition, since FNMA is the largest and most visible player in the home mortgage game. FIRREA was passed as part of an omnibus set of legislation passed after the savings and loan crisis. It regulates, among other things, the due diligence required by lenders in real estate–based lending. Since the largest quantity of real estate loans are home mortgages, it is assumed sometimes that FIRREA only applies to such mortgages, but indeed much of what is in FIRREA applies to the whole spectrum of real estate lending.
4. Title XI of the Financial Institutions Reform, Recovery, and Enforcement Act of 1989 (FIRREA), Pub. L. 101—73, 103 Stat. 183, 12 U.S.C. 3331 et seq. (1989).
5. Oddly, Bayesian statistics is not taught in appraisal curriculum, but this is in effect what appraisers do.
6. There is actually a lot of debate about this topic in academic and practitioner circles. Wouldn't the most probable price be the highest one bid? Or what about the lowest one offered? Or what about the second-best bidder? These are ponderable questions best left for scholars.
7. Of course, savvy buyers are always on the lookout for these!
8. There is an excellent and informative chapter on this very topic in the recently published book *Corridor Valuation*, from the US Appraisal Institute, the Appraisal Institute of Canada, and the International Right of Way Association.
9. One of my favorites is Fanning, Stephen F., *Market Analysis for Real Estate*, 2nd ed. (Chicago: Appraisal Institute).

Chapter 7

1. This phenomenon was driven home by a passage in the book *Freakonomics by* Steven Levitt and Stephen Dubner. They were interested in the paradox that real estate agents were willing to hold their own properties on the market for slightly longer, to maximize selling price, than they would for clients' properties.
2. *Lucas v. South Carolina Coastal Council*, 505 U.S. 1003 (1992).
3. These options were actually listed by Justice Brennan in a footnote.
4. An avigation easement is the rights to land and take off at a nearby airport. We once assisted a property owner who owned a recording studio

and found that a railroad bridge was going to be built within 10 feet of his outer wall.

5. Yes, this was actually an important factor in a recent analysis.
6. Gravity models are concepts and tools in economic geography to aid in determining the area from which a property will draw customers.
7. Adapted from Fanning, Stephen F., *Market Analysis for Real Estate: Concepts and Applications in Valuation and Highest and Best Use* (Chicago: Appraisal Institute, 2005), 15.

Chapter 8

1. www.agweb.com/farmland-value-guide.
2. 26 CFR 20.2032A-4, Method of valuing farm real property.
3. *The Land Report*, published by The American Landowner, www.landreport.com, and www.businessinsider.com. Many of these holdings are very dynamic—wealthy landowners tend to accumulate more property over time. The ordering of this list and the total acreage owned by top landowners may have changed since this was written.
4. The statistically minded will recognize this as the upper tail of a two-tailed 95% distribution. Since real estate values are not symmetrically distributed, and the upper bound is theoretically (although not practically) limitless, the range of the upper 2½% is far greater than the range of any other 2½% slice of the distribution. This makes for some fascinating analytical issues.
5. Since I know you're curious, their current property tax bill is $1,130,373.61.
6. In 2018, to stem the tide of foreigners "buying up" that country, the New Zealand parliament passed highly restrictive prohibitions against such investments by non–New Zealanders.
7. I have had the pleasure of contributing to several.
8. MTBE, a common gas additive from decades ago, may test positive one day and not test at all the next.
9. Florida, Richard, *The Rise of the Creative Class* (New York: Perseus, 2002).

Chapter 9

1. As you may imagine, a sudden negative externality often manifests in a damage claim by impacted parties.

Chapter 12

1. For the uninitiated, IRR is the discount rate that would cause the NPV to equal zero. If an investment has a positive NPV, then the IRR must be higher than the discount rate used in the analysis.

Chapter 15

1. Although studies show that even inaccurate tax assessor values can be used to find true market value as long as they are consistent.

Chapter 16

1. http://www.freddiemac.com/singlefamily/purchasemarket/sell/rural_properties_QA.html, viewed December 3, 2018.

Chapter 17

1. The EB-5 program provides a "green card" in trade for an investment of $900,000 that creates 10 US jobs, or $500,000 invested in a targeted area.

Chapter 19

1. Section 856, Internal Revenue Code.
2. http://www.finra.org/investors/alerts/public-non-traded-reits-careful-review.
3. https://www.sec.gov/oiea/investor-alerts-bulletins/ib_nontradedreits.html.

Chapter 20

1. FNMA Selling Guide Section B4-1.4-04 (2014).

Chapter 21

1. "Accounting by creditors for the impairment of a loan."
2. *Federal Register* 55, no. 163, August 22, 1990.

Index

Page numbers followed by "f" and "t" refer to figures and tables, respectively.

M

N

O

P

Q

About the Author

DR. JOHN A. KILPATRICK is the Managing Director of Greenfield Advisors, headquartered in Seattle, and also serves as a Director of the Washington State Economic Development Finance Authority and as the Director of Greenfield's private REIT fund, ACCRE LLC. Dr. Kilpatrick is the co-holder of a patent on Automated Valuation Models., and has published extensively in real estate finance and related fields. He holds a Ph.D. in Finance from the University of South Carolina.